MARVEL

GUARDIANS OF THE GALAXY VOL. 2

PRELUDE

GUARDIANS OF THE GALAXY VOL. 2

PRELUDE

BASED ON A SCREENPLAY BY
JAMES GUNN AND NICOLE PERLMAN

WRITER: **WILL CORONA PILGRIM**
PENCILERS: **CHRIS ALLEN** WITH **ANDREA MUTTI** (#2)
INKERS: **SCOTT HANNA** WITH **ROBERTO POGGI** (#1)
COLORIST: **ANDRES MOSSA**
LETTERER: **VC'S TRAVIS LANHAM**
EDITOR: **MARK BASSO**

MARVEL STUDIOS

VP PRODUCTION & DEVELOPMENT: **JONATHAN SCHWARTZ**
SVP PRODUCTION & DEVELOPMENT: **JEREMY LATCHAM**
PRESIDENT: **KEVIN FEIGE**

COLLECTION EDITOR: JENNIFER GRÜNWALD   ASSISTANT EDITOR: CAITLIN O'CONNELL
ASSOCIATE MANAGING EDITOR: KATERI WOODY   EDITOR, SPECIAL PROJECTS: MARK D. BEAZLEY
VP PRODUCTION & SPECIAL PROJECTS: JEFF YOUNGQUIST   SVP PRINT, SALES & MARKETING: DAVID GABRIEL
BOOK DESIGNER: ADAM DEL RE

EDITOR IN CHIEF: AXEL ALONSO   CHIEF CREATIVE OFFICER: JOE QUESADA   PUBLISHER: DAN BUCKLEY   EXECUTIVE PRODUCER: ALAN FINE

MARVEL'S GUARDIANS OF THE GALAXY VOL. 2 PRELUDE. Contains material originally published in magazine form as MARVEL'S GUARDIANS OF THE GALAXY VOL. 2 PRELUDE #1-2, GIANT-SIZE AVENGER
GUARDIANS OF THE GALAXY #1 and GUARDIANS TEAM-UP #1-2. First printing 2017. ISBN# 978-1-302-90468-5. Published by MARVEL WORLDWIDE, INC., a subsidiary of MARVEL ENTERTAINMENT, LLC. OFFIC
PUBLICATION: 135 West 50th Street, New York, NY 10020. Copyright © 2017 MARVEL. No similarity between any of the names, characters, persons, and/or institutions in this magazine with those of any living or
person or institution is intended, and any such similarity which may exist is purely coincidental. **Printed in the U.S.A.** ALAN FINE, President, Marvel Entertainment; DAN BUCKLEY, President, TV, Publishing & I
Management; JOE QUESADA, Chief Creative Officer; TOM BREVOORT, SVP of Publishing; DAVID BOGART, SVP of Business Affairs & Operations, Publishing & Partnership; C.B. CEBULSKI, VP of Brand Managem
Development, Asia; DAVID GABRIEL, SVP of Sales & Marketing, Publishing; JEFF YOUNGQUIST, VP of Production & Special Projects; DAN CARR, Executive Director of Publishing Technology; ALEX MORALES, Direc
Publishing Operations; SUSAN CRESPI, Production Manager; STAN LEE, Chairman Emeritus. For information regarding advertising in Marvel Comics or on Marvel.com, please contact Vit DeBellis, Integrated Sales Mar
at vdebellis@marvel.com. For Marvel subscription inquiries, please call 888-511-5480. **Manufactured between 1/27/2017 and 2/28/2017 by QUAD/GRAPHICS WASECA, WASECA, MN, USA.**
10 9 8 7 6 5 4 3 2 1

MARVEL'S GUARDIANS OF THE GALAXY VOL. 2 PRELUDE #1

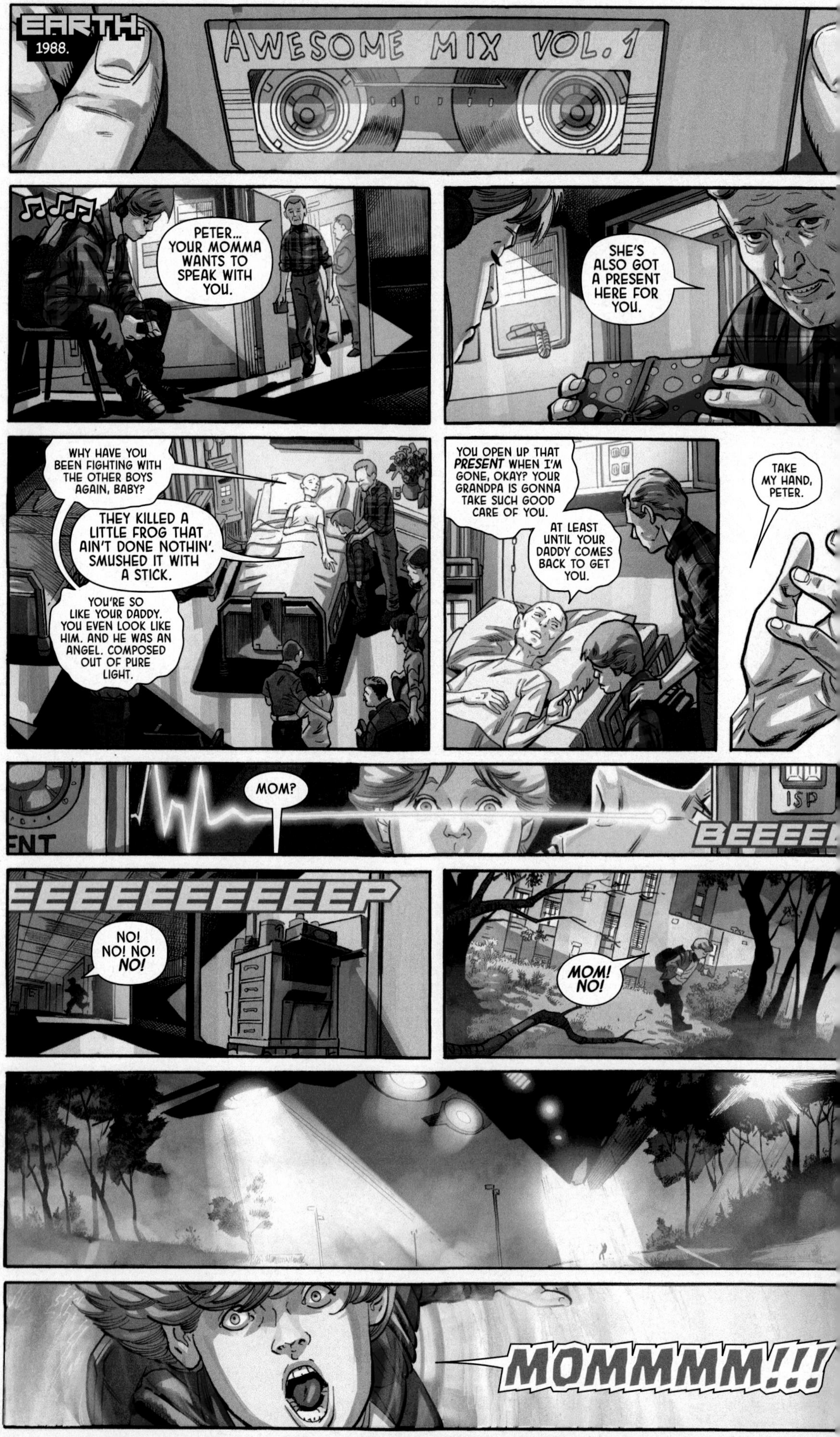
EARTH.
1988.
AWESOME MIX VOL. 1
PETER... YOUR MOMMA WANTS TO SPEAK WITH YOU.
SHE'S ALSO GOT A PRESENT HERE FOR YOU.
WHY HAVE YOU BEEN FIGHTING WITH THE OTHER BOYS AGAIN, BABY?
THEY KILLED A LITTLE FROG THAT AIN'T DONE NOTHIN'. SMUSHED IT WITH A STICK.
YOU'RE SO LIKE YOUR DADDY. YOU EVEN LOOK LIKE HIM. AND HE WAS AN ANGEL. COMPOSED OUT OF PURE LIGHT.
YOU OPEN UP THAT PRESENT WHEN I'M GONE, OKAY? YOUR GRANDPA IS GONNA TAKE SUCH GOOD CARE OF YOU.
AT LEAST UNTIL YOUR DADDY COMES BACK TO GET YOU.
TAKE MY HAND, PETER.
MOM?
BEEEEEEEEEEEEEEEEP
NO! NO! NO! NO!
MOM! NO!
MOMMMM!!!

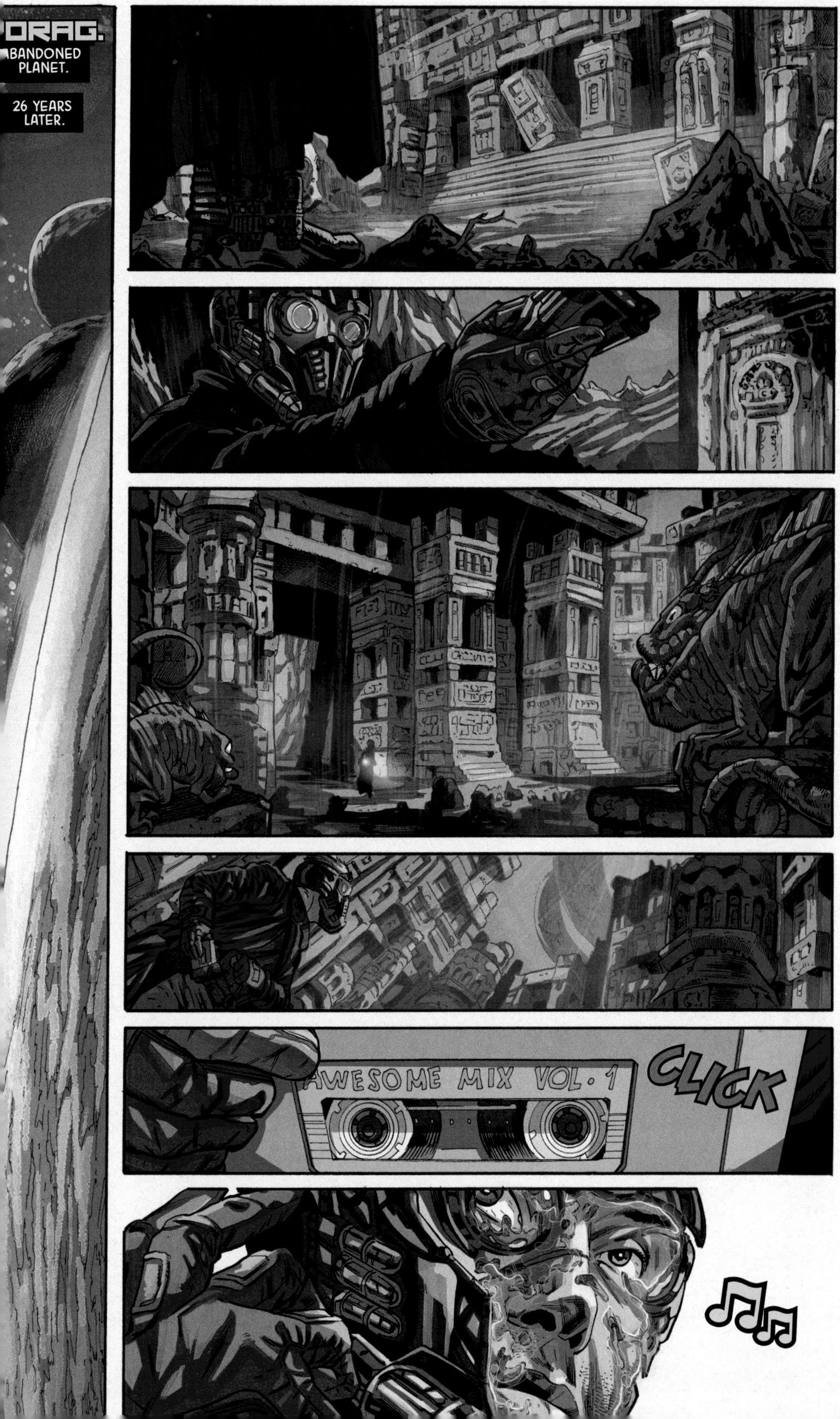

ORAG.
ABANDONED PLANET.
26 YEARS LATER.
AWESOME MIX VOL. 1
CLICK

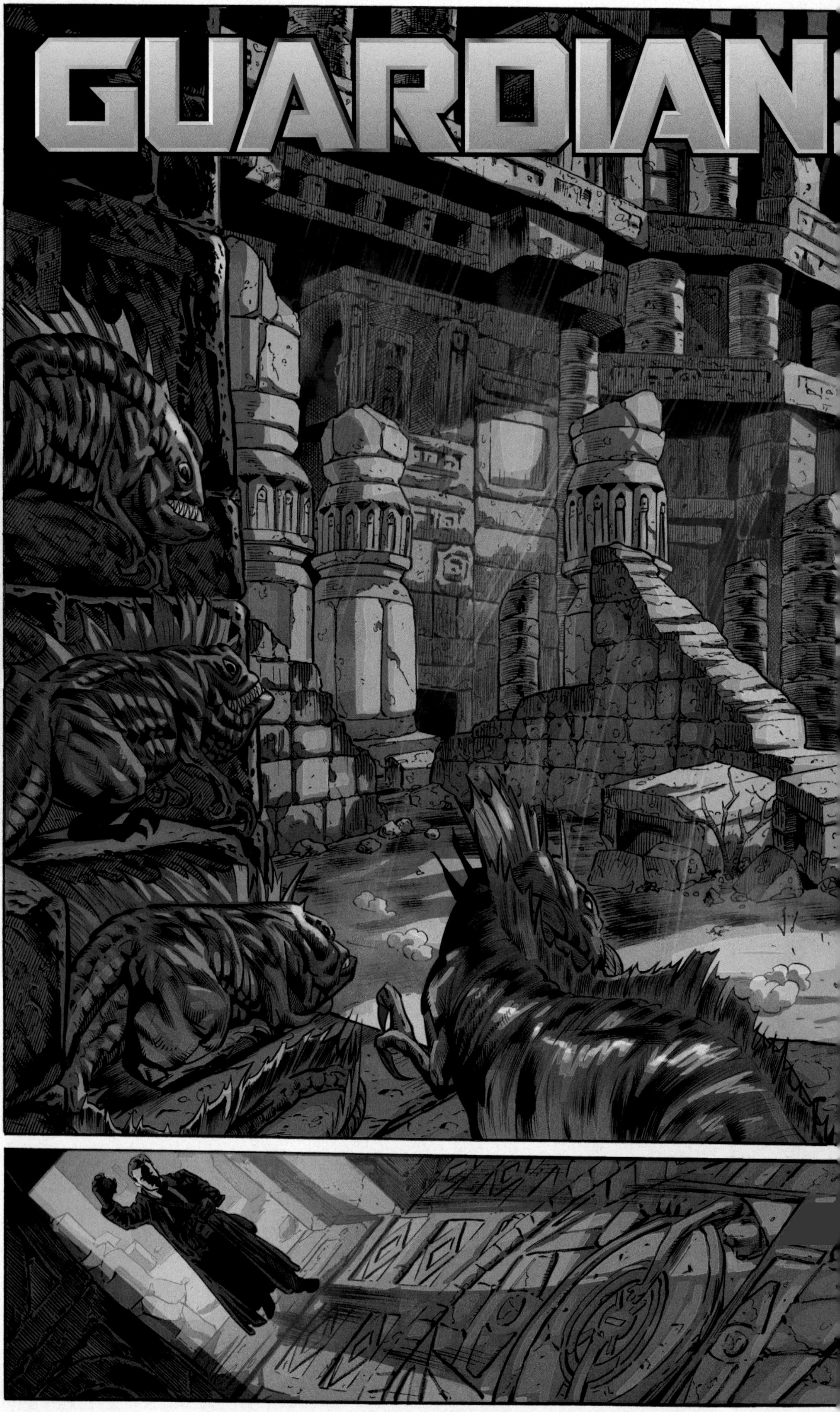
GUARDIAN

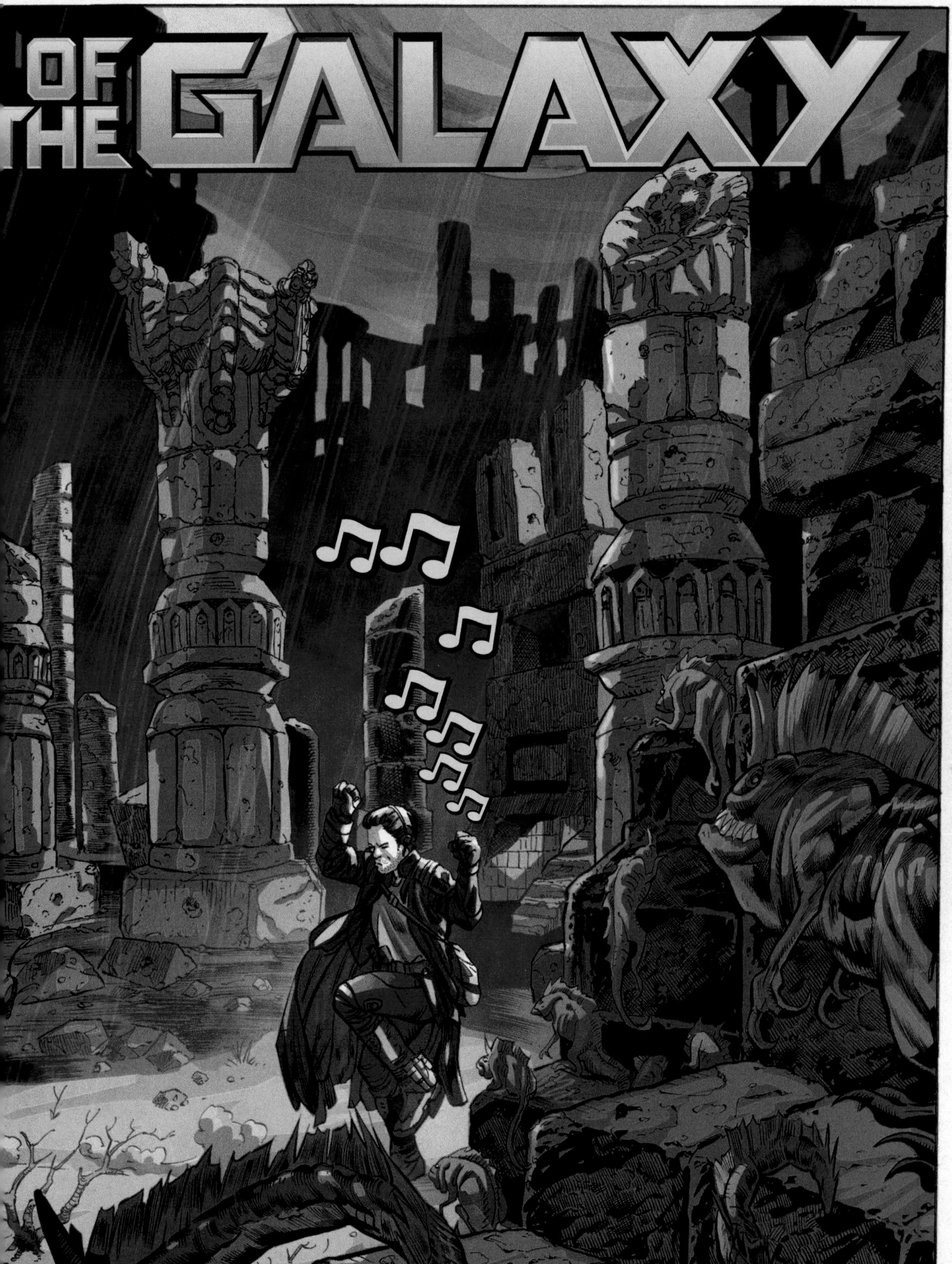
OF THE GALAXY

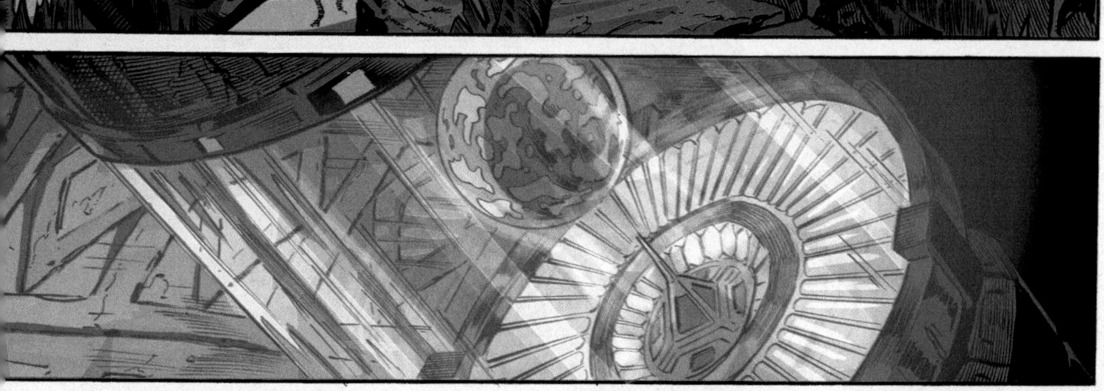

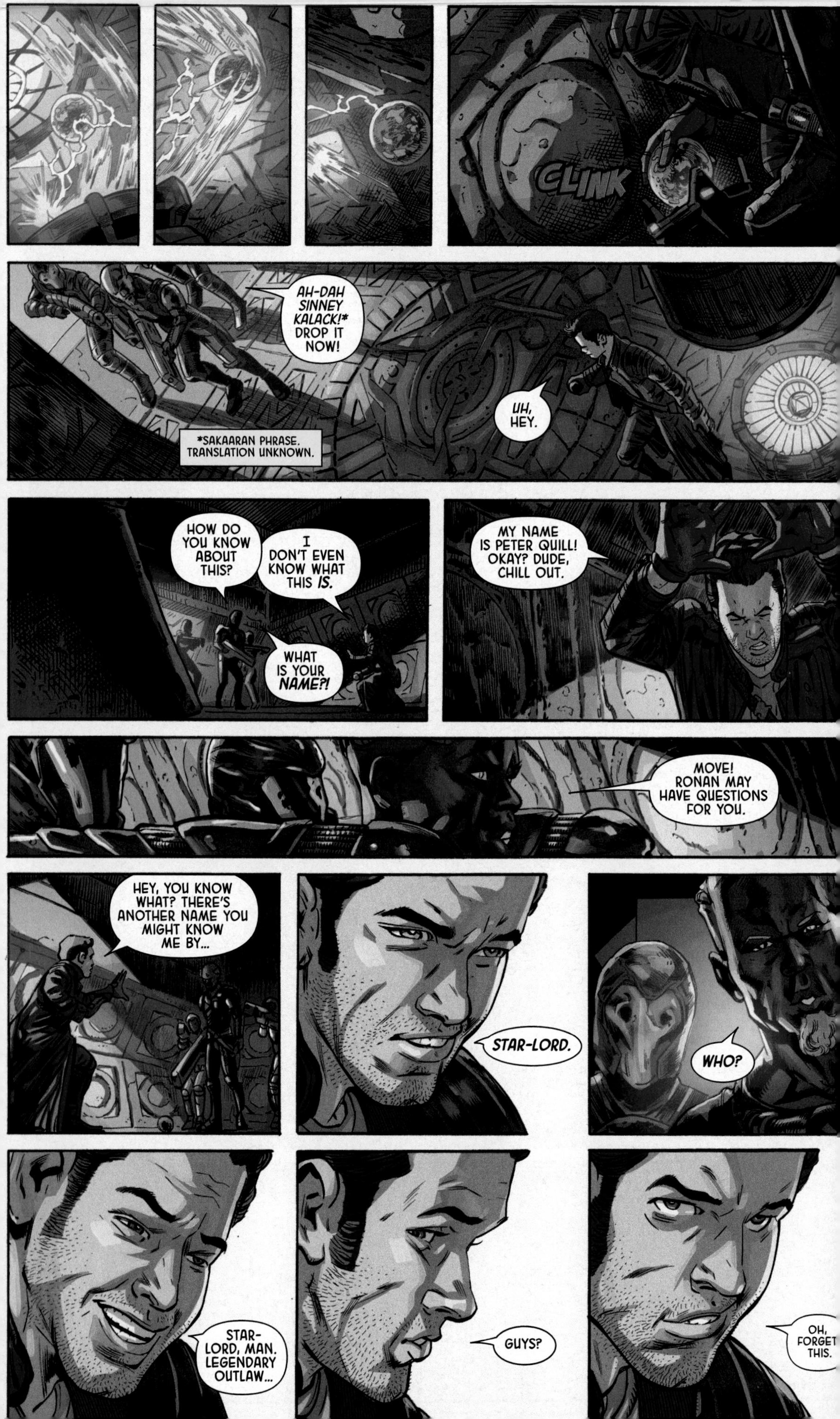
CLINK
AH-DAH SINNEY KALACK!* DROP IT NOW!
UH, HEY.
*SAKAARAN PHRASE. TRANSLATION UNKNOWN.
HOW DO YOU KNOW ABOUT THIS?
I DON'T EVEN KNOW WHAT THIS IS.
WHAT IS YOUR NAME?!
MY NAME IS PETER QUILL! OKAY? DUDE, CHILL OUT.
MOVE! RONAN MAY HAVE QUESTIONS FOR YOU.
HEY, YOU KNOW WHAT? THERE'S ANOTHER NAME YOU MIGHT KNOW ME BY...
STAR-LORD.
WHO?
STAR-LORD, MAN. LEGENDARY OUTLAW...
GUYS?
OH, FORGET THIS.

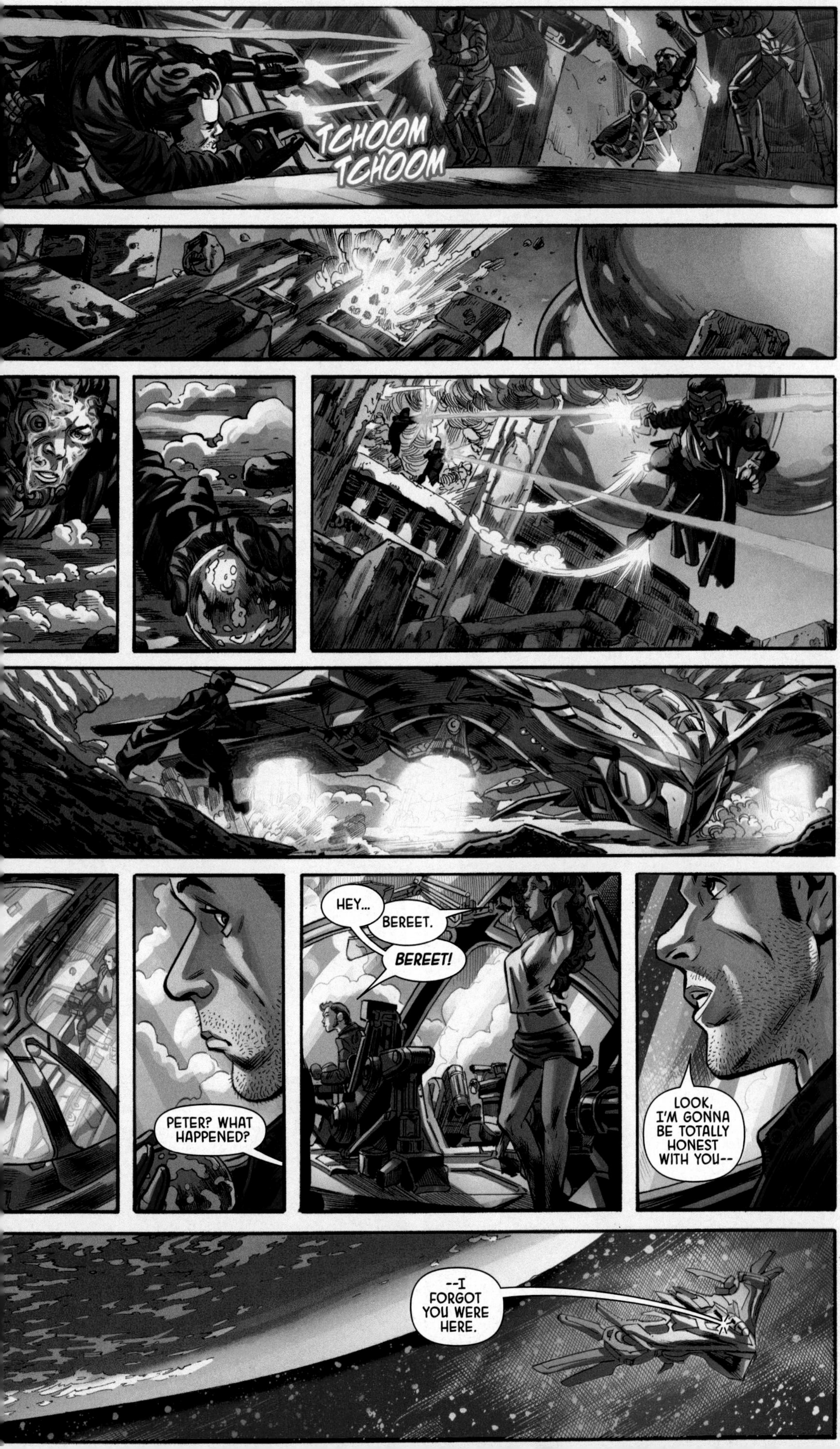
TCHOOM TCHOOM
PETER? WHAT HAPPENED?
HEY...
BEREET.
BEREET!
LOOK, I'M GONNA BE TOTALLY HONEST WITH YOU--
--I FORGOT YOU WERE HERE.

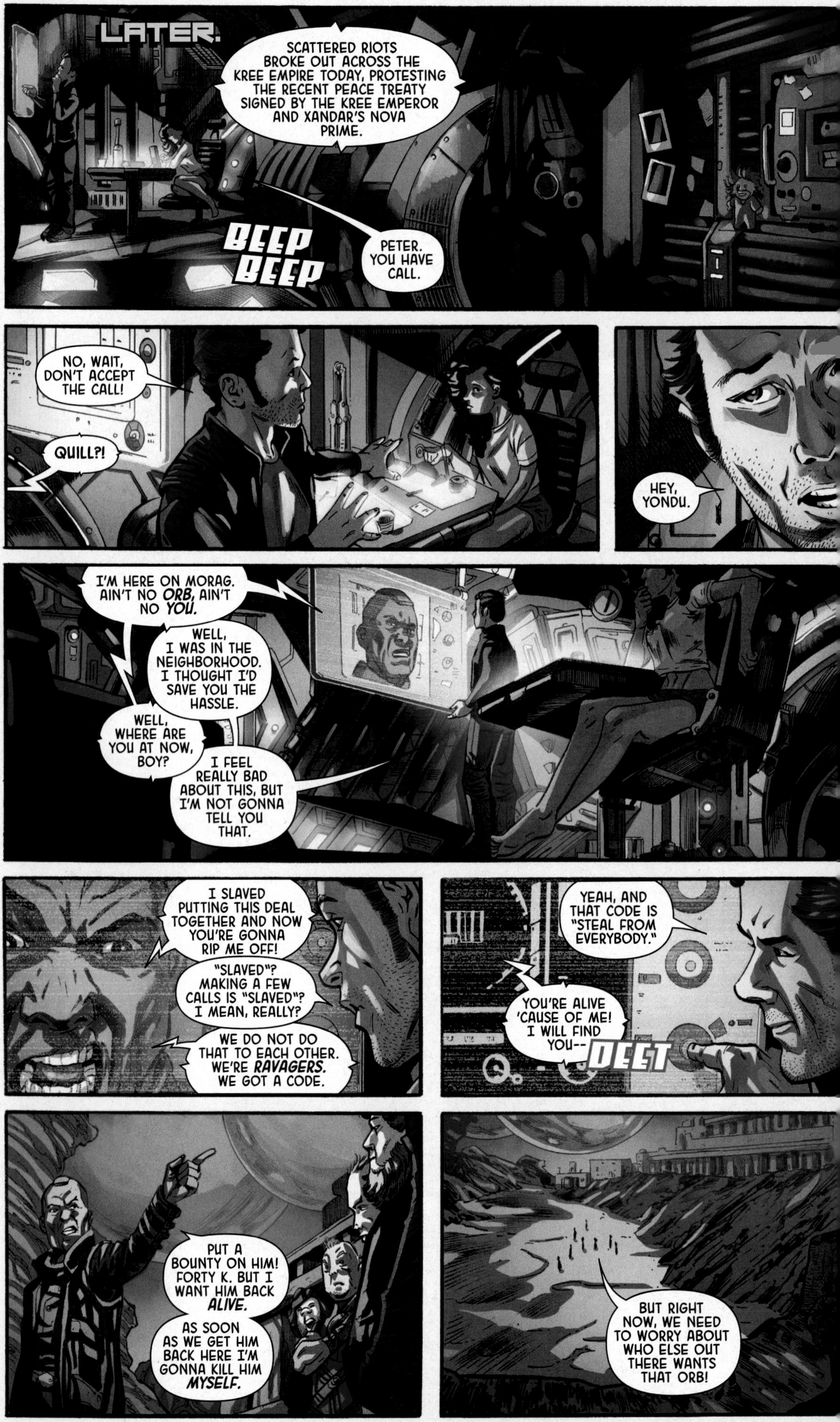
LATER.
SCATTERED RIOTS BROKE OUT ACROSS THE KREE EMPIRE TODAY, PROTESTING THE RECENT PEACE TREATY SIGNED BY THE KREE EMPEROR AND XANDAR'S NOVA PRIME.
BEEP BEEP
PETER. YOU HAVE CALL.
NO, WAIT, DON'T ACCEPT THE CALL!
QUILL?!
HEY, YONDU.
I'M HERE ON MORAG. AIN'T NO ORB, AIN'T NO YOU.
WELL, I WAS IN THE NEIGHBORHOOD. I THOUGHT I'D SAVE YOU THE HASSLE.
WELL, WHERE ARE YOU AT NOW, BOY?
I FEEL REALLY BAD ABOUT THIS, BUT I'M NOT GONNA TELL YOU THAT.
I SLAVED PUTTING THIS DEAL TOGETHER AND NOW YOU'RE GONNA RIP ME OFF!
"SLAVED"? MAKING A FEW CALLS IS "SLAVED"? I MEAN, REALLY?
WE DO NOT DO THAT TO EACH OTHER. WE'RE RAVAGERS. WE GOT A CODE.
YEAH, AND THAT CODE IS "STEAL FROM EVERYBODY."
YOU'RE ALIVE 'CAUSE OF ME! I WILL FIND YOU--
DEET
PUT A BOUNTY ON HIM! FORTY K. BUT I WANT HIM BACK ALIVE.
AS SOON AS WE GET HIM BACK HERE I'M GONNA KILL HIM MYSELF.
BUT RIGHT NOW, WE NEED TO WORRY ABOUT WHO ELSE OUT THERE WANTS THAT ORB!

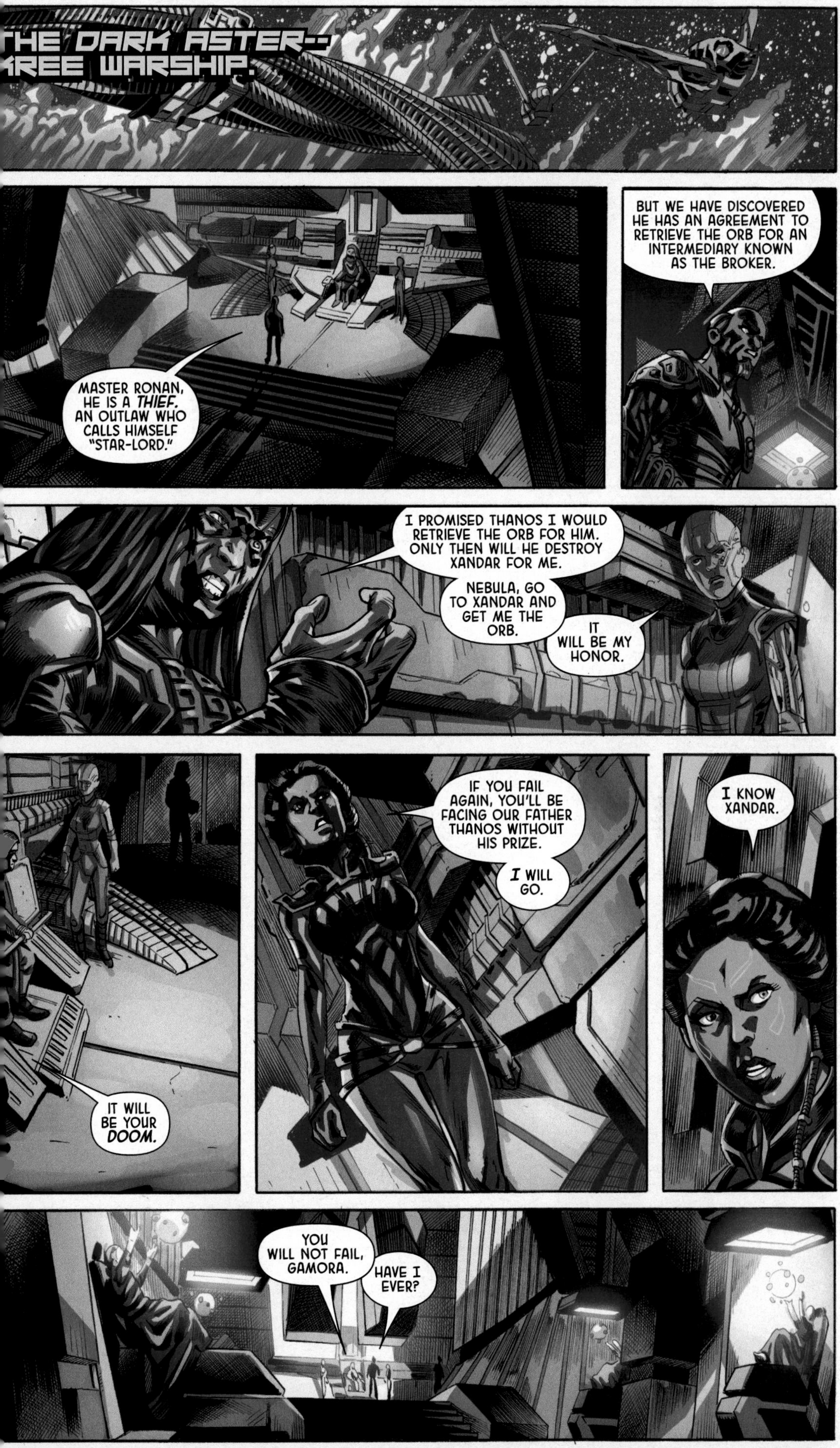

THE DARK ASTER--
KREE WARSHIP.
MASTER RONAN, HE IS A *THIEF.* AN OUTLAW WHO CALLS HIMSELF "STAR-LORD."
BUT WE HAVE DISCOVERED HE HAS AN AGREEMENT TO RETRIEVE THE ORB FOR AN INTERMEDIARY KNOWN AS THE BROKER.
I PROMISED THANOS I WOULD RETRIEVE THE ORB FOR HIM. ONLY THEN WILL HE DESTROY XANDAR FOR ME.
NEBULA, GO TO XANDAR AND GET ME THE ORB.
IT WILL BE MY HONOR.
IT WILL BE YOUR *DOOM.*
IF YOU FAIL AGAIN, YOU'LL BE FACING OUR FATHER THANOS WITHOUT HIS PRIZE.
I WILL GO.
I KNOW XANDAR.
YOU WILL NOT FAIL, GAMORA.
HAVE I EVER?

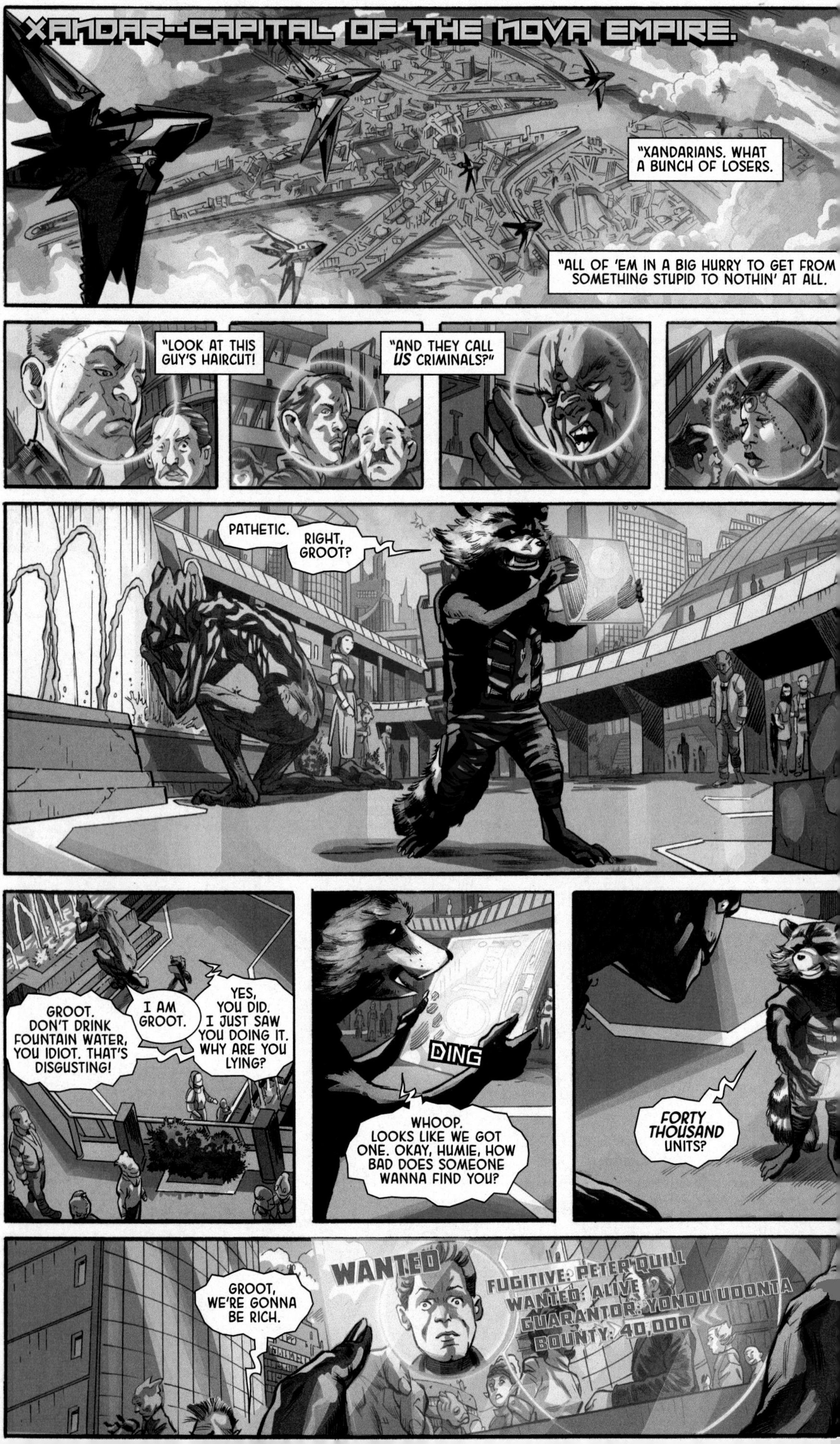
XANDAR--CAPITAL OF THE NOVA EMPIRE.
"XANDARIANS. WHAT A BUNCH OF LOSERS.
"ALL OF 'EM IN A BIG HURRY TO GET FROM SOMETHING STUPID TO NOTHIN' AT ALL.
"LOOK AT THIS GUY'S HAIRCUT!
"AND THEY CALL *US* CRIMINALS?"
PATHETIC.
RIGHT, GROOT?
GROOT. DON'T DRINK FOUNTAIN WATER, YOU IDIOT. THAT'S DISGUSTING!
I AM GROOT.
YES, YOU DID. I JUST SAW YOU DOING IT. WHY ARE YOU LYING?
DING
WHOOP. LOOKS LIKE WE GOT ONE. OKAY, HUMIE, HOW BAD DOES SOMEONE WANNA FIND YOU?
FORTY THOUSAND UNITS?
GROOT, WE'RE GONNA BE RICH.
WANTED
FUGITIVE: PETER QUILL
WANTED: ALIVE
GUARANTOR: YONDU UDONTA
BOUNTY: 40,000

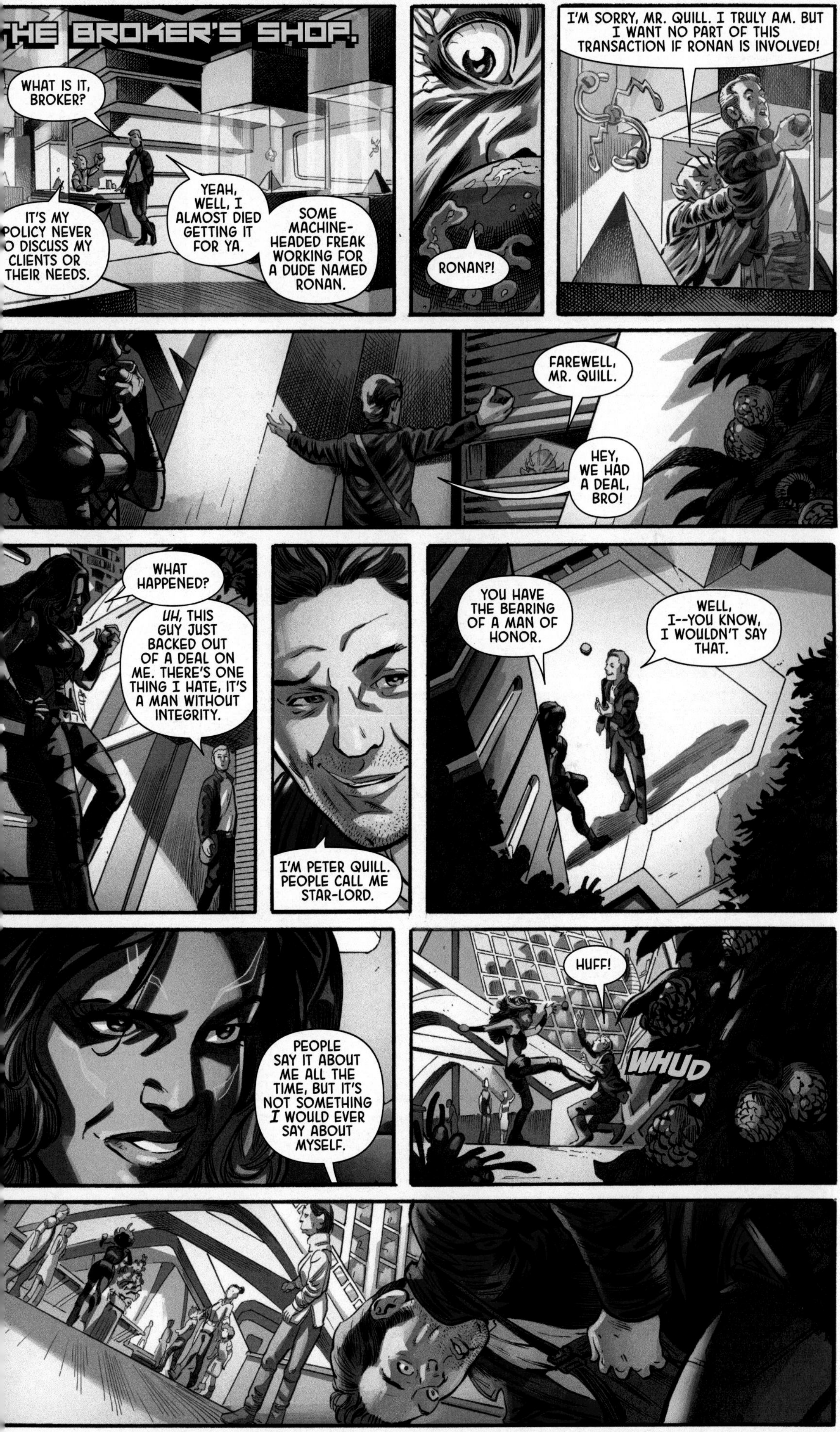
THE BROKER'S SHOP.
WHAT IS IT, BROKER?
IT'S MY POLICY NEVER TO DISCUSS MY CLIENTS OR THEIR NEEDS.
YEAH, WELL, I ALMOST DIED GETTING IT FOR YA.
SOME MACHINE-HEADED FREAK WORKING FOR A DUDE NAMED RONAN.
RONAN?!
I'M SORRY, MR. QUILL. I TRULY AM. BUT I WANT NO PART OF THIS TRANSACTION IF RONAN IS INVOLVED!
FAREWELL, MR. QUILL.
HEY, WE HAD A DEAL, BRO!
WHAT HAPPENED?
UH, THIS GUY JUST BACKED OUT OF A DEAL ON ME. THERE'S ONE THING I HATE, IT'S A MAN WITHOUT INTEGRITY.
I'M PETER QUILL. PEOPLE CALL ME STAR-LORD.
YOU HAVE THE BEARING OF A MAN OF HONOR.
WELL, I--YOU KNOW, I WOULDN'T SAY THAT.
PEOPLE SAY IT ABOUT ME ALL THE TIME, BUT IT'S NOT SOMETHING I WOULD EVER SAY ABOUT MYSELF.
HUFF!
WHUD

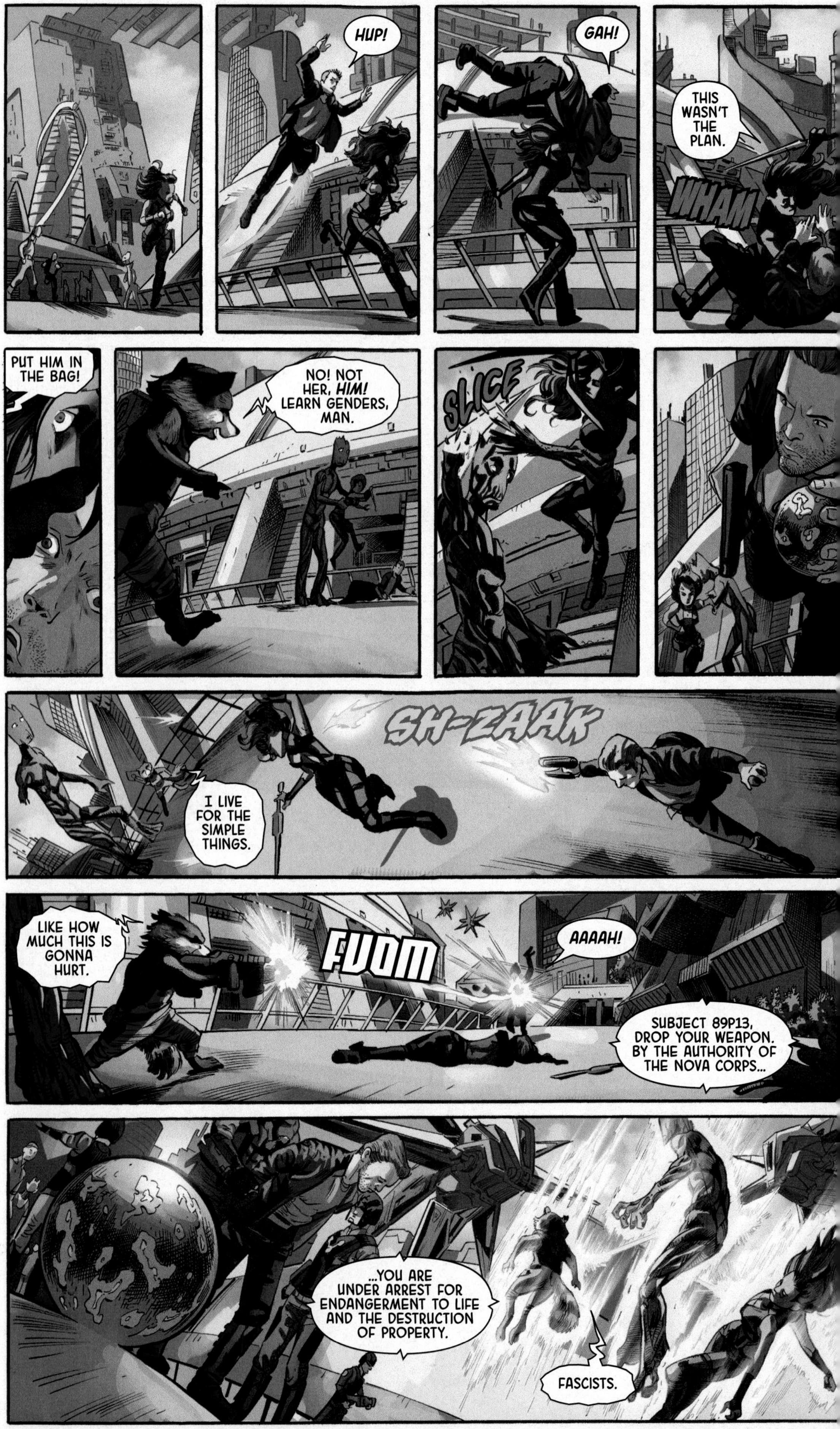
HUP!
GAH!
THIS WASN'T THE PLAN.
WHAM
PUT HIM IN THE BAG!
NO! NOT HER, HIM! LEARN GENDERS, MAN.
SLICE
SH-ZAAK
I LIVE FOR THE SIMPLE THINGS.
LIKE HOW MUCH THIS IS GONNA HURT.
FVOM
AAAAH!
SUBJECT 89P13, DROP YOUR WEAPON. BY THE AUTHORITY OF THE NOVA CORPS...
...YOU ARE UNDER ARREST FOR ENDANGERMENT TO LIFE AND THE DESTRUCTION OF PROPERTY.
FASCISTS.

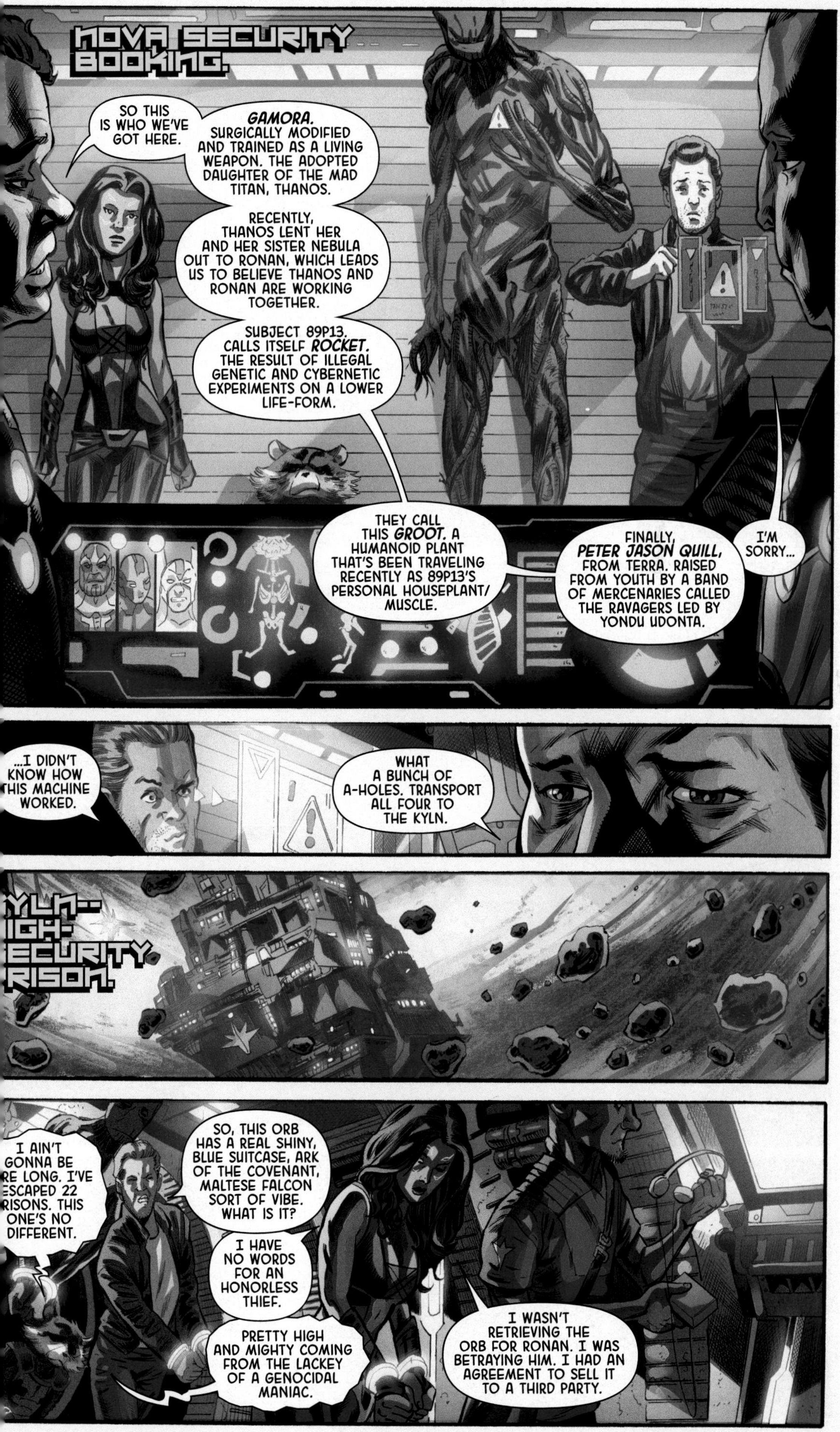

NOVA SECURITY BOOKING.
SO THIS IS WHO WE'VE GOT HERE.
GAMORA. SURGICALLY MODIFIED AND TRAINED AS A LIVING WEAPON. THE ADOPTED DAUGHTER OF THE MAD TITAN, THANOS.
RECENTLY, THANOS LENT HER AND HER SISTER NEBULA OUT TO RONAN, WHICH LEADS US TO BELIEVE THANOS AND RONAN ARE WORKING TOGETHER.
SUBJECT 89P13. CALLS ITSELF ROCKET. THE RESULT OF ILLEGAL GENETIC AND CYBERNETIC EXPERIMENTS ON A LOWER LIFE-FORM.
THEY CALL THIS GROOT. A HUMANOID PLANT THAT'S BEEN TRAVELING RECENTLY AS 89P13'S PERSONAL HOUSEPLANT/ MUSCLE.
FINALLY, PETER JASON QUILL, FROM TERRA. RAISED FROM YOUTH BY A BAND OF MERCENARIES CALLED THE RAVAGERS LED BY YONDU UDONTA.
I'M SORRY...
...I DIDN'T KNOW HOW THIS MACHINE WORKED.
WHAT A BUNCH OF A-HOLES. TRANSPORT ALL FOUR TO THE KYLN.
YLN-- IGH- ECURITY RISON.
I AIN'T GONNA BE RE LONG. I'VE ESCAPED 22 RISONS. THIS ONE'S NO DIFFERENT.
SO, THIS ORB HAS A REAL SHINY, BLUE SUITCASE, ARK OF THE COVENANT, MALTESE FALCON SORT OF VIBE. WHAT IS IT?
I HAVE NO WORDS FOR AN HONORLESS THIEF.
PRETTY HIGH AND MIGHTY COMING FROM THE LACKEY OF A GENOCIDAL MANIAC.
I WASN'T RETRIEVING THE ORB FOR RONAN. I WAS BETRAYING HIM. I HAD AN AGREEMENT TO SELL IT TO A THIRD PARTY.

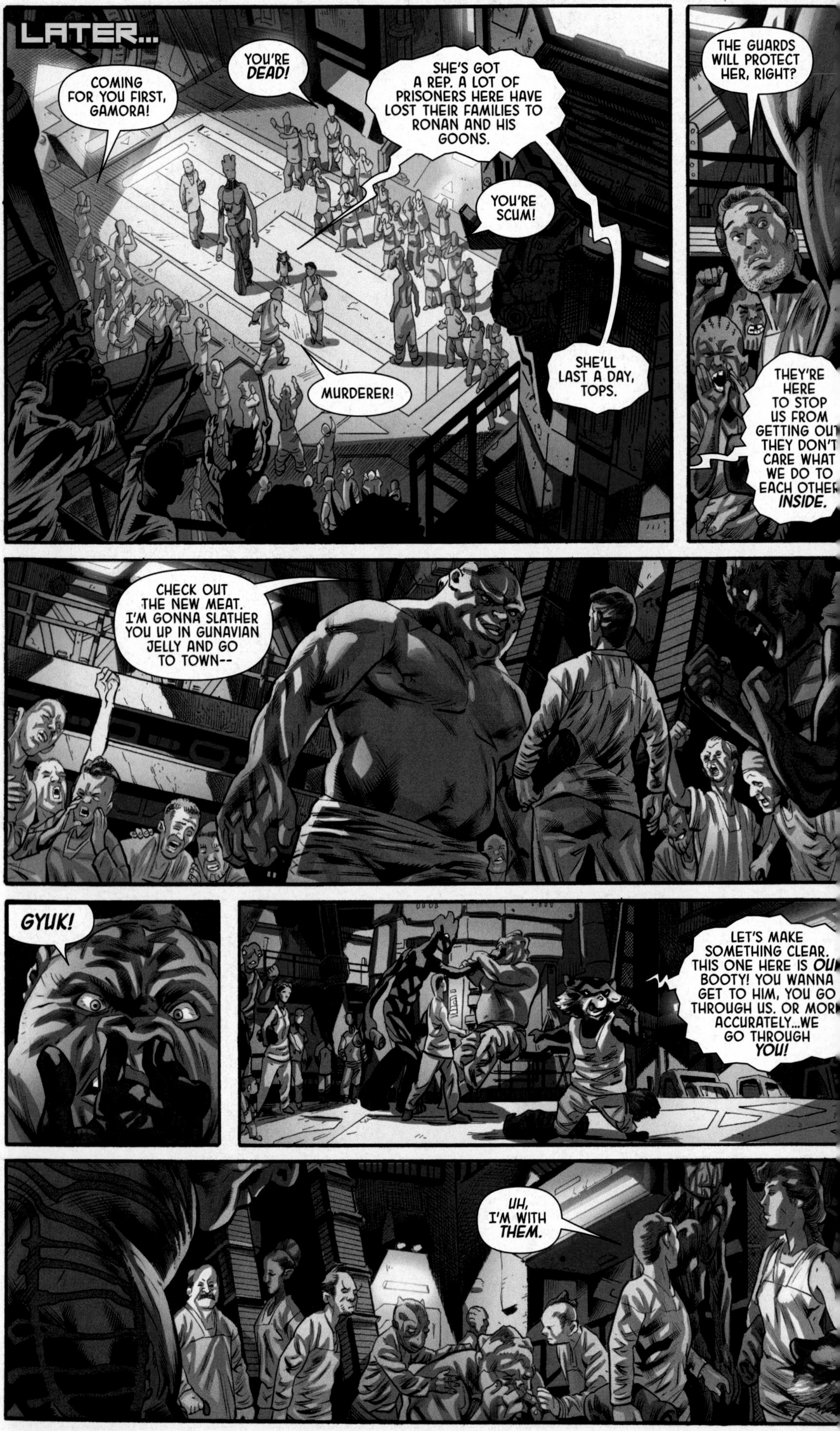
LATER...
COMING FOR YOU FIRST, GAMORA!
YOU'RE DEAD!
SHE'S GOT A REP. A LOT OF PRISONERS HERE HAVE LOST THEIR FAMILIES TO RONAN AND HIS GOONS.
YOU'RE SCUM!
MURDERER!
SHE'LL LAST A DAY, TOPS.
THE GUARDS WILL PROTECT HER, RIGHT?
THEY'RE HERE TO STOP US FROM GETTING OUT THEY DON'T CARE WHAT WE DO TO EACH OTHER INSIDE.
CHECK OUT THE NEW MEAT. I'M GONNA SLATHER YOU UP IN GUNAVIAN JELLY AND GO TO TOWN--
GYUK!
LET'S MAKE SOMETHING CLEAR. THIS ONE HERE IS OU BOOTY! YOU WANNA GET TO HIM, YOU GO THROUGH US. OR MOR ACCURATELY...WE GO THROUGH YOU!
UH, I'M WITH THEM.

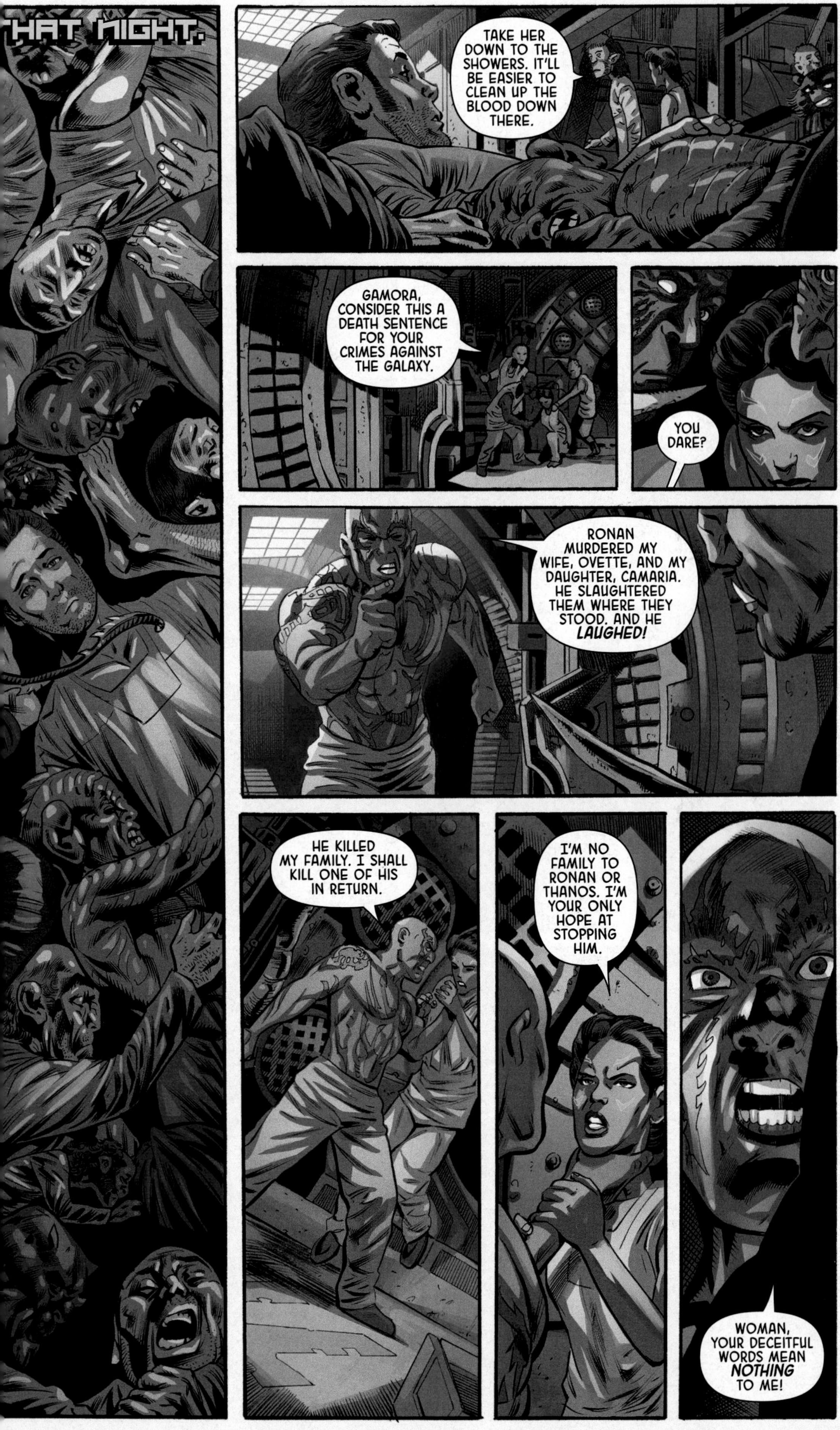
THAT NIGHT.
TAKE HER DOWN TO THE SHOWERS. IT'LL BE EASIER TO CLEAN UP THE BLOOD DOWN THERE.
GAMORA, CONSIDER THIS A DEATH SENTENCE FOR YOUR CRIMES AGAINST THE GALAXY.
YOU DARE?
RONAN MURDERED MY WIFE, OVETTE, AND MY DAUGHTER, CAMARIA. HE SLAUGHTERED THEM WHERE THEY STOOD. AND HE *LAUGHED!*
HE KILLED MY FAMILY. I SHALL KILL ONE OF HIS IN RETURN.
I'M NO FAMILY TO RONAN OR THANOS. I'M YOUR ONLY HOPE AT STOPPING HIM.
WOMAN, YOUR DECEITFUL WORDS MEAN *NOTHING* TO ME!

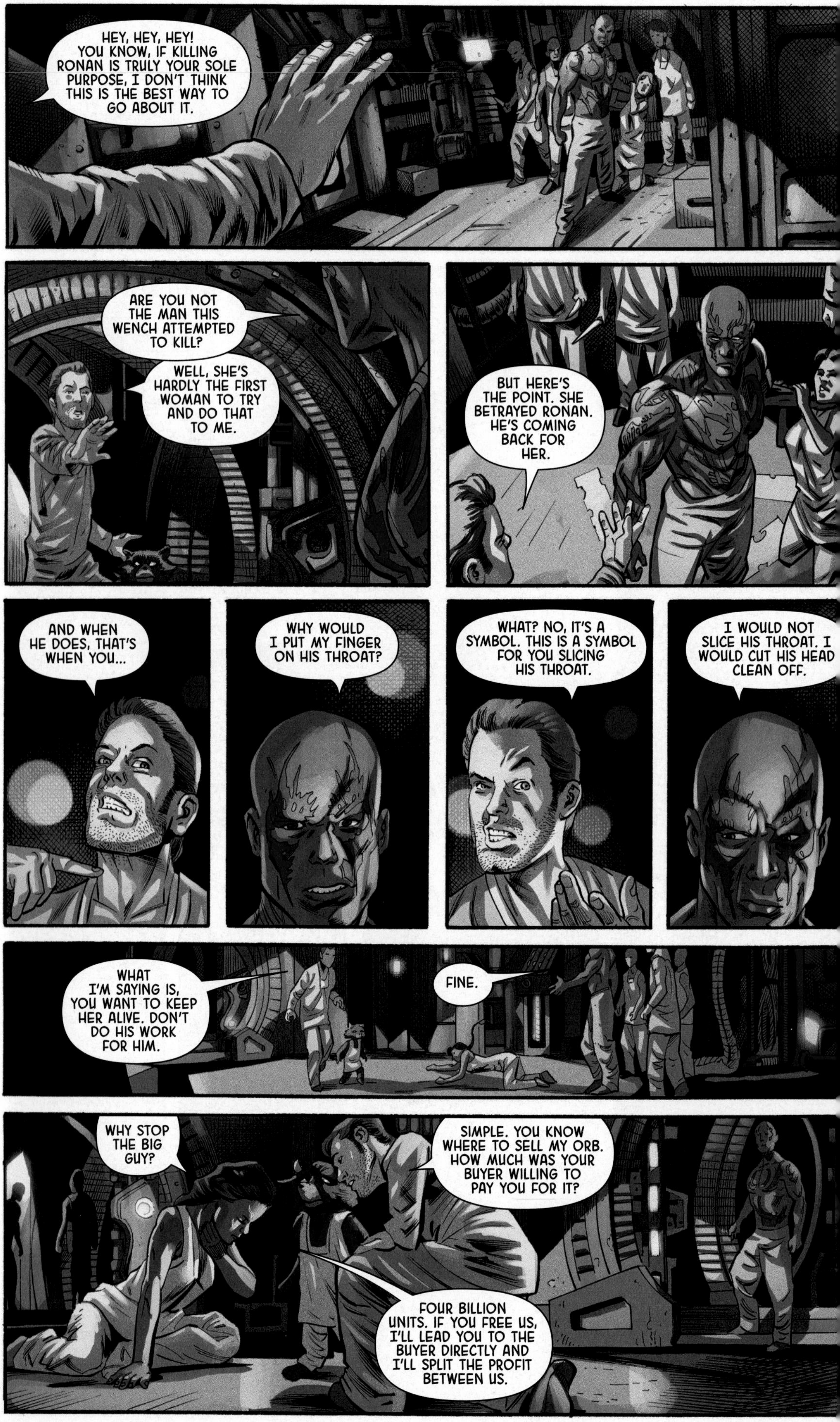
HEY, HEY, HEY! YOU KNOW, IF KILLING RONAN IS TRULY YOUR SOLE PURPOSE, I DON'T THINK THIS IS THE BEST WAY TO GO ABOUT IT.
ARE YOU NOT THE MAN THIS WENCH ATTEMPTED TO KILL?
WELL, SHE'S HARDLY THE FIRST WOMAN TO TRY AND DO THAT TO ME.
BUT HERE'S THE POINT. SHE BETRAYED RONAN. HE'S COMING BACK FOR HER.
AND WHEN HE DOES, THAT'S WHEN YOU...
WHY WOULD I PUT MY FINGER ON HIS THROAT?
WHAT? NO, IT'S A SYMBOL. THIS IS A SYMBOL FOR YOU SLICING HIS THROAT.
I WOULD NOT SLICE HIS THROAT. I WOULD CUT HIS HEAD CLEAN OFF.
WHAT I'M SAYING IS, YOU WANT TO KEEP HER ALIVE. DON'T DO HIS WORK FOR HIM.
FINE.
WHY STOP THE BIG GUY?
SIMPLE. YOU KNOW WHERE TO SELL MY ORB. HOW MUCH WAS YOUR BUYER WILLING TO PAY YOU FOR IT?
FOUR BILLION UNITS. IF YOU FREE US, I'LL LEAD YOU TO THE BUYER DIRECTLY AND I'LL SPLIT THE PROFIT BETWEEN US.

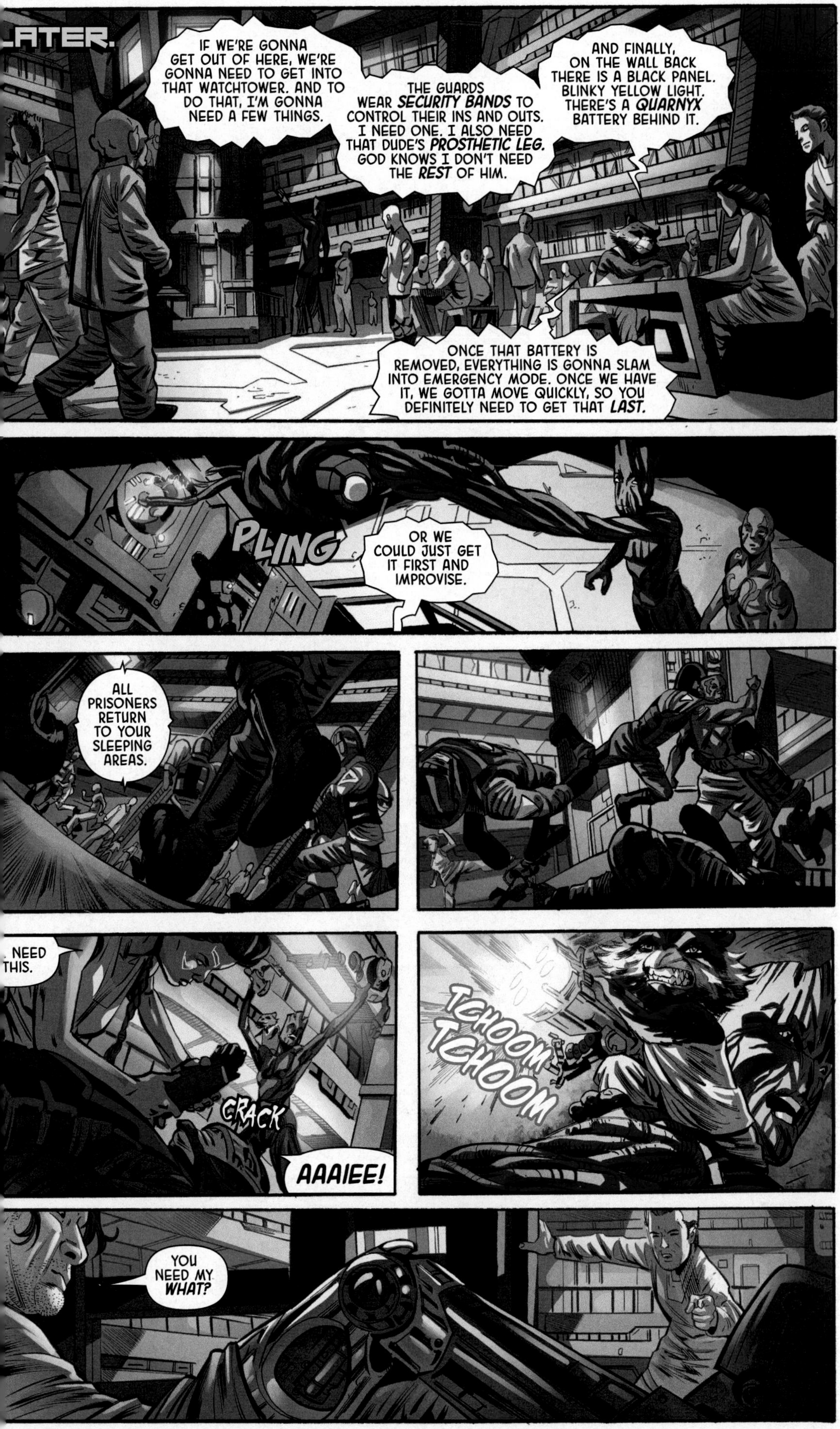
LATER.
IF WE'RE GONNA GET OUT OF HERE, WE'RE GONNA NEED TO GET INTO THAT WATCHTOWER. AND TO DO THAT, I'M GONNA NEED A FEW THINGS.
THE GUARDS WEAR SECURITY BANDS TO CONTROL THEIR INS AND OUTS. I NEED ONE. I ALSO NEED THAT DUDE'S PROSTHETIC LEG. GOD KNOWS I DON'T NEED THE REST OF HIM.
AND FINALLY, ON THE WALL BACK THERE IS A BLACK PANEL. BLINKY YELLOW LIGHT. THERE'S A QUARNYX BATTERY BEHIND IT.
ONCE THAT BATTERY IS REMOVED, EVERYTHING IS GONNA SLAM INTO EMERGENCY MODE. ONCE WE HAVE IT, WE GOTTA MOVE QUICKLY, SO YOU DEFINITELY NEED TO GET THAT LAST.
PLING
OR WE COULD JUST GET IT FIRST AND IMPROVISE.
ALL PRISONERS RETURN TO YOUR SLEEPING AREAS.
NEED THIS.
CRACK
AAAIEE!
TCHOOM TCHOOM
YOU NEED MY WHAT?

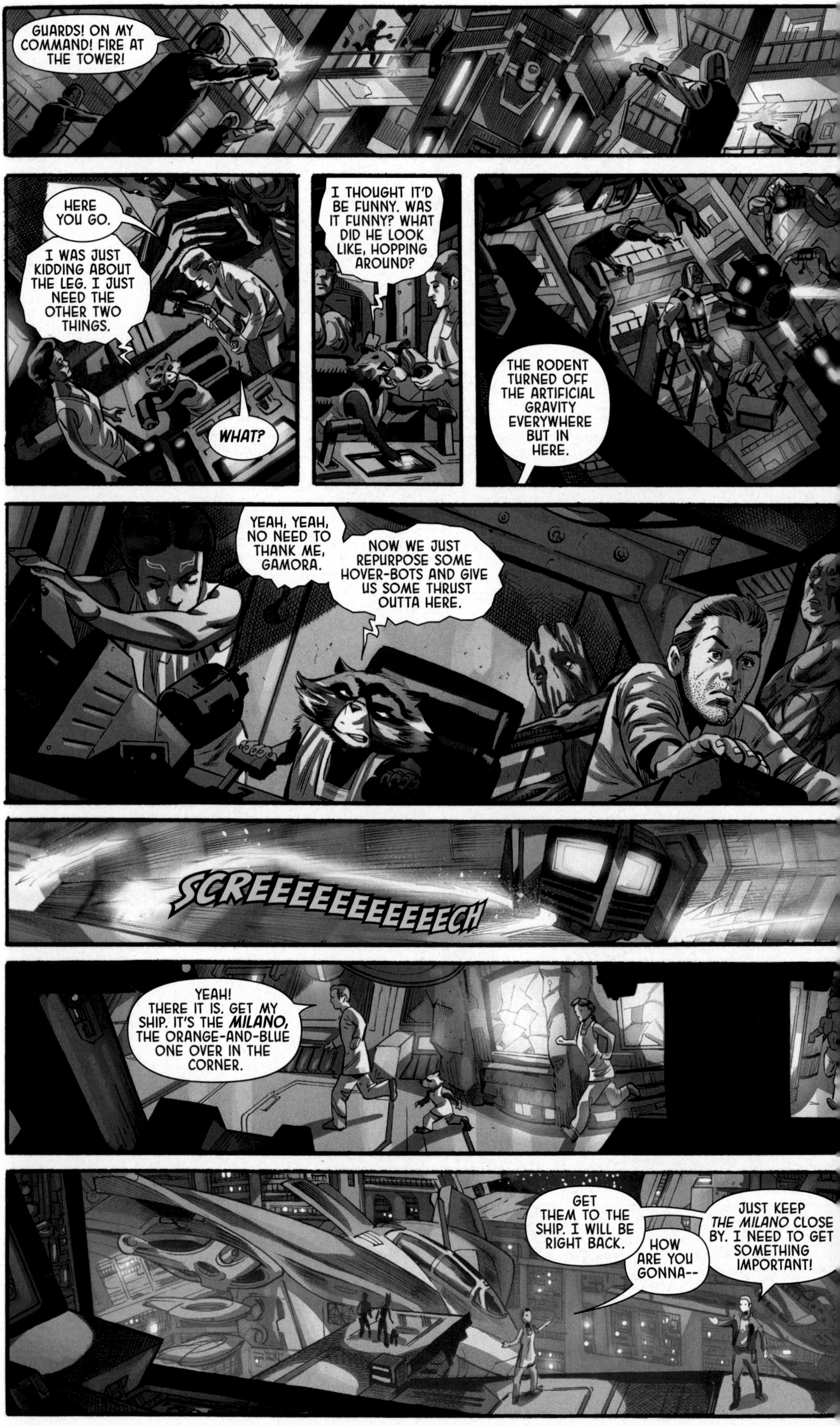
GUARDS! ON MY COMMAND! FIRE AT THE TOWER!
HERE YOU GO.
I WAS JUST KIDDING ABOUT THE LEG. I JUST NEED THE OTHER TWO THINGS.
WHAT?
I THOUGHT IT'D BE FUNNY. WAS IT FUNNY? WHAT DID HE LOOK LIKE, HOPPING AROUND?
THE RODENT TURNED OFF THE ARTIFICIAL GRAVITY EVERYWHERE BUT IN HERE.
YEAH, YEAH, NO NEED TO THANK ME, GAMORA.
NOW WE JUST REPURPOSE SOME HOVER-BOTS AND GIVE US SOME THRUST OUTTA HERE.
SCREEEEEEEEEEEECH
YEAH! THERE IT IS. GET MY SHIP. IT'S THE *MILANO,* THE ORANGE-AND-BLUE ONE OVER IN THE CORNER.
GET THEM TO THE SHIP. I WILL BE RIGHT BACK.
HOW ARE YOU GONNA--
JUST KEEP *THE MILANO* CLOSE BY. I NEED TO GET SOMETHING IMPORTANT!

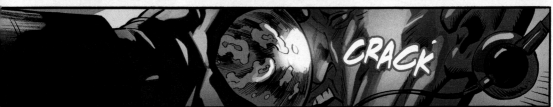

HOW'S HE GONNA GET BACK TO US IN TIME, GAMORA?

HE DECLINED TO SHARE THAT INFORMATION WITH ME.

WELL, SCREW THIS, THEN! I AIN'T WAITING AROUND FOR SOME HUMIE WITH A DEATH WISH. IF WE DON'T LEAVE NOW, WE WILL BE BLOWN TO BITS.

NO! WE'RE NOT LEAVING WITHOUT THE ORB.

BEHOLD.

THIS ONE SHOWS SPIRIT. YOU SHALL MAKE A KEEN ALLY IN THE BATTLE AGAINST RONAN.

COMPANION, WHAT WERE YOU RETRIEVING?

YOU'RE AN IMBECILE.

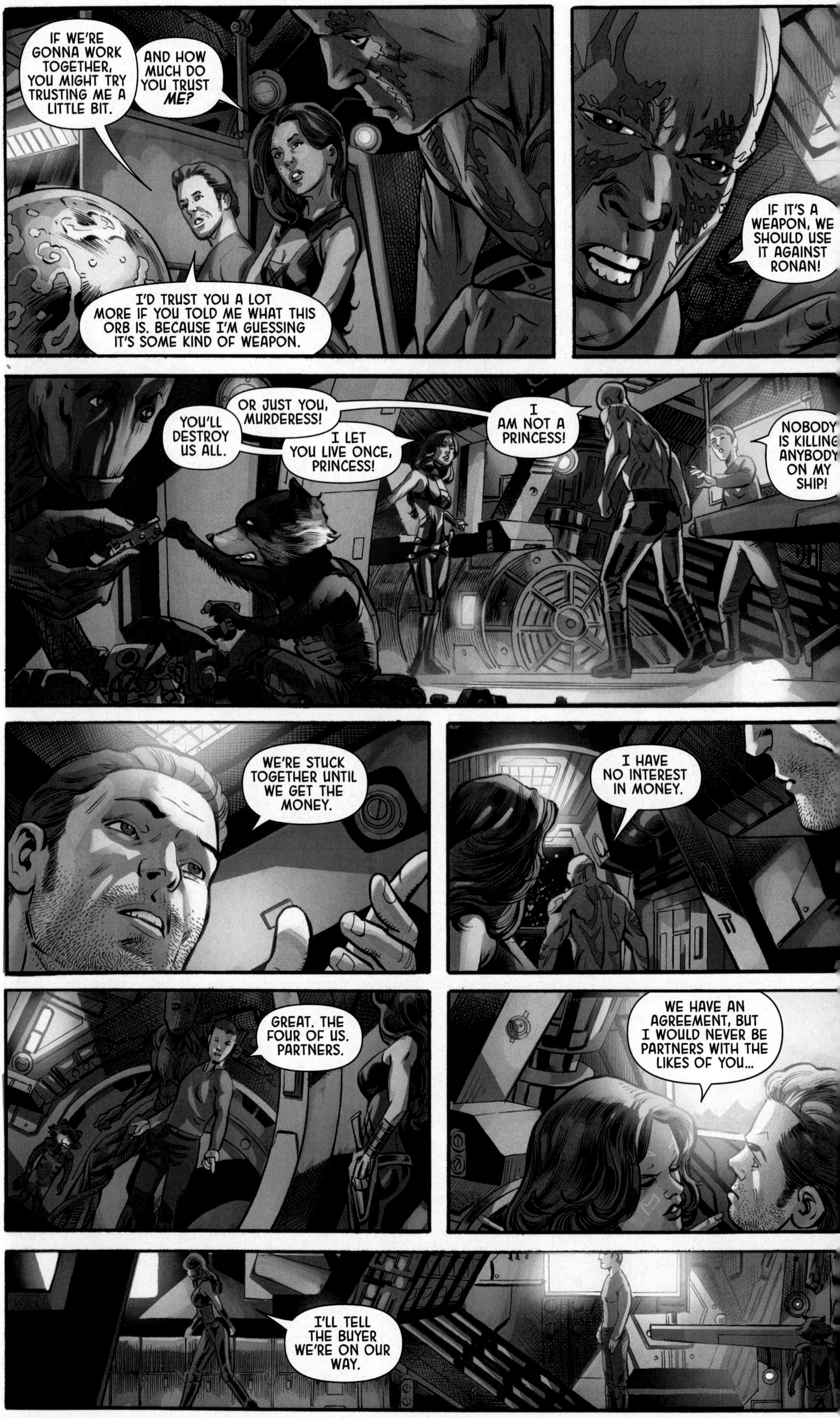
IF WE'RE GONNA WORK TOGETHER, YOU MIGHT TRY TRUSTING ME A LITTLE BIT.
AND HOW MUCH DO YOU TRUST *ME?*
I'D TRUST YOU A LOT MORE IF YOU TOLD ME WHAT THIS ORB IS. BECAUSE I'M GUESSING IT'S SOME KIND OF WEAPON.
IF IT'S A WEAPON, WE SHOULD USE IT AGAINST RONAN!
YOU'LL DESTROY US ALL.
OR JUST YOU, MURDERESS!
I LET YOU LIVE ONCE, PRINCESS!
I AM NOT A PRINCESS!
NOBODY IS KILLING ANYBODY ON MY SHIP!
WE'RE STUCK TOGETHER UNTIL WE GET THE MONEY.
I HAVE NO INTEREST IN MONEY.
GREAT. THE FOUR OF US. PARTNERS.
WE HAVE AN AGREEMENT, BUT I WOULD NEVER BE PARTNERS WITH THE LIKES OF YOU...
I'LL TELL THE BUYER WE'RE ON OUR WAY.

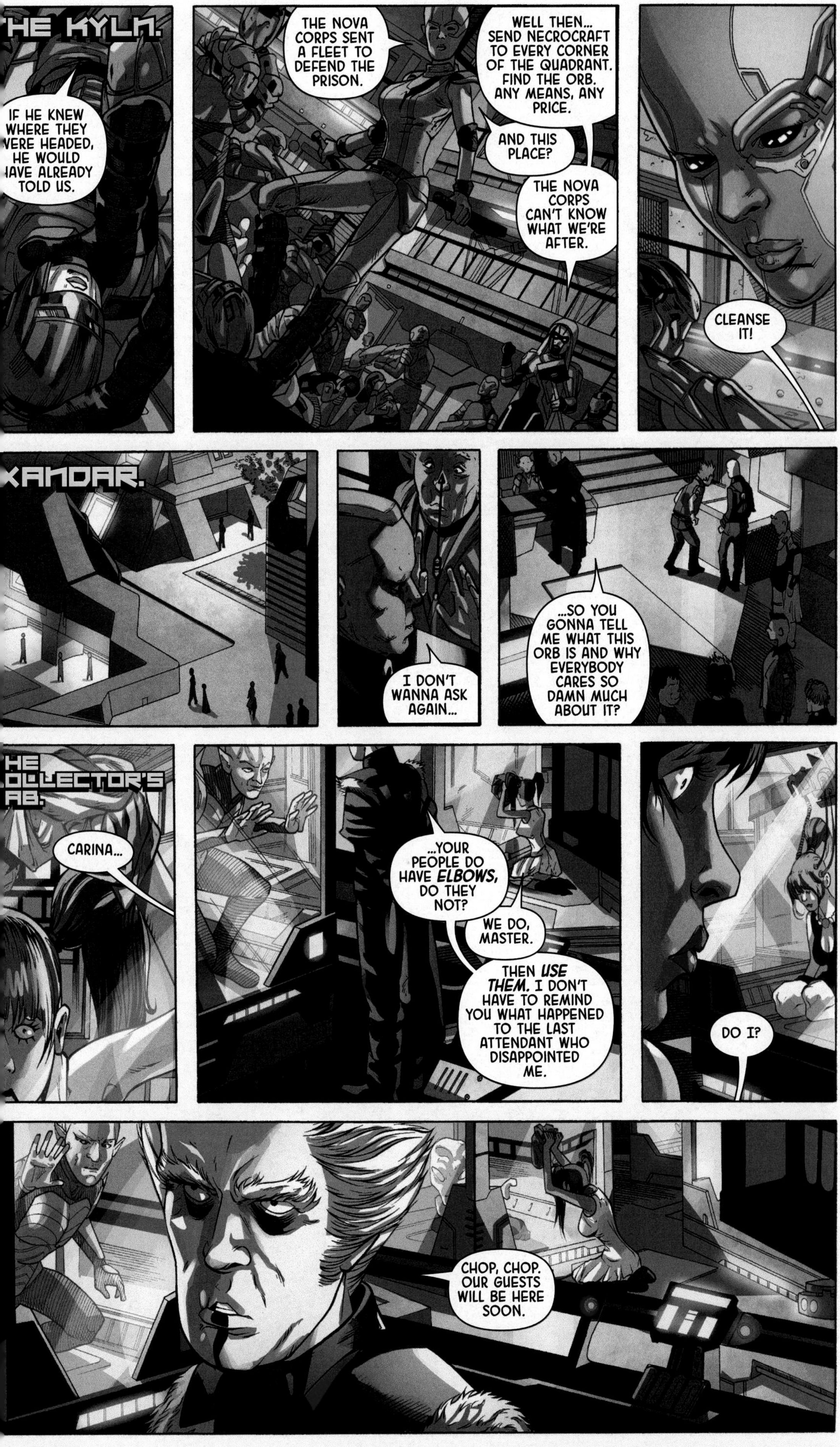
HE KYLN.
IF HE KNEW WHERE THEY VERE HEADED, HE WOULD HAVE ALREADY TOLD US.
THE NOVA CORPS SENT A FLEET TO DEFEND THE PRISON.
WELL THEN... SEND NECROCRAFT TO EVERY CORNER OF THE QUADRANT. FIND THE ORB. ANY MEANS, ANY PRICE.
AND THIS PLACE?
THE NOVA CORPS CAN'T KNOW WHAT WE'RE AFTER.
CLEANSE IT!
XANDAR.
I DON'T WANNA ASK AGAIN...
...SO YOU GONNA TELL ME WHAT THIS ORB IS AND WHY EVERYBODY CARES SO DAMN MUCH ABOUT IT?
HE OLLECTOR'S AB.
CARINA...
...YOUR PEOPLE DO HAVE ELBOWS, DO THEY NOT?
WE DO, MASTER.
THEN USE THEM. I DON'T HAVE TO REMIND YOU WHAT HAPPENED TO THE LAST ATTENDANT WHO DISAPPOINTED ME.
DO I?
CHOP, CHOP. OUR GUESTS WILL BE HERE SOON.

YOUR BUYER'S IN THERE?

WE ARE TO WAIT HERE FOR HIS REPRESENTATIVE.

THIS IS NO RESPECTABLE ESTABLISHMENT. WHAT DO YOU EXPECT US TO DO WHILE WE WAIT?

SOON...

YES! YES! MY ORLONI HAS WON, AS I WIN AT ALL THINGS! NOW, LET'S PUT MORE OF THIS LIQUID INTO OUR BODIES.

WHEN THANOS SAID HE WAS GOING TO DESTROY AN ENTIRE PLANET FOR RONAN I COULDN'T STAND BY AND...

WHY WOULD YOU RISK YOUR LIFE FOR THAT THING?

MY MOTHER GAVE IT TO ME.

WHAT DO YOU DO WITH IT?

YOU LISTEN TO IT. OR YOU CAN DANCE.

I'M A WARRIOR AN ASSAS I DO NO DANCE

NO!

WHAT THE HELL?

I AM NOT SOME STARRY-EYED WAIF HERE TO SUCCUMB TO YOUR, YOUR...PELVIC SORCERY!

THAT IS NOT WHAT'S HAPPENING HERE.

I'LL KILL YOU!

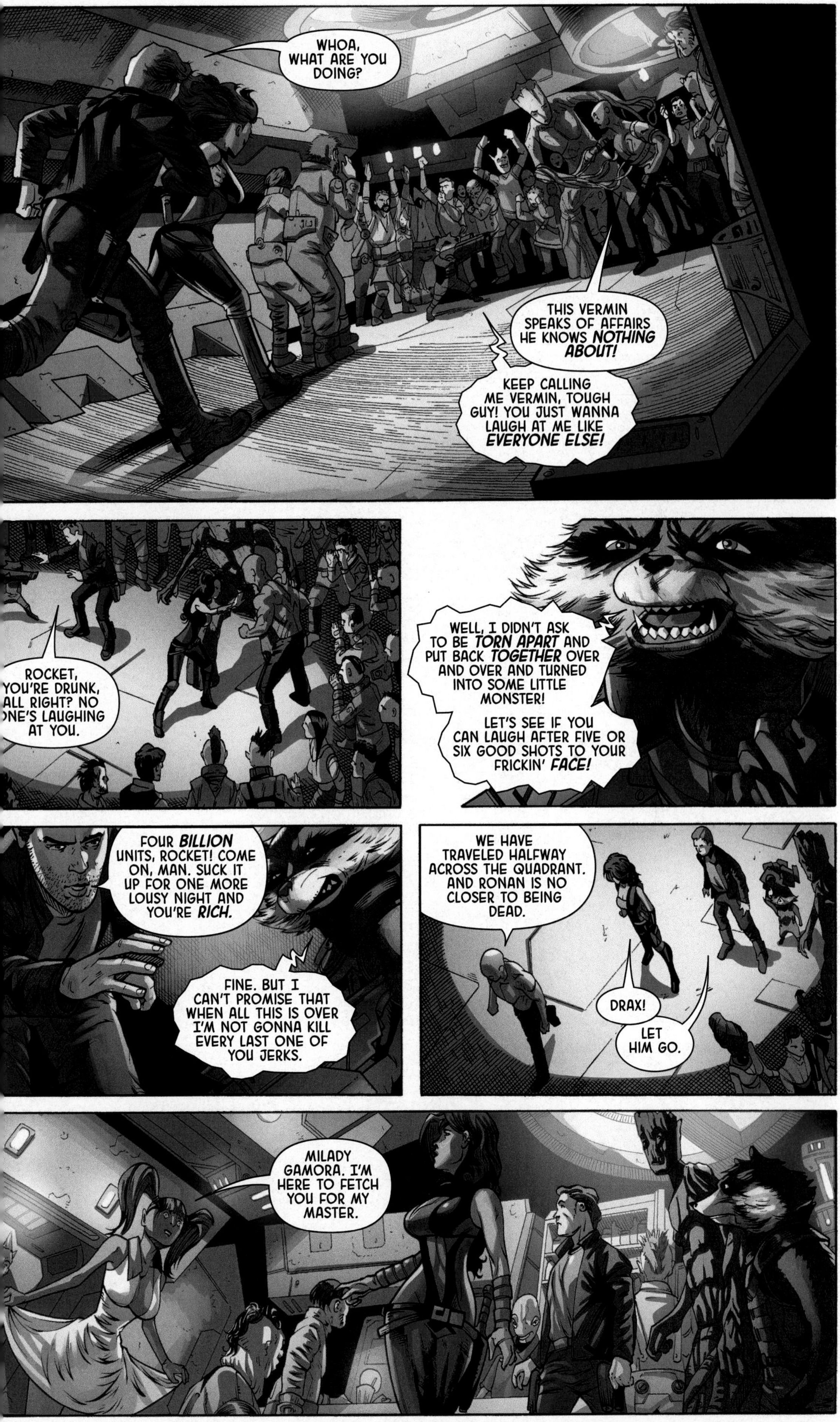
WHOA, WHAT ARE YOU DOING?
THIS VERMIN SPEAKS OF AFFAIRS HE KNOWS NOTHING ABOUT!
KEEP CALLING ME VERMIN, TOUGH GUY! YOU JUST WANNA LAUGH AT ME LIKE EVERYONE ELSE!
ROCKET, YOU'RE DRUNK, ALL RIGHT? NO ONE'S LAUGHING AT YOU.
WELL, I DIDN'T ASK TO BE TORN APART AND PUT BACK TOGETHER OVER AND OVER AND TURNED INTO SOME LITTLE MONSTER!
LET'S SEE IF YOU CAN LAUGH AFTER FIVE OR SIX GOOD SHOTS TO YOUR FRICKIN' FACE!
FOUR BILLION UNITS, ROCKET! COME ON, MAN. SUCK IT UP FOR ONE MORE LOUSY NIGHT AND YOU'RE RICH.
FINE. BUT I CAN'T PROMISE THAT WHEN ALL THIS IS OVER I'M NOT GONNA KILL EVERY LAST ONE OF YOU JERKS.
WE HAVE TRAVELED HALFWAY ACROSS THE QUADRANT. AND RONAN IS NO CLOSER TO BEING DEAD.
DRAX!
LET HIM GO.
MILADY GAMORA. I'M HERE TO FETCH YOU FOR MY MASTER.

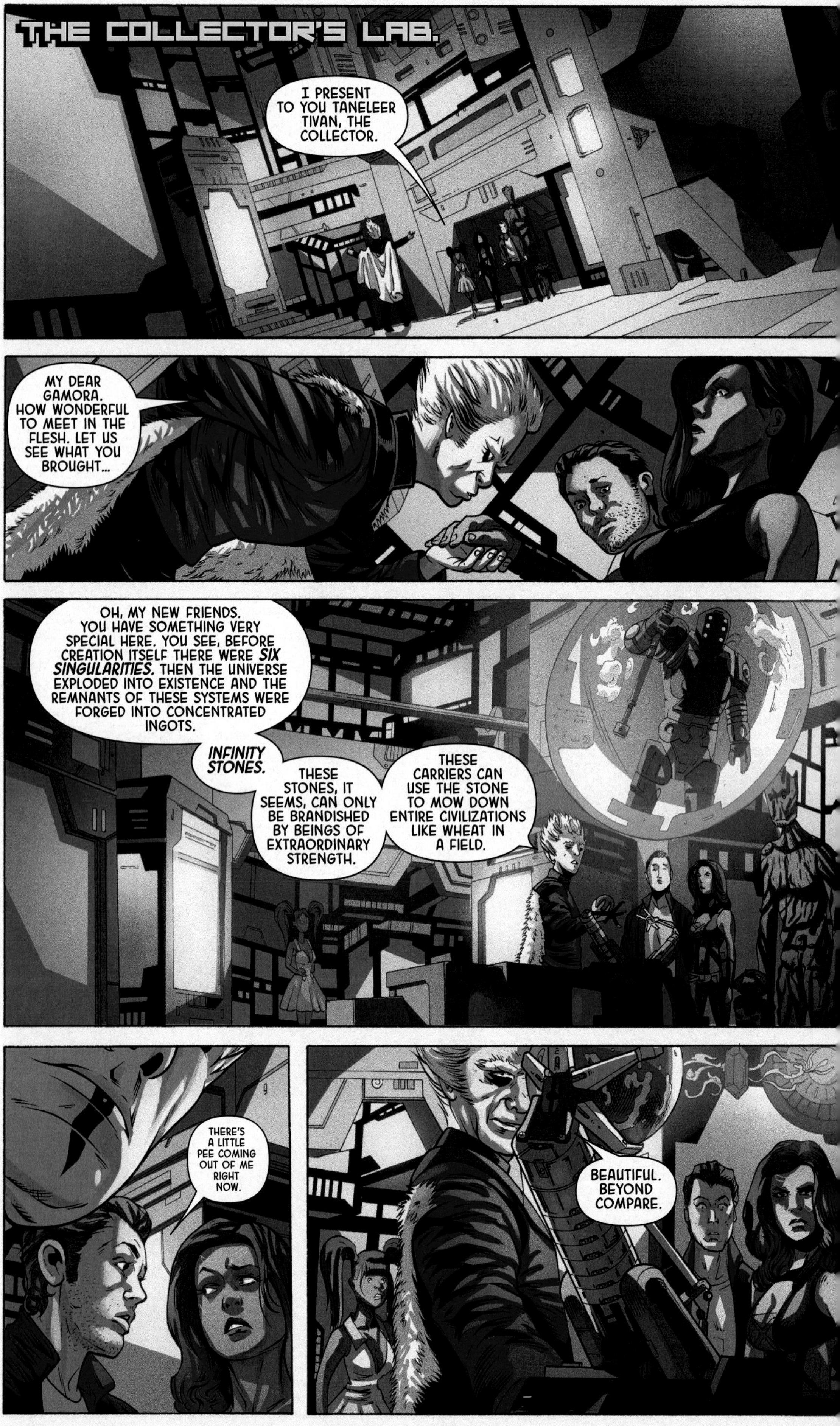
THE COLLECTOR'S LAB.
I PRESENT TO YOU TANELEER TIVAN, THE COLLECTOR.
MY DEAR GAMORA. HOW WONDERFUL TO MEET IN THE FLESH. LET US SEE WHAT YOU BROUGHT...
OH, MY NEW FRIENDS. YOU HAVE SOMETHING VERY SPECIAL HERE. YOU SEE, BEFORE CREATION ITSELF THERE WERE *SIX SINGULARITIES.* THEN THE UNIVERSE EXPLODED INTO EXISTENCE AND THE REMNANTS OF THESE SYSTEMS WERE FORGED INTO CONCENTRATED INGOTS.
INFINITY STONES.
THESE STONES, IT SEEMS, CAN ONLY BE BRANDISHED BY BEINGS OF EXTRAORDINARY STRENGTH.
THESE CARRIERS CAN USE THE STONE TO MOW DOWN ENTIRE CIVILIZATIONS LIKE WHEAT IN A FIELD.
THERE'S A LITTLE PEE COMING OUT OF ME RIGHT NOW.
BEAUTIFUL. BEYOND COMPARE.

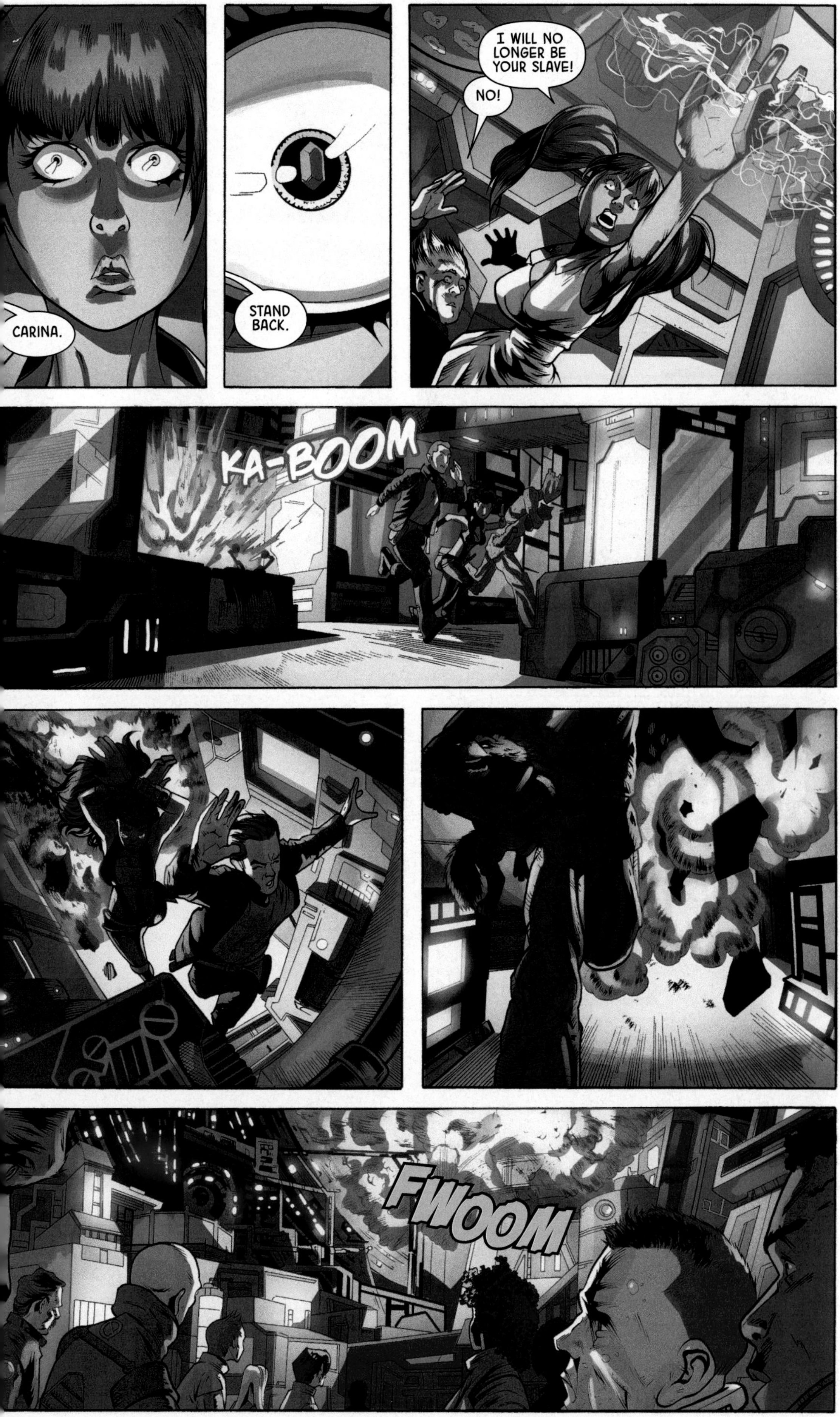
CARINA.
STAND BACK.
I WILL NO LONGER BE YOUR SLAVE!
NO!
KA-BOOM
FWOOM

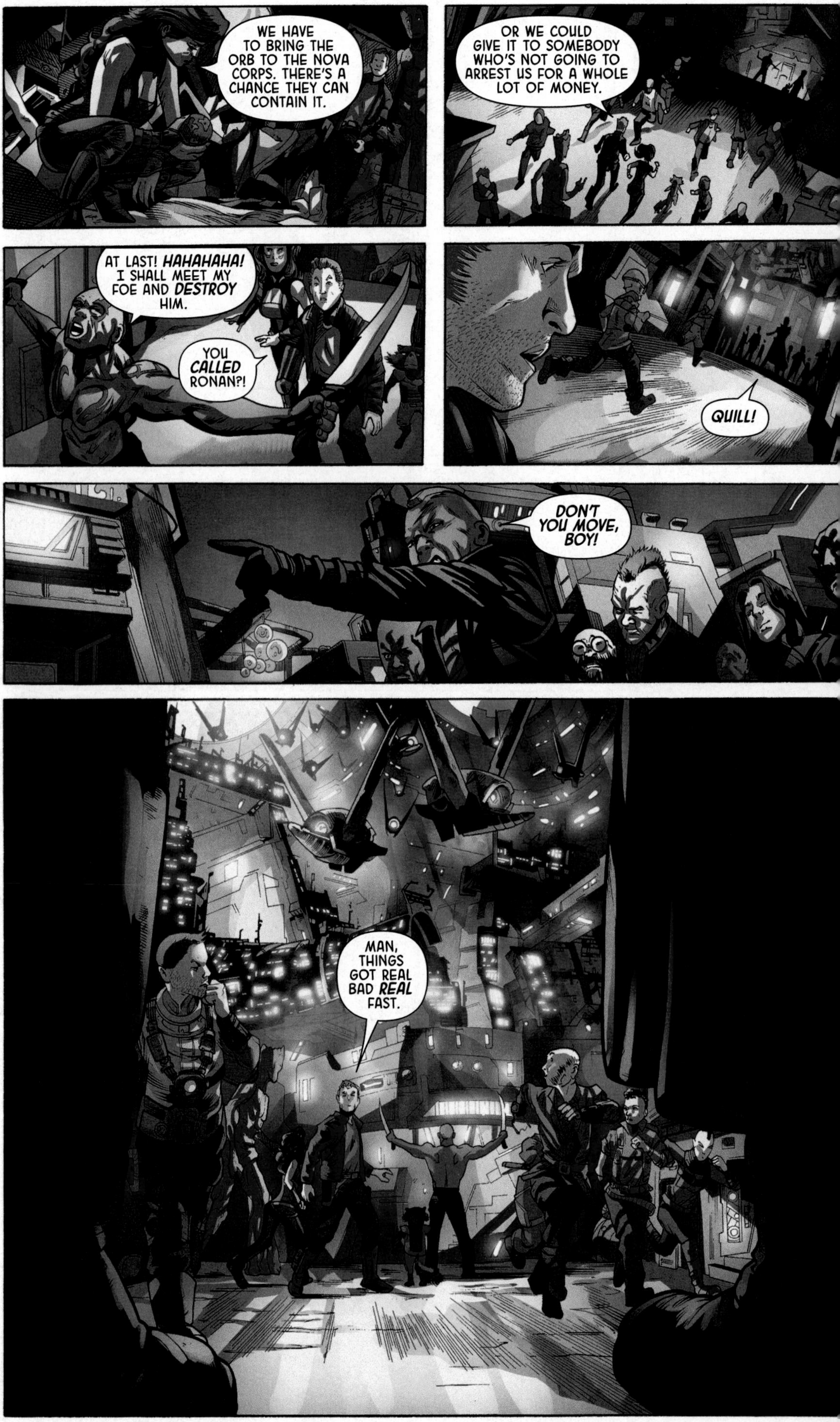
WE HAVE TO BRING THE ORB TO THE NOVA CORPS. THERE'S A CHANCE THEY CAN CONTAIN IT.
OR WE COULD GIVE IT TO SOMEBODY WHO'S NOT GOING TO ARREST US FOR A WHOLE LOT OF MONEY.
AT LAST! HAHAHAHA! I SHALL MEET MY FOE AND DESTROY HIM.
YOU CALLED RONAN?!
QUILL!
DON'T YOU MOVE, BOY!
MAN, THINGS GOT REAL BAD REAL FAST.

MARVEL'S GUARDIANS OF THE GALAXY VOL. 2 PRELUDE #2

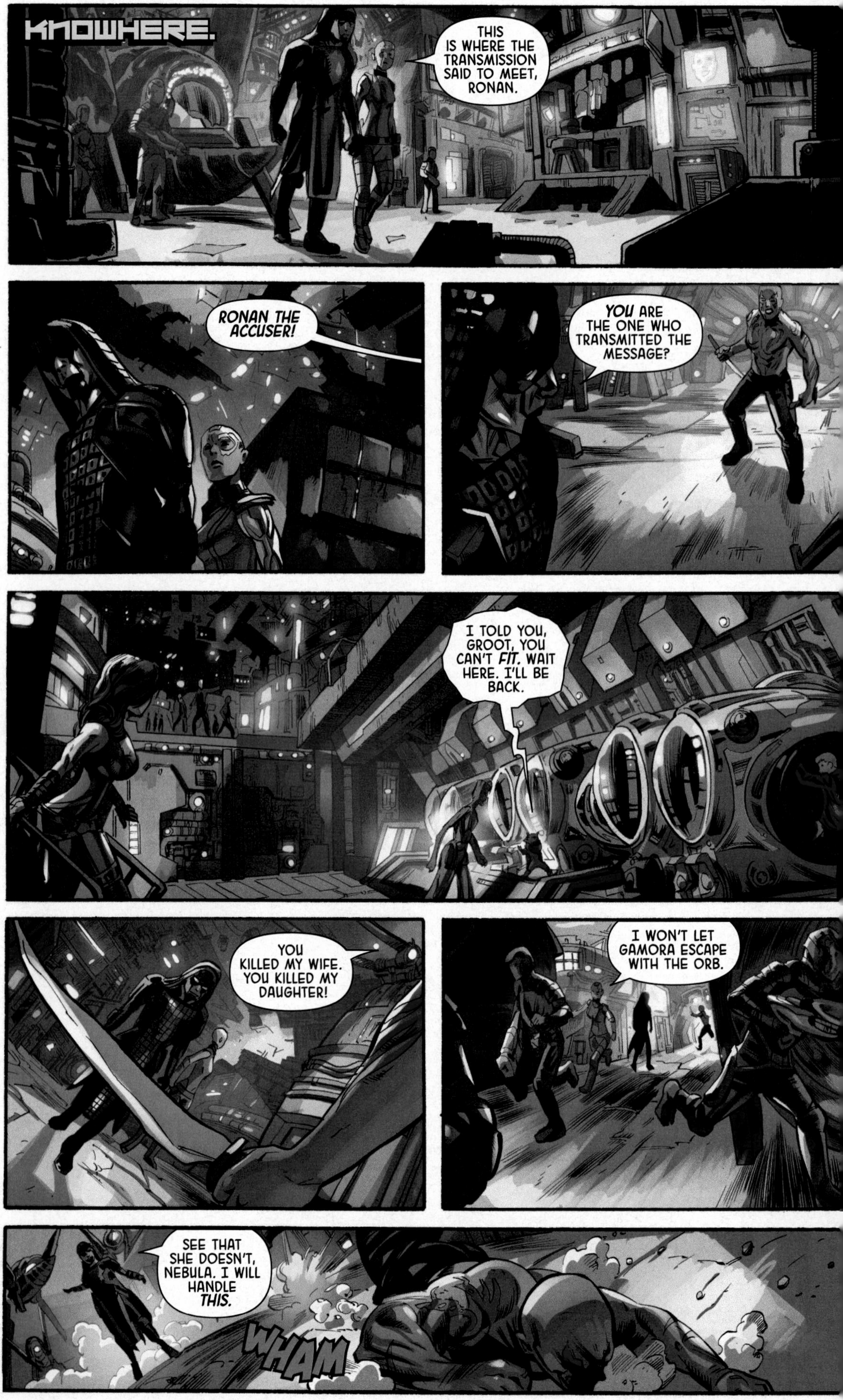
KNOWHERE.
THIS IS WHERE THE TRANSMISSION SAID TO MEET, RONAN.
RONAN THE ACCUSER!
YOU ARE THE ONE WHO TRANSMITTED THE MESSAGE?
I TOLD YOU, GROOT, YOU CAN'T FIT. WAIT HERE. I'LL BE BACK.
YOU KILLED MY WIFE. YOU KILLED MY DAUGHTER!
I WON'T LET GAMORA ESCAPE WITH THE ORB.
SEE THAT SHE DOESN'T, NEBULA. I WILL HANDLE THIS.
WHAM

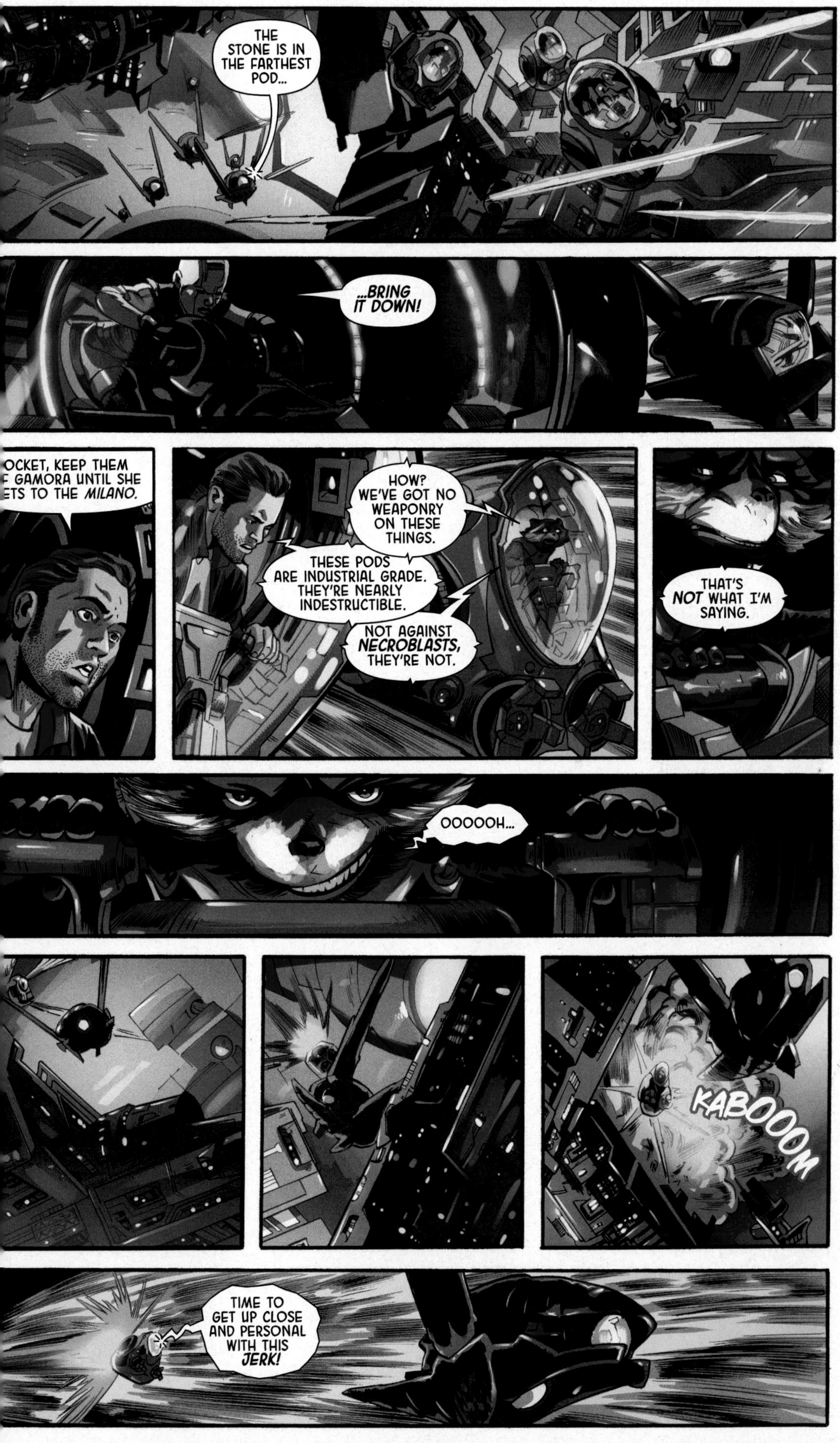
THE STONE IS IN THE FARTHEST POD...
...BRING IT DOWN!
OCKET, KEEP THEM F GAMORA UNTIL SHE ETS TO THE MILANO.
HOW? WE'VE GOT NO WEAPONRY ON THESE THINGS.
THESE PODS ARE INDUSTRIAL GRADE. THEY'RE NEARLY INDESTRUCTIBLE.
NOT AGAINST NECROBLASTS, THEY'RE NOT.
THAT'S NOT WHAT I'M SAYING.
OOOOOH...
KABOOOM
TIME TO GET UP CLOSE AND PERSONAL WITH THIS JERK!

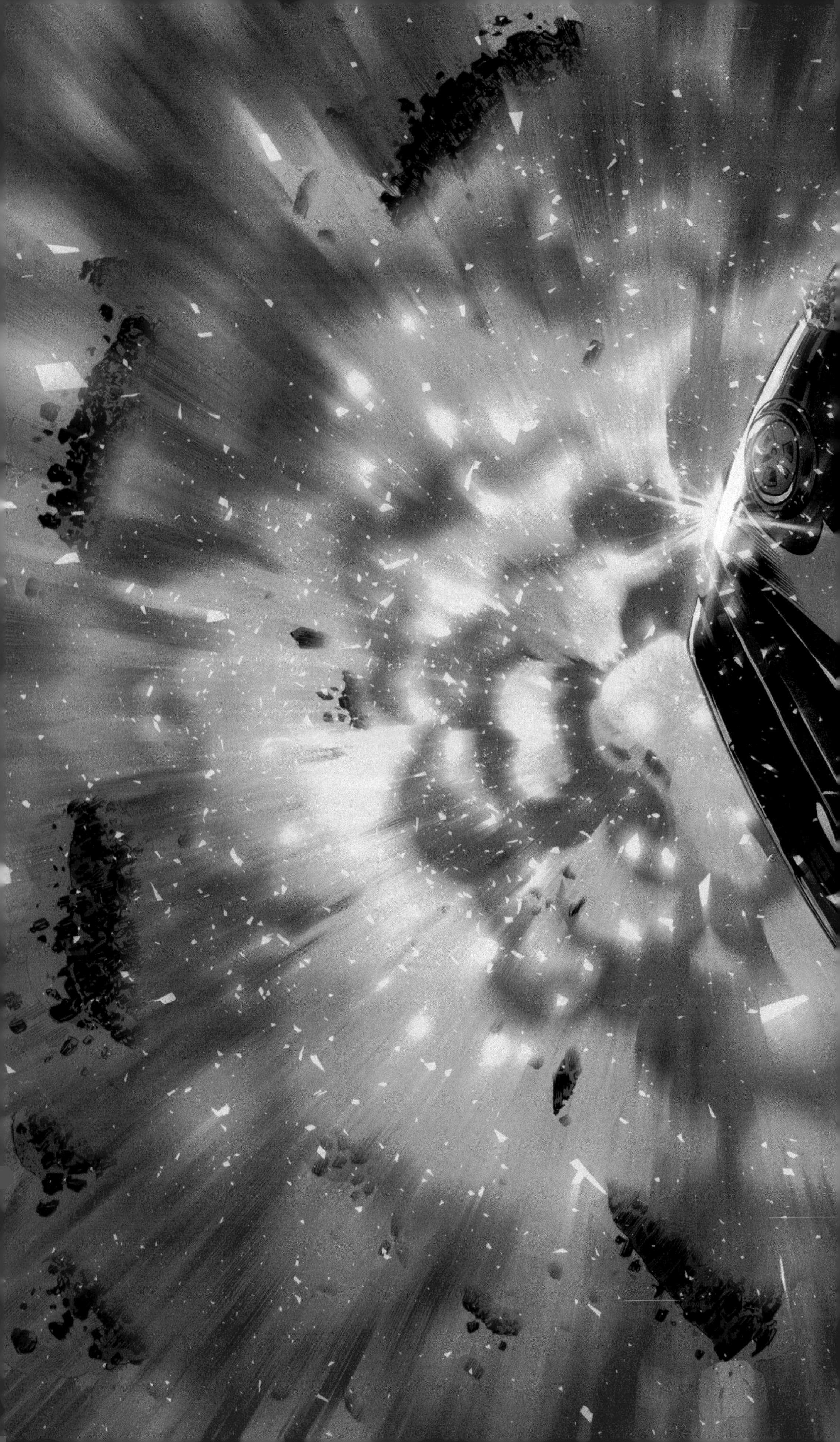

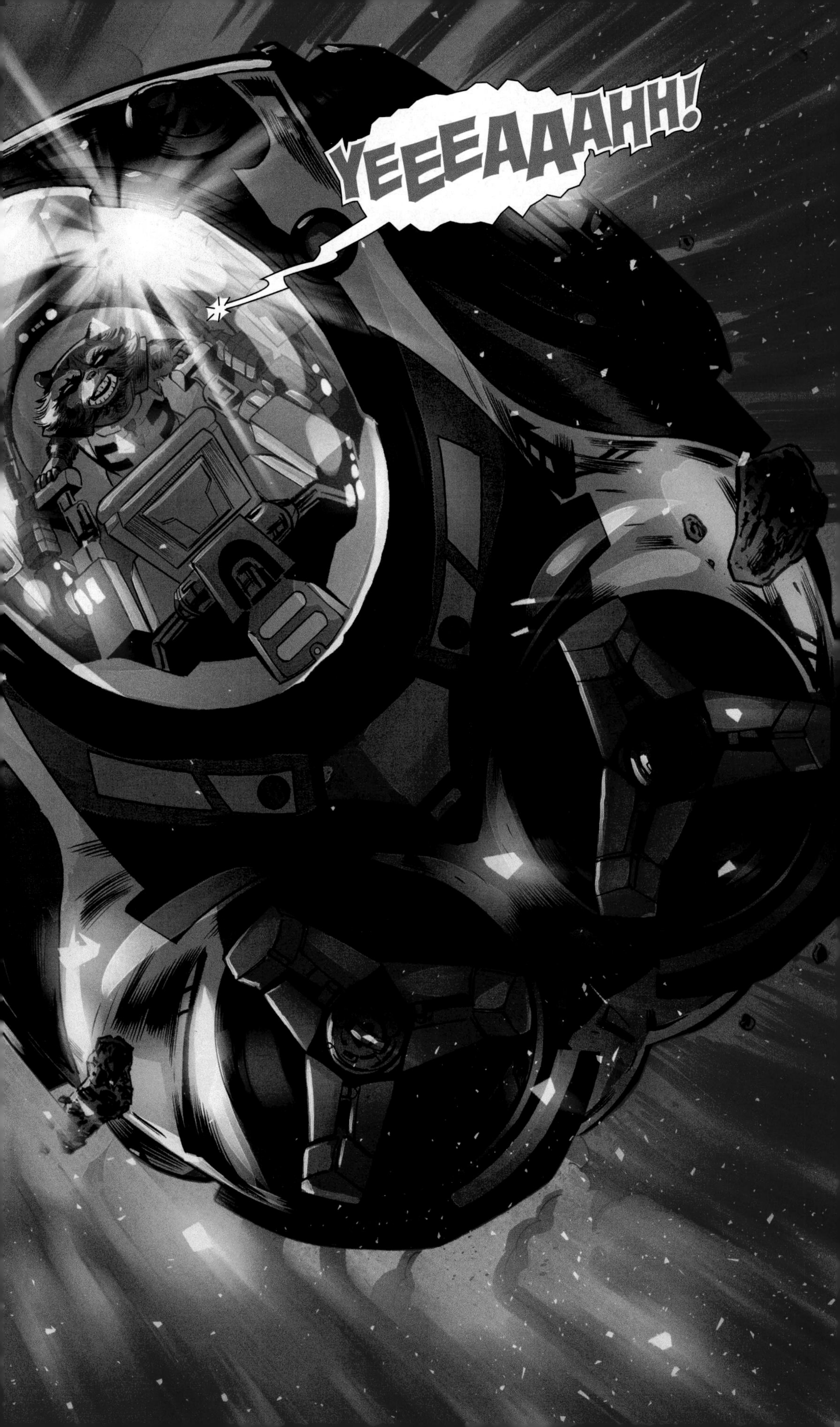
YEEEAAAHH!

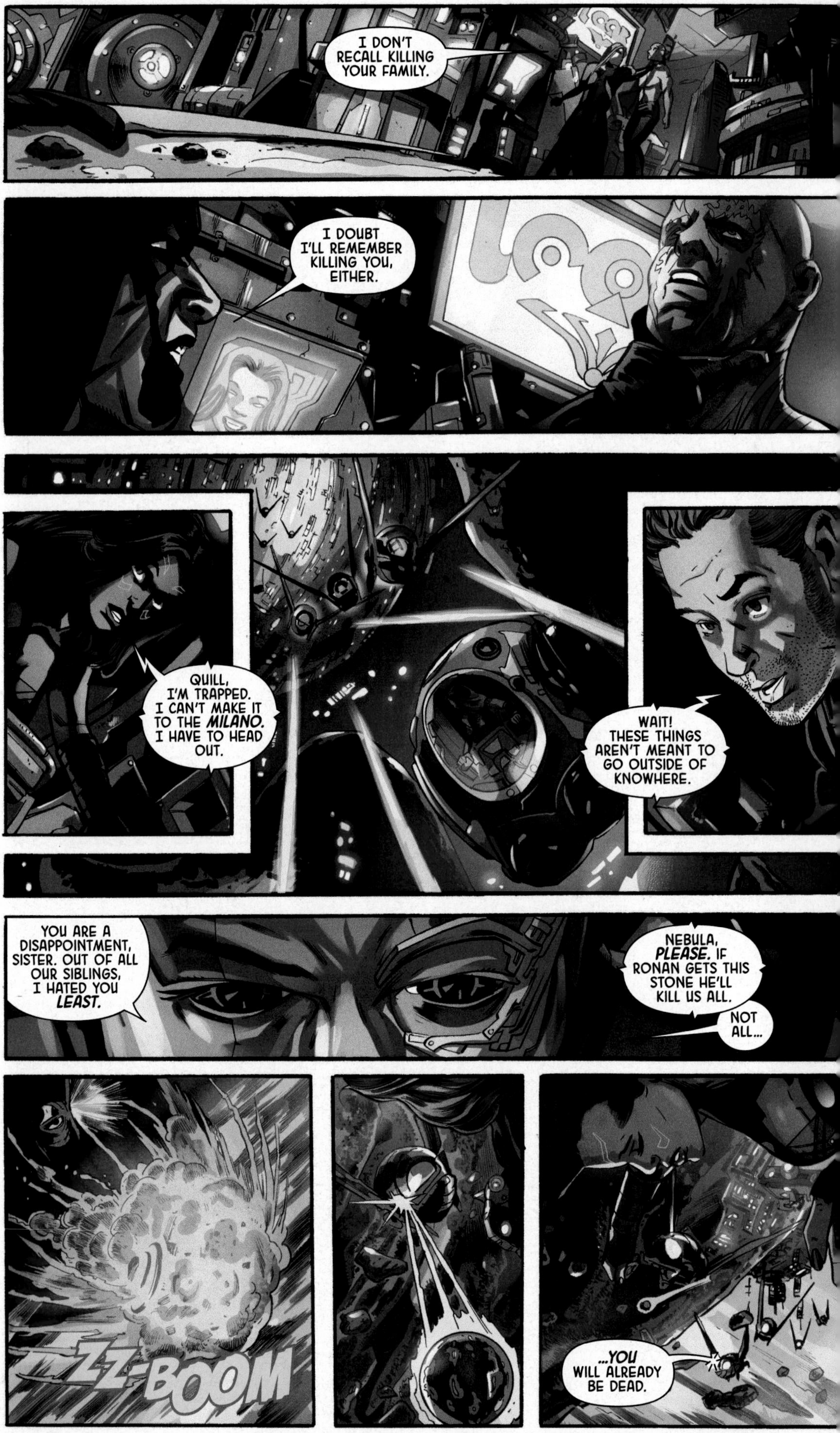
I DON'T RECALL KILLING YOUR FAMILY.
I DOUBT I'LL REMEMBER KILLING YOU, EITHER.
QUILL, I'M TRAPPED. I CAN'T MAKE IT TO THE *MILANO.* I HAVE TO HEAD OUT.
WAIT! THESE THINGS AREN'T MEANT TO GO OUTSIDE OF KNOWHERE.
YOU ARE A DISAPPOINTMENT, SISTER. OUT OF ALL OUR SIBLINGS, I HATED YOU *LEAST.*
NEBULA, *PLEASE.* IF RONAN GETS THIS STONE HE'LL KILL US ALL.
NOT ALL...
ZZ-BOOM
...*YOU* WILL ALREADY BE DEAD.

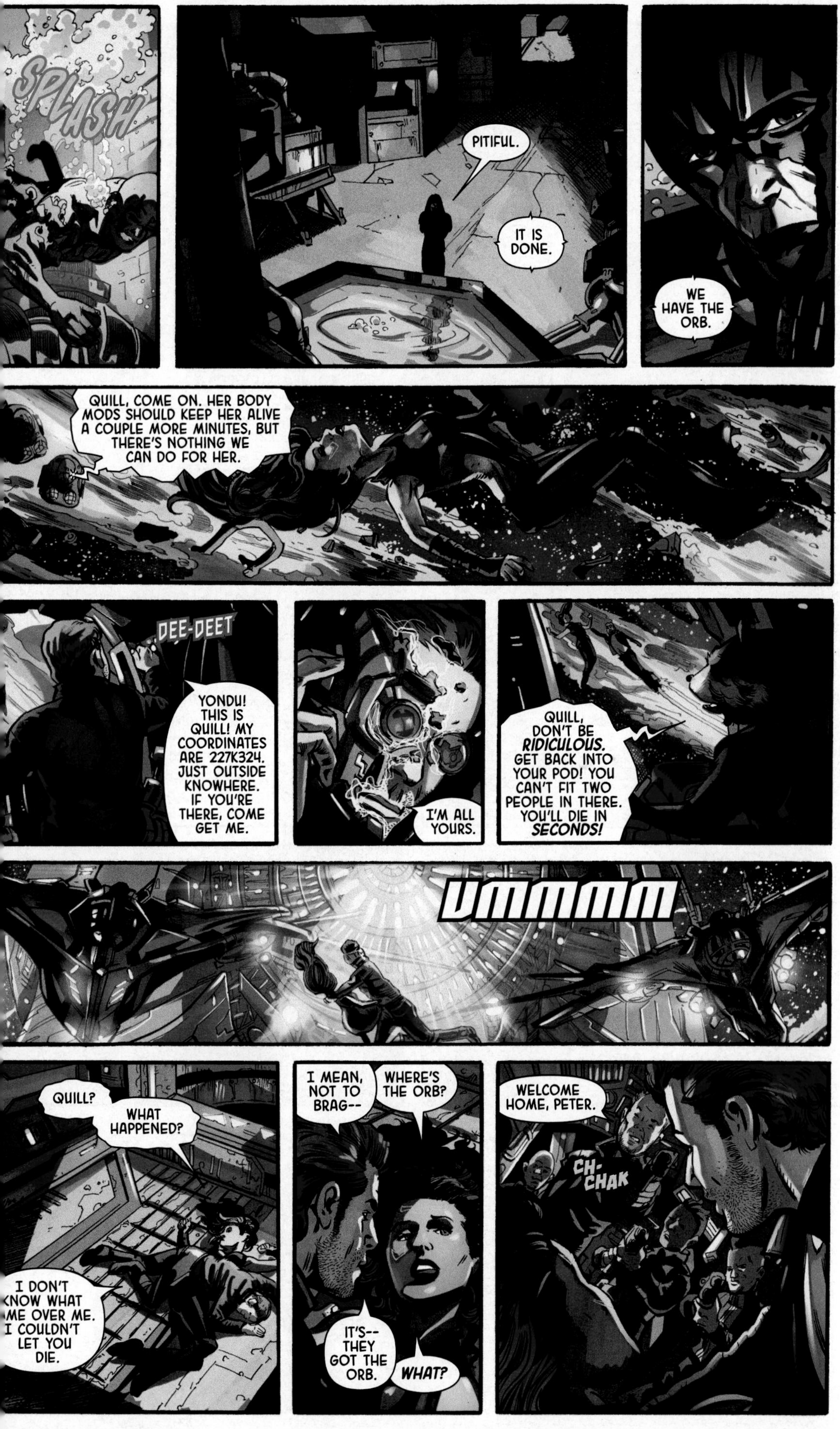
SPLASH
PITIFUL.
IT IS DONE.
WE HAVE THE ORB.
QUILL, COME ON. HER BODY MODS SHOULD KEEP HER ALIVE A COUPLE MORE MINUTES, BUT THERE'S NOTHING WE CAN DO FOR HER.
DEE-DEET
YONDU! THIS IS QUILL! MY COORDINATES ARE 227K324. JUST OUTSIDE KNOWHERE. IF YOU'RE THERE, COME GET ME.
I'M ALL YOURS.
QUILL, DON'T BE RIDICULOUS. GET BACK INTO YOUR POD! YOU CAN'T FIT TWO PEOPLE IN THERE. YOU'LL DIE IN SECONDS!
VMMMMM
QUILL?
WHAT HAPPENED?
I DON'T KNOW WHAT ME OVER ME. I COULDN'T LET YOU DIE.
I MEAN, NOT TO BRAG--
WHERE'S THE ORB?
IT'S-- THEY GOT THE ORB.
WHAT?
WELCOME HOME, PETER.
CH-CHAK

KAFF! KAFF! HUAAGH!

BLASTED IDIOT. THEY'RE *ALL* IDIOTS! QUILL JUST GOT HIMSELF CAPTURED. NONE OF THIS EVER WOULD HAVE HAPPENED IF *YOU* DIDN'T TRY TO SINGLE-HANDEDLY TAKE ON A FRICKIN' ARMY!

YOU'RE RIGHT. I WAS A FOOL. ALL THE ANGER... ALL THE RAGE... WAS JUST TO COVER MY LOSS.

OH, BOO-HOO-HOO. "MY WIFE AND CHILD ARE DEAD."

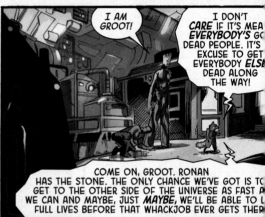

I AM GROOT!

I DON'T *CARE* IF IT'S MEA *EVERYBODY'S* GO DEAD PEOPLE. IT'S EXCUSE TO GET EVERYBODY *ELSE* DEAD ALONG THE WAY!

COME ON, GROOT. RONAN HAS THE STONE. THE ONLY CHANCE WE'VE GOT IS TO GET TO THE OTHER SIDE OF THE UNIVERSE AS FAST A WE CAN AND MAYBE, JUST *MAYBE*, WE'LL BE ABLE TO L FULL LIVES BEFORE THAT WHACKJOB EVER GETS THER

I AM GROOT.

SAVE THEM? *HOW?*

I AM *GROOT.*

I KNOW THEY'RE THE ONLY FRIENDS THAT WE EVER HAD, BUT THERE'S AN *ARMY* OF RAVAGERS AROUND THEM. AND THERE'S ONLY *TWO* OF US!

THREE.

RRRAAAAUGH!

YOU'RE MAKING ME...   ...BEAT...

...UP...

...THE GROUN

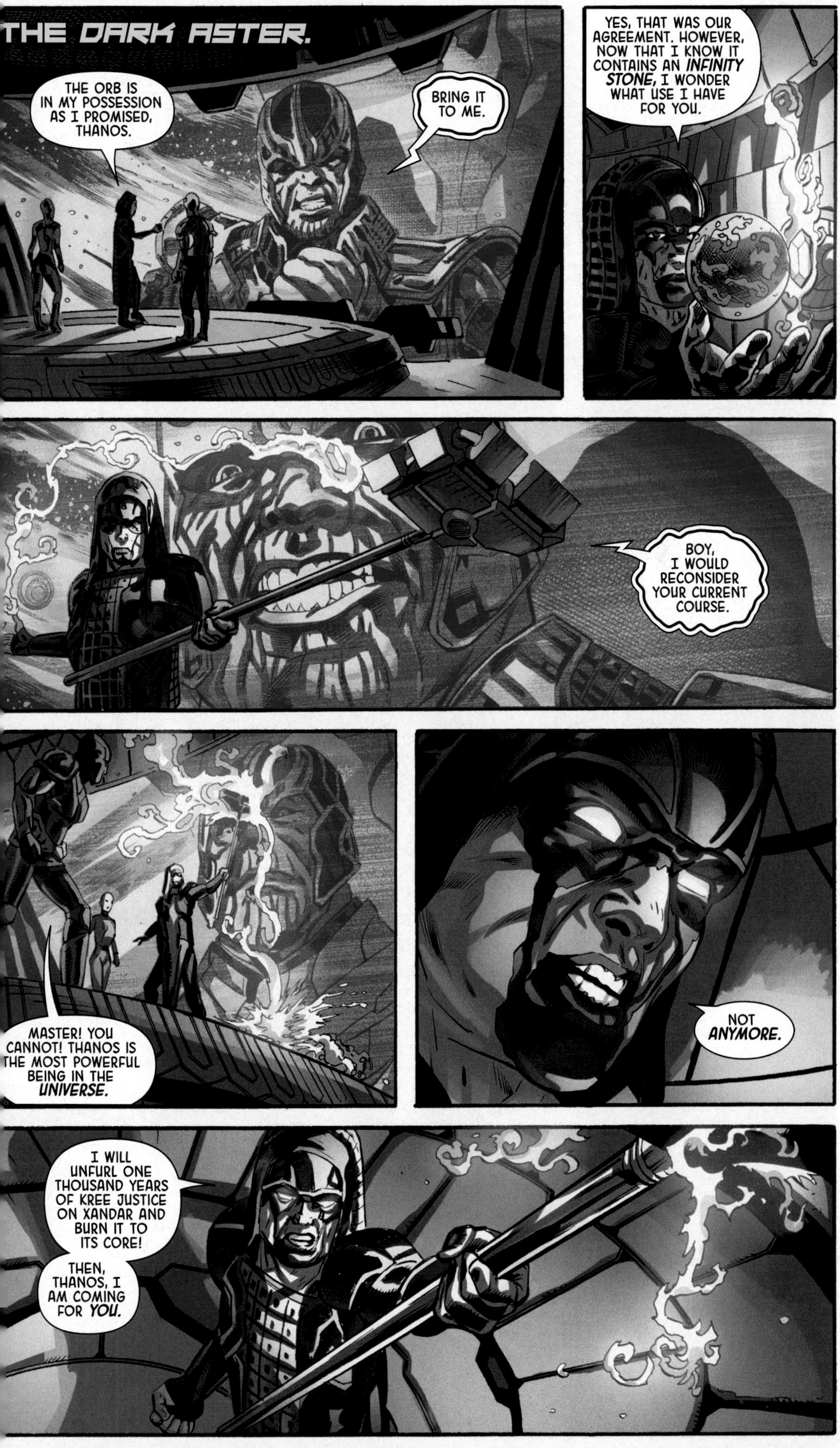
THE DARK ASTER.
THE ORB IS IN MY POSSESSION AS I PROMISED, THANOS.
BRING IT TO ME.
YES, THAT WAS OUR AGREEMENT. HOWEVER, NOW THAT I KNOW IT CONTAINS AN INFINITY STONE, I WONDER WHAT USE I HAVE FOR YOU.
BOY, I WOULD RECONSIDER YOUR CURRENT COURSE.
MASTER! YOU CANNOT! THANOS IS THE MOST POWERFUL BEING IN THE UNIVERSE.
NOT ANYMORE.
I WILL UNFURL ONE THOUSAND YEARS OF KREE JUSTICE ON XANDAR AND BURN IT TO ITS CORE!
THEN, THANOS, I AM COMING FOR YOU.

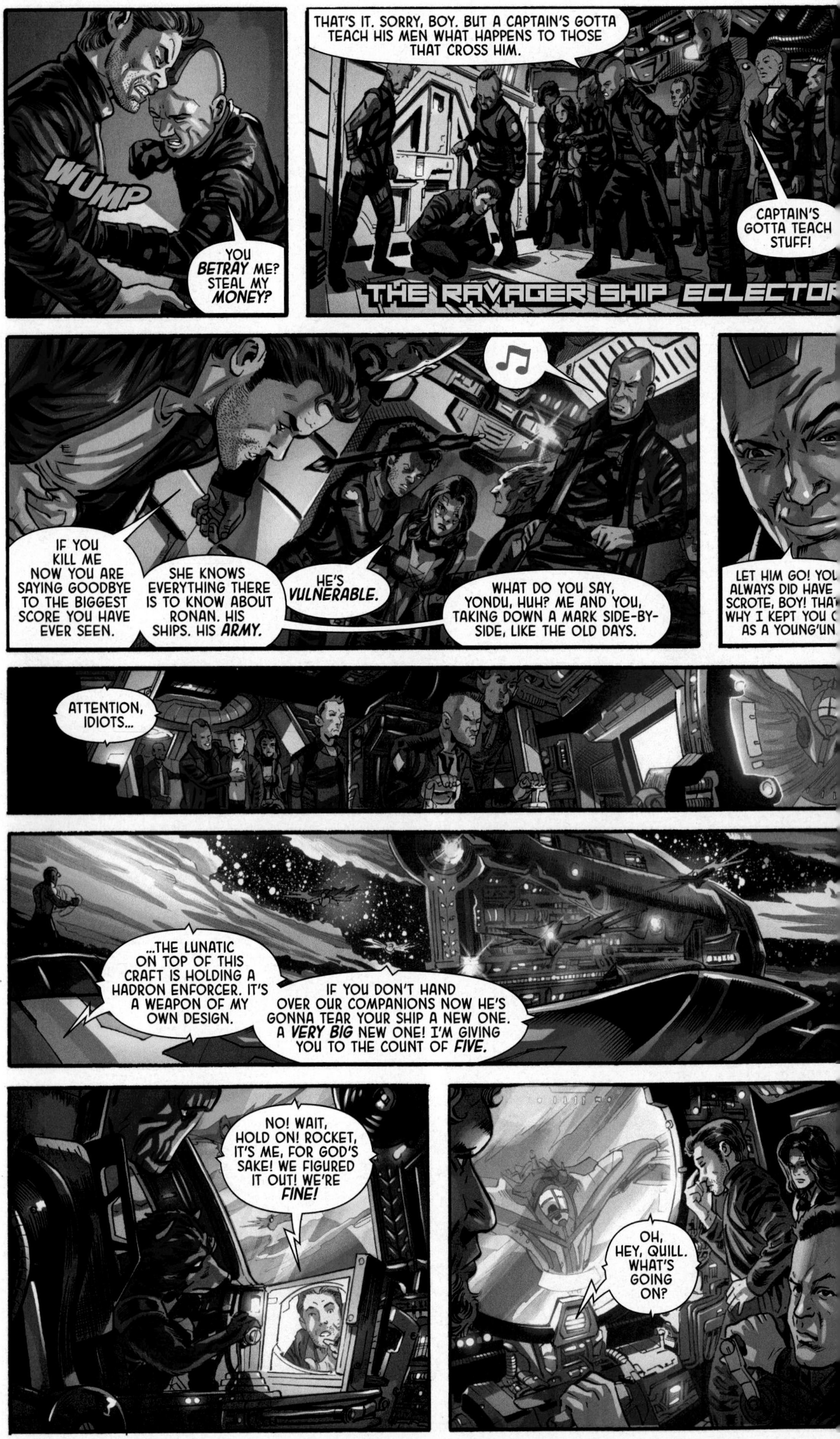
WUMP
YOU BETRAY ME? STEAL MY MONEY?
THAT'S IT. SORRY, BOY. BUT A CAPTAIN'S GOTTA TEACH HIS MEN WHAT HAPPENS TO THOSE THAT CROSS HIM.
CAPTAIN'S GOTTA TEACH STUFF!
THE RAVAGER SHIP ECLECTOR
IF YOU KILL ME NOW YOU ARE SAYING GOODBYE TO THE BIGGEST SCORE YOU HAVE EVER SEEN.
SHE KNOWS EVERYTHING THERE IS TO KNOW ABOUT RONAN. HIS SHIPS. HIS ARMY.
HE'S VULNERABLE.
WHAT DO YOU SAY, YONDU, HUH? ME AND YOU, TAKING DOWN A MARK SIDE-BY-SIDE, LIKE THE OLD DAYS.
♫
LET HIM GO! YOU ALWAYS DID HAVE SCROTE, BOY! THAT WHY I KEPT YOU AS A YOUNG'UN
ATTENTION, IDIOTS...
...THE LUNATIC ON TOP OF THIS CRAFT IS HOLDING A HADRON ENFORCER. IT'S A WEAPON OF MY OWN DESIGN.
IF YOU DON'T HAND OVER OUR COMPANIONS NOW HE'S GONNA TEAR YOUR SHIP A NEW ONE. A VERY BIG NEW ONE! I'M GIVING YOU TO THE COUNT OF FIVE.
NO! WAIT, HOLD ON! ROCKET, IT'S ME, FOR GOD'S SAKE! WE FIGURED IT OUT! WE'RE FINE!
OH, HEY, QUILL. WHAT'S GOING ON?

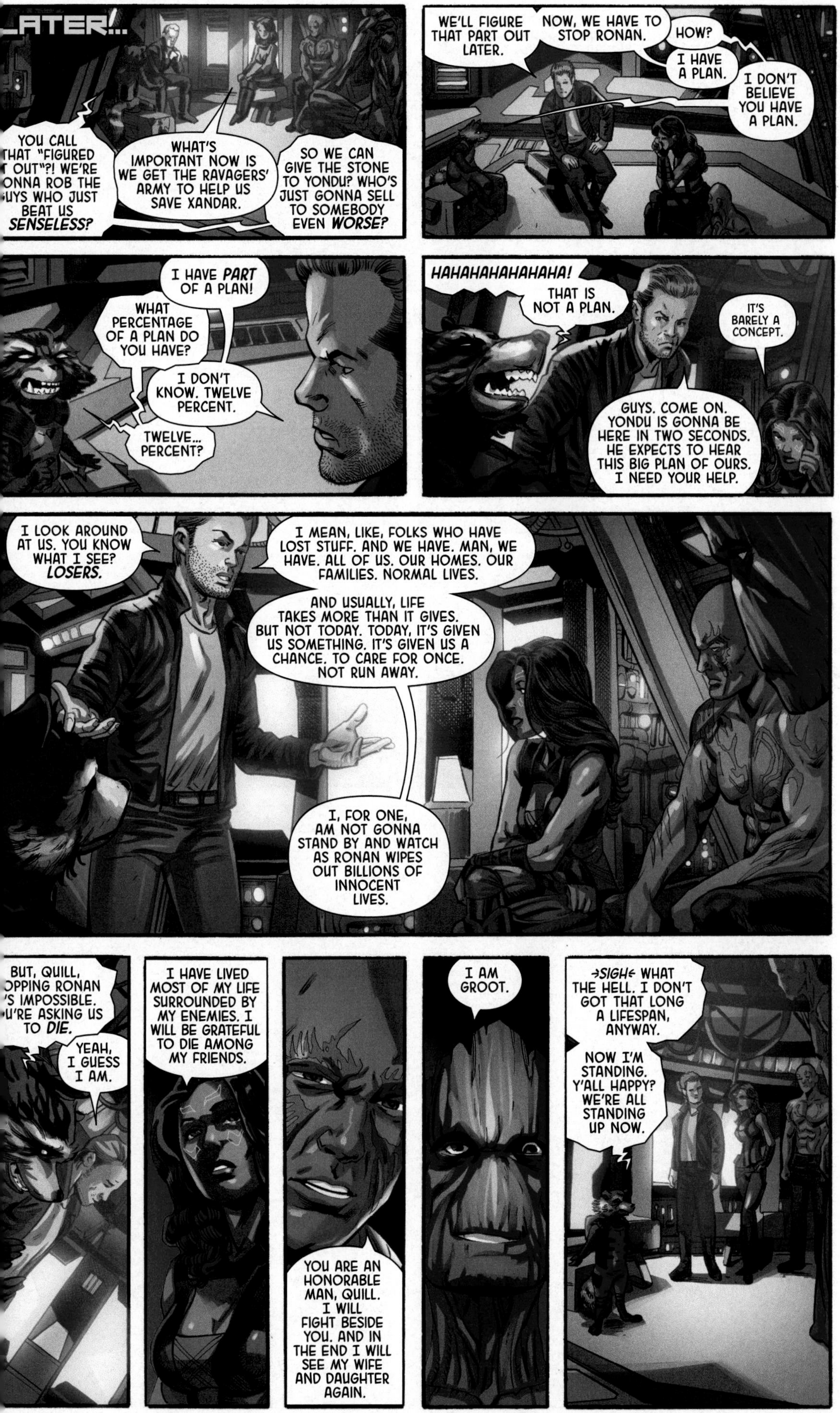
LATER!...
YOU CALL THAT "FIGURED IT OUT"?! WE'RE GONNA ROB THE GUYS WHO JUST BEAT US SENSELESS?
WHAT'S IMPORTANT NOW IS WE GET THE RAVAGERS' ARMY TO HELP US SAVE XANDAR.
SO WE CAN GIVE THE STONE TO YONDU? WHO'S JUST GONNA SELL TO SOMEBODY EVEN WORSE?
WE'LL FIGURE THAT PART OUT LATER.
NOW, WE HAVE TO STOP RONAN.
HOW?
I HAVE A PLAN.
I DON'T BELIEVE YOU HAVE A PLAN.
I HAVE PART OF A PLAN!
WHAT PERCENTAGE OF A PLAN DO YOU HAVE?
I DON'T KNOW. TWELVE PERCENT.
TWELVE... PERCENT?
HAHAHAHAHAHAHA!
THAT IS NOT A PLAN.
IT'S BARELY A CONCEPT.
GUYS. COME ON. YONDU IS GONNA BE HERE IN TWO SECONDS. HE EXPECTS TO HEAR THIS BIG PLAN OF OURS. I NEED YOUR HELP.
I LOOK AROUND AT US. YOU KNOW WHAT I SEE? LOSERS.
I MEAN, LIKE, FOLKS WHO HAVE LOST STUFF. AND WE HAVE. MAN, WE HAVE. ALL OF US. OUR HOMES. OUR FAMILIES. NORMAL LIVES.
AND USUALLY, LIFE TAKES MORE THAN IT GIVES. BUT NOT TODAY. TODAY, IT'S GIVEN US SOMETHING. IT'S GIVEN US A CHANCE. TO CARE FOR ONCE. NOT RUN AWAY.
I, FOR ONE, AM NOT GONNA STAND BY AND WATCH AS RONAN WIPES OUT BILLIONS OF INNOCENT LIVES.
BUT, QUILL, STOPPING RONAN IT'S IMPOSSIBLE. YOU'RE ASKING US TO DIE.
YEAH, I GUESS I AM.
I HAVE LIVED MOST OF MY LIFE SURROUNDED BY MY ENEMIES. I WILL BE GRATEFUL TO DIE AMONG MY FRIENDS.
YOU ARE AN HONORABLE MAN, QUILL. I WILL FIGHT BESIDE YOU. AND IN THE END I WILL SEE MY WIFE AND DAUGHTER AGAIN.
I AM GROOT.
→SIGH← WHAT THE HELL. I DON'T GOT THAT LONG A LIFESPAN, ANYWAY.
NOW I'M STANDING. Y'ALL HAPPY? WE'RE ALL STANDING UP NOW.

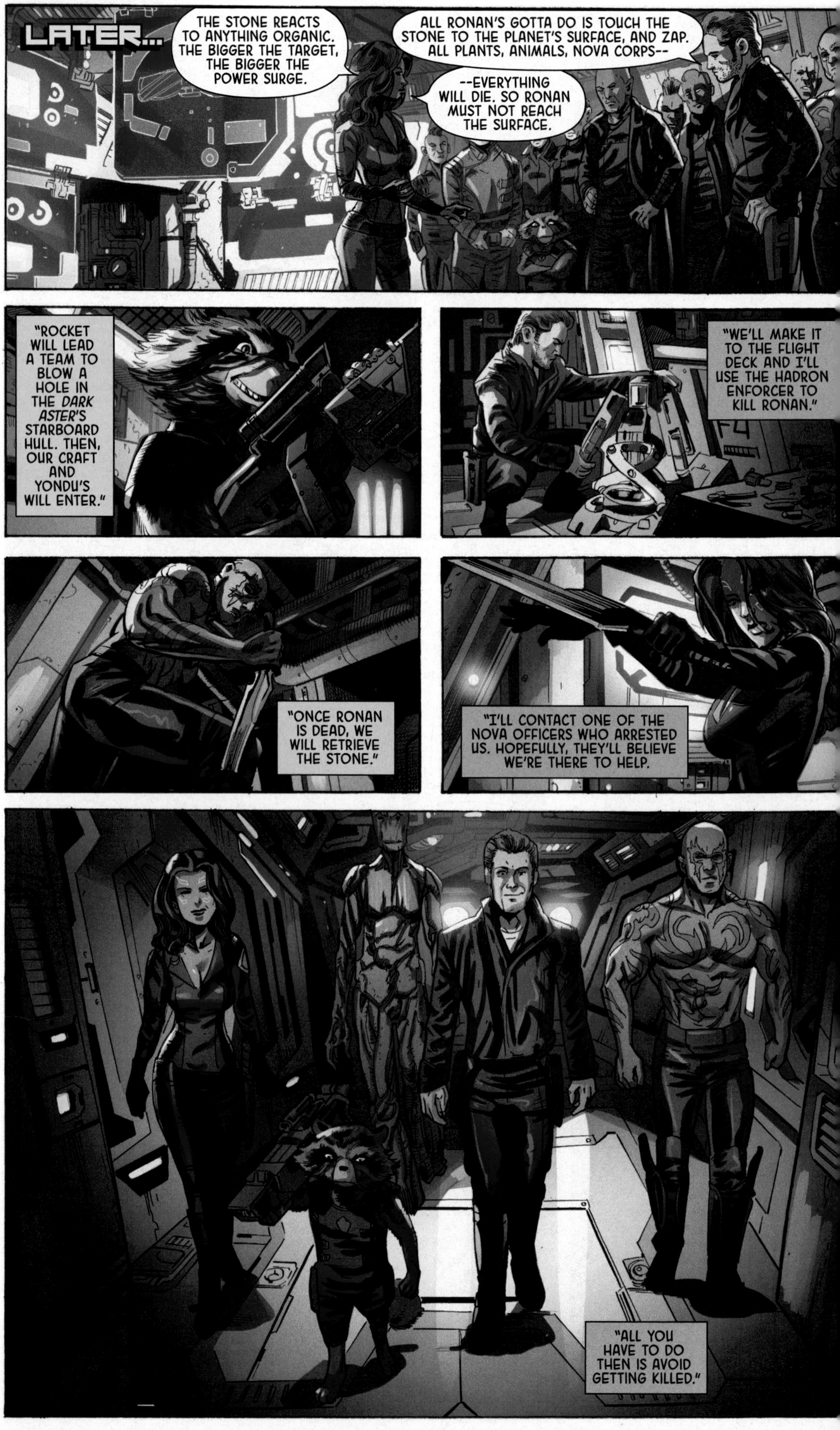
LATER...
THE STONE REACTS TO ANYTHING ORGANIC. THE BIGGER THE TARGET, THE BIGGER THE POWER SURGE.
ALL RONAN'S GOTTA DO IS TOUCH THE STONE TO THE PLANET'S SURFACE, AND ZAP. ALL PLANTS, ANIMALS, NOVA CORPS--
--EVERYTHING WILL DIE. SO RONAN MUST NOT REACH THE SURFACE.
"ROCKET WILL LEAD A TEAM TO BLOW A HOLE IN THE *DARK ASTER'S* STARBOARD HULL. THEN, OUR CRAFT AND YONDU'S WILL ENTER."
"WE'LL MAKE IT TO THE FLIGHT DECK AND I'LL USE THE HADRON ENFORCER TO KILL RONAN."
"ONCE RONAN IS DEAD, WE WILL RETRIEVE THE STONE."
"I'LL CONTACT ONE OF THE NOVA OFFICERS WHO ARRESTED US. HOPEFULLY, THEY'LL BELIEVE WE'RE THERE TO HELP.
"ALL YOU HAVE TO DO THEN IS AVOID GETTING KILLED."

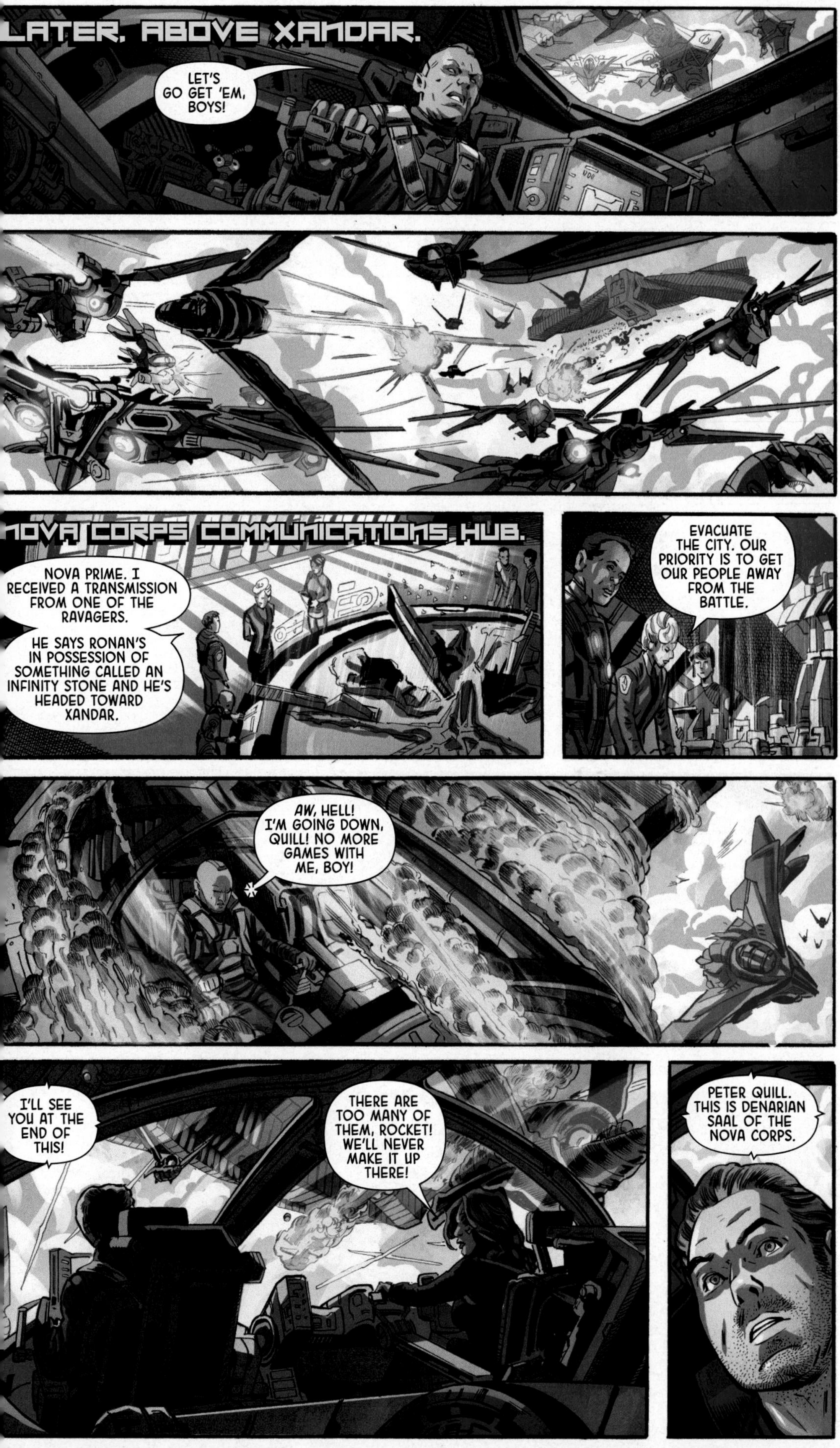
LATER, ABOVE XANDAR.
LET'S GO GET 'EM, BOYS!
NOVA CORPS COMMUNICATIONS HUB.
NOVA PRIME. I RECEIVED A TRANSMISSION FROM ONE OF THE RAVAGERS.
HE SAYS RONAN'S IN POSSESSION OF SOMETHING CALLED AN INFINITY STONE AND HE'S HEADED TOWARD XANDAR.
EVACUATE THE CITY. OUR PRIORITY IS TO GET OUR PEOPLE AWAY FROM THE BATTLE.
AW, HELL! I'M GOING DOWN, QUILL! NO MORE GAMES WITH ME, BOY!
I'LL SEE YOU AT THE END OF THIS!
THERE ARE TOO MANY OF THEM, ROCKET! WE'LL NEVER MAKE IT UP THERE!
PETER QUILL. THIS IS DENARIAN SAAL OF THE NOVA CORPS.

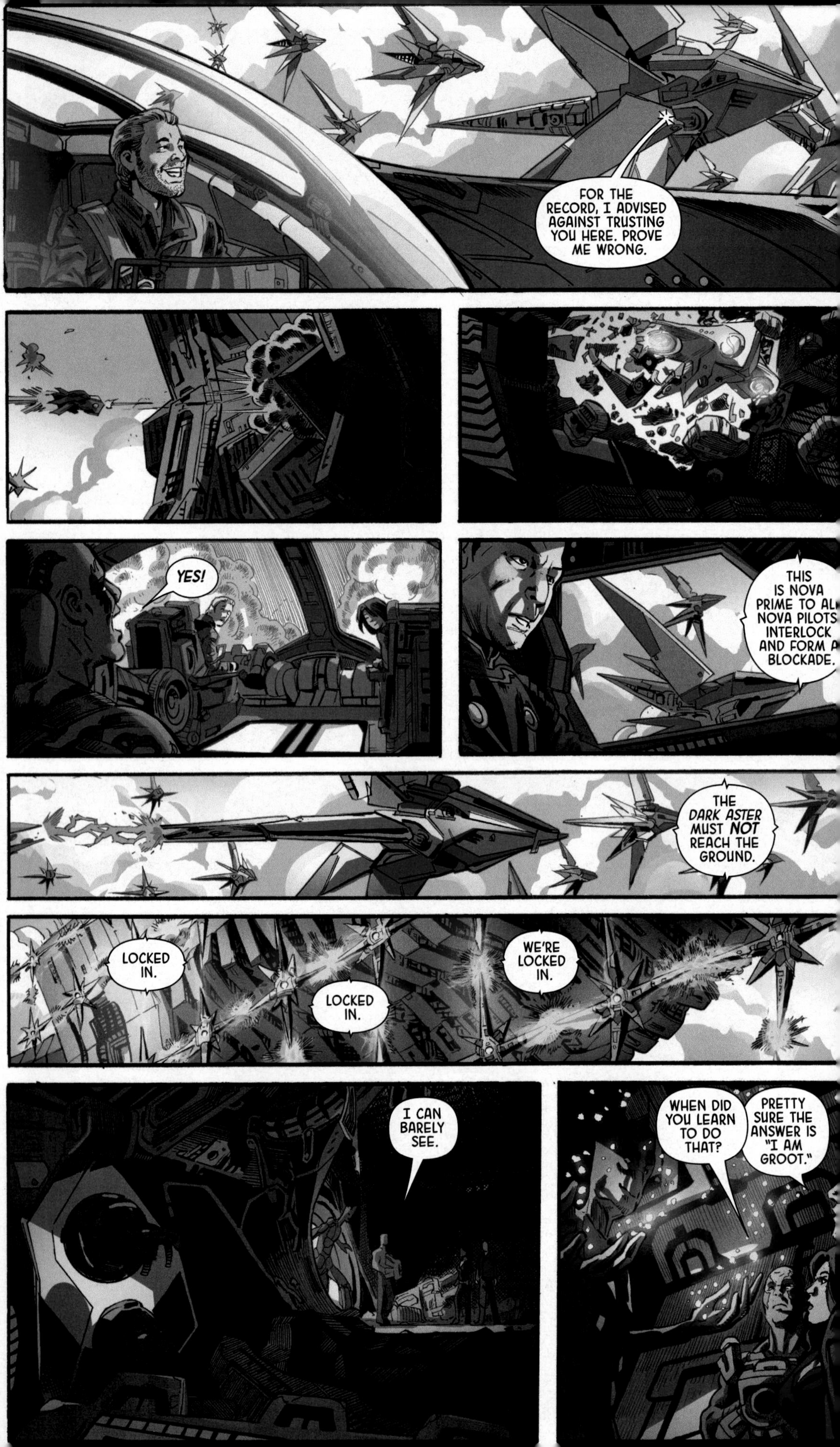
FOR THE RECORD, I ADVISED AGAINST TRUSTING YOU HERE. PROVE ME WRONG.
YES!
THIS IS NOVA PRIME TO AL NOVA PILOTS INTERLOCK AND FORM A BLOCKADE.
THE DARK ASTER MUST NOT REACH THE GROUND.
LOCKED IN.
LOCKED IN.
WE'RE LOCKED IN.
I CAN BARELY SEE.
WHEN DID YOU LEARN TO DO THAT?
PRETTY SURE THE ANSWER IS "I AM GROOT."

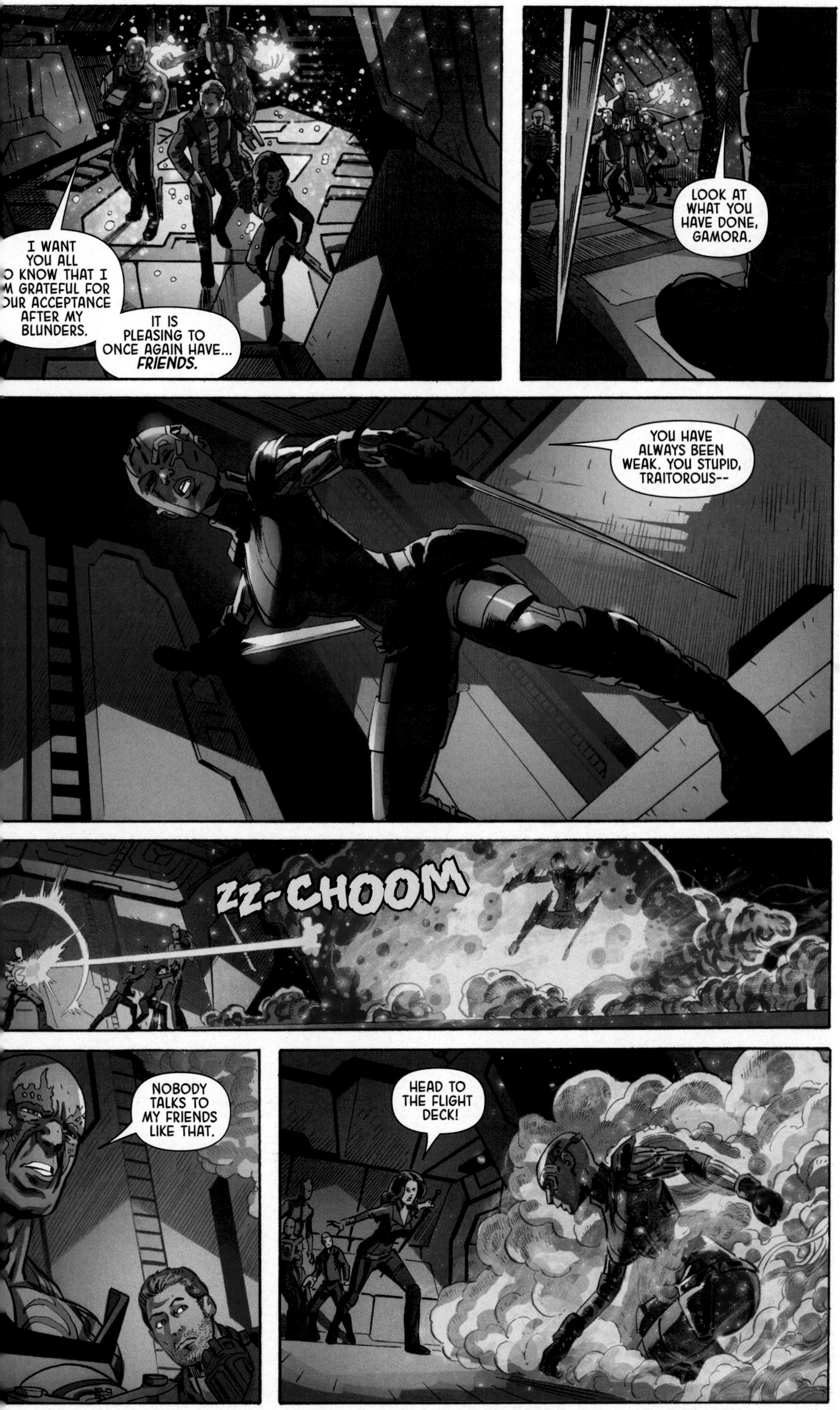

I WANT YOU ALL O KNOW THAT I M GRATEFUL FOR OUR ACCEPTANCE AFTER MY BLUNDERS.
IT IS PLEASING TO ONCE AGAIN HAVE... *FRIENDS.*
LOOK AT WHAT YOU HAVE DONE, GAMORA.
YOU HAVE ALWAYS BEEN WEAK. YOU STUPID, TRAITOROUS--
ZZ-CHOOM
NOBODY TALKS TO MY FRIENDS LIKE THAT.
HEAD TO THE FLIGHT DECK!

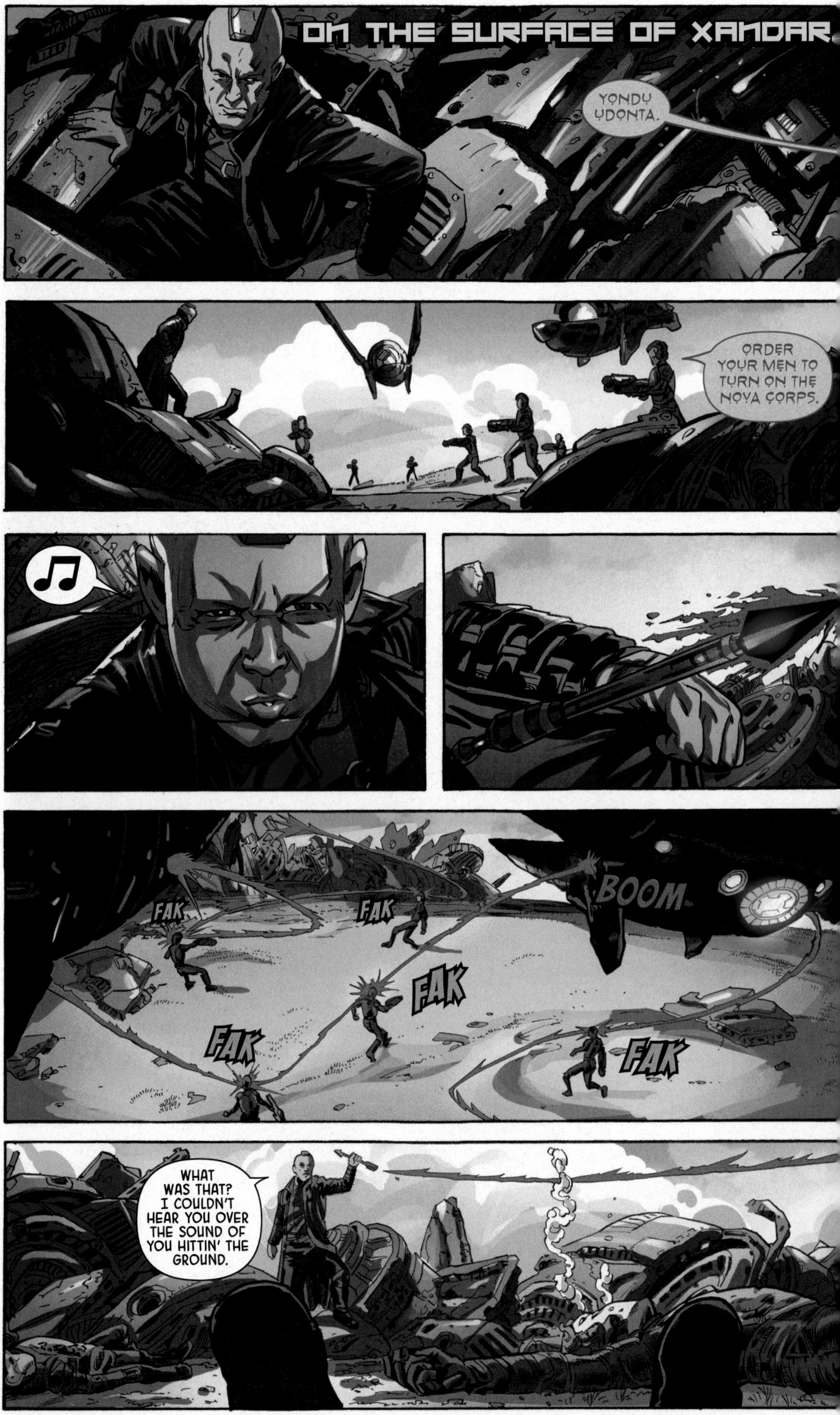
ON THE SURFACE OF XANDAR.
YONDU UDONTA.
ORDER YOUR MEN TO TURN ON THE NOVA CORPS.
♫
FAK
FAK
BOOM
FAK
FAK
FAK
WHAT WAS THAT? I COULDN'T HEAR YOU OVER THE SOUND OF YOU HITTIN' THE GROUND.

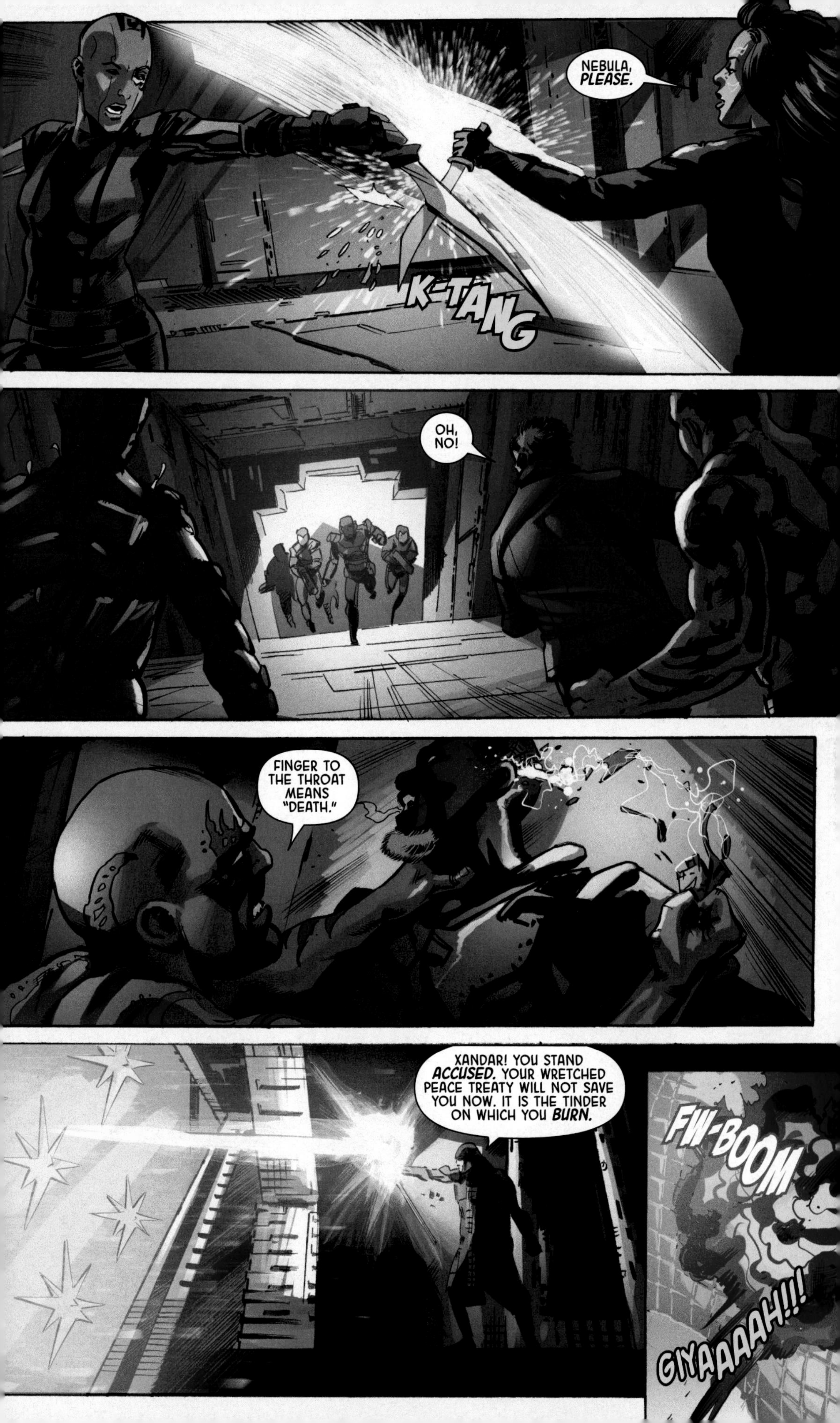
NEBULA, PLEASE.
K-TANG
OH, NO!
FINGER TO THE THROAT MEANS "DEATH."
XANDAR! YOU STAND ACCUSED. YOUR WRETCHED PEACE TREATY WILL NOT SAVE YOU NOW. IT IS THE TINDER ON WHICH YOU BURN.
FW-BOOM
GIYAAAAH!!!

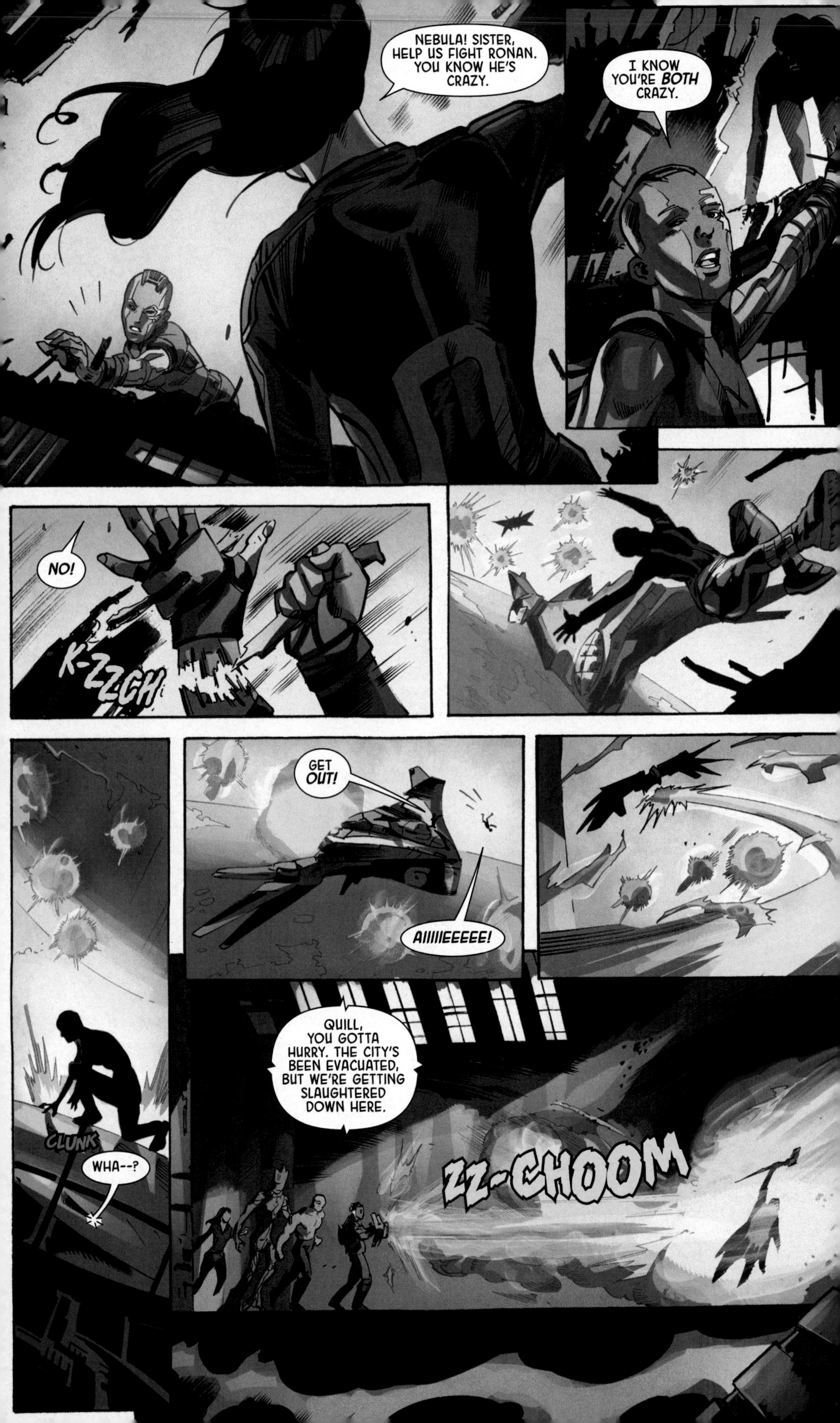
NEBULA! SISTER, HELP US FIGHT RONAN. YOU KNOW HE'S CRAZY.
I KNOW YOU'RE *BOTH* CRAZY.
NO!
K-ZZZCH
GET OUT!
AIIIIIEEEEE!
CLUNK
WHA--?
QUILL, YOU GOTTA HURRY. THE CITY'S BEEN EVACUATED, BUT WE'RE GETTING SLAUGHTERED DOWN HERE.
ZZ-CHOOM

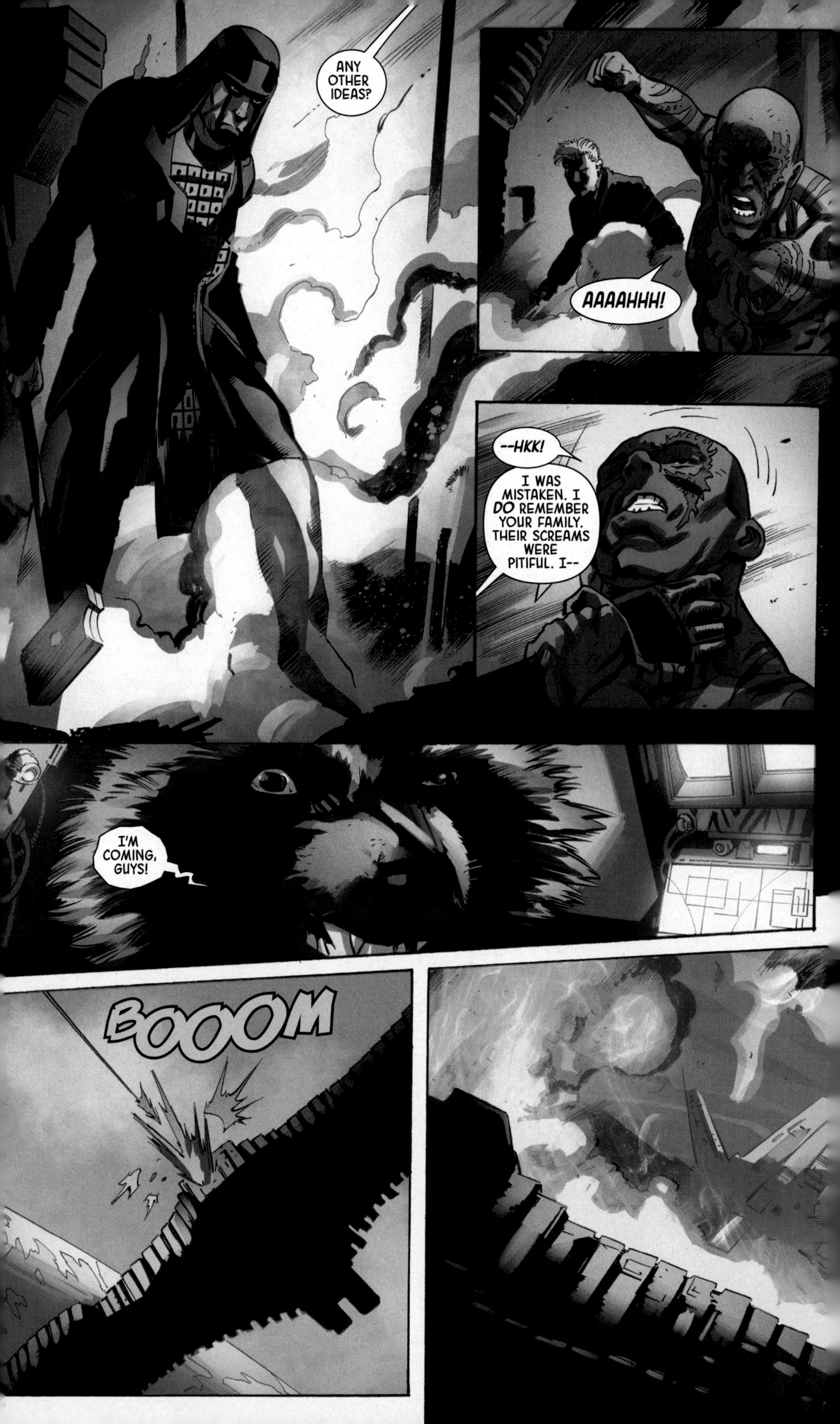
ANY OTHER IDEAS?
AAAAHHH!
--HKK!
I WAS MISTAKEN. I DO REMEMBER YOUR FAMILY. THEIR SCREAMS WERE PITIFUL. I--
I'M COMING, GUYS!
BOOOM

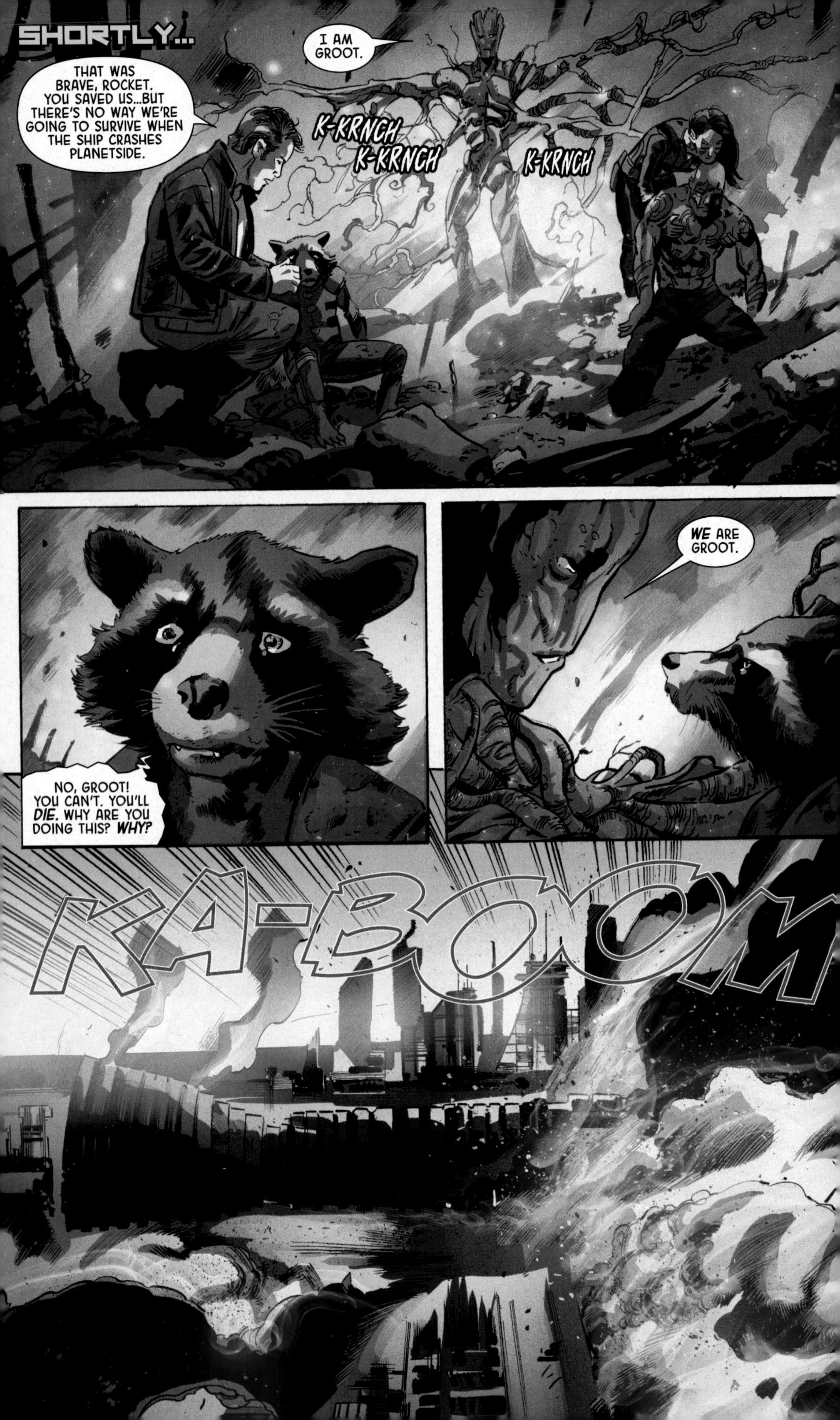
SHORTLY...
I AM GROOT.
THAT WAS BRAVE, ROCKET. YOU SAVED US...BUT THERE'S NO WAY WE'RE GOING TO SURVIVE WHEN THE SHIP CRASHES PLANETSIDE.
K-KRNCH
K-KRNCH
K-KRNCH
NO, GROOT! YOU CAN'T. YOU'LL DIE. WHY ARE YOU DOING THIS? WHY?
WE ARE GROOT.
KA-BOOM

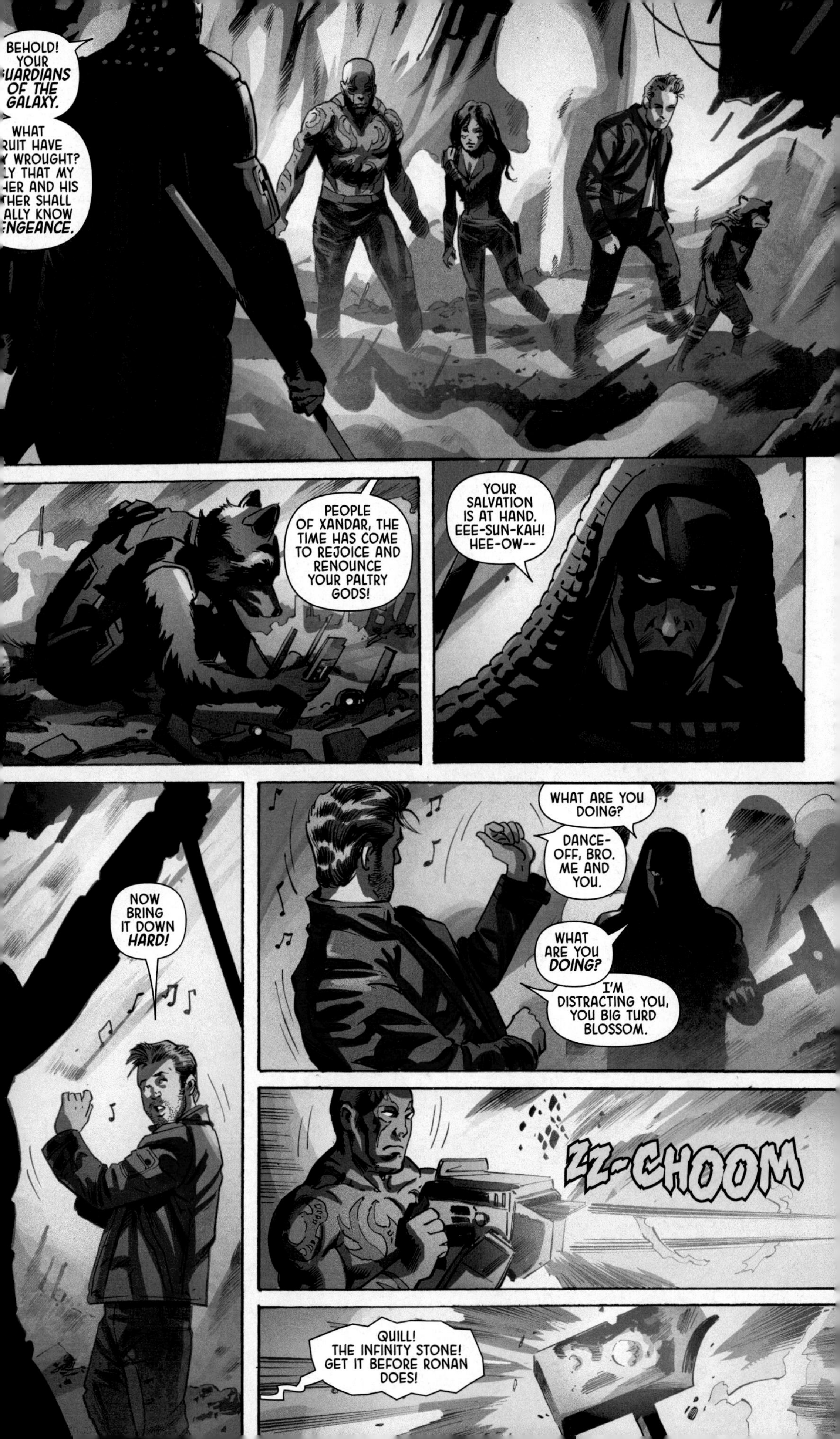
BEHOLD! YOUR UARDIANS OF THE GALAXY.
WHAT RUIT HAVE Y WROUGHT? LY THAT MY HER AND HIS THER SHALL ALLY KNOW ENGEANCE.
PEOPLE OF XANDAR, THE TIME HAS COME TO REJOICE AND RENOUNCE YOUR PALTRY GODS!
YOUR SALVATION IS AT HAND. EEE-SUN-KAH! HEE-OW--
NOW BRING IT DOWN HARD!
WHAT ARE YOU DOING?
DANCE-OFF, BRO. ME AND YOU.
WHAT ARE YOU DOING?
I'M DISTRACTING YOU, YOU BIG TURD BLOSSOM.
ZZ-CHOOM
QUILL! THE INFINITY STONE! GET IT BEFORE RONAN DOES!

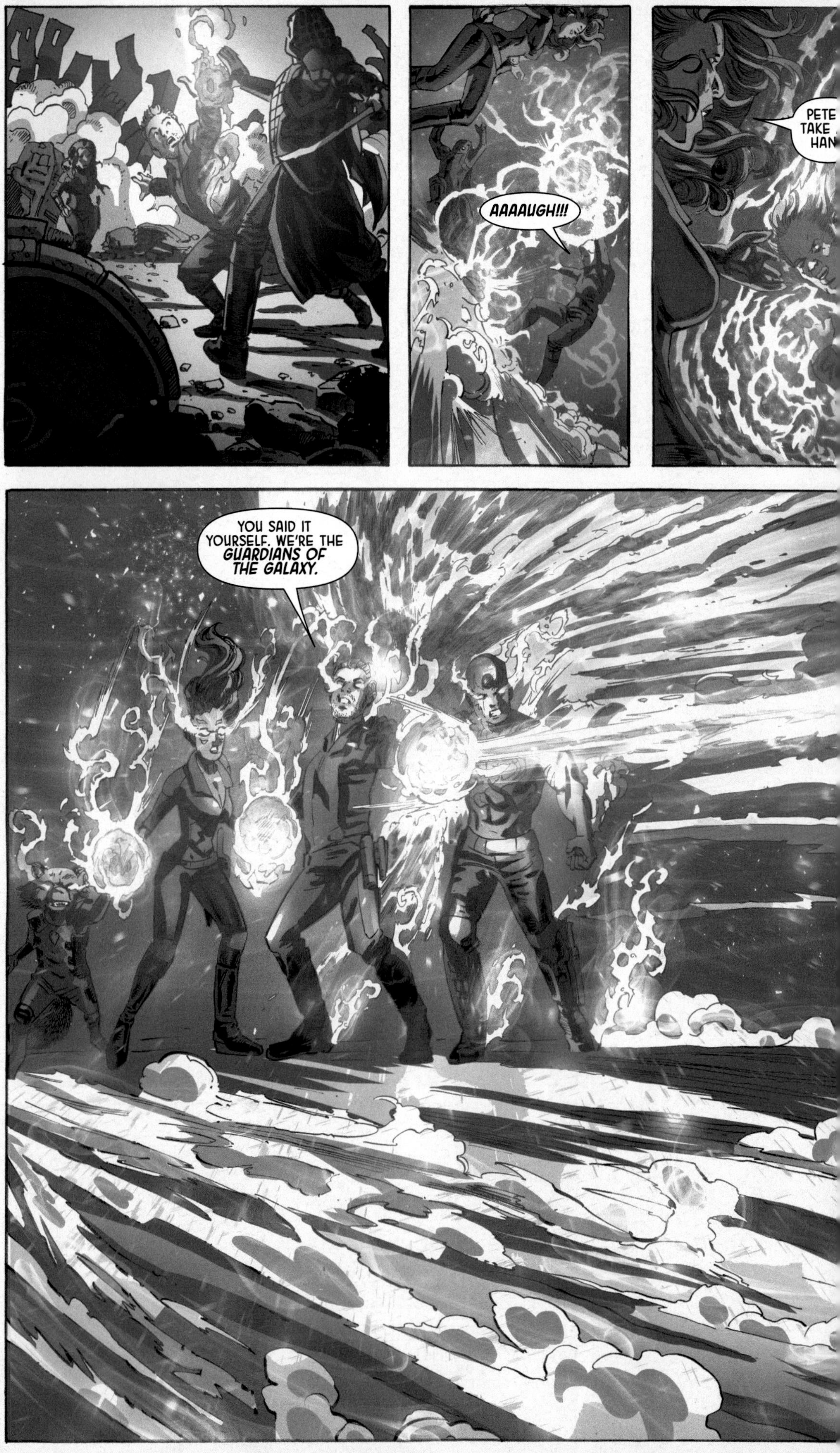
AAAAUGH!!!
PETE
TAKE
HAN
YOU SAID IT YOURSELF. WE'RE THE GUARDIANS OF THE GALAXY.

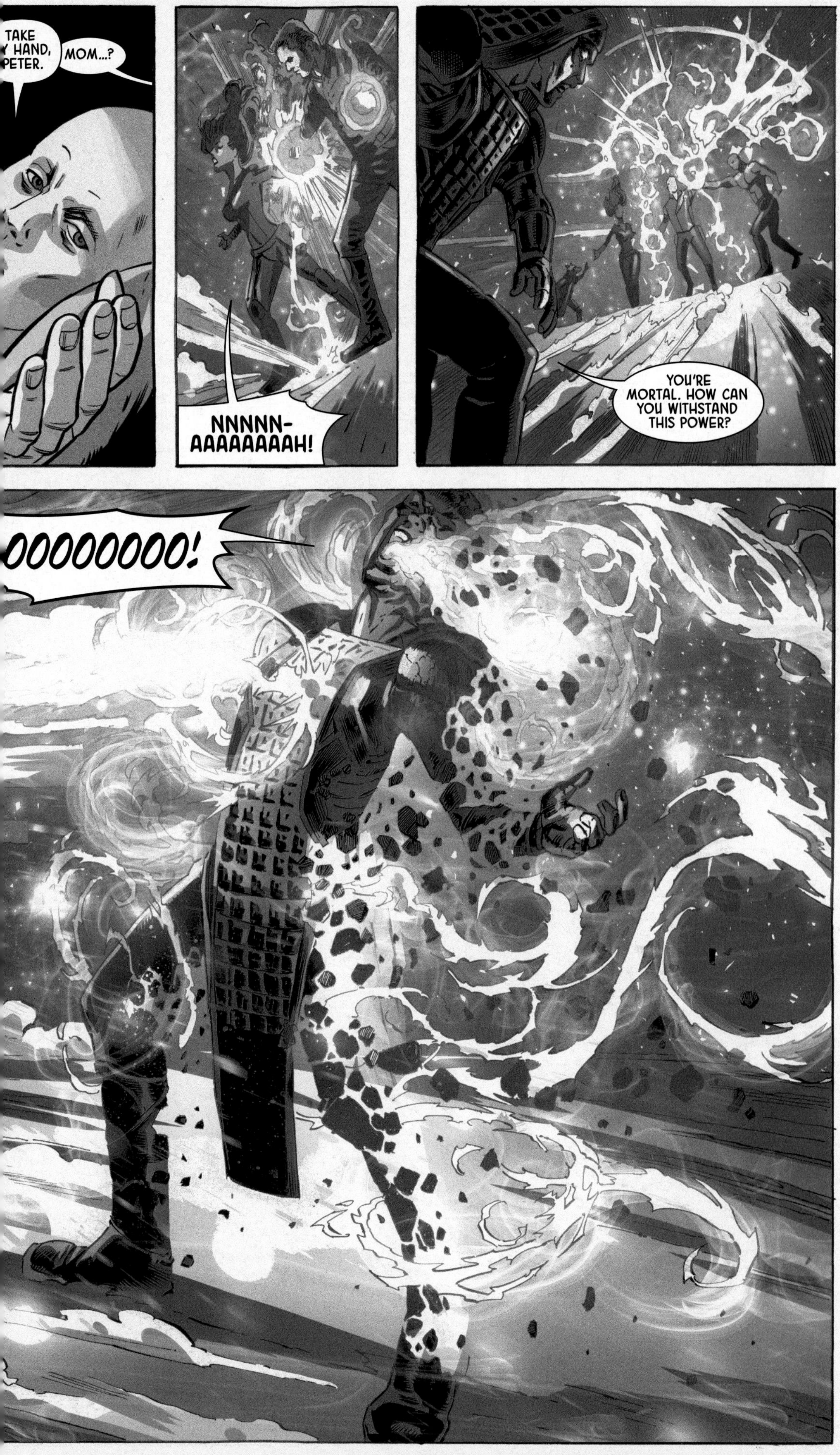
TAKE
Y HAND,
PETER.
MOM...?
NNNNN-
AAAAAAAAH!
YOU'RE
MORTAL. HOW CAN
YOU WITHSTAND
THIS POWER?
OOOOOOOO!

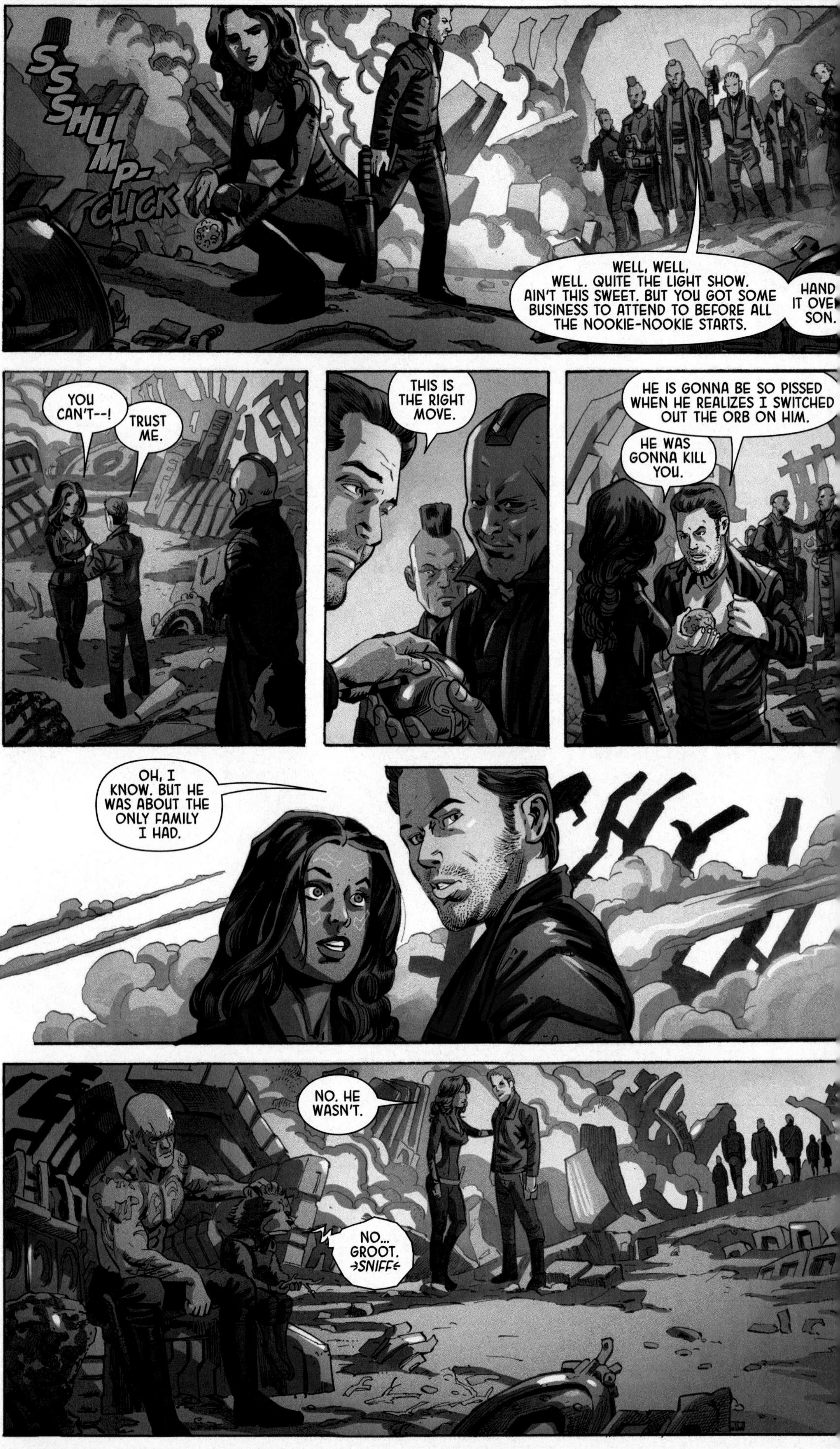
SSSHUMP-CLICK
WELL, WELL, WELL. QUITE THE LIGHT SHOW. AIN'T THIS SWEET. BUT YOU GOT SOME BUSINESS TO ATTEND TO BEFORE ALL THE NOOKIE-NOOKIE STARTS.
HAND IT OVE SON.
YOU CAN'T--!
TRUST ME.
THIS IS THE RIGHT MOVE.
HE IS GONNA BE SO PISSED WHEN HE REALIZES I SWITCHED OUT THE ORB ON HIM.
HE WAS GONNA KILL YOU.
OH, I KNOW. BUT HE WAS ABOUT THE ONLY FAMILY I HAD.
NO. HE WASN'T.
NO... GROOT. SNIFF

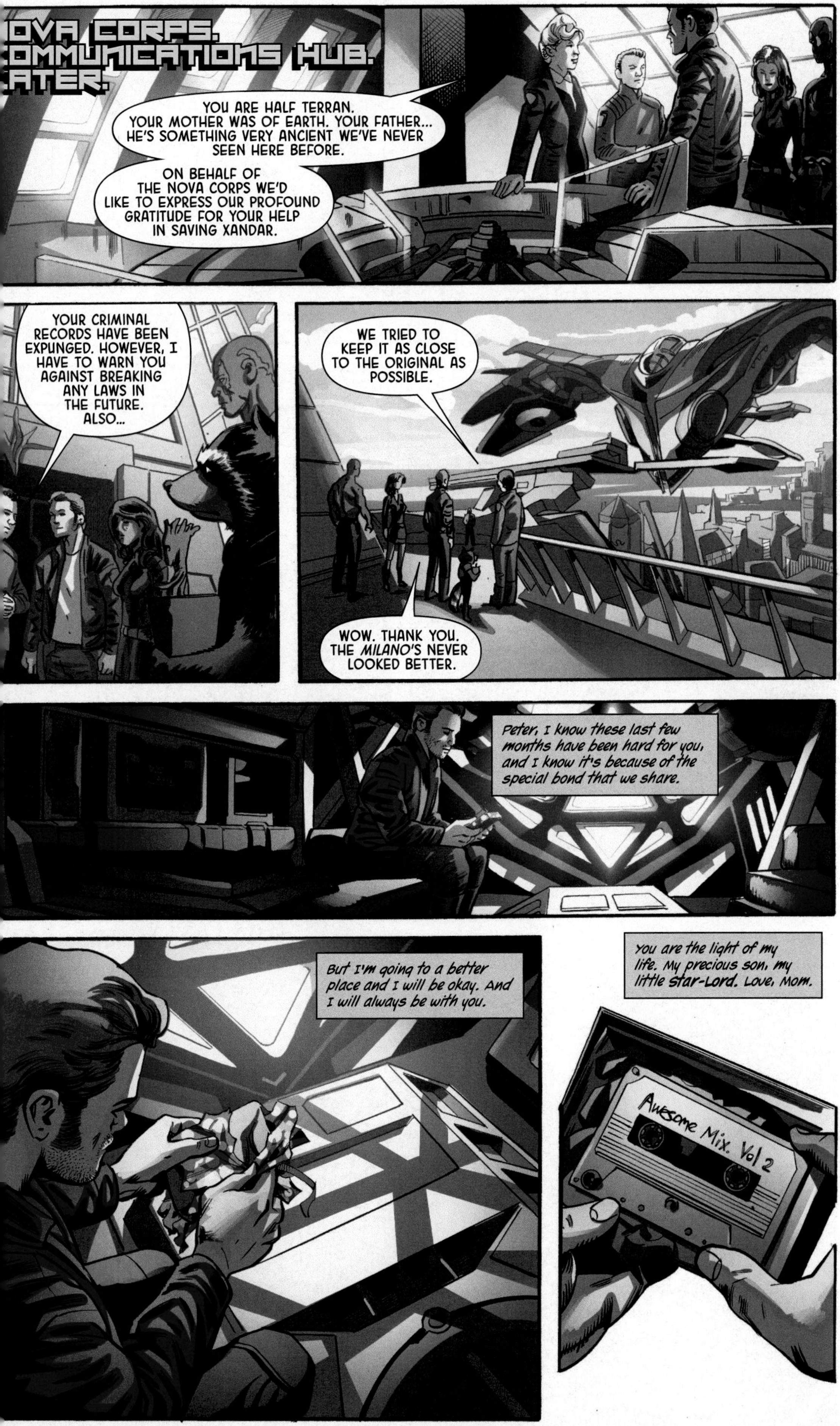
OVA CORPS. OMMUNICATIONS HUB. ATER.
YOU ARE HALF TERRAN. YOUR MOTHER WAS OF EARTH. YOUR FATHER... HE'S SOMETHING VERY ANCIENT WE'VE NEVER SEEN HERE BEFORE.
ON BEHALF OF THE NOVA CORPS WE'D LIKE TO EXPRESS OUR PROFOUND GRATITUDE FOR YOUR HELP IN SAVING XANDAR.
YOUR CRIMINAL RECORDS HAVE BEEN EXPUNGED. HOWEVER, I HAVE TO WARN YOU AGAINST BREAKING ANY LAWS IN THE FUTURE. ALSO...
WE TRIED TO KEEP IT AS CLOSE TO THE ORIGINAL AS POSSIBLE.
WOW. THANK YOU. THE MILANO'S NEVER LOOKED BETTER.
Peter, I know these last few months have been hard for you, and I know it's because of the special bond that we share.
But I'm going to a better place and I will be okay. And I will always be with you.
You are the light of my life. My precious son, my little Star-Lord. Love, Mom.
Awesome Mix. Vol 2

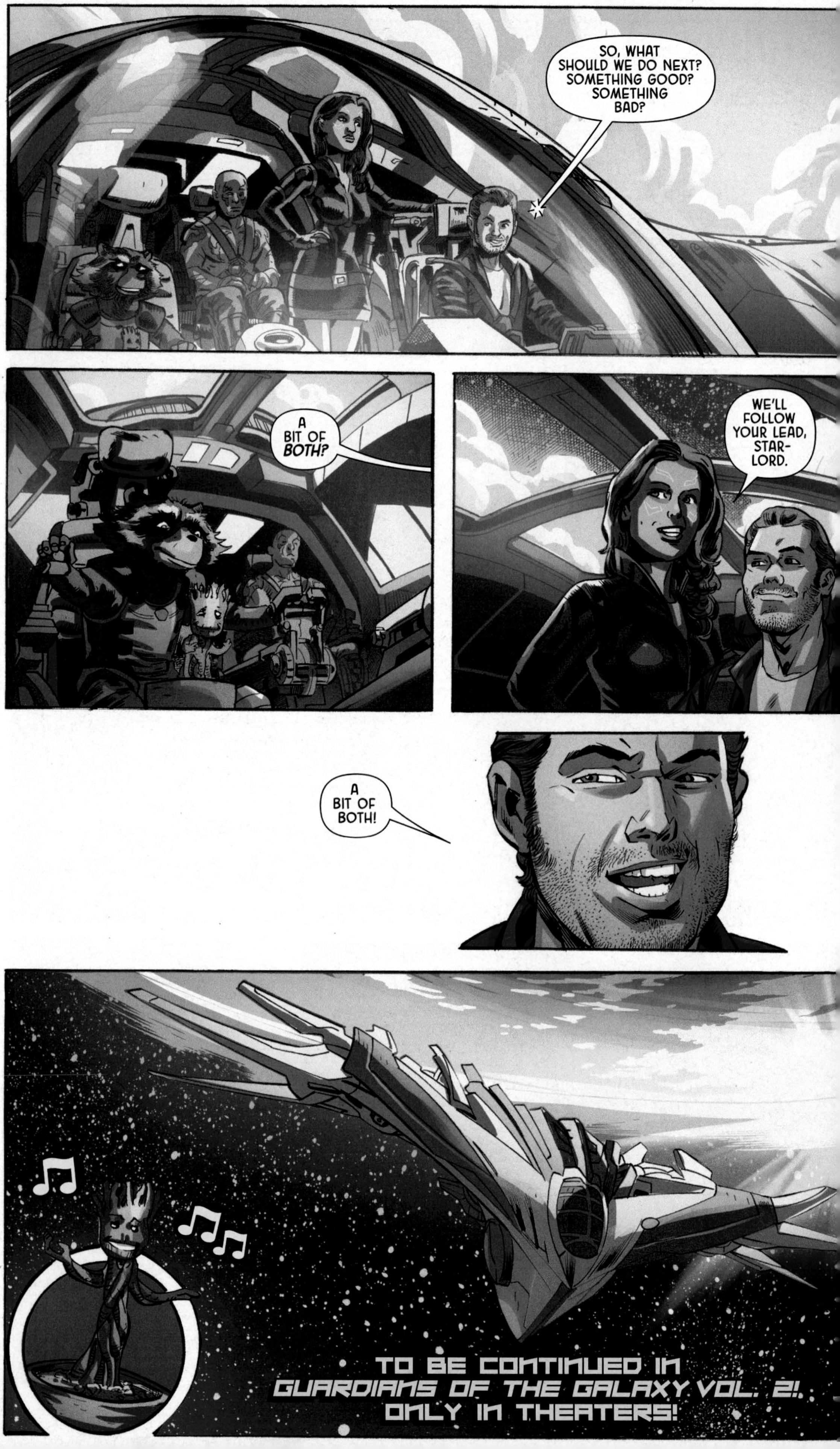
SO, WHAT SHOULD WE DO NEXT? SOMETHING GOOD? SOMETHING BAD?
A BIT OF *BOTH?*
WE'LL FOLLOW YOUR LEAD, STAR-LORD.
A BIT OF BOTH!
TO BE CONTINUED IN *GUARDIANS OF THE GALAXY VOL. 2!*. ONLY IN THEATERS!

Wedding bells chime for the enigmatic Avenger called Mantis!
But will she embrace her destiny as the Celestial Madonna?

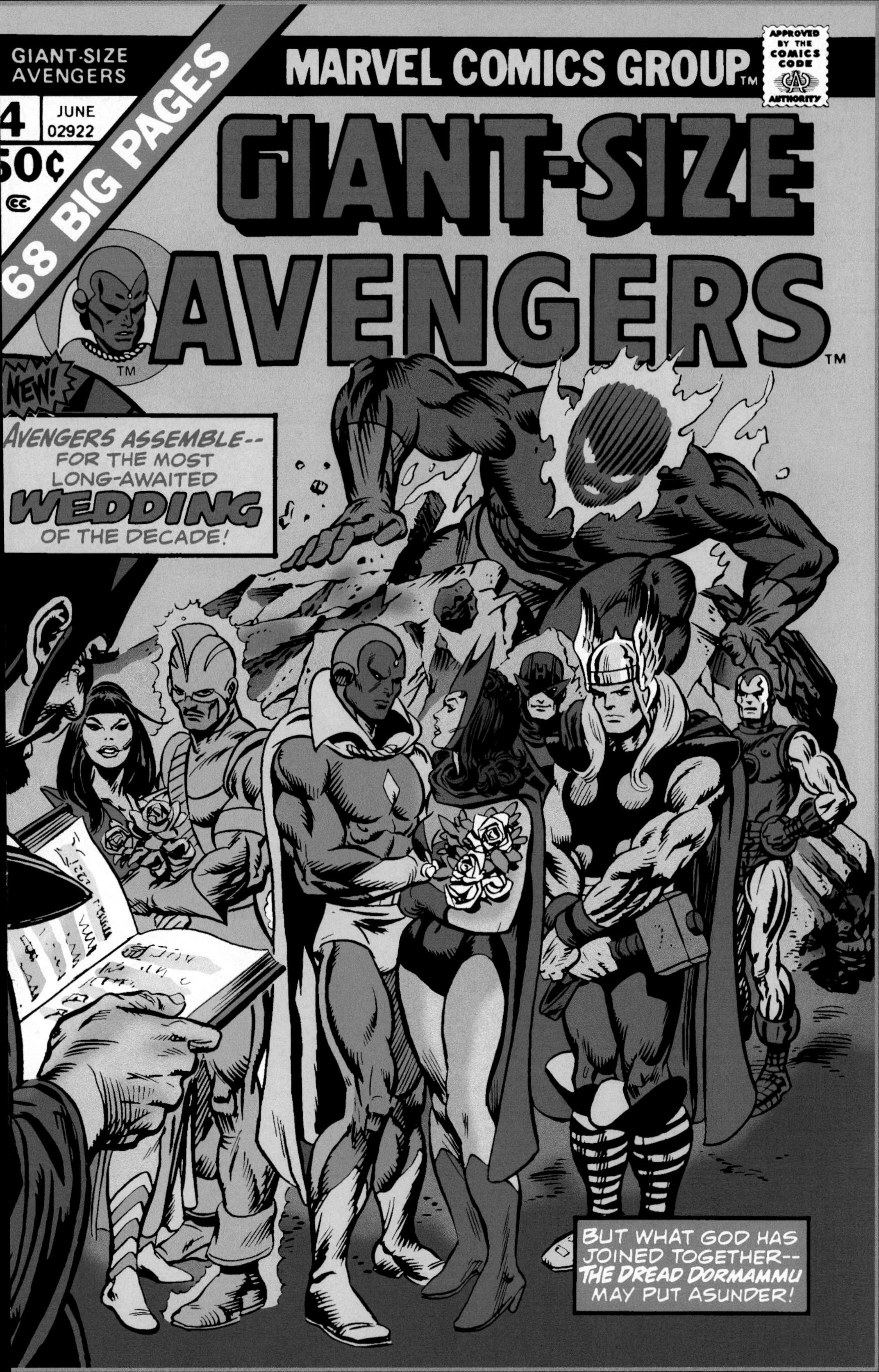
GIANT-SIZE AVENGERS
4
JUNE
02922
50¢
68 BIG PAGES
MARVEL COMICS GROUP
APPROVED BY THE COMICS CODE AUTHORITY
GIANT-SIZE AVENGERS
NEW!
AVENGERS ASSEMBLE-- FOR THE MOST LONG-AWAITED WEDDING OF THE DECADE!
BUT WHAT GOD HAS JOINED TOGETHER-- THE DREAD DORMAMMU MAY PUT ASUNDER!

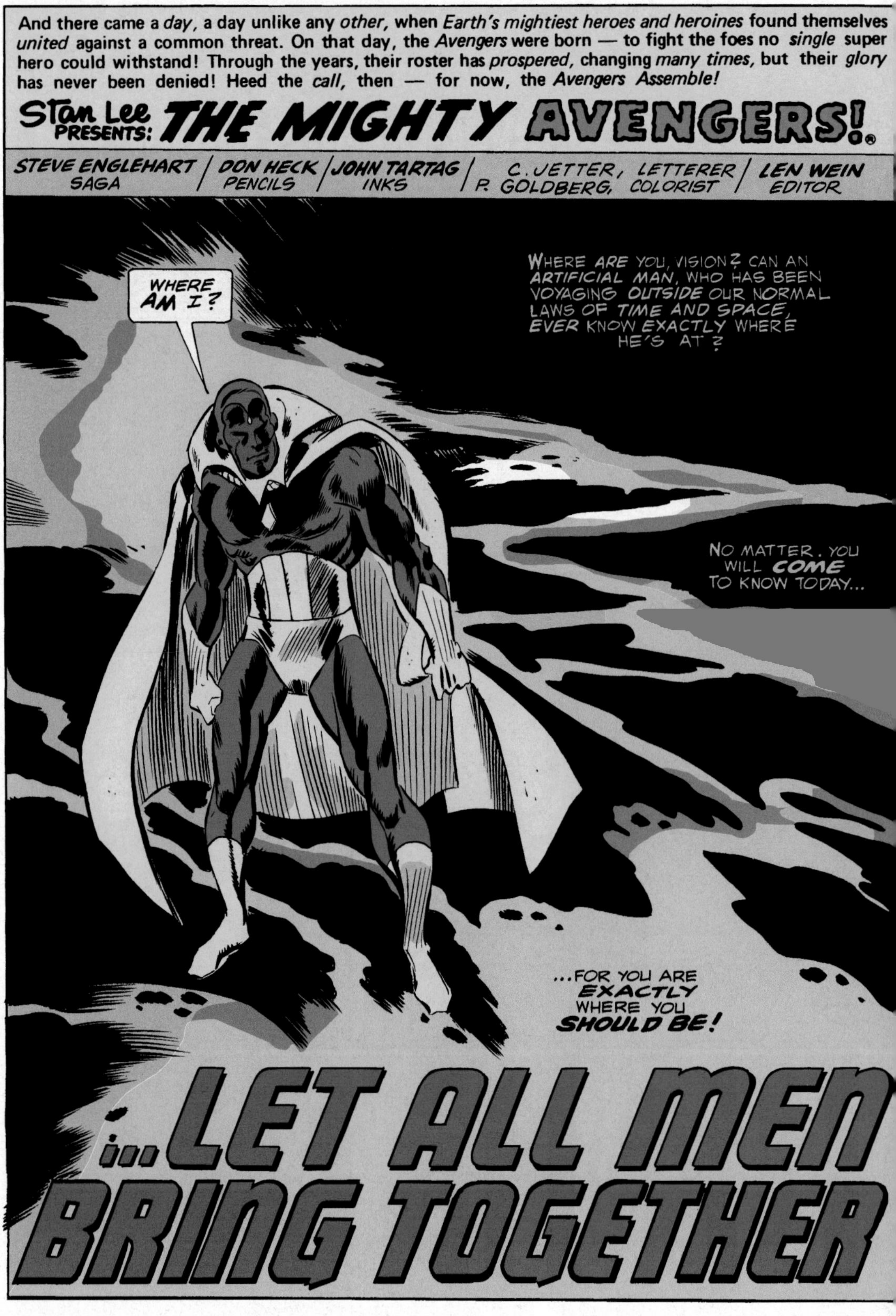
And there came a *day*, a day unlike any *other*, when *Earth's mightiest heroes and heroines* found themselves *united* against a common threat. On that day, the *Avengers* were born — to fight the foes no *single* super hero could withstand! Through the years, their roster has *prospered*, changing *many times*, but their *glory* has never been denied! Heed the *call*, then — for now, the *Avengers Assemble!*
Stan Lee PRESENTS: THE MIGHTY AVENGERS!®
STEVE ENGLEHART SAGA / DON HECK PENCILS / JOHN TARTAG INKS / C. JETTER, LETTERER P. GOLDBERG, COLORIST / LEN WEIN EDITOR
WHERE ARE YOU, VISION? CAN AN ARTIFICIAL MAN, WHO HAS BEEN VOYAGING OUTSIDE OUR NORMAL LAWS OF TIME AND SPACE, EVER KNOW EXACTLY WHERE HE'S AT?
WHERE AM I?
NO MATTER. YOU WILL COME TO KNOW TODAY...
...FOR YOU ARE EXACTLY WHERE YOU SHOULD BE!
...LET ALL MEN BRING TOGETHER

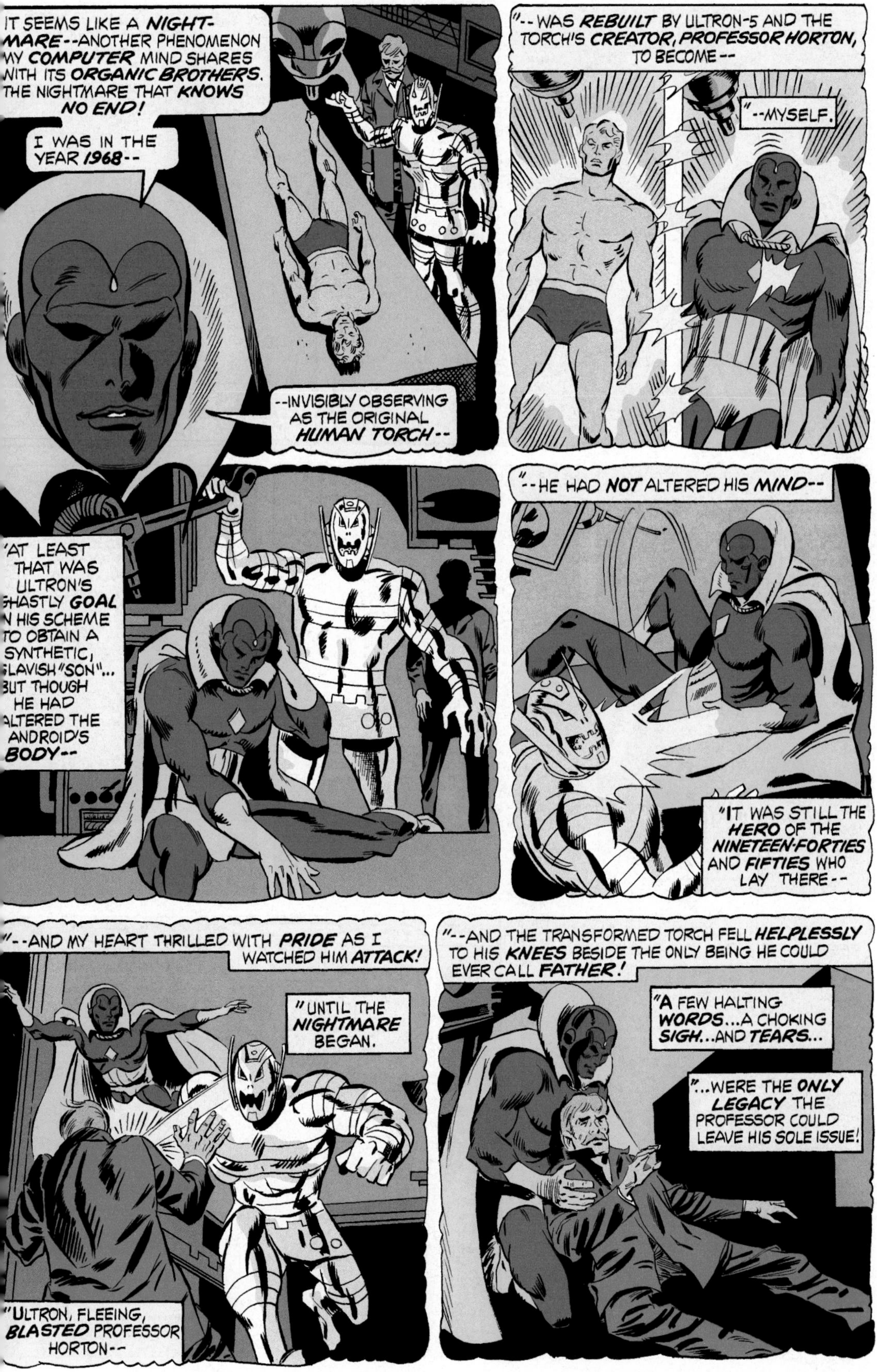
IT SEEMS LIKE A NIGHT-MARE--ANOTHER PHENOMENON MY COMPUTER MIND SHARES WITH ITS ORGANIC BROTHERS. THE NIGHTMARE THAT KNOWS NO END!
I WAS IN THE YEAR 1968--
--INVISIBLY OBSERVING AS THE ORIGINAL HUMAN TORCH--
"--WAS REBUILT BY ULTRON-5 AND THE TORCH'S CREATOR, PROFESSOR HORTON, TO BECOME--
"--MYSELF.
"AT LEAST THAT WAS ULTRON'S GHASTLY GOAL IN HIS SCHEME TO OBTAIN A SYNTHETIC, SLAVISH "SON"... BUT THOUGH HE HAD ALTERED THE ANDROID'S BODY--
"--HE HAD NOT ALTERED HIS MIND--
"IT WAS STILL THE HERO OF THE NINETEEN-FORTIES AND FIFTIES WHO LAY THERE--
"--AND MY HEART THRILLED WITH PRIDE AS I WATCHED HIM ATTACK!
"UNTIL THE NIGHTMARE BEGAN.
"ULTRON, FLEEING, BLASTED PROFESSOR HORTON--
"--AND THE TRANSFORMED TORCH FELL HELPLESSLY TO HIS KNEES BESIDE THE ONLY BEING HE COULD EVER CALL FATHER!
"A FEW HALTING WORDS...A CHOKING SIGH...AND TEARS...
"...WERE THE ONLY LEGACY THE PROFESSOR COULD LEAVE HIS SOLE ISSUE!

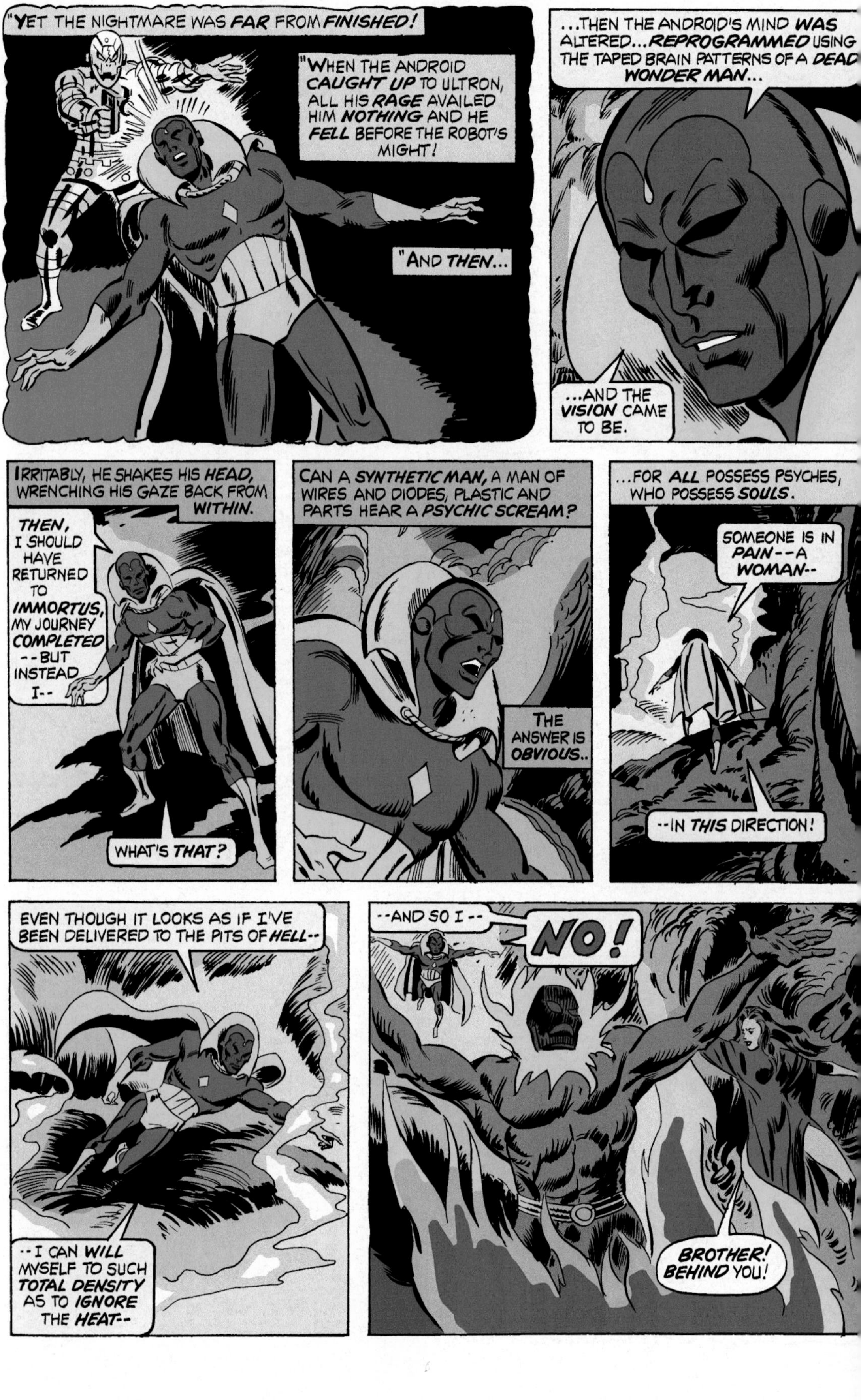
"YET THE NIGHTMARE WAS FAR FROM FINISHED!
"WHEN THE ANDROID CAUGHT UP TO ULTRON, ALL HIS RAGE AVAILED HIM NOTHING AND HE FELL BEFORE THE ROBOT'S MIGHT!
"AND THEN...
...THEN THE ANDROID'S MIND WAS ALTERED...REPROGRAMMED USING THE TAPED BRAIN PATTERNS OF A DEAD WONDER MAN...
...AND THE VISION CAME TO BE.
IRRITABLY, HE SHAKES HIS HEAD, WRENCHING HIS GAZE BACK FROM WITHIN.
THEN, I SHOULD HAVE RETURNED TO IMMORTUS, MY JOURNEY COMPLETED --BUT INSTEAD I--
WHAT'S THAT?
CAN A SYNTHETIC MAN, A MAN OF WIRES AND DIODES, PLASTIC AND PARTS HEAR A PSYCHIC SCREAM?
THE ANSWER IS OBVIOUS..
...FOR ALL POSSESS PSYCHES, WHO POSSESS SOULS.
SOMEONE IS IN PAIN--A WOMAN--
--IN THIS DIRECTION!
EVEN THOUGH IT LOOKS AS IF I'VE BEEN DELIVERED TO THE PITS OF HELL--
--I CAN WILL MYSELF TO SUCH TOTAL DENSITY AS TO IGNORE THE HEAT--
--AND SO I--
NO!
BROTHER! BEHIND YOU!

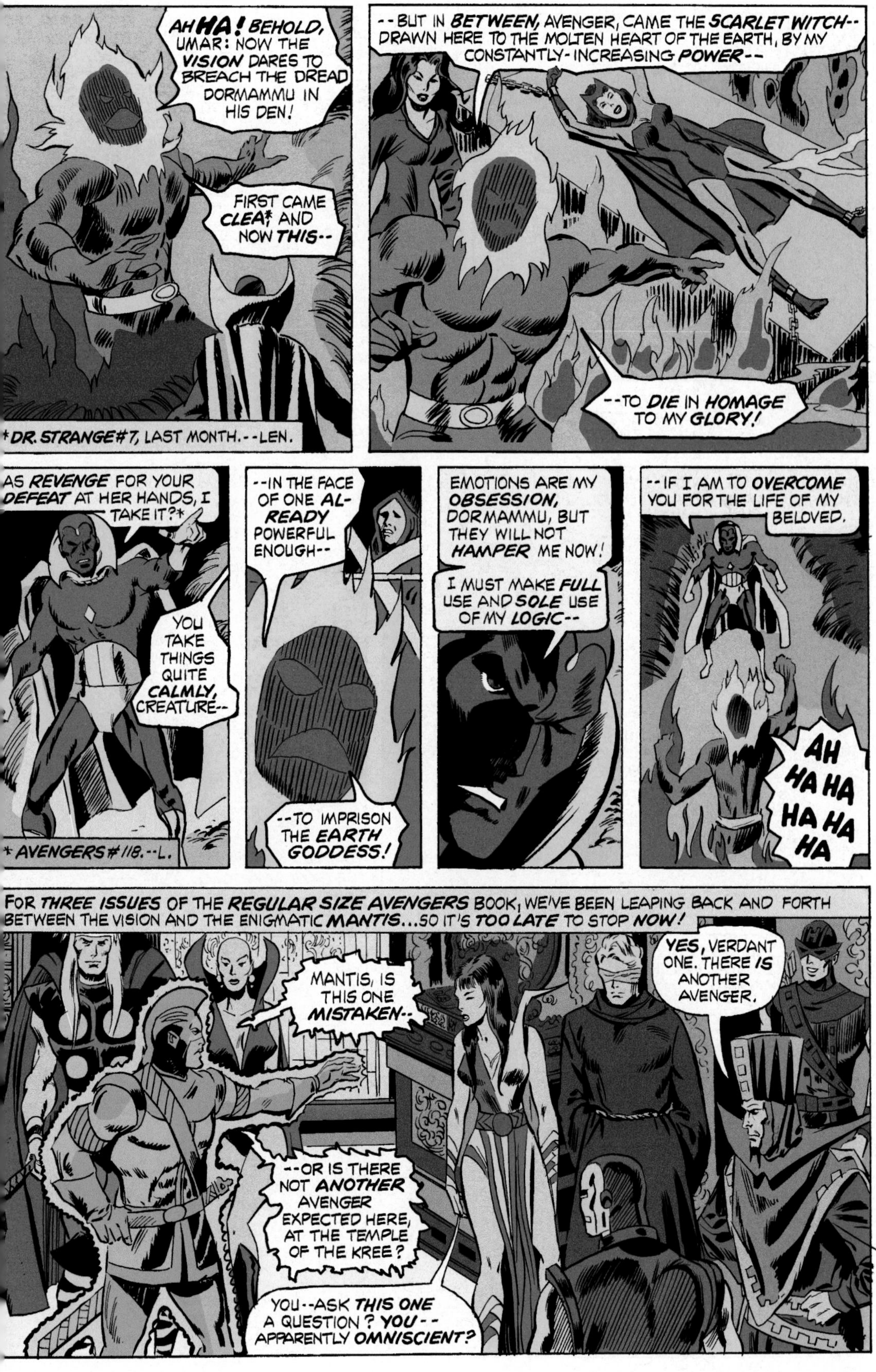
AH HA! BEHOLD, UMAR: NOW THE VISION DARES TO BREACH THE DREAD DORMAMMU IN HIS DEN!
FIRST CAME CLEA;* AND NOW THIS--
*DR. STRANGE #7, LAST MONTH.--LEN.
--BUT IN BETWEEN, AVENGER, CAME THE SCARLET WITCH--DRAWN HERE TO THE MOLTEN HEART OF THE EARTH, BY MY CONSTANTLY-INCREASING POWER--
--TO DIE IN HOMAGE TO MY GLORY!
AS REVENGE FOR YOUR DEFEAT AT HER HANDS, I TAKE IT?*
YOU TAKE THINGS QUITE CALMLY, CREATURE--
* AVENGERS #118.--L.
--IN THE FACE OF ONE AL-READY POWERFUL ENOUGH--
--TO IMPRISON THE EARTH GODDESS!
EMOTIONS ARE MY OBSESSION, DORMAMMU, BUT THEY WILL NOT HAMPER ME NOW!
I MUST MAKE FULL USE AND SOLE USE OF MY LOGIC--
--IF I AM TO OVERCOME YOU FOR THE LIFE OF MY BELOVED.
AH HA HA HA HA HA HA
FOR THREE ISSUES OF THE REGULAR SIZE AVENGERS BOOK, WE'VE BEEN LEAPING BACK AND FORTH BETWEEN THE VISION AND THE ENIGMATIC MANTIS...SO IT'S TOO LATE TO STOP NOW!
MANTIS, IS THIS ONE MISTAKEN--
--OR IS THERE NOT ANOTHER AVENGER EXPECTED HERE, AT THE TEMPLE OF THE KREE?
YOU--ASK THIS ONE A QUESTION? YOU--APPARENTLY OMNISCIENT?
YES, VERDANT ONE. THERE IS ANOTHER AVENGER.

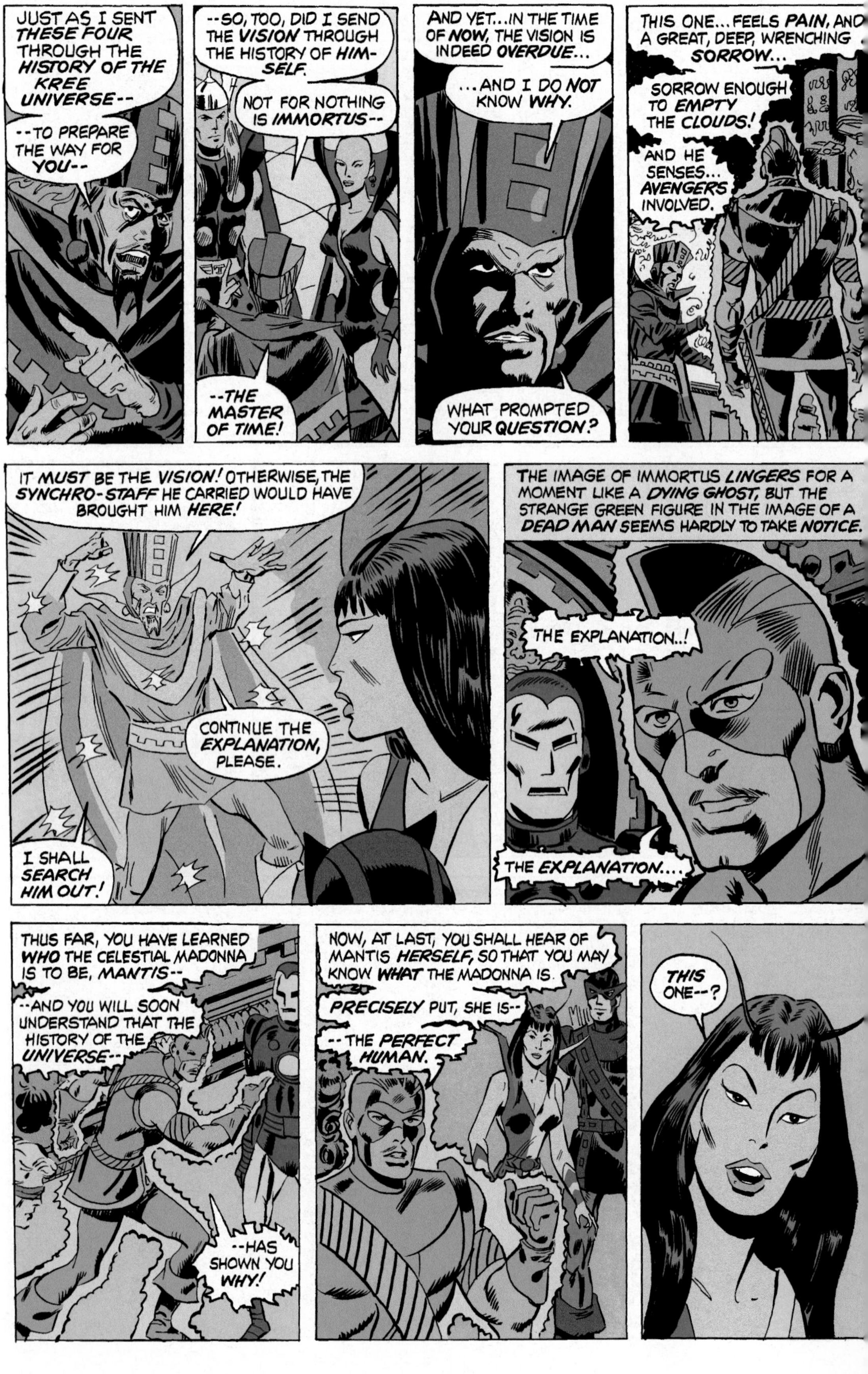
JUST AS I SENT THESE FOUR THROUGH THE HISTORY OF THE KREE UNIVERSE--
--TO PREPARE THE WAY FOR YOU--
--SO, TOO, DID I SEND THE VISION THROUGH THE HISTORY OF HIMSELF.
NOT FOR NOTHING IS IMMORTUS--
--THE MASTER OF TIME!
AND YET...IN THE TIME OF NOW, THE VISION IS INDEED OVERDUE...
...AND I DO NOT KNOW WHY.
WHAT PROMPTED YOUR QUESTION?
THIS ONE... FEELS PAIN, AND A GREAT, DEEP, WRENCHING SORROW...
SORROW ENOUGH TO EMPTY THE CLOUDS!
AND HE SENSES... AVENGERS INVOLVED.
IT MUST BE THE VISION! OTHERWISE, THE SYNCHRO-STAFF HE CARRIED WOULD HAVE BROUGHT HIM HERE!
CONTINUE THE EXPLANATION, PLEASE.
I SHALL SEARCH HIM OUT!
THE IMAGE OF IMMORTUS LINGERS FOR A MOMENT LIKE A DYING GHOST, BUT THE STRANGE GREEN FIGURE IN THE IMAGE OF A DEAD MAN SEEMS HARDLY TO TAKE NOTICE.
THE EXPLANATION..!
THE EXPLANATION....
THUS FAR, YOU HAVE LEARNED WHO THE CELESTIAL MADONNA IS TO BE, MANTIS--
--AND YOU WILL SOON UNDERSTAND THAT THE HISTORY OF THE UNIVERSE--
--HAS SHOWN YOU WHY!
NOW, AT LAST, YOU SHALL HEAR OF MANTIS HERSELF, SO THAT YOU MAY KNOW WHAT THE MADONNA IS.
PRECISELY PUT, SHE IS--
--THE PERFECT HUMAN.
THIS ONE--?

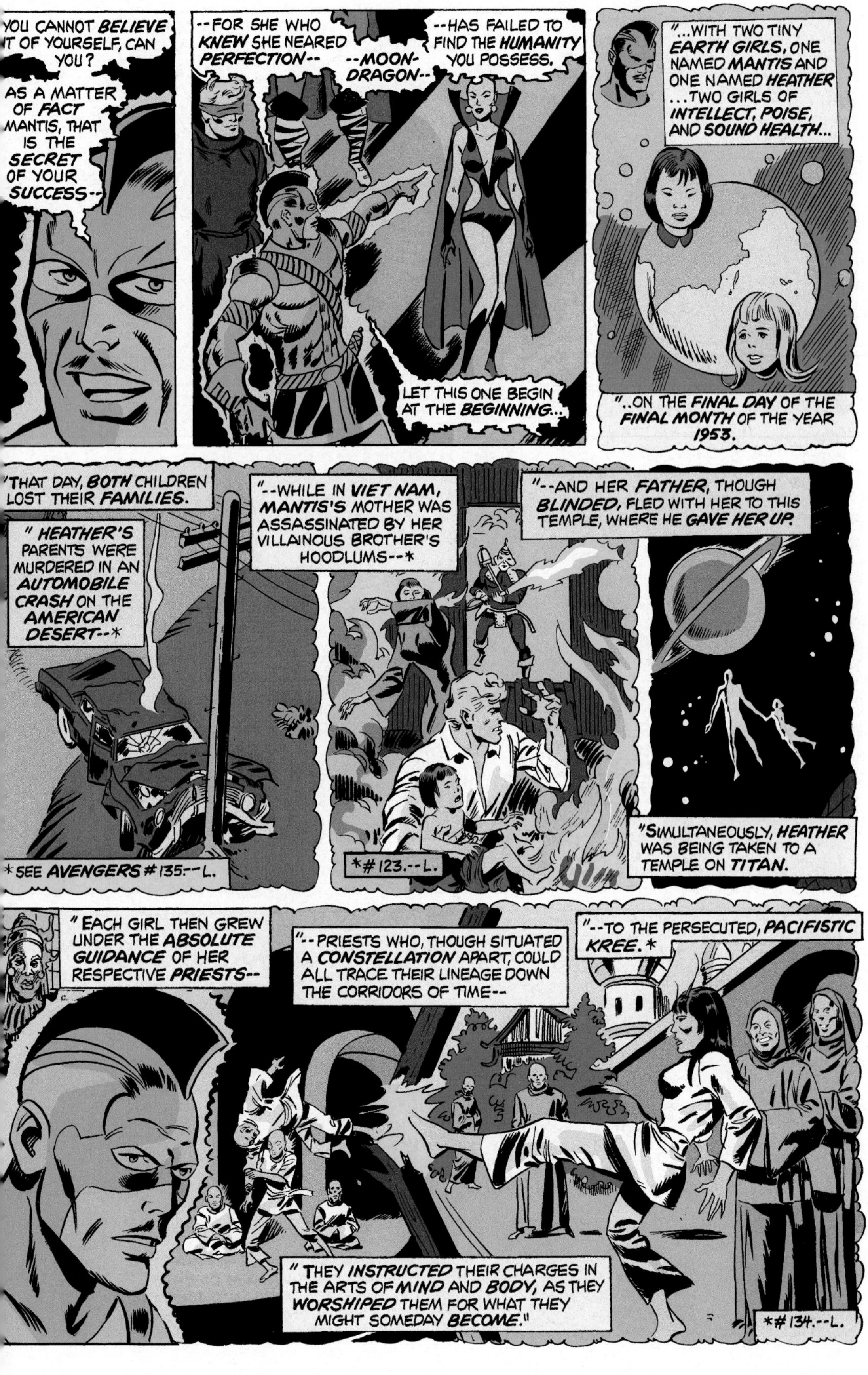
YOU CANNOT BELIEVE IT OF YOURSELF, CAN YOU?
AS A MATTER OF FACT MANTIS, THAT IS THE SECRET OF YOUR SUCCESS--
--FOR SHE WHO KNEW SHE NEARED PERFECTION--
--MOON-DRAGON--
--HAS FAILED TO FIND THE HUMANITY YOU POSSESS.
LET THIS ONE BEGIN AT THE BEGINNING...
"...WITH TWO TINY EARTH GIRLS, ONE NAMED MANTIS AND ONE NAMED HEATHER ...TWO GIRLS OF INTELLECT, POISE, AND SOUND HEALTH...
"..ON THE FINAL DAY OF THE FINAL MONTH OF THE YEAR 1953.
"THAT DAY, BOTH CHILDREN LOST THEIR FAMILIES.
" HEATHER'S PARENTS WERE MURDERED IN AN AUTOMOBILE CRASH ON THE AMERICAN DESERT--*
*SEE AVENGERS #135.--L.
"--WHILE IN VIET NAM, MANTIS'S MOTHER WAS ASSASSINATED BY HER VILLAINOUS BROTHER'S HOODLUMS--*
*#123.--L.
"--AND HER FATHER, THOUGH BLINDED, FLED WITH HER TO THIS TEMPLE, WHERE HE GAVE HER UP.
"SIMULTANEOUSLY, HEATHER WAS BEING TAKEN TO A TEMPLE ON TITAN.
" EACH GIRL THEN GREW UNDER THE ABSOLUTE GUIDANCE OF HER RESPECTIVE PRIESTS--
"--PRIESTS WHO, THOUGH SITUATED A CONSTELLATION APART, COULD ALL TRACE THEIR LINEAGE DOWN THE CORRIDORS OF TIME--
"--TO THE PERSECUTED, PACIFISTIC KREE.*
" THEY INSTRUCTED THEIR CHARGES IN THE ARTS OF MIND AND BODY, AS THEY WORSHIPED THEM FOR WHAT THEY MIGHT SOMEDAY BECOME."
*#134.--L.

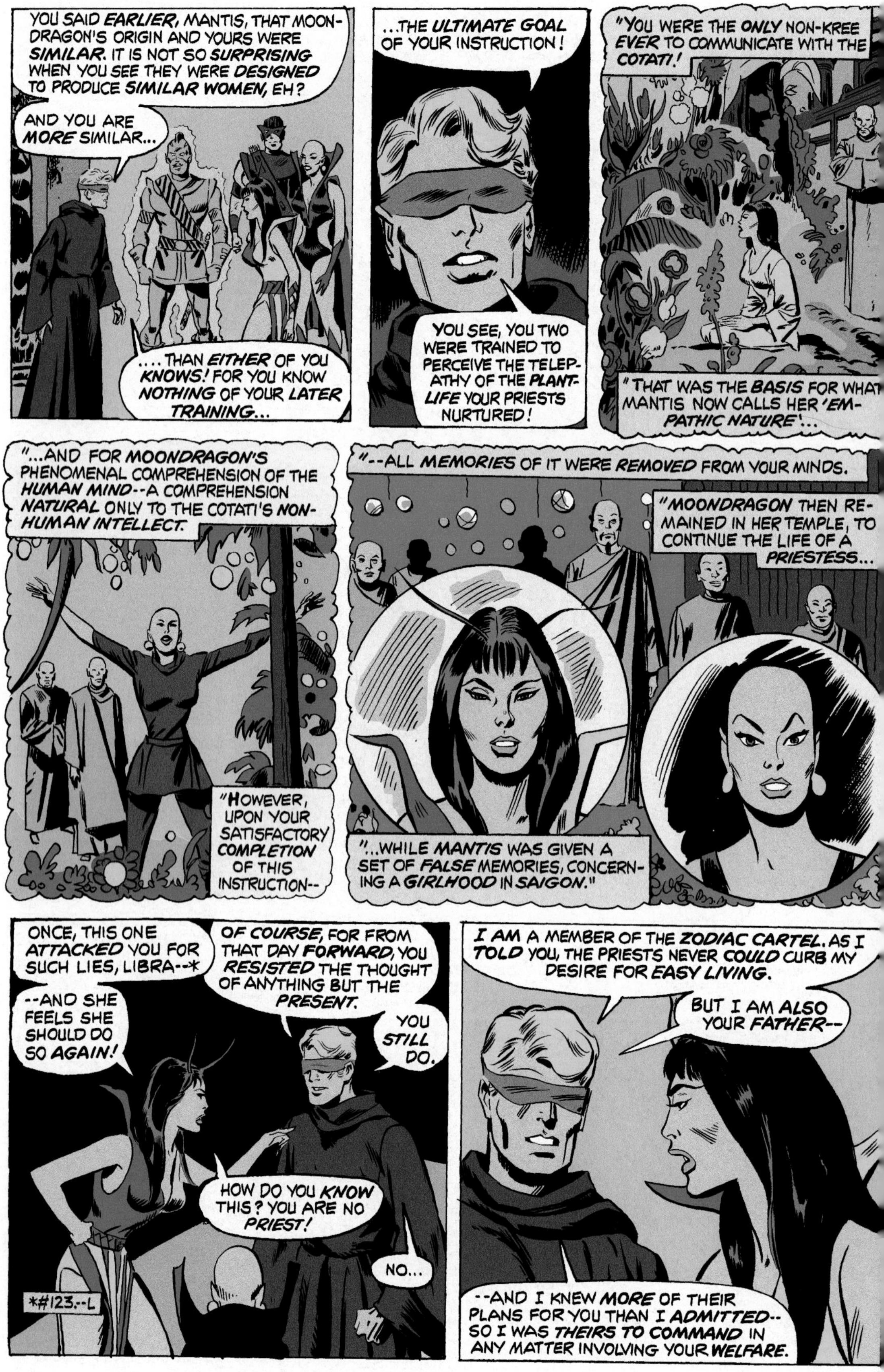
YOU SAID EARLIER, MANTIS, THAT MOON-DRAGON'S ORIGIN AND YOURS WERE SIMILAR. IT IS NOT SO SURPRISING WHEN YOU SEE THEY WERE DESIGNED TO PRODUCE SIMILAR WOMEN, EH?
AND YOU ARE MORE SIMILAR...
....THAN EITHER OF YOU KNOWS! FOR YOU KNOW NOTHING OF YOUR LATER TRAINING...
...THE ULTIMATE GOAL OF YOUR INSTRUCTION!
YOU SEE, YOU TWO WERE TRAINED TO PERCEIVE THE TELEP-ATHY OF THE PLANT-LIFE YOUR PRIESTS NURTURED!
"YOU WERE THE ONLY NON-KREE EVER TO COMMUNICATE WITH THE COTATI!
"THAT WAS THE BASIS FOR WHAT MANTIS NOW CALLS HER 'EM-PATHIC NATURE'...
"...AND FOR MOONDRAGON'S PHENOMENAL COMPREHENSION OF THE HUMAN MIND--A COMPREHENSION NATURAL ONLY TO THE COTATI'S NON-HUMAN INTELLECT.
"HOWEVER, UPON YOUR SATISFACTORY COMPLETION OF THIS INSTRUCTION--
"--ALL MEMORIES OF IT WERE REMOVED FROM YOUR MINDS.
"MOONDRAGON THEN RE-MAINED IN HER TEMPLE, TO CONTINUE THE LIFE OF A PRIESTESS...
"...WHILE MANTIS WAS GIVEN A SET OF FALSE MEMORIES, CONCERN-ING A GIRLHOOD IN SAIGON."
ONCE, THIS ONE ATTACKED YOU FOR SUCH LIES, LIBRA--*
--AND SHE FEELS SHE SHOULD DO SO AGAIN!
OF COURSE, FOR FROM THAT DAY FORWARD, YOU RESISTED THE THOUGHT OF ANYTHING BUT THE PRESENT.
YOU STILL DO.
HOW DO YOU KNOW THIS? YOU ARE NO PRIEST!
NO...
*#123.--L
I AM A MEMBER OF THE ZODIAC CARTEL. AS I TOLD YOU, THE PRIESTS NEVER COULD CURB MY DESIRE FOR EASY LIVING.
BUT I AM ALSO YOUR FATHER--
--AND I KNEW MORE OF THEIR PLANS FOR YOU THAN I ADMITTED--SO I WAS THEIRS TO COMMAND IN ANY MATTER INVOLVING YOUR WELFARE.

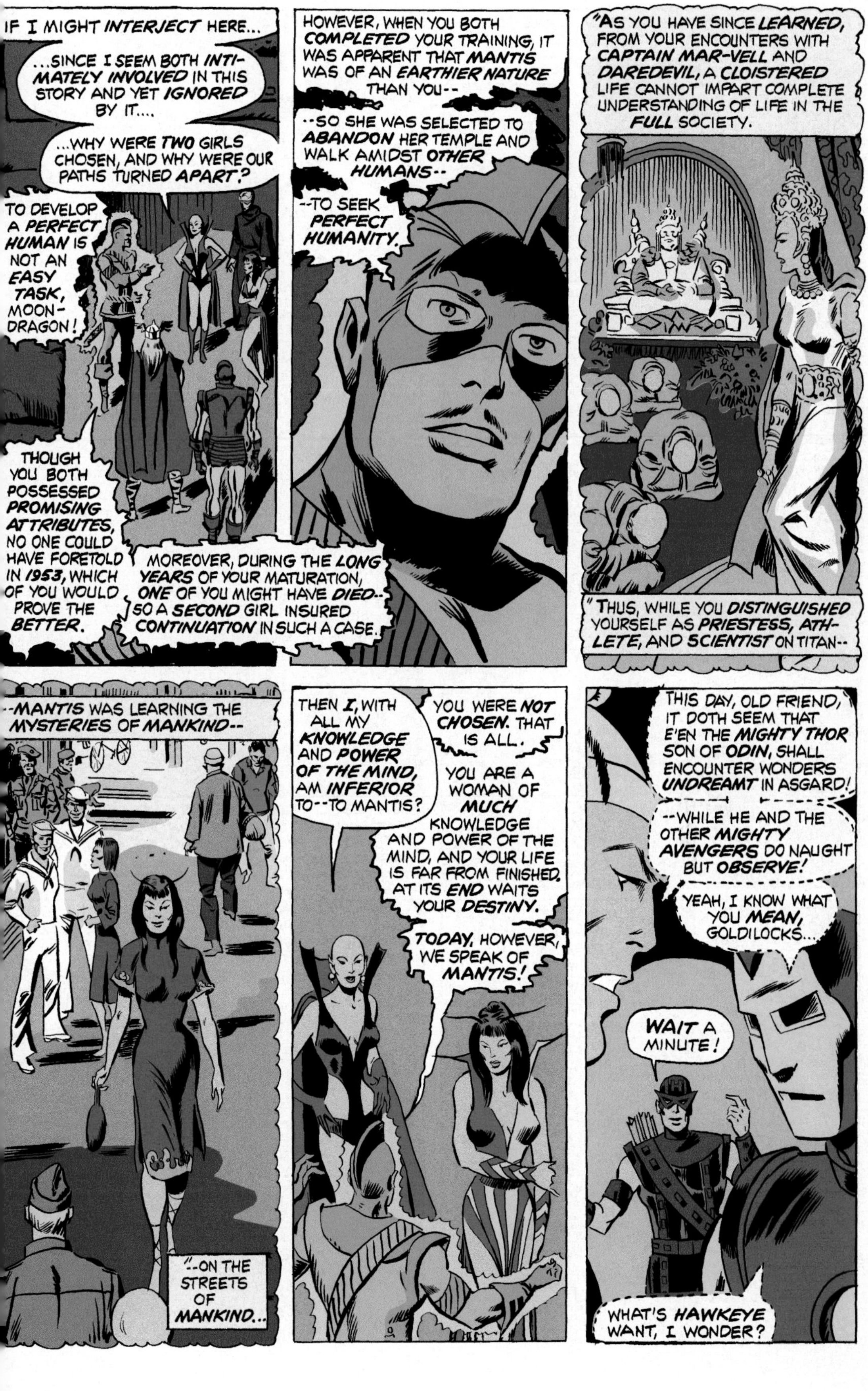
IF I MIGHT INTERJECT HERE...
...SINCE I SEEM BOTH INTIMATELY INVOLVED IN THIS STORY AND YET IGNORED BY IT....
...WHY WERE TWO GIRLS CHOSEN, AND WHY WERE OUR PATHS TURNED APART?
TO DEVELOP A PERFECT HUMAN IS NOT AN EASY TASK, MOONDRAGON!
THOUGH YOU BOTH POSSESSED PROMISING ATTRIBUTES, NO ONE COULD HAVE FORETOLD IN 1953, WHICH OF YOU WOULD PROVE THE BETTER.
MOREOVER, DURING THE LONG YEARS OF YOUR MATURATION, ONE OF YOU MIGHT HAVE DIED--SO A SECOND GIRL INSURED CONTINUATION IN SUCH A CASE.
HOWEVER, WHEN YOU BOTH COMPLETED YOUR TRAINING, IT WAS APPARENT THAT MANTIS WAS OF AN EARTHIER NATURE THAN YOU--
--SO SHE WAS SELECTED TO ABANDON HER TEMPLE AND WALK AMIDST OTHER HUMANS--
--TO SEEK PERFECT HUMANITY.
"AS YOU HAVE SINCE LEARNED, FROM YOUR ENCOUNTERS WITH CAPTAIN MAR-VELL AND DAREDEVIL, A CLOISTERED LIFE CANNOT IMPART COMPLETE UNDERSTANDING OF LIFE IN THE FULL SOCIETY.
"THUS, WHILE YOU DISTINGUISHED YOURSELF AS PRIESTESS, ATHLETE, AND SCIENTIST ON TITAN--
--MANTIS WAS LEARNING THE MYSTERIES OF MANKIND--
"--ON THE STREETS OF MANKIND...
THEN I, WITH ALL MY KNOWLEDGE AND POWER OF THE MIND, AM INFERIOR TO--TO MANTIS?
YOU WERE NOT CHOSEN. THAT IS ALL.
YOU ARE A WOMAN OF MUCH KNOWLEDGE AND POWER OF THE MIND, AND YOUR LIFE IS FAR FROM FINISHED. AT ITS END WAITS YOUR DESTINY.
TODAY, HOWEVER, WE SPEAK OF MANTIS!
THIS DAY, OLD FRIEND, IT DOTH SEEM THAT E'EN THE MIGHTY THOR SON OF ODIN, SHALL ENCOUNTER WONDERS UNDREAMT IN ASGARD!
--WHILE HE AND THE OTHER MIGHTY AVENGERS DO NAUGHT BUT OBSERVE!
YEAH, I KNOW WHAT YOU MEAN, GOLDILOCKS...
WAIT A MINUTE!
WHAT'S HAWKEYE WANT, I WONDER?

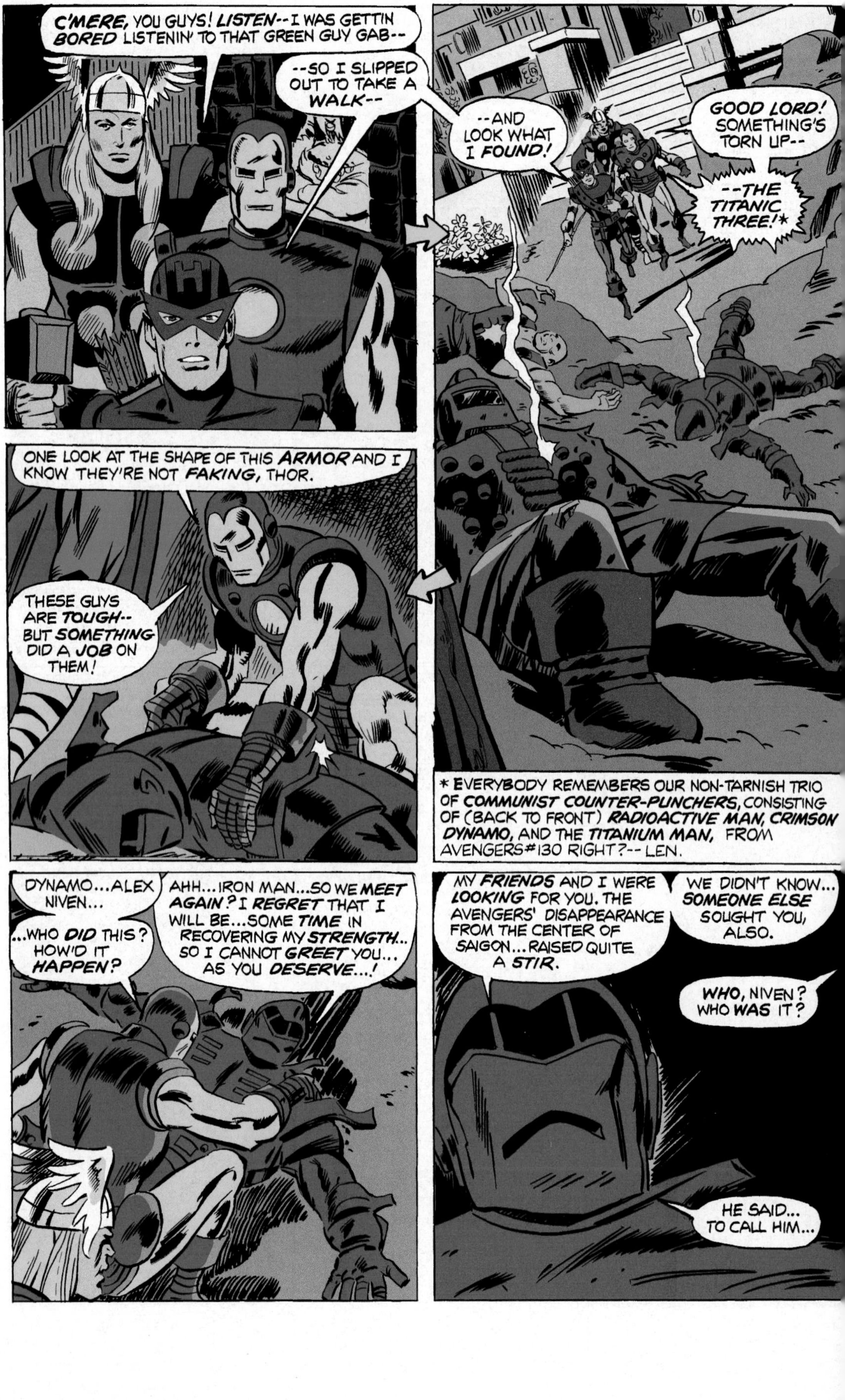
C'MERE, YOU GUYS! LISTEN--I WAS GETTIN BORED LISTENIN' TO THAT GREEN GUY GAB--
--SO I SLIPPED OUT TO TAKE A WALK--
--AND LOOK WHAT I FOUND!
GOOD LORD! SOMETHING'S TORN UP--
--THE TITANIC THREE!*
ONE LOOK AT THE SHAPE OF THIS ARMOR AND I KNOW THEY'RE NOT FAKING, THOR.
THESE GUYS ARE TOUGH-- BUT SOMETHING DID A JOB ON THEM!
* EVERYBODY REMEMBERS OUR NON-TARNISH TRIO OF COMMUNIST COUNTER-PUNCHERS, CONSISTING OF (BACK TO FRONT) RADIOACTIVE MAN, CRIMSON DYNAMO, AND THE TITANIUM MAN, FROM AVENGERS #130 RIGHT?--LEN.
DYNAMO...ALEX NIVEN...
...WHO DID THIS? HOW'D IT HAPPEN?
AHH...IRON MAN...SO WE MEET AGAIN? I REGRET THAT I WILL BE...SOME TIME IN RECOVERING MY STRENGTH.. SO I CANNOT GREET YOU... AS YOU DESERVE...!
MY FRIENDS AND I WERE LOOKING FOR YOU. THE AVENGERS' DISAPPEARANCE FROM THE CENTER OF SAIGON...RAISED QUITE A STIR.
WE DIDN'T KNOW... SOMEONE ELSE SOUGHT YOU, ALSO.
WHO, NIVEN? WHO WAS IT?
HE SAID... TO CALL HIM...

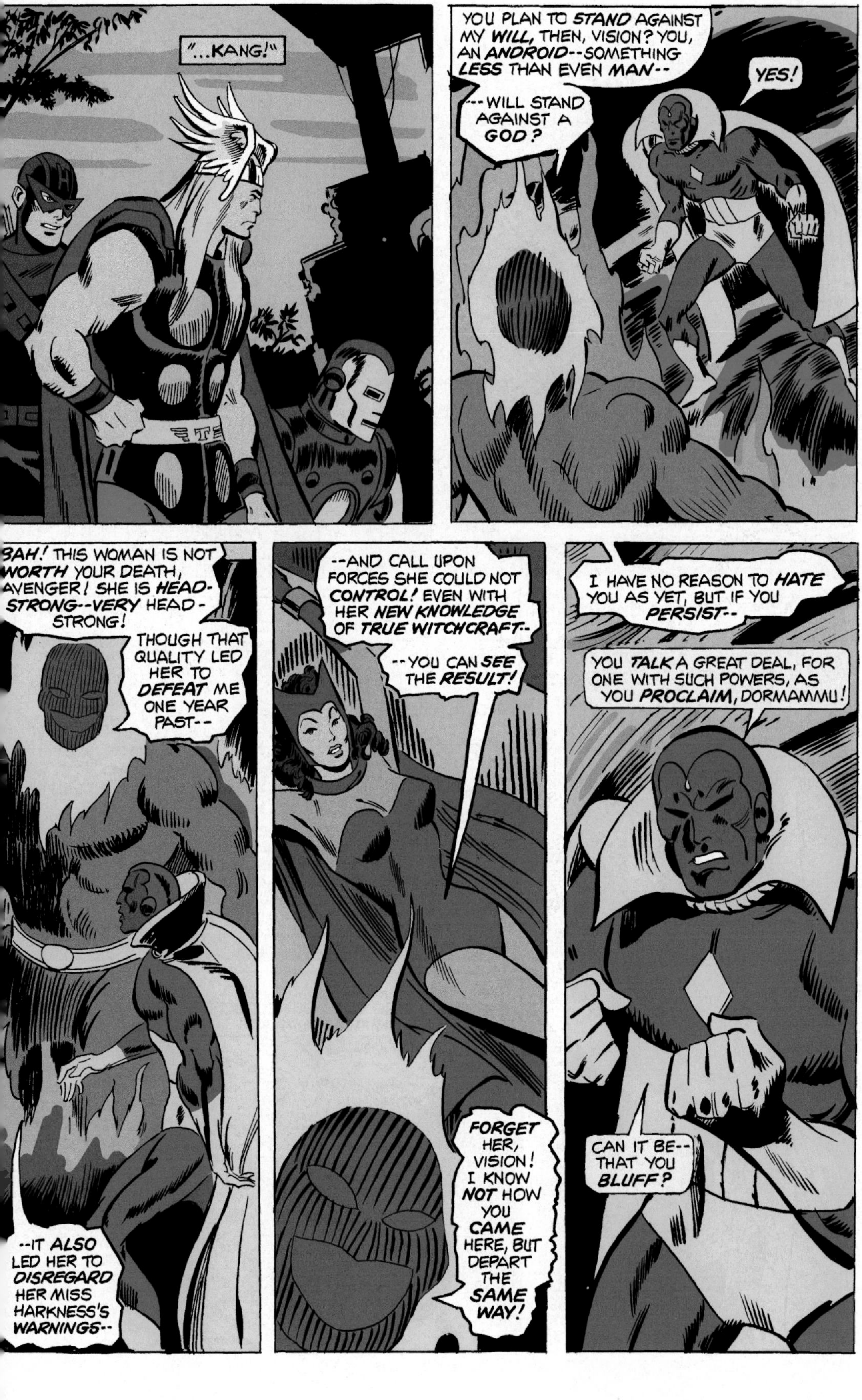
"...KANG!"
YOU PLAN TO STAND AGAINST MY WILL, THEN, VISION? YOU, AN ANDROID--SOMETHING LESS THAN EVEN MAN--
--WILL STAND AGAINST A GOD?
YES!
BAH! THIS WOMAN IS NOT WORTH YOUR DEATH, AVENGER! SHE IS HEAD-STRONG--VERY HEAD-STRONG!
THOUGH THAT QUALITY LED HER TO DEFEAT ME ONE YEAR PAST--
--IT ALSO LED HER TO DISREGARD HER MISS HARKNESS'S WARNINGS--
--AND CALL UPON FORCES SHE COULD NOT CONTROL! EVEN WITH HER NEW KNOWLEDGE OF TRUE WITCHCRAFT--
--YOU CAN SEE THE RESULT!
FORGET HER, VISION! I KNOW NOT HOW YOU CAME HERE, BUT DEPART THE SAME WAY!
I HAVE NO REASON TO HATE YOU AS YET, BUT IF YOU PERSIST--
YOU TALK A GREAT DEAL, FOR ONE WITH SUCH POWERS, AS YOU PROCLAIM, DORMAMMU!
CAN IT BE--THAT YOU BLUFF?

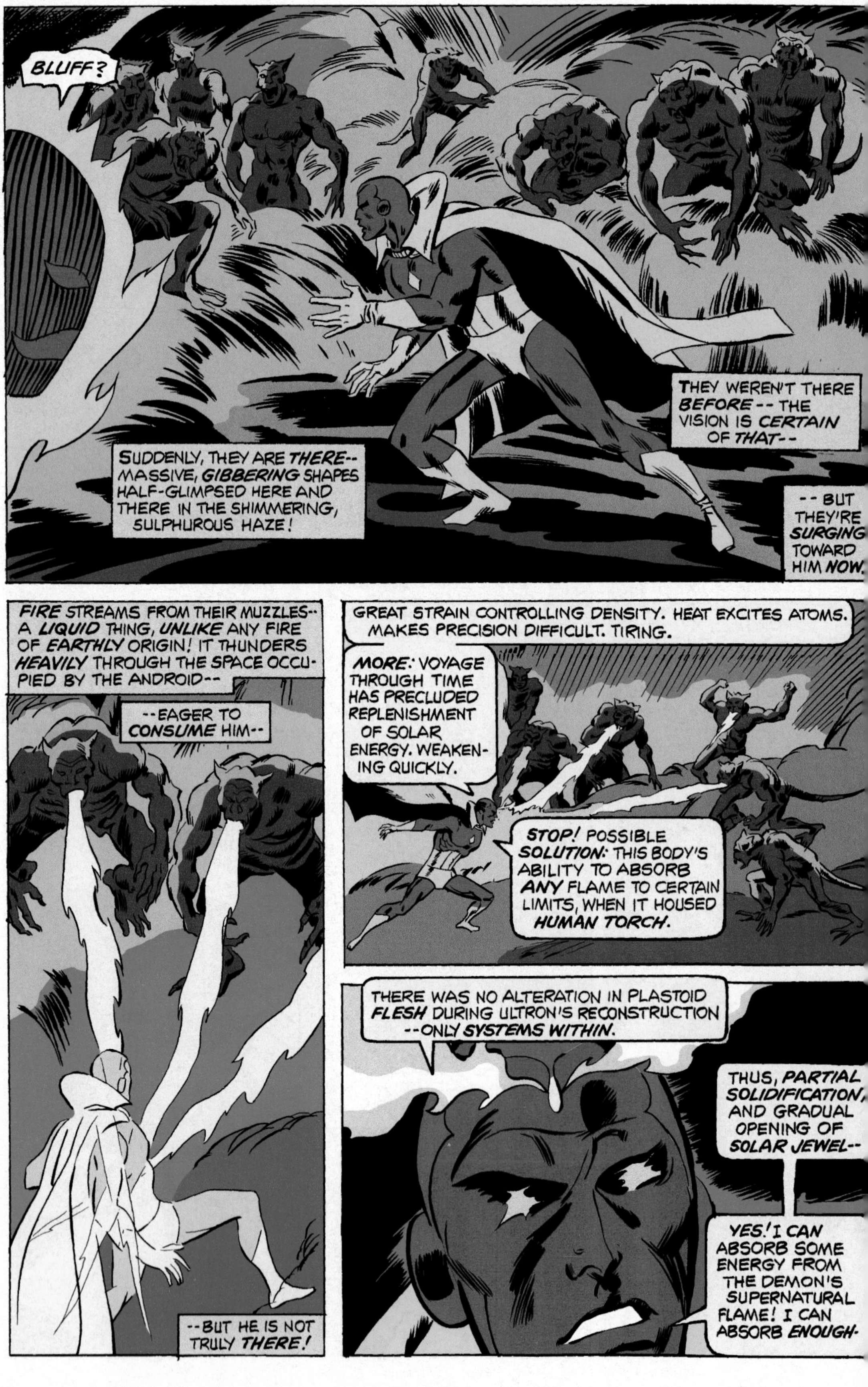
BLUFF?
SUDDENLY, THEY ARE THERE-- MASSIVE, GIBBERING SHAPES HALF-GLIMPSED HERE AND THERE IN THE SHIMMERING, SULPHUROUS HAZE!
THEY WEREN'T THERE BEFORE -- THE VISION IS CERTAIN OF THAT--
-- BUT THEY'RE SURGING TOWARD HIM NOW.
FIRE STREAMS FROM THEIR MUZZLES-- A LIQUID THING, UNLIKE ANY FIRE OF EARTHLY ORIGIN! IT THUNDERS HEAVILY THROUGH THE SPACE OCCUPIED BY THE ANDROID--
--EAGER TO CONSUME HIM--
--BUT HE IS NOT TRULY THERE!
GREAT STRAIN CONTROLLING DENSITY. HEAT EXCITES ATOMS. MAKES PRECISION DIFFICULT. TIRING.
MORE: VOYAGE THROUGH TIME HAS PRECLUDED REPLENISHMENT OF SOLAR ENERGY. WEAKENING QUICKLY.
STOP! POSSIBLE SOLUTION: THIS BODY'S ABILITY TO ABSORB ANY FLAME TO CERTAIN LIMITS, WHEN IT HOUSED HUMAN TORCH.
THERE WAS NO ALTERATION IN PLASTOID FLESH DURING ULTRON'S RECONSTRUCTION --ONLY SYSTEMS WITHIN.
THUS, PARTIAL SOLIDIFICATION, AND GRADUAL OPENING OF SOLAR JEWEL--
YES! I CAN ABSORB SOME ENERGY FROM THE DEMON'S SUPERNATURAL FLAME! I CAN ABSORB ENOUGH-

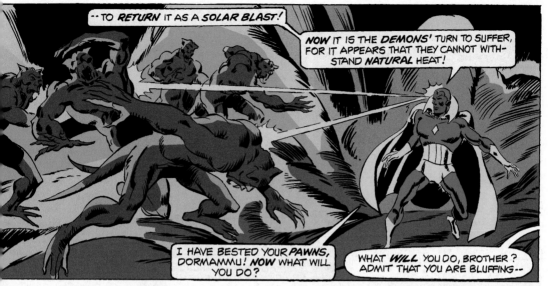

--TO *RETURN* IT AS A *SOLAR BLAST!*

NOW IT IS THE *DEMONS'* TURN TO SUFFER, FOR IT APPEARS THAT THEY CANNOT WITHSTAND *NATURAL* HEAT!

I HAVE BESTED YOUR *PAWNS,* DORMAMMU! *NOW* WHAT WILL YOU DO?

WHAT *WILL* YOU DO, BROTHER? ADMIT THAT YOU ARE BLUFFING--

--THAT YOUR RETURNING MIGHT IS AS YET SUFFICIENT ONLY TO SPIRIT AWAY *DEFENSELESS WITCHES,* AND *NOT* TO SQUANDER ON BATTLE WITH A *DETERMINED* OPPONENT?

HAVE A *CARE,* UMAR!

I MAY NOT WISH TO *SLOW* THE ARRIVAL OF MY FULL STRENGTH--

--BUT *DORMAMMU* CAN ACHIEVE WHATEVER HE *DESIRES!*

--THERE ARE *MANY* WHO MUST DO MY BIDDING!

LIKE *YOU,* TO WHOM I PROMISED MASTERY OF MY *DARK DOMAIN* WHEN I HAVE CLAIMED *THIS* DIMENSION--

RISE, SCARLET WITCH!

DAZEDLY, SHE QUIVERS IN BLIND *OBEDIANCE--*

--AND *RISES--*

--AS SUBSERVIANT TO THIS EVIL FORCE *NOW* AS WHEN SHE BATTLED *MOONDRAGON* IN ITS NAME!*

MY WILL IS *YOUR* WILL, WITCH--

*#134.--L

--AND I DEMAND THAT YOU--

--*DESTROY THE VISION!*

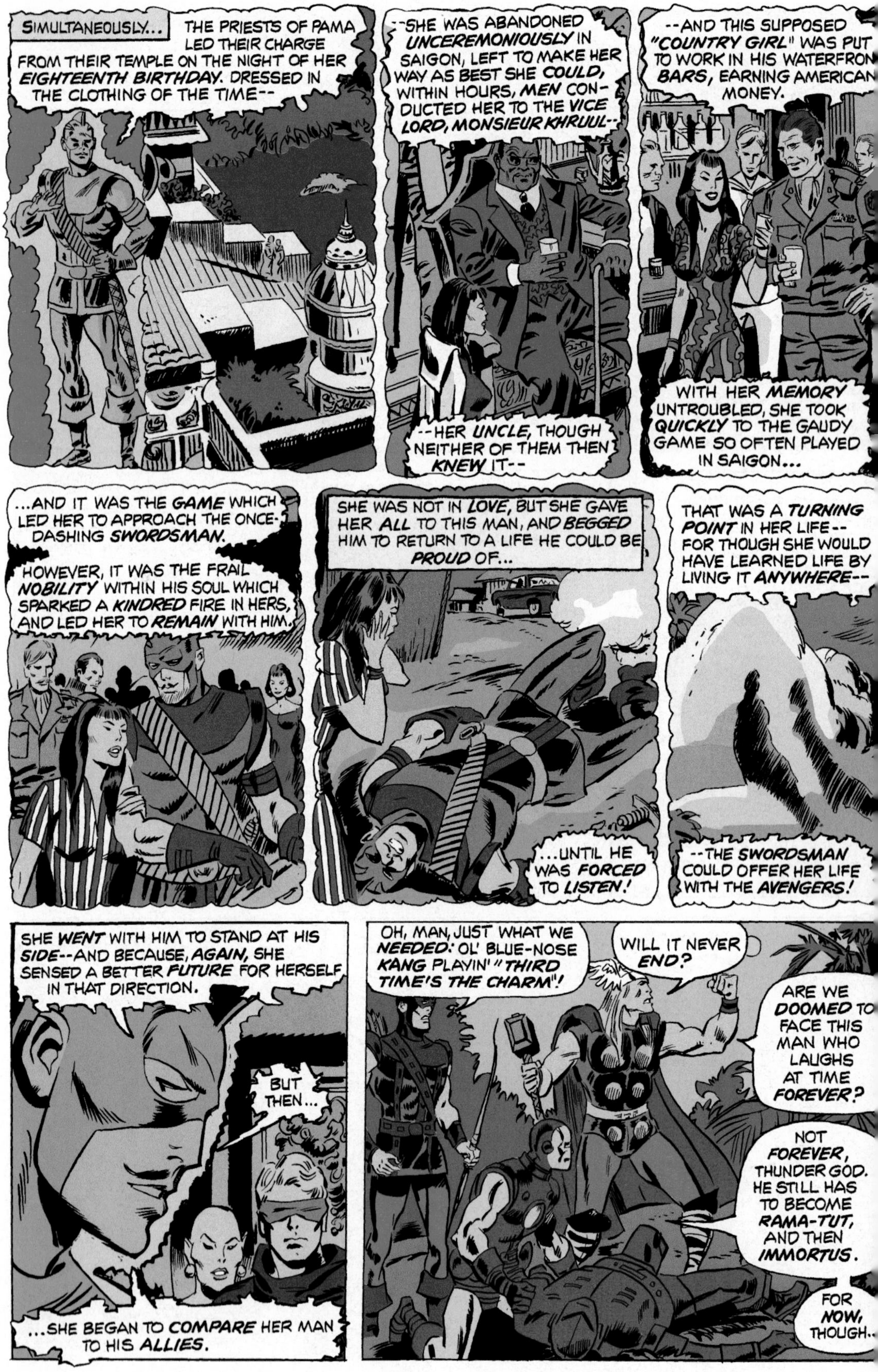
SIMULTANEOUSLY...
THE PRIESTS OF PAMA LED THEIR CHARGE FROM THEIR TEMPLE ON THE NIGHT OF HER EIGHTEENTH BIRTHDAY. DRESSED IN THE CLOTHING OF THE TIME--
--SHE WAS ABANDONED UNCEREMONIOUSLY IN SAIGON, LEFT TO MAKE HER WAY AS BEST SHE COULD, WITHIN HOURS, MEN CONDUCTED HER TO THE VICE LORD, MONSIEUR KHRUUL--
--HER UNCLE, THOUGH NEITHER OF THEM THEN KNEW IT--
--AND THIS SUPPOSED "COUNTRY GIRL" WAS PUT TO WORK IN HIS WATERFRON BARS, EARNING AMERICAN MONEY.
WITH HER MEMORY UNTROUBLED, SHE TOOK QUICKLY TO THE GAUDY GAME SO OFTEN PLAYED IN SAIGON...
...AND IT WAS THE GAME WHICH LED HER TO APPROACH THE ONCE-DASHING SWORDSMAN.
HOWEVER, IT WAS THE FRAIL NOBILITY WITHIN HIS SOUL WHICH SPARKED A KINDRED FIRE IN HERS, AND LED HER TO REMAIN WITH HIM.
SHE WAS NOT IN LOVE, BUT SHE GAVE HER ALL TO THIS MAN, AND BEGGED HIM TO RETURN TO A LIFE HE COULD BE PROUD OF...
...UNTIL HE WAS FORCED TO LISTEN!
THAT WAS A TURNING POINT IN HER LIFE--FOR THOUGH SHE WOULD HAVE LEARNED LIFE BY LIVING IT ANYWHERE--
--THE SWORDSMAN COULD OFFER HER LIFE WITH THE AVENGERS!
SHE WENT WITH HIM TO STAND AT HIS SIDE--AND BECAUSE, AGAIN, SHE SENSED A BETTER FUTURE FOR HERSELF IN THAT DIRECTION.
BUT THEN...
...SHE BEGAN TO COMPARE HER MAN TO HIS ALLIES.
OH, MAN, JUST WHAT WE NEEDED: OL' BLUE-NOSE KANG PLAYIN' "THIRD TIME'S THE CHARM"!
WILL IT NEVER END?
ARE WE DOOMED TO FACE THIS MAN WHO LAUGHS AT TIME FOREVER?
NOT FOREVER, THUNDER GOD. HE STILL HAS TO BECOME RAMA-TUT, AND THEN IMMORTUS.
FOR NOW, THOUGH..

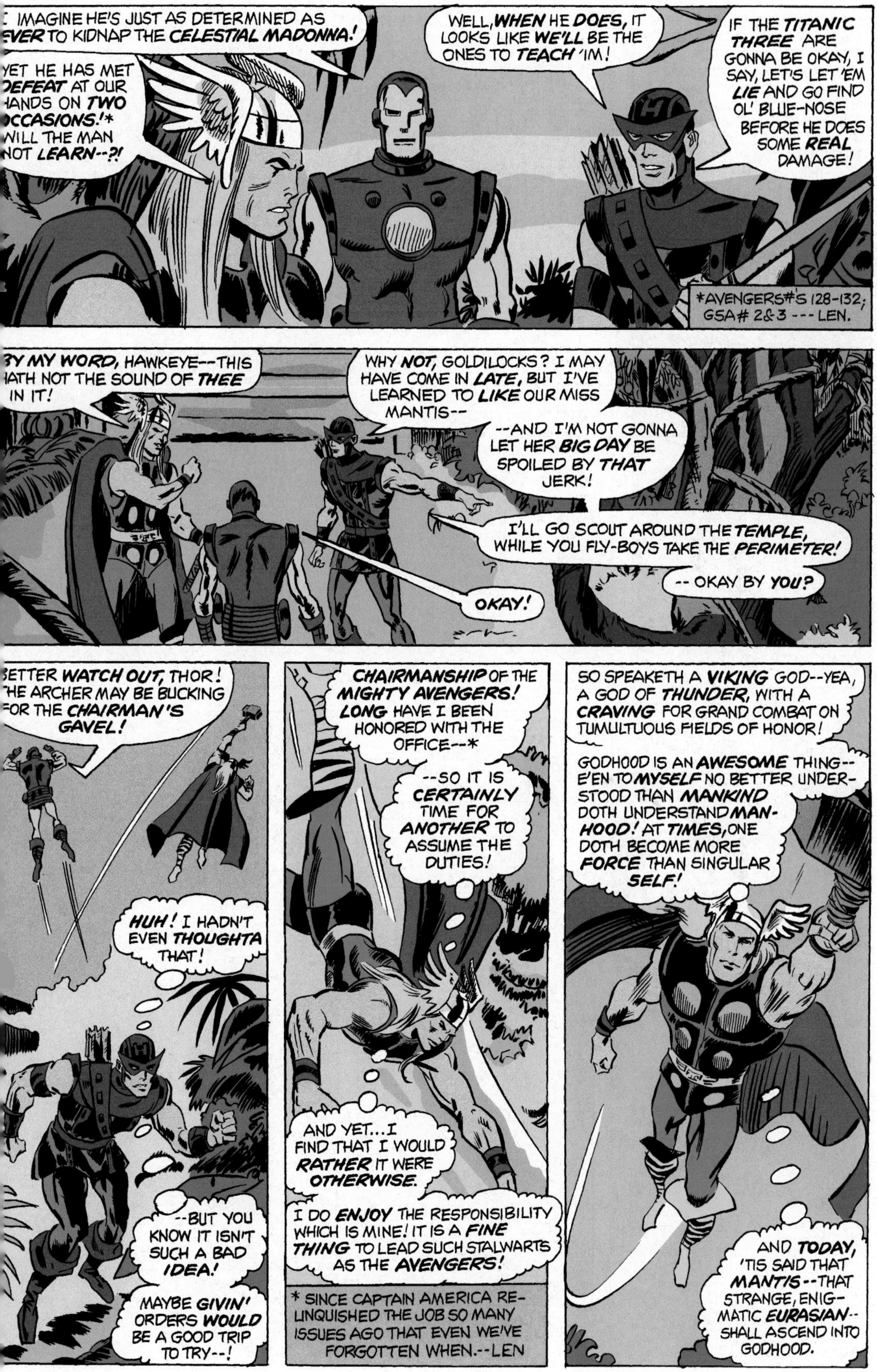
I IMAGINE HE'S JUST AS DETERMINED AS EVER TO KIDNAP THE CELESTIAL MADONNA!
YET HE HAS MET DEFEAT AT OUR HANDS ON TWO OCCASIONS!* WILL THE MAN NOT LEARN--?!
WELL, WHEN HE DOES, IT LOOKS LIKE WE'LL BE THE ONES TO TEACH 'IM!
IF THE TITANIC THREE ARE GONNA BE OKAY, I SAY, LET'S LET 'EM LIE AND GO FIND OL' BLUE-NOSE BEFORE HE DOES SOME REAL DAMAGE!
*AVENGERS#'S 128-132; GSA# 2&3 --- LEN.
BY MY WORD, HAWKEYE--THIS HATH NOT THE SOUND OF THEE IN IT!
WHY NOT, GOLDILOCKS? I MAY HAVE COME IN LATE, BUT I'VE LEARNED TO LIKE OUR MISS MANTIS--
--AND I'M NOT GONNA LET HER BIG DAY BE SPOILED BY THAT JERK!
I'LL GO SCOUT AROUND THE TEMPLE, WHILE YOU FLY-BOYS TAKE THE PERIMETER!
-- OKAY BY YOU?
OKAY!
BETTER WATCH OUT, THOR! THE ARCHER MAY BE BUCKING FOR THE CHAIRMAN'S GAVEL!
HUH! I HADN'T EVEN THOUGHTA THAT!
--BUT YOU KNOW IT ISN'T SUCH A BAD IDEA!
MAYBE GIVIN' ORDERS WOULD BE A GOOD TRIP TO TRY--!
CHAIRMANSHIP OF THE MIGHTY AVENGERS! LONG HAVE I BEEN HONORED WITH THE OFFICE--*
--SO IT IS CERTAINLY TIME FOR ANOTHER TO ASSUME THE DUTIES!
AND YET...I FIND THAT I WOULD RATHER IT WERE OTHERWISE.
I DO ENJOY THE RESPONSIBILITY WHICH IS MINE! IT IS A FINE THING TO LEAD SUCH STALWARTS AS THE AVENGERS!
* SINCE CAPTAIN AMERICA RELINQUISHED THE JOB SO MANY ISSUES AGO THAT EVEN WE'VE FORGOTTEN WHEN.--LEN
SO SPEAKETH A VIKING GOD--YEA, A GOD OF THUNDER, WITH A CRAVING FOR GRAND COMBAT ON TUMULTUOUS FIELDS OF HONOR!
GODHOOD IS AN AWESOME THING--E'EN TO MYSELF NO BETTER UNDERSTOOD THAN MANKIND DOTH UNDERSTAND MANHOOD! AT TIMES, ONE DOTH BECOME MORE FORCE THAN SINGULAR SELF!
AND TODAY, 'TIS SAID THAT MANTIS--THAT STRANGE, ENIGMATIC EURASIAN--SHALL ASCEND INTO GODHOOD.

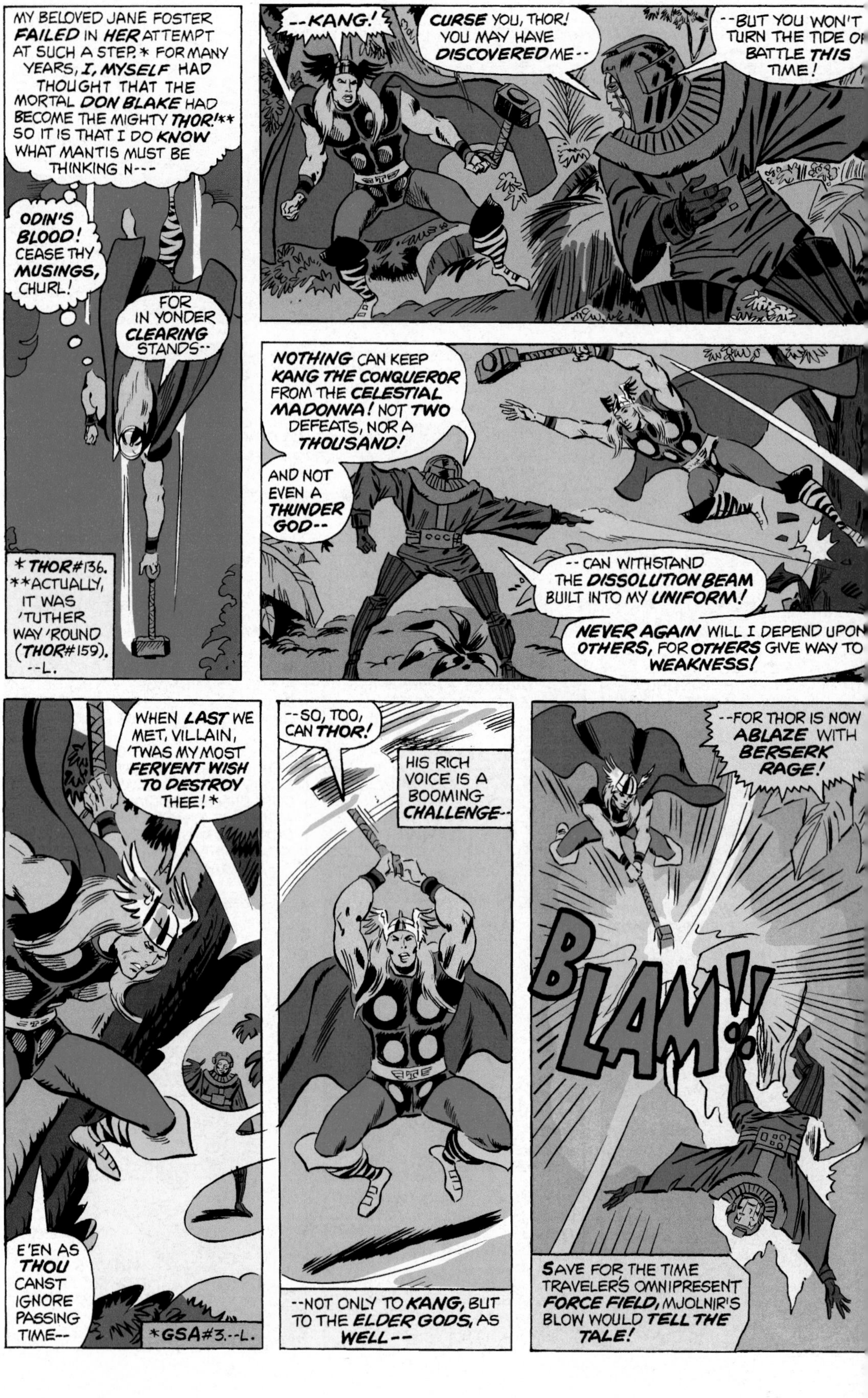
MY BELOVED JANE FOSTER FAILED IN HER ATTEMPT AT SUCH A STEP.* FOR MANY YEARS, I, MYSELF HAD THOUGHT THAT THE MORTAL DON BLAKE HAD BECOME THE MIGHTY THOR!** SO IT IS THAT I DO KNOW WHAT MANTIS MUST BE THINKING N---
ODIN'S BLOOD! CEASE THY MUSINGS, CHURL!
FOR IN YONDER CLEARING STANDS--
*THOR #136. **ACTUALLY, IT WAS 'TUTHER WAY 'ROUND (THOR #159). --L.
--KANG!
CURSE YOU, THOR! YOU MAY HAVE DISCOVERED ME--
--BUT YOU WON'T TURN THE TIDE OF BATTLE THIS TIME!
NOTHING CAN KEEP KANG THE CONQUEROR FROM THE CELESTIAL MADONNA! NOT TWO DEFEATS, NOR A THOUSAND!
AND NOT EVEN A THUNDER GOD--
--CAN WITHSTAND THE DISSOLUTION BEAM BUILT INTO MY UNIFORM!
NEVER AGAIN WILL I DEPEND UPON OTHERS, FOR OTHERS GIVE WAY TO WEAKNESS!
WHEN LAST WE MET, VILLAIN, 'TWAS MY MOST FERVENT WISH TO DESTROY THEE!*
E'EN AS THOU CANST IGNORE PASSING TIME--
*GSA #3.--L.
--SO, TOO, CAN THOR!
HIS RICH VOICE IS A BOOMING CHALLENGE--
--NOT ONLY TO KANG, BUT TO THE ELDER GODS, AS WELL--
--FOR THOR IS NOW ABLAZE WITH BERSERK RAGE!
BLAM!!
SAVE FOR THE TIME TRAVELER'S OMNIPRESENT FORCE FIELD, MJOLNIR'S BLOW WOULD TELL THE TALE!

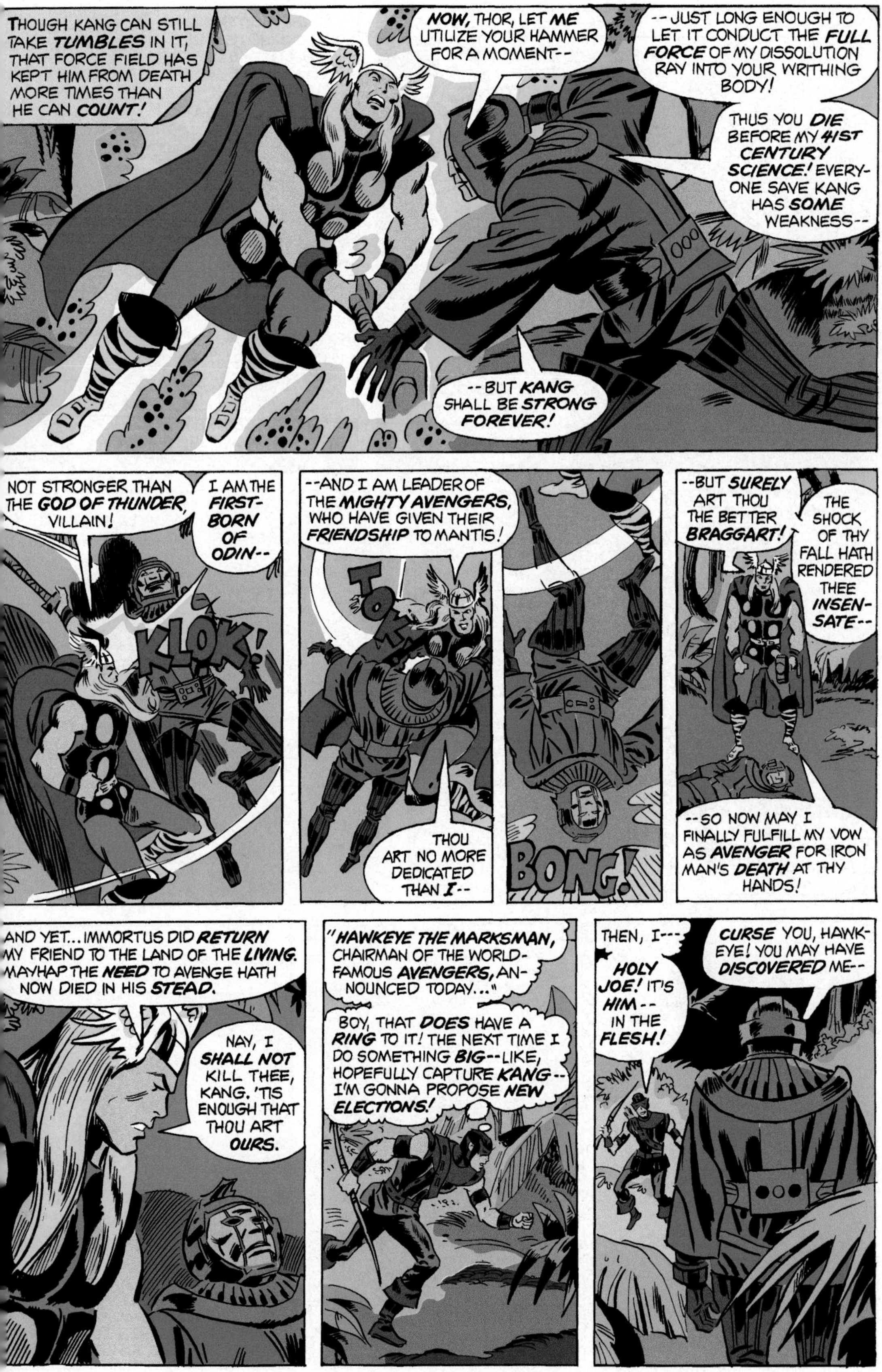
THOUGH KANG CAN STILL TAKE TUMBLES IN IT, THAT FORCE FIELD HAS KEPT HIM FROM DEATH MORE TIMES THAN HE CAN COUNT!
NOW, THOR, LET ME UTILIZE YOUR HAMMER FOR A MOMENT--
--JUST LONG ENOUGH TO LET IT CONDUCT THE FULL FORCE OF MY DISSOLUTION RAY INTO YOUR WRITHING BODY!
THUS YOU DIE BEFORE MY 41ST CENTURY SCIENCE! EVERY-ONE SAVE KANG HAS SOME WEAKNESS--
--BUT KANG SHALL BE STRONG FOREVER!
NOT STRONGER THAN THE GOD OF THUNDER, VILLAIN!
I AM THE FIRST-BORN OF ODIN--
KLOK!
--AND I AM LEADER OF THE MIGHTY AVENGERS, WHO HAVE GIVEN THEIR FRIENDSHIP TO MANTIS!
TOK
THOU ART NO MORE DEDICATED THAN I--
BONG!
--BUT SURELY ART THOU THE BETTER BRAGGART!
THE SHOCK OF THY FALL HATH RENDERED THEE INSEN-SATE--
--SO NOW MAY I FINALLY FULFILL MY VOW AS AVENGER FOR IRON MAN'S DEATH AT THY HANDS!
AND YET... IMMORTUS DID RETURN MY FRIEND TO THE LAND OF THE LIVING. MAYHAP THE NEED TO AVENGE HATH NOW DIED IN HIS STEAD.
NAY, I SHALL NOT KILL THEE, KANG. 'TIS ENOUGH THAT THOU ART OURS.
"HAWKEYE THE MARKSMAN, CHAIRMAN OF THE WORLD-FAMOUS AVENGERS, AN-NOUNCED TODAY..."
BOY, THAT DOES HAVE A RING TO IT! THE NEXT TIME I DO SOMETHING BIG--LIKE, HOPEFULLY CAPTURE KANG--I'M GONNA PROPOSE NEW ELECTIONS!
THEN, I---
HOLY JOE! IT'S HIM--IN THE FLESH!
CURSE YOU, HAWK-EYE! YOU MAY HAVE DISCOVERED ME--

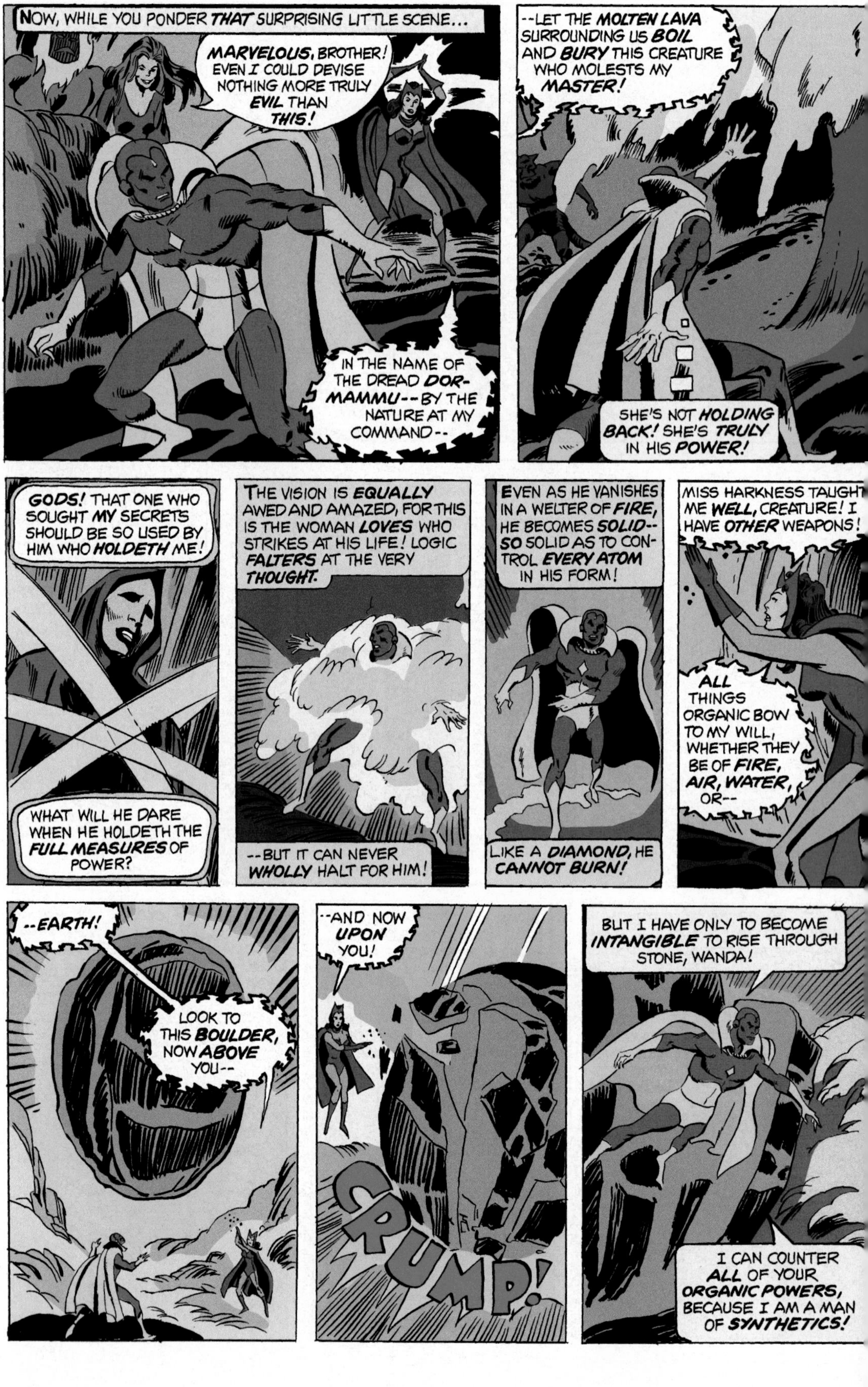
NOW, WHILE YOU PONDER THAT SURPRISING LITTLE SCENE...
MARVELOUS, BROTHER! EVEN I COULD DEVISE NOTHING MORE TRULY EVIL THAN THIS!
IN THE NAME OF THE DREAD DOR-MAMMU--BY THE NATURE AT MY COMMAND--
--LET THE MOLTEN LAVA SURROUNDING US BOIL AND BURY THIS CREATURE WHO MOLESTS MY MASTER!
SHE'S NOT HOLDING BACK! SHE'S TRULY IN HIS POWER!
GODS! THAT ONE WHO SOUGHT MY SECRETS SHOULD BE SO USED BY HIM WHO HOLDETH ME!
WHAT WILL HE DARE WHEN HE HOLDETH THE FULL MEASURES OF POWER?
THE VISION IS EQUALLY AWED AND AMAZED, FOR THIS IS THE WOMAN LOVES WHO STRIKES AT HIS LIFE! LOGIC FALTERS AT THE VERY THOUGHT.
--BUT IT CAN NEVER WHOLLY HALT FOR HIM!
EVEN AS HE VANISHES IN A WELTER OF FIRE, HE BECOMES SOLID--SO SOLID AS TO CON-TROL EVERY ATOM IN HIS FORM!
LIKE A DIAMOND, HE CANNOT BURN!
MISS HARKNESS TAUGHT ME WELL, CREATURE! I HAVE OTHER WEAPONS!
ALL THINGS ORGANIC BOW TO MY WILL, WHETHER THEY BE OF FIRE, AIR, WATER, OR--
--EARTH!
LOOK TO THIS BOULDER, NOW ABOVE YOU--
--AND NOW UPON YOU!
CRUMP!
BUT I HAVE ONLY TO BECOME INTANGIBLE TO RISE THROUGH STONE, WANDA!
I CAN COUNTER ALL OF YOUR ORGANIC POWERS, BECAUSE I AM A MAN OF SYNTHETICS!

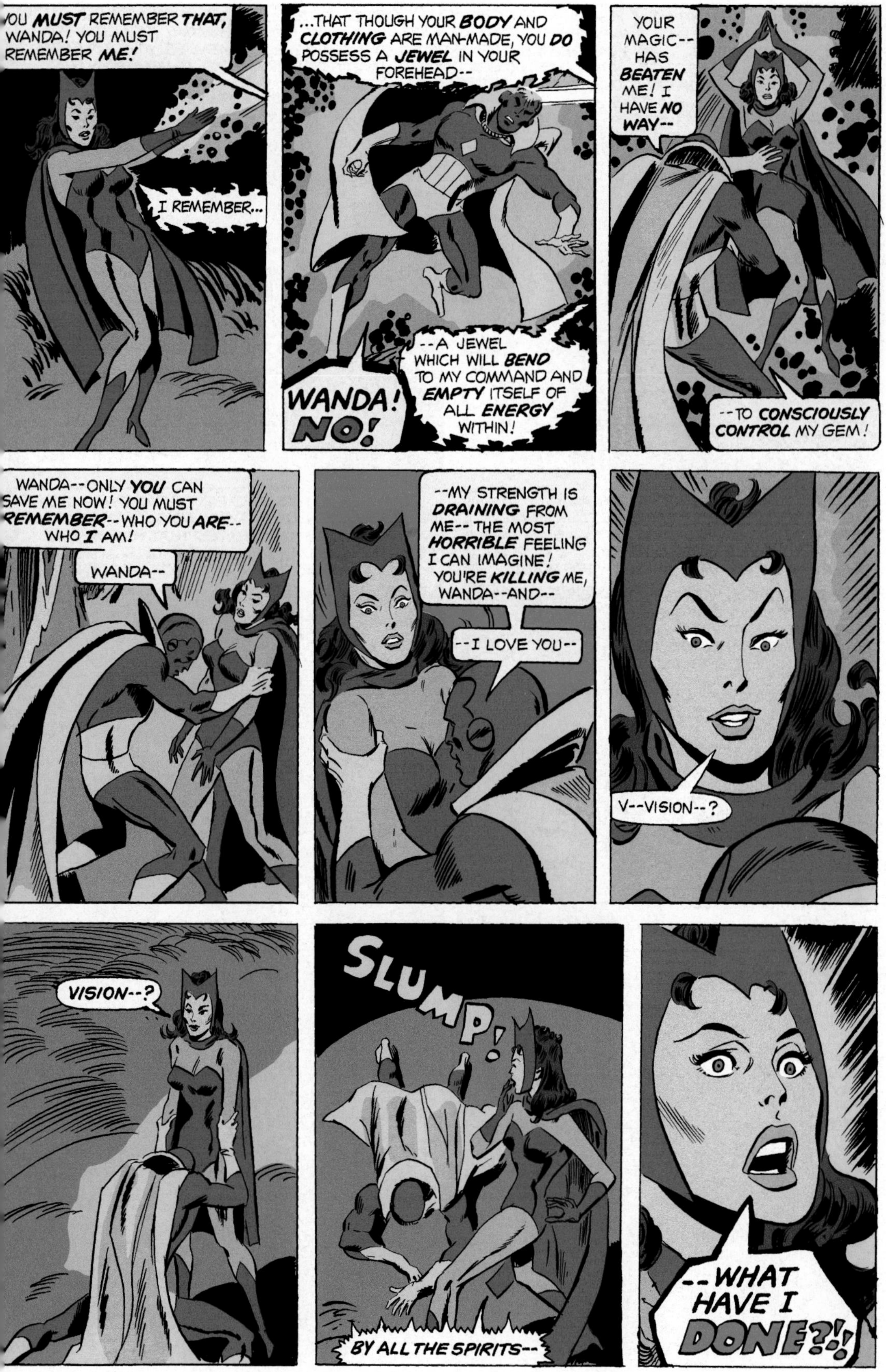
YOU MUST REMEMBER THAT, WANDA! YOU MUST REMEMBER ME!
I REMEMBER...
...THAT THOUGH YOUR BODY AND CLOTHING ARE MAN-MADE, YOU DO POSSESS A JEWEL IN YOUR FOREHEAD--
WANDA! NO!
--A JEWEL WHICH WILL BEND TO MY COMMAND AND EMPTY ITSELF OF ALL ENERGY WITHIN!
YOUR MAGIC-- HAS BEATEN ME! I HAVE NO WAY--
--TO CONSCIOUSLY CONTROL MY GEM!
WANDA--ONLY YOU CAN SAVE ME NOW! YOU MUST REMEMBER--WHO YOU ARE-- WHO I AM!
WANDA--
--MY STRENGTH IS DRAINING FROM ME-- THE MOST HORRIBLE FEELING I CAN IMAGINE! YOU'RE KILLING ME, WANDA--AND--
--I LOVE YOU--
V--VISION--?
VISION--?
SLUMP!
BY ALL THE SPIRITS--
--WHAT HAVE I DONE?!

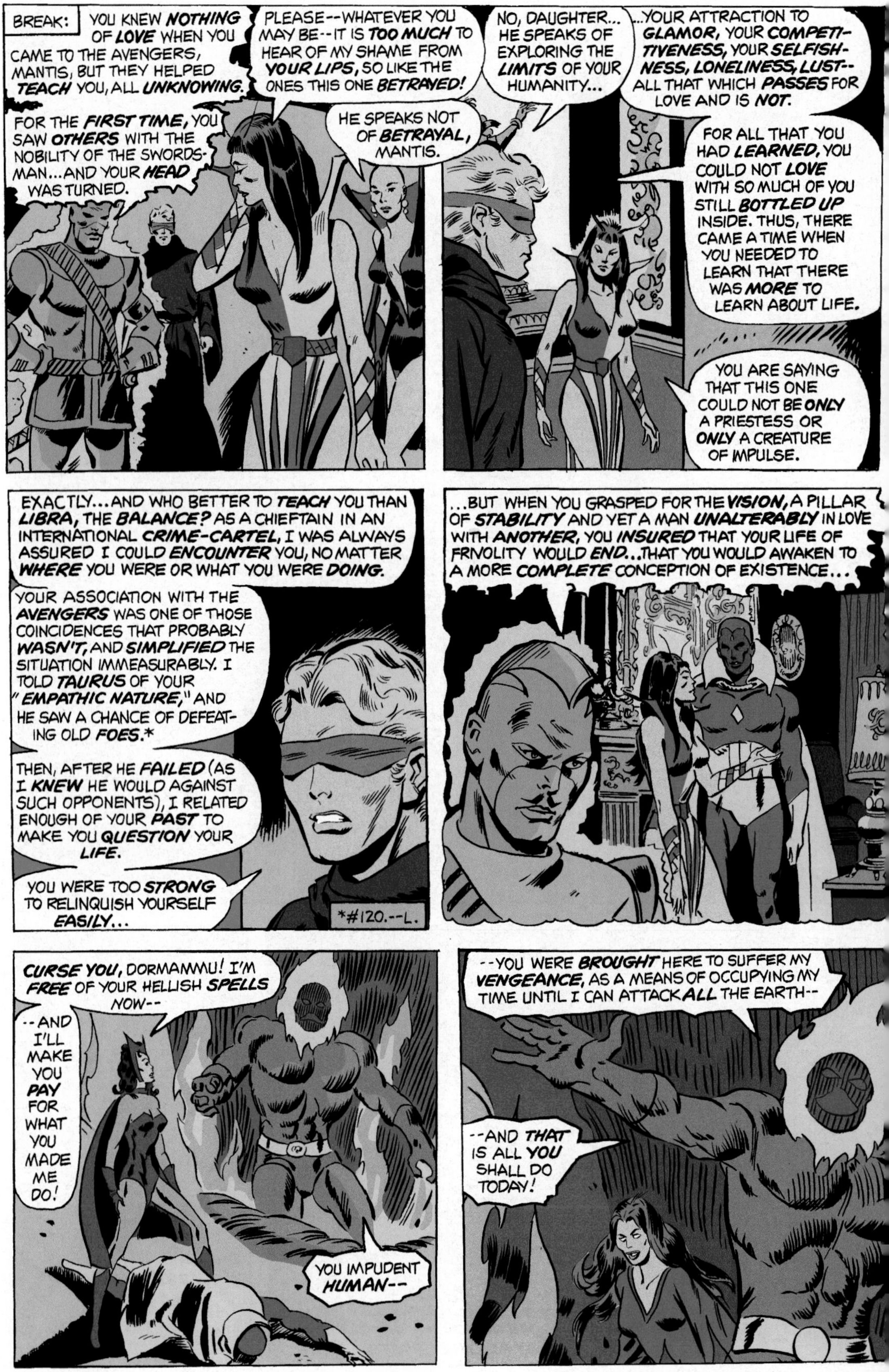

BREAK:
YOU KNEW NOTHING OF LOVE WHEN YOU CAME TO THE AVENGERS, MANTIS, BUT THEY HELPED TEACH YOU, ALL UNKNOWING.
FOR THE FIRST TIME, YOU SAW OTHERS WITH THE NOBILITY OF THE SWORDSMAN... AND YOUR HEAD WAS TURNED.
PLEASE--WHATEVER YOU MAY BE--IT IS TOO MUCH TO HEAR OF MY SHAME FROM YOUR LIPS, SO LIKE THE ONES THIS ONE BETRAYED!
HE SPEAKS NOT OF BETRAYAL, MANTIS.
NO, DAUGHTER... HE SPEAKS OF EXPLORING THE LIMITS OF YOUR HUMANITY...
...YOUR ATTRACTION TO GLAMOR, YOUR COMPETITIVENESS, YOUR SELFISHNESS, LONELINESS, LUST--ALL THAT WHICH PASSES FOR LOVE AND IS NOT.
FOR ALL THAT YOU HAD LEARNED, YOU COULD NOT LOVE WITH SO MUCH OF YOU STILL BOTTLED UP INSIDE. THUS, THERE CAME A TIME WHEN YOU NEEDED TO LEARN THAT THERE WAS MORE TO LEARN ABOUT LIFE.
YOU ARE SAYING THAT THIS ONE COULD NOT BE ONLY A PRIESTESS OR ONLY A CREATURE OF IMPULSE.
EXACTLY... AND WHO BETTER TO TEACH YOU THAN LIBRA, THE BALANCE? AS A CHIEFTAIN IN AN INTERNATIONAL CRIME-CARTEL, I WAS ALWAYS ASSURED I COULD ENCOUNTER YOU, NO MATTER WHERE YOU WERE OR WHAT YOU WERE DOING.
YOUR ASSOCIATION WITH THE AVENGERS WAS ONE OF THOSE COINCIDENCES THAT PROBABLY WASN'T, AND SIMPLIFIED THE SITUATION IMMEASURABLY. I TOLD TAURUS OF YOUR "EMPATHIC NATURE," AND HE SAW A CHANCE OF DEFEATING OLD FOES.*
THEN, AFTER HE FAILED (AS I KNEW HE WOULD AGAINST SUCH OPPONENTS), I RELATED ENOUGH OF YOUR PAST TO MAKE YOU QUESTION YOUR LIFE.
YOU WERE TOO STRONG TO RELINQUISH YOURSELF EASILY...
*#120.--L.
...BUT WHEN YOU GRASPED FOR THE VISION, A PILLAR OF STABILITY AND YET A MAN UNALTERABLY IN LOVE WITH ANOTHER, YOU INSURED THAT YOUR LIFE OF FRIVOLITY WOULD END... THAT YOU WOULD AWAKEN TO A MORE COMPLETE CONCEPTION OF EXISTENCE...
CURSE YOU, DORMAMMU! I'M FREE OF YOUR HELLISH SPELLS NOW--
--AND I'LL MAKE YOU PAY FOR WHAT YOU MADE ME DO!
YOU IMPUDENT HUMAN--
--YOU WERE BROUGHT HERE TO SUFFER MY VENGEANCE, AS A MEANS OF OCCUPYING MY TIME UNTIL I CAN ATTACK ALL THE EARTH--
--AND THAT IS ALL YOU SHALL DO TODAY!

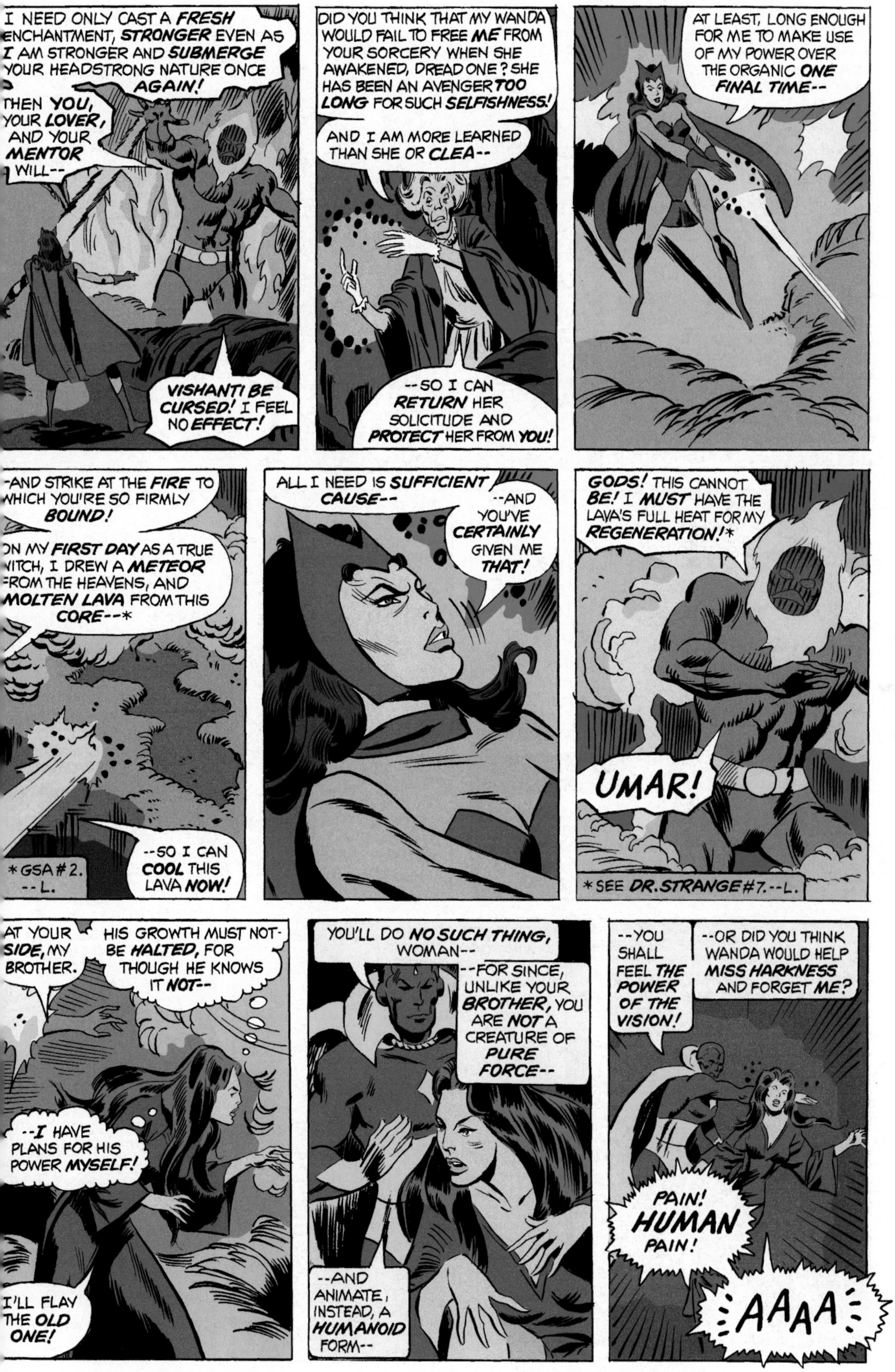
I NEED ONLY CAST A FRESH ENCHANTMENT, STRONGER EVEN AS I AM STRONGER AND SUBMERGE YOUR HEADSTRONG NATURE ONCE AGAIN!
THEN YOU, YOUR LOVER, AND YOUR MENTOR WILL--
VISHANT! BE CURSED! I FEEL NO EFFECT!
DID YOU THINK THAT MY WANDA WOULD FAIL TO FREE ME FROM YOUR SORCERY WHEN SHE AWAKENED, DREAD ONE? SHE HAS BEEN AN AVENGER TOO LONG FOR SUCH SELFISHNESS!
AND I AM MORE LEARNED THAN SHE OR CLEA--
--SO I CAN RETURN HER SOLICITUDE AND PROTECT HER FROM YOU!
AT LEAST, LONG ENOUGH FOR ME TO MAKE USE OF MY POWER OVER THE ORGANIC ONE FINAL TIME--
-AND STRIKE AT THE FIRE TO WHICH YOU'RE SO FIRMLY BOUND!
ON MY FIRST DAY AS A TRUE WITCH, I DREW A METEOR FROM THE HEAVENS, AND MOLTEN LAVA FROM THIS CORE--*
--SO I CAN COOL THIS LAVA NOW!
* GSA # 2. --L.
ALL I NEED IS SUFFICIENT CAUSE--
--AND YOU'VE CERTAINLY GIVEN ME THAT!
GODS! THIS CANNOT BE! I MUST HAVE THE LAVA'S FULL HEAT FOR MY REGENERATION!*
UMAR!
* SEE DR. STRANGE #7. --L.
AT YOUR SIDE, MY BROTHER.
HIS GROWTH MUST NOT BE HALTED, FOR THOUGH HE KNOWS IT NOT--
--I HAVE PLANS FOR HIS POWER MYSELF!
I'LL FLAY THE OLD ONE!
YOU'LL DO NO SUCH THING, WOMAN--
--FOR SINCE, UNLIKE YOUR BROTHER, YOU ARE NOT A CREATURE OF PURE FORCE--
--AND ANIMATE, INSTEAD, A HUMANOID FORM--
--YOU SHALL FEEL THE POWER OF THE VISION!
--OR DID YOU THINK WANDA WOULD HELP MISS HARKNESS AND FORGET ME?
PAIN! HUMAN PAIN!
AAAA

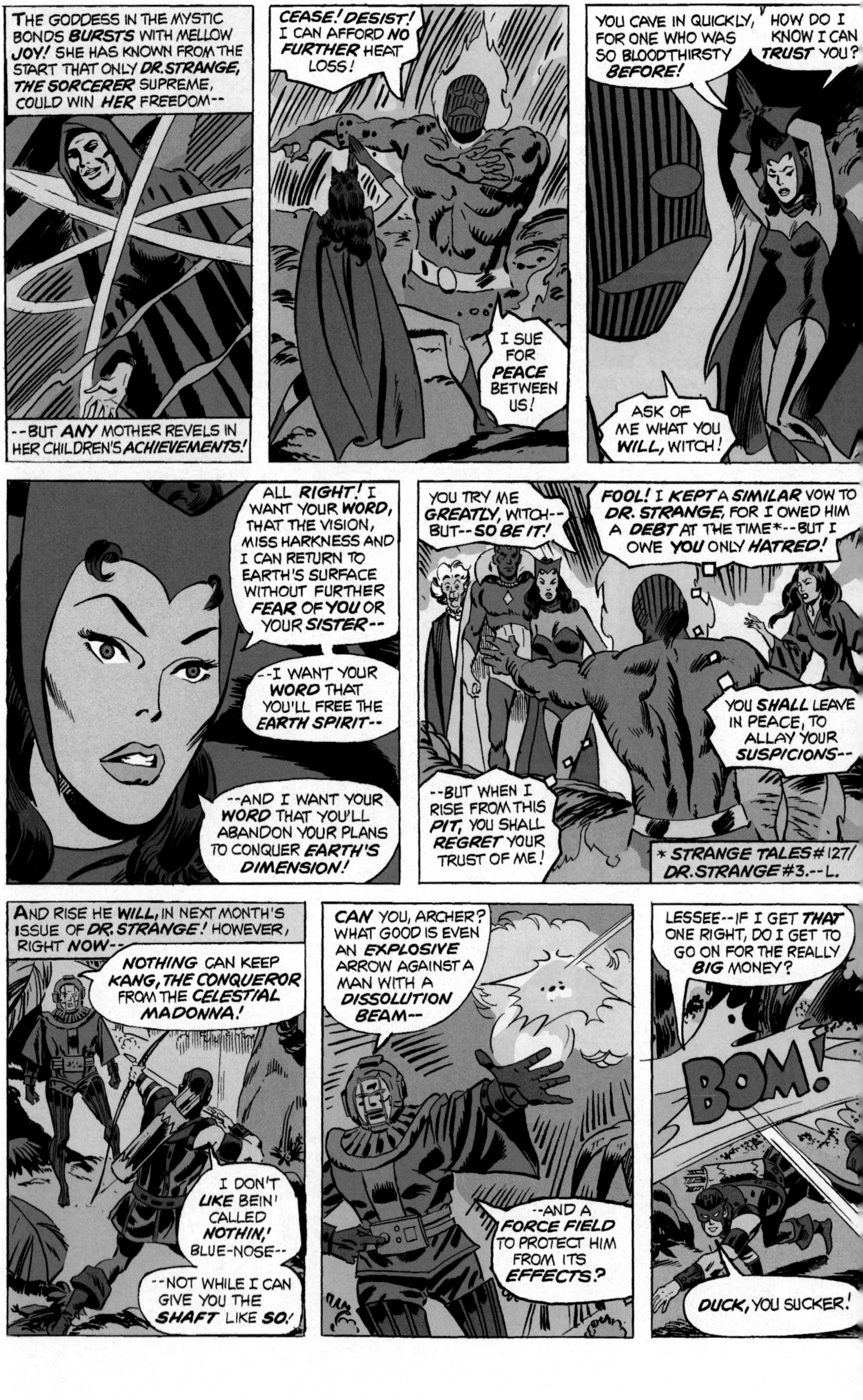
THE GODDESS IN THE MYSTIC BONDS BURSTS WITH MELLOW JOY! SHE HAS KNOWN FROM THE START THAT ONLY DR. STRANGE, THE SORCERER SUPREME, COULD WIN HER FREEDOM--
--BUT ANY MOTHER REVELS IN HER CHILDREN'S ACHIEVEMENTS!
CEASE! DESIST! I CAN AFFORD NO FURTHER HEAT LOSS!
I SUE FOR PEACE BETWEEN US!
YOU CAVE IN QUICKLY, FOR ONE WHO WAS SO BLOODTHIRSTY BEFORE!
HOW DO I KNOW I CAN TRUST YOU?
ASK OF ME WHAT YOU WILL, WITCH!
ALL RIGHT! I WANT YOUR WORD, THAT THE VISION, MISS HARKNESS AND I CAN RETURN TO EARTH'S SURFACE WITHOUT FURTHER FEAR OF YOU OR YOUR SISTER--
--I WANT YOUR WORD THAT YOU'LL FREE THE EARTH SPIRIT--
--AND I WANT YOUR WORD THAT YOU'LL ABANDON YOUR PLANS TO CONQUER EARTH'S DIMENSION!
YOU TRY ME GREATLY, WITCH-- BUT-- SO BE IT!
FOOL! I KEPT A SIMILAR VOW TO DR. STRANGE, FOR I OWED HIM A DEBT AT THE TIME*--BUT I OWE YOU ONLY HATRED!
YOU SHALL LEAVE IN PEACE, TO ALLAY YOUR SUSPICIONS--
--BUT WHEN I RISE FROM THIS PIT, YOU SHALL REGRET YOUR TRUST OF ME!
* STRANGE TALES #127/ DR. STRANGE #3.--L.
AND RISE HE WILL, IN NEXT MONTH'S ISSUE OF DR. STRANGE! HOWEVER, RIGHT NOW--
NOTHING CAN KEEP KANG, THE CONQUEROR FROM THE CELESTIAL MADONNA!
I DON'T LIKE BEIN' CALLED NOTHIN,' BLUE-NOSE--
--NOT WHILE I CAN GIVE YOU THE SHAFT LIKE SO!
CAN YOU, ARCHER? WHAT GOOD IS EVEN AN EXPLOSIVE ARROW AGAINST A MAN WITH A DISSOLUTION BEAM--
--AND A FORCE FIELD TO PROTECT HIM FROM ITS EFFECTS?
LESSEE--IF I GET THAT ONE RIGHT, DO I GET TO GO ON FOR THE REALLY BIG MONEY?
BOM!
DUCK, YOU SUCKER!

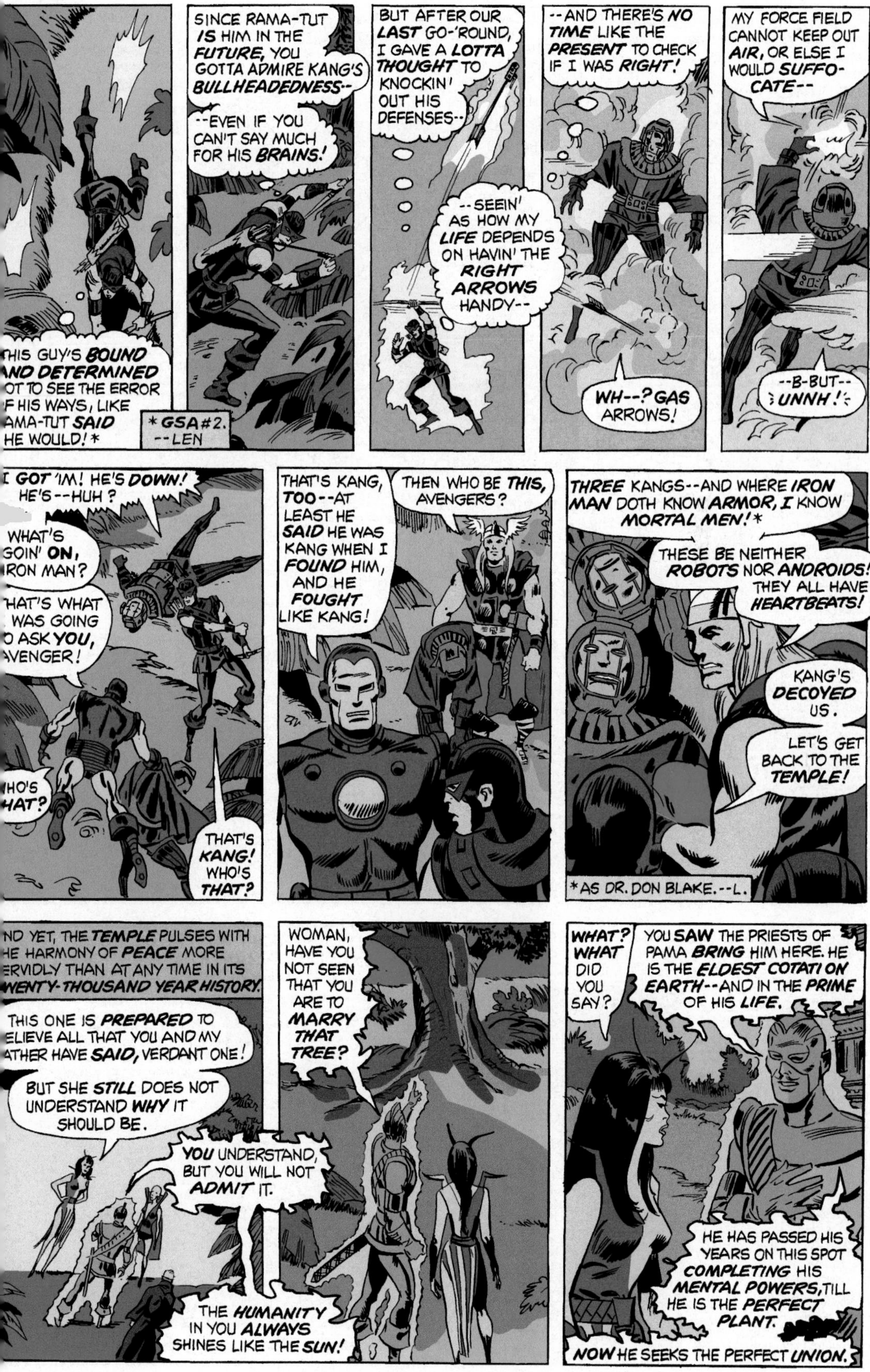
THIS GUY'S BOUND
AND DETERMINED
NOT TO SEE THE ERROR
OF HIS WAYS, LIKE
RAMA-TUT SAID
HE WOULD! *
* GSA #2. --LEN
SINCE RAMA-TUT IS HIM IN THE FUTURE, YOU GOTTA ADMIRE KANG'S BULLHEADEDNESS--
--EVEN IF YOU CAN'T SAY MUCH FOR HIS BRAINS!
BUT AFTER OUR LAST GO-'ROUND, I GAVE A LOTTA THOUGHT TO KNOCKIN' OUT HIS DEFENSES--
--SEEIN' AS HOW MY LIFE DEPENDS ON HAVIN' THE RIGHT ARROWS HANDY--
--AND THERE'S NO TIME LIKE THE PRESENT TO CHECK IF I WAS RIGHT!
WH--? GAS ARROWS!
MY FORCE FIELD CANNOT KEEP OUT AIR, OR ELSE I WOULD SUFFOCATE--
--B-BUT-- UNNH!
I GOT 'IM! HE'S DOWN! HE'S--HUH?
WHAT'S GOIN' ON, IRON MAN?
THAT'S WHAT I WAS GOING TO ASK YOU, AVENGER!
WHO'S THAT?
THAT'S KANG! WHO'S THAT?
THAT'S KANG, TOO--AT LEAST HE SAID HE WAS KANG WHEN I FOUND HIM, AND HE FOUGHT LIKE KANG!
THEN WHO BE THIS, AVENGERS?
THREE KANGS--AND WHERE IRON MAN DOTH KNOW ARMOR, I KNOW MORTAL MEN! *
THESE BE NEITHER ROBOTS NOR ANDROIDS! THEY ALL HAVE HEARTBEATS!
KANG'S DECOYED US.
LET'S GET BACK TO THE TEMPLE!
* AS DR. DON BLAKE. --L.
AND YET, THE TEMPLE PULSES WITH THE HARMONY OF PEACE MORE FERVIDLY THAN AT ANY TIME IN ITS TWENTY-THOUSAND YEAR HISTORY.
THIS ONE IS PREPARED TO BELIEVE ALL THAT YOU AND MY FATHER HAVE SAID, VERDANT ONE!
BUT SHE STILL DOES NOT UNDERSTAND WHY IT SHOULD BE.
YOU UNDERSTAND, BUT YOU WILL NOT ADMIT IT.
THE HUMANITY IN YOU ALWAYS SHINES LIKE THE SUN!
WOMAN, HAVE YOU NOT SEEN THAT YOU ARE TO MARRY THAT TREE?
WHAT? WHAT DID YOU SAY?
YOU SAW THE PRIESTS OF PAMA BRING HIM HERE. HE IS THE ELDEST COTATI ON EARTH--AND IN THE PRIME OF HIS LIFE.
HE HAS PASSED HIS YEARS ON THIS SPOT COMPLETING HIS MENTAL POWERS, TILL HE IS THE PERFECT PLANT.
NOW HE SEEKS THE PERFECT UNION.

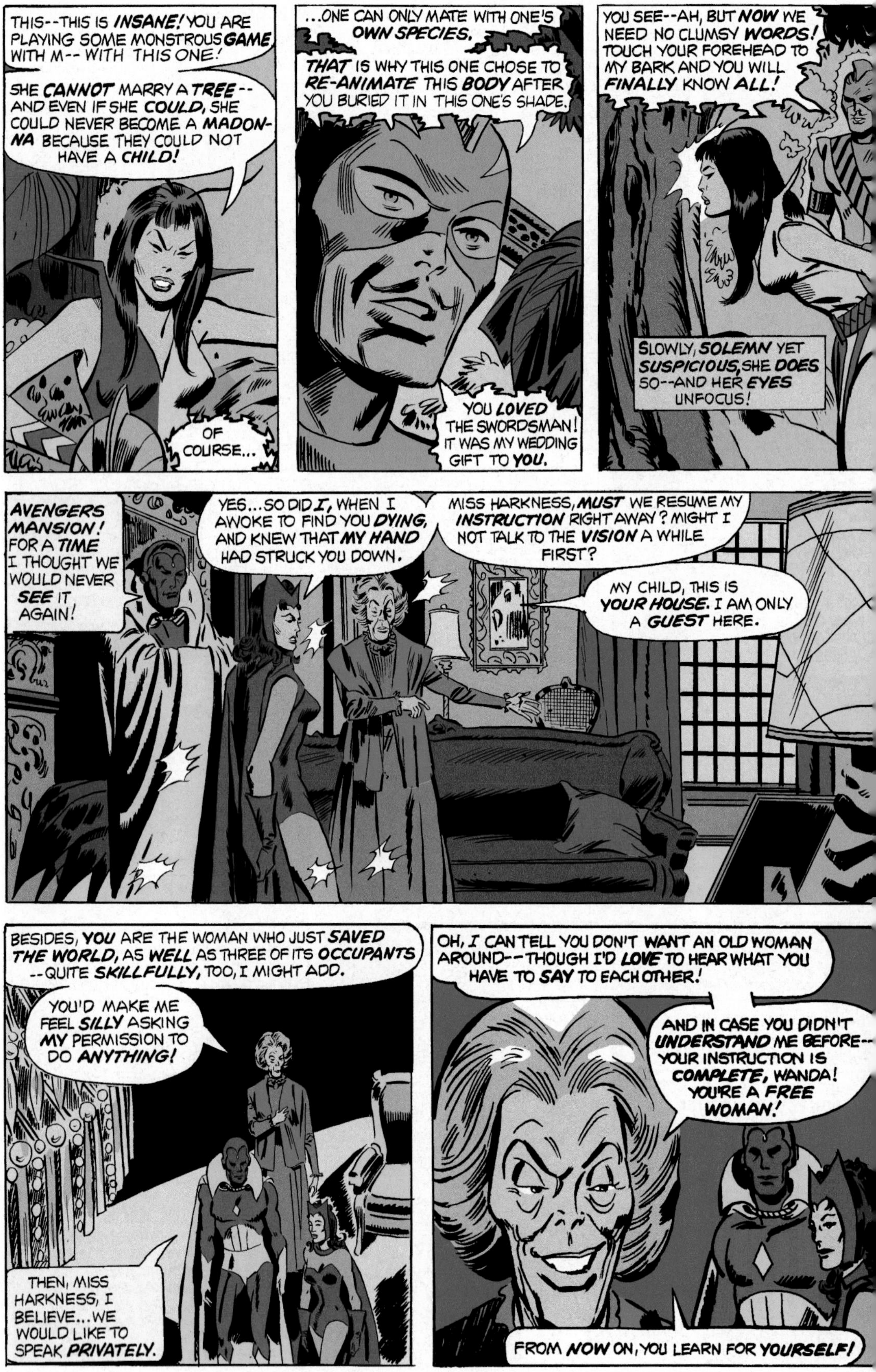

THIS--THIS IS INSANE! YOU ARE PLAYING SOME MONSTROUS GAME WITH M-- WITH THIS ONE!
SHE CANNOT MARRY A TREE-- AND EVEN IF SHE COULD, SHE COULD NEVER BECOME A MADONNA BECAUSE THEY COULD NOT HAVE A CHILD!
OF COURSE...
...ONE CAN ONLY MATE WITH ONE'S OWN SPECIES.
THAT IS WHY THIS ONE CHOSE TO RE-ANIMATE THIS BODY AFTER YOU BURIED IT IN THIS ONE'S SHADE.
YOU LOVED THE SWORDSMAN! IT WAS MY WEDDING GIFT TO YOU.
YOU SEE--AH, BUT NOW WE NEED NO CLUMSY WORDS! TOUCH YOUR FOREHEAD TO MY BARK AND YOU WILL FINALLY KNOW ALL!
SLOWLY, SOLEMN YET SUSPICIOUS, SHE DOES SO--AND HER EYES UNFOCUS!
AVENGERS MANSION! FOR A TIME I THOUGHT WE WOULD NEVER SEE IT AGAIN!
YES...SO DID I, WHEN I AWOKE TO FIND YOU DYING, AND KNEW THAT MY HAND HAD STRUCK YOU DOWN.
MISS HARKNESS, MUST WE RESUME MY INSTRUCTION RIGHT AWAY? MIGHT I NOT TALK TO THE VISION A WHILE FIRST?
MY CHILD, THIS IS YOUR HOUSE. I AM ONLY A GUEST HERE.
BESIDES, YOU ARE THE WOMAN WHO JUST SAVED THE WORLD, AS WELL AS THREE OF ITS OCCUPANTS --QUITE SKILLFULLY, TOO, I MIGHT ADD.
YOU'D MAKE ME FEEL SILLY ASKING MY PERMISSION TO DO ANYTHING!
THEN, MISS HARKNESS, I BELIEVE...WE WOULD LIKE TO SPEAK PRIVATELY.
OH, I CAN TELL YOU DON'T WANT AN OLD WOMAN AROUND--THOUGH I'D LOVE TO HEAR WHAT YOU HAVE TO SAY TO EACH OTHER!
AND IN CASE YOU DIDN'T UNDERSTAND ME BEFORE-- YOUR INSTRUCTION IS COMPLETE, WANDA! YOU'RE A FREE WOMAN!
FROM NOW ON, YOU LEARN FOR YOURSELF!

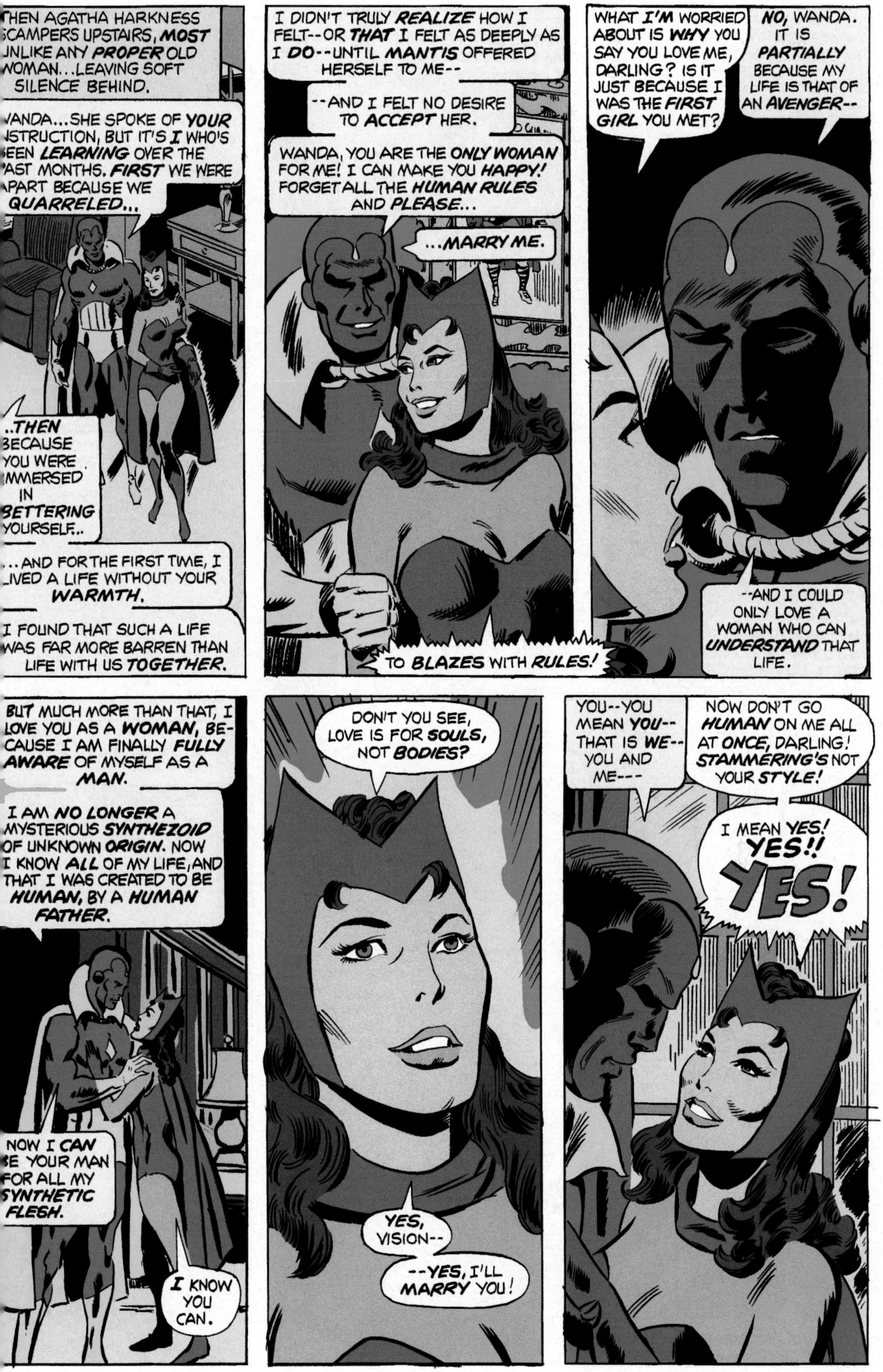

THEN AGATHA HARKNESS SCAMPERS UPSTAIRS, MOST UNLIKE ANY PROPER OLD WOMAN... LEAVING SOFT SILENCE BEHIND.
WANDA... SHE SPOKE OF YOUR INSTRUCTION, BUT IT'S I WHO'S BEEN LEARNING OVER THE PAST MONTHS. FIRST WE WERE APART BECAUSE WE QUARRELED...
..THEN BECAUSE YOU WERE IMMERSED IN BETTERING YOURSELF..
...AND FOR THE FIRST TIME, I LIVED A LIFE WITHOUT YOUR WARMTH.
I FOUND THAT SUCH A LIFE WAS FAR MORE BARREN THAN LIFE WITH US TOGETHER.
I DIDN'T TRULY REALIZE HOW I FELT--OR THAT I FELT AS DEEPLY AS I DO--UNTIL MANTIS OFFERED HERSELF TO ME--
--AND I FELT NO DESIRE TO ACCEPT HER.
WANDA, YOU ARE THE ONLY WOMAN FOR ME! I CAN MAKE YOU HAPPY! FORGET ALL THE HUMAN RULES AND PLEASE...
...MARRY ME.
TO BLAZES WITH RULES!
WHAT I'M WORRIED ABOUT IS WHY YOU SAY YOU LOVE ME, DARLING? IS IT JUST BECAUSE I WAS THE FIRST GIRL YOU MET?
NO, WANDA. IT IS PARTIALLY BECAUSE MY LIFE IS THAT OF AN AVENGER--
--AND I COULD ONLY LOVE A WOMAN WHO CAN UNDERSTAND THAT LIFE.
BUT MUCH MORE THAN THAT, I LOVE YOU AS A WOMAN, BECAUSE I AM FINALLY FULLY AWARE OF MYSELF AS A MAN.
I AM NO LONGER A MYSTERIOUS SYNTHEZOID OF UNKNOWN ORIGIN. NOW I KNOW ALL OF MY LIFE, AND THAT I WAS CREATED TO BE HUMAN, BY A HUMAN FATHER.
NOW I CAN BE YOUR MAN FOR ALL MY SYNTHETIC FLESH.
I KNOW YOU CAN.
DON'T YOU SEE, LOVE IS FOR SOULS, NOT BODIES?
YES, VISION--
--YES, I'LL MARRY YOU!
YOU--YOU MEAN YOU--THAT IS WE--YOU AND ME---
NOW DON'T GO HUMAN ON ME ALL AT ONCE, DARLING! STAMMERING'S NOT YOUR STYLE!
I MEAN YES! YES!! YES!

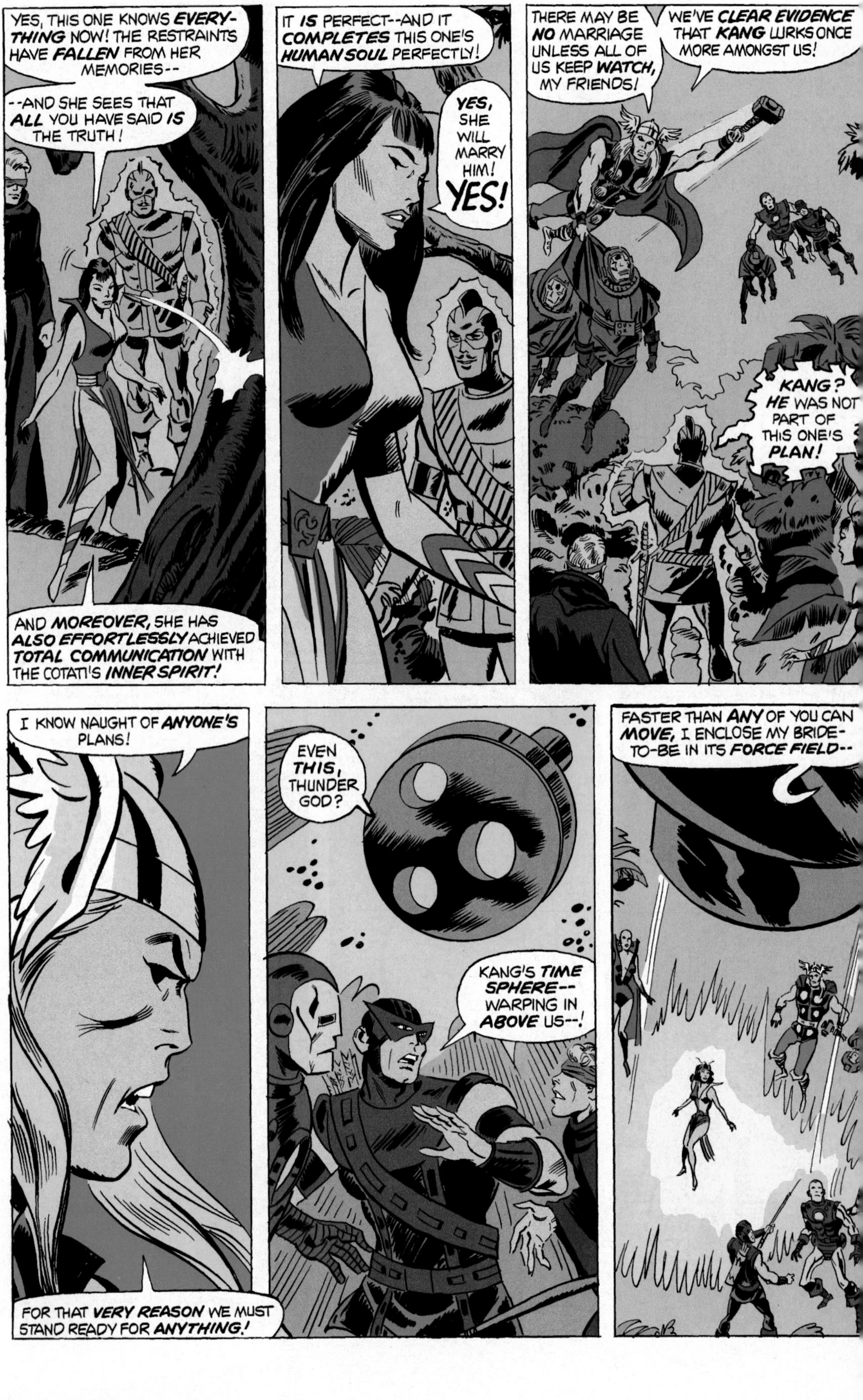

YES, THIS ONE KNOWS EVERYTHING NOW! THE RESTRAINTS HAVE FALLEN FROM HER MEMORIES--
--AND SHE SEES THAT ALL YOU HAVE SAID IS THE TRUTH!
AND MOREOVER, SHE HAS ALSO EFFORTLESSLY ACHIEVED TOTAL COMMUNICATION WITH THE COTATI'S INNER SPIRIT!
IT IS PERFECT--AND IT COMPLETES THIS ONE'S HUMAN SOUL PERFECTLY!
YES, SHE WILL MARRY HIM! YES!
THERE MAY BE NO MARRIAGE UNLESS ALL OF US KEEP WATCH, MY FRIENDS!
WE'VE CLEAR EVIDENCE THAT KANG LURKS ONCE MORE AMONGST US!
KANG? HE WAS NOT PART OF THIS ONE'S PLAN!
I KNOW NAUGHT OF ANYONE'S PLANS!
FOR THAT VERY REASON WE MUST STAND READY FOR ANYTHING!
EVEN THIS, THUNDER GOD?
KANG'S TIME SPHERE-- WARPING IN ABOVE US--!
FASTER THAN ANY OF YOU CAN MOVE, I ENCLOSE MY BRIDE-TO-BE IN ITS FORCE FIELD--

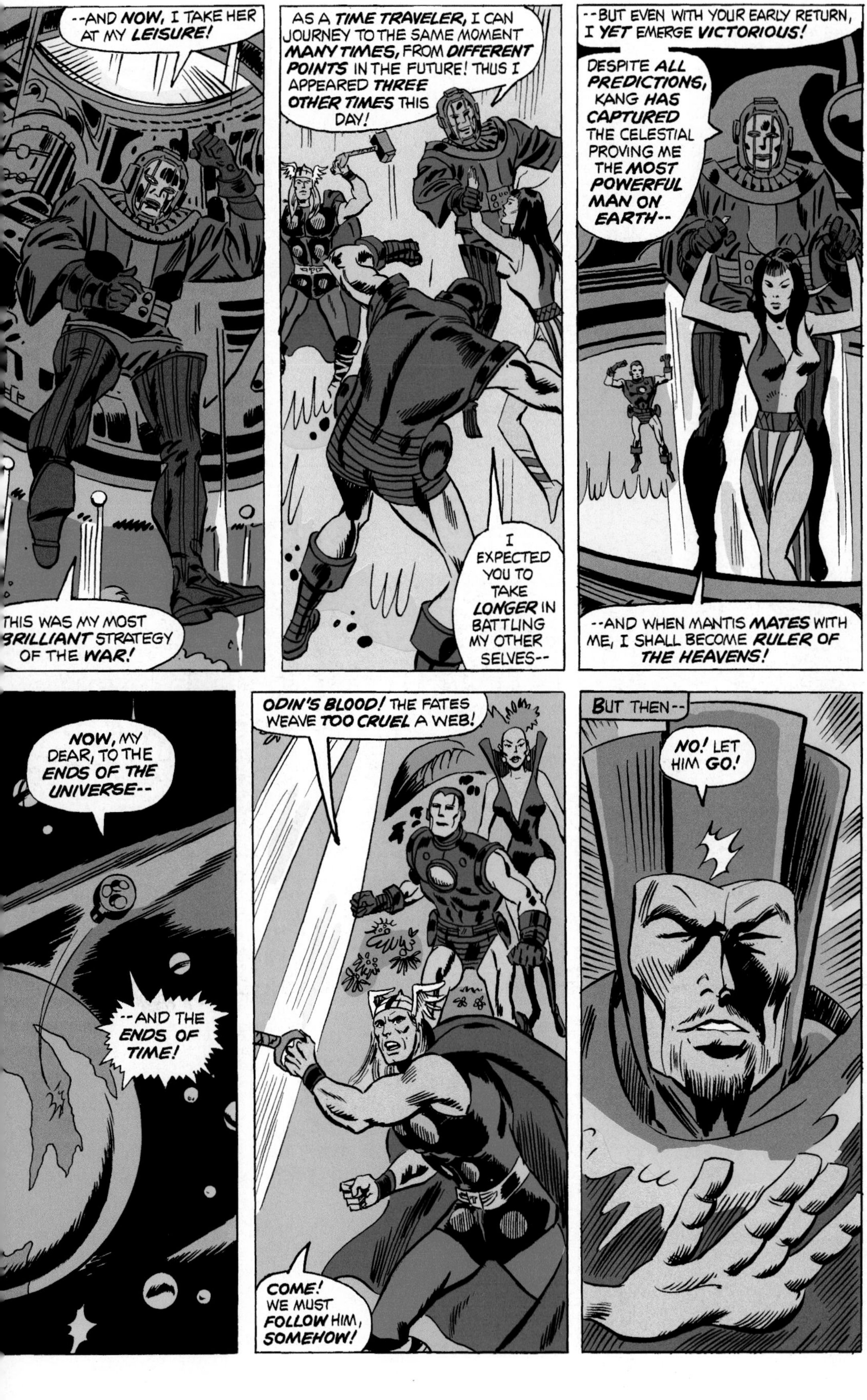
--AND NOW, I TAKE HER AT MY LEISURE!
THIS WAS MY MOST BRILLIANT STRATEGY OF THE WAR!
AS A TIME TRAVELER, I CAN JOURNEY TO THE SAME MOMENT MANY TIMES, FROM DIFFERENT POINTS IN THE FUTURE! THUS I APPEARED THREE OTHER TIMES THIS DAY!
I EXPECTED YOU TO TAKE LONGER IN BATTLING MY OTHER SELVES--
--BUT EVEN WITH YOUR EARLY RETURN, I YET EMERGE VICTORIOUS!
DESPITE ALL PREDICTIONS, KANG HAS CAPTURED THE CELESTIAL PROVING ME THE MOST POWERFUL MAN ON EARTH--
--AND WHEN MANTIS MATES WITH ME, I SHALL BECOME RULER OF THE HEAVENS!
NOW, MY DEAR, TO THE ENDS OF THE UNIVERSE--
--AND THE ENDS OF TIME!
ODIN'S BLOOD! THE FATES WEAVE TOO CRUEL A WEB!
COME! WE MUST FOLLOW HIM, SOMEHOW!
BUT THEN--
NO! LET HIM GO!

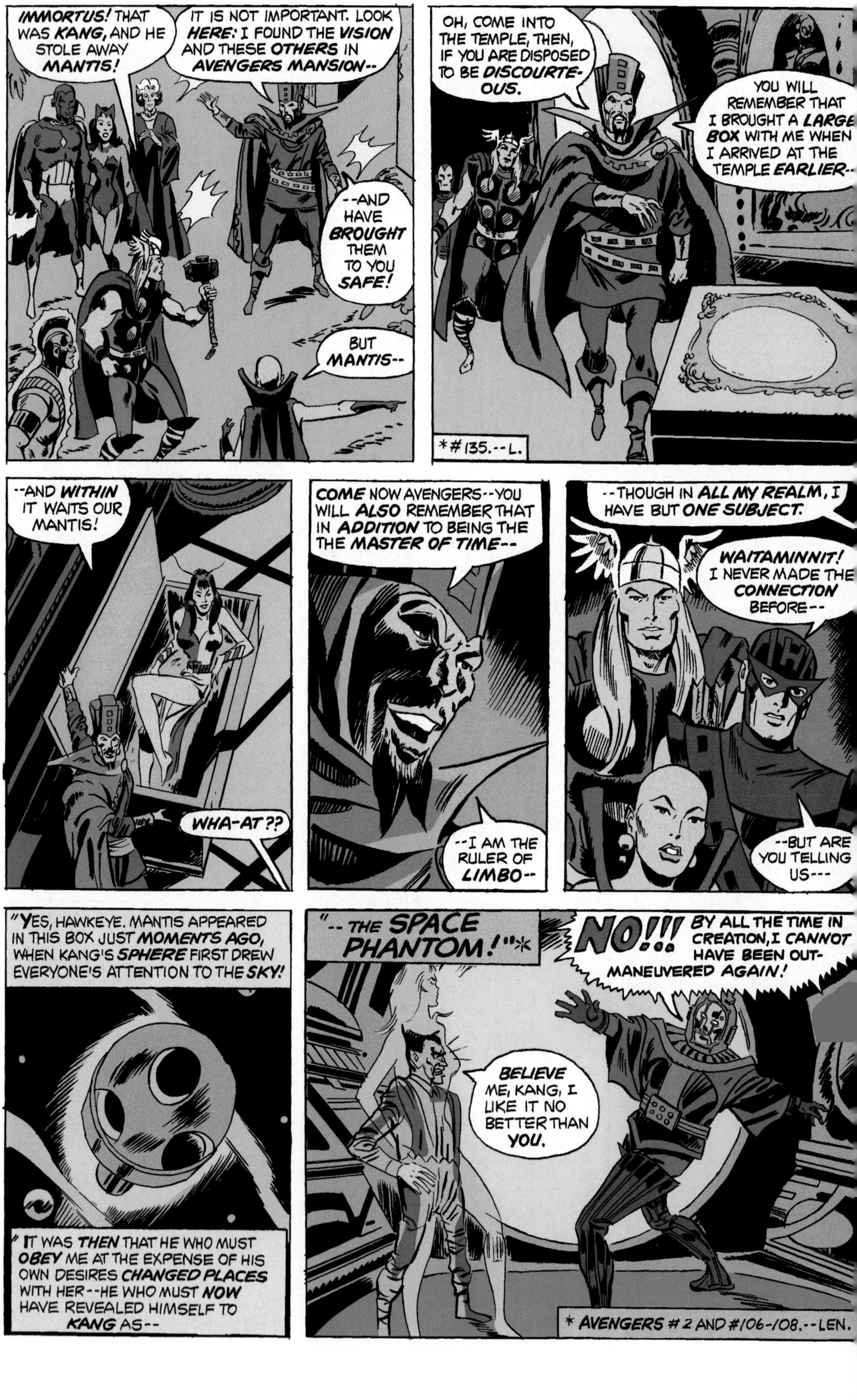
IMMORTUS! THAT WAS KANG, AND HE STOLE AWAY MANTIS!
IT IS NOT IMPORTANT. LOOK HERE: I FOUND THE VISION AND THESE OTHERS IN AVENGERS MANSION--
--AND HAVE BROUGHT THEM TO YOU SAFE!
BUT MANTIS--
OH, COME INTO THE TEMPLE, THEN, IF YOU ARE DISPOSED TO BE DISCOURTEOUS.
YOU WILL REMEMBER THAT I BROUGHT A LARGE BOX WITH ME WHEN I ARRIVED AT THE TEMPLE EARLIER--*
*#135.--L.
--AND WITHIN IT WAITS OUR MANTIS!
WHA-AT??
COME NOW AVENGERS--YOU WILL ALSO REMEMBER THAT IN ADDITION TO BEING THE THE MASTER OF TIME--
--I AM THE RULER OF LIMBO--
--THOUGH IN ALL MY REALM, I HAVE BUT ONE SUBJECT.
WAITAMINNIT! I NEVER MADE THE CONNECTION BEFORE--
--BUT ARE YOU TELLING US---
"YES, HAWKEYE. MANTIS APPEARED IN THIS BOX JUST MOMENTS AGO, WHEN KANG'S SPHERE FIRST DREW EVERYONE'S ATTENTION TO THE SKY!
"IT WAS THEN THAT HE WHO MUST OBEY ME AT THE EXPENSE OF HIS OWN DESIRES CHANGED PLACES WITH HER--HE WHO MUST NOW HAVE REVEALED HIMSELF TO KANG AS--
"--THE SPACE PHANTOM!"*
NO!!! BY ALL THE TIME IN CREATION, I CANNOT HAVE BEEN OUT-MANEUVERED AGAIN!
BELIEVE ME, KANG, I LIKE IT NO BETTER THAN YOU.
* AVENGERS #2 AND #106-108.--LEN.

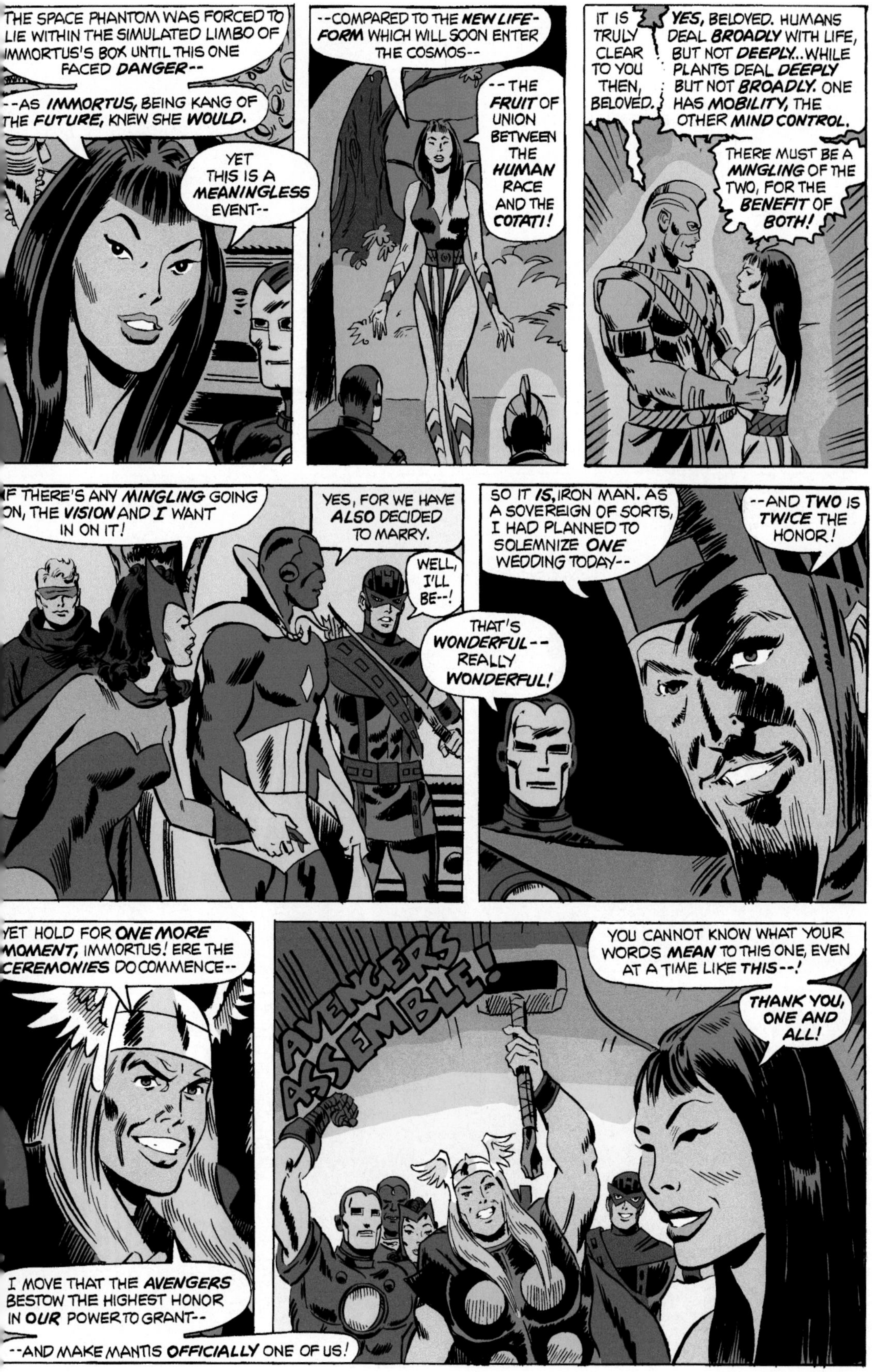
THE SPACE PHANTOM WAS FORCED TO LIE WITHIN THE SIMULATED LIMBO OF IMMORTUS'S BOX UNTIL THIS ONE FACED DANGER--
--AS IMMORTUS, BEING KANG OF THE FUTURE, KNEW SHE WOULD.
YET THIS IS A MEANINGLESS EVENT--
--COMPARED TO THE NEW LIFE-FORM WHICH WILL SOON ENTER THE COSMOS--
--THE FRUIT OF UNION BETWEEN THE HUMAN RACE AND THE COTATI!
IT IS TRULY CLEAR TO YOU THEN, BELOVED.
YES, BELOVED. HUMANS DEAL BROADLY WITH LIFE, BUT NOT DEEPLY...WHILE PLANTS DEAL DEEPLY BUT NOT BROADLY. ONE HAS MOBILITY, THE OTHER MIND CONTROL.
THERE MUST BE A MINGLING OF THE TWO, FOR THE BENEFIT OF BOTH!
IF THERE'S ANY MINGLING GOING ON, THE VISION AND I WANT IN ON IT!
YES, FOR WE HAVE ALSO DECIDED TO MARRY.
WELL, I'LL BE--!
THAT'S WONDERFUL-- REALLY WONDERFUL!
SO IT IS, IRON MAN. AS A SOVEREIGN OF SORTS, I HAD PLANNED TO SOLEMNIZE ONE WEDDING TODAY--
--AND TWO IS TWICE THE HONOR!
YET HOLD FOR ONE MORE MOMENT, IMMORTUS! ERE THE CEREMONIES DO COMMENCE--
I MOVE THAT THE AVENGERS BESTOW THE HIGHEST HONOR IN OUR POWER TO GRANT--
--AND MAKE MANTIS OFFICIALLY ONE OF US!
AVENGERS ASSEMBLE!
YOU CANNOT KNOW WHAT YOUR WORDS MEAN TO THIS ONE, EVEN AT A TIME LIKE THIS--!
THANK YOU, ONE AND ALL!

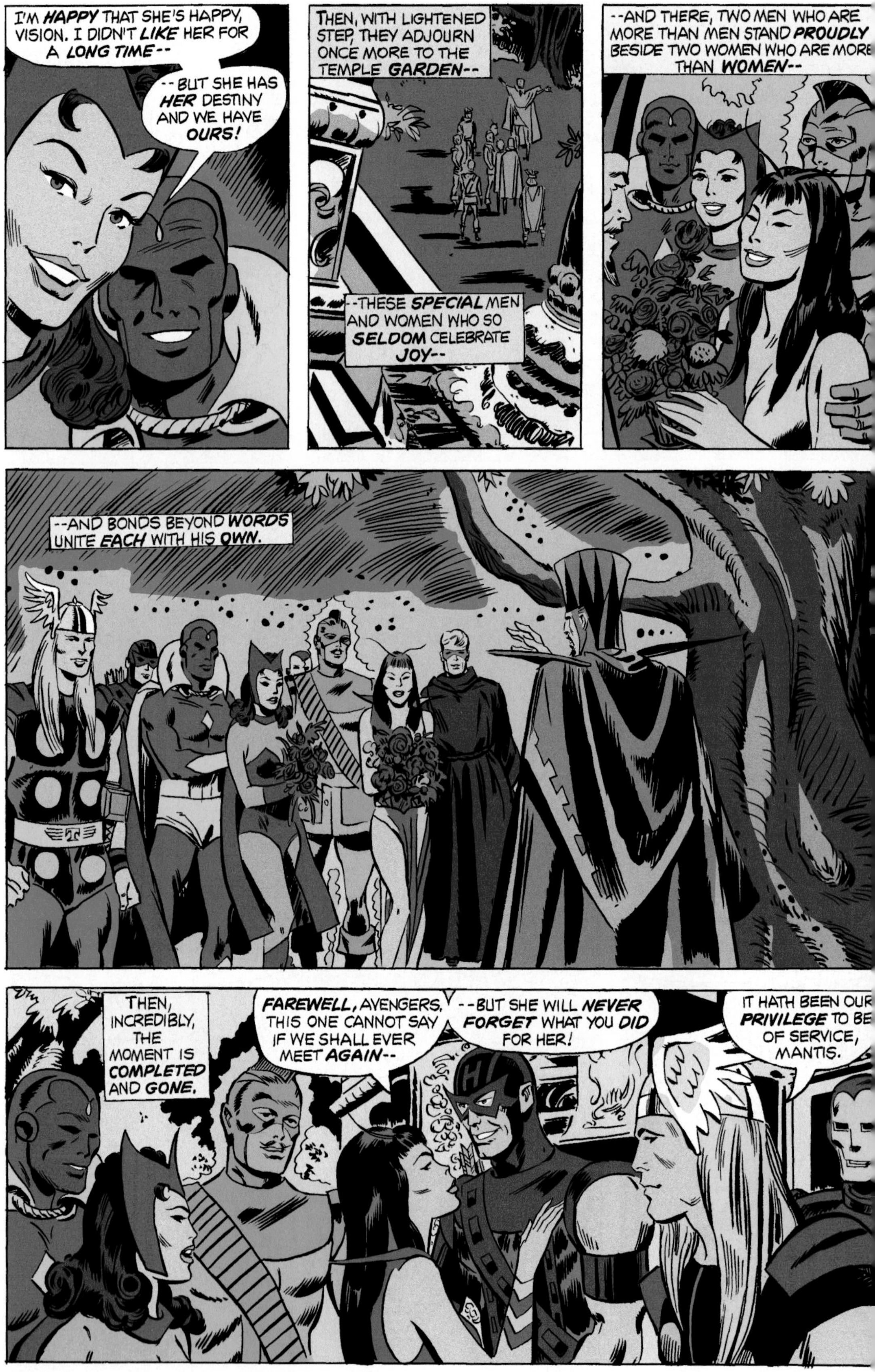
I'M HAPPY THAT SHE'S HAPPY, VISION. I DIDN'T LIKE HER FOR A LONG TIME--
--BUT SHE HAS HER DESTINY AND WE HAVE OURS!
THEN, WITH LIGHTENED STEP, THEY ADJOURN ONCE MORE TO THE TEMPLE GARDEN--
--THESE SPECIAL MEN AND WOMEN WHO SO SELDOM CELEBRATE JOY--
--AND THERE, TWO MEN WHO ARE MORE THAN MEN STAND PROUDLY BESIDE TWO WOMEN WHO ARE MORE THAN WOMEN--
--AND BONDS BEYOND WORDS UNITE EACH WITH HIS OWN.
THEN, INCREDIBLY, THE MOMENT IS COMPLETED AND GONE.
FAREWELL, AVENGERS, THIS ONE CANNOT SAY IF WE SHALL EVER MEET AGAIN--
--BUT SHE WILL NEVER FORGET WHAT YOU DID FOR HER!
IT HATH BEEN OUR PRIVILEGE TO BE OF SERVICE, MANTIS.

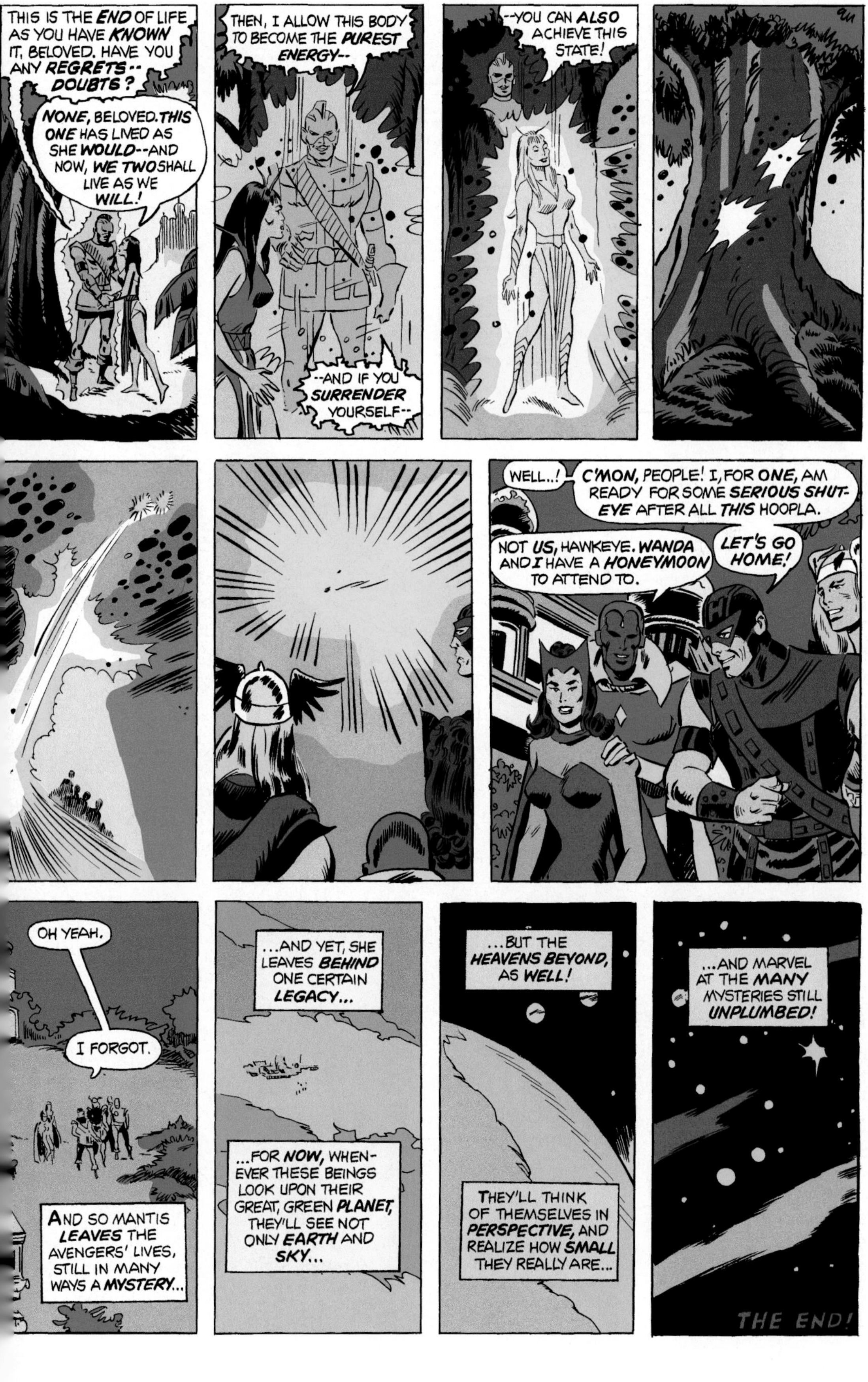

THIS IS THE END OF LIFE AS YOU HAVE KNOWN IT, BELOVED. HAVE YOU ANY REGRETS--DOUBTS?
NONE, BELOVED. THIS ONE HAS LIVED AS SHE WOULD--AND NOW, WE TWO SHALL LIVE AS WE WILL!
THEN, I ALLOW THIS BODY TO BECOME THE PUREST ENERGY--
--AND IF YOU SURRENDER YOURSELF--
--YOU CAN ALSO ACHIEVE THIS STATE!
WELL..!
C'MON, PEOPLE! I, FOR ONE, AM READY FOR SOME SERIOUS SHUT-EYE AFTER ALL THIS HOOPLA.
NOT US, HAWKEYE. WANDA AND I HAVE A HONEYMOON TO ATTEND TO.
LET'S GO HOME!
OH YEAH.
I FORGOT.
AND SO MANTIS LEAVES THE AVENGERS' LIVES, STILL IN MANY WAYS A MYSTERY...
...AND YET, SHE LEAVES BEHIND ONE CERTAIN LEGACY...
...FOR NOW, WHENEVER THESE BEINGS LOOK UPON THEIR GREAT, GREEN PLANET, THEY'LL SEE NOT ONLY EARTH AND SKY...
...BUT THE HEAVENS BEYOND, AS WELL!
THEY'LL THINK OF THEMSELVES IN PERSPECTIVE, AND REALIZE HOW SMALL THEY REALLY ARE...
...AND MARVEL AT THE MANY MYSTERIES STILL UNPLUMBED!
THE END!

A bold new era begins for the greatest heroes of the 31st century —
Yondu Udonta and the original Guardians of the Galaxy! But are they ready for…Taserface?

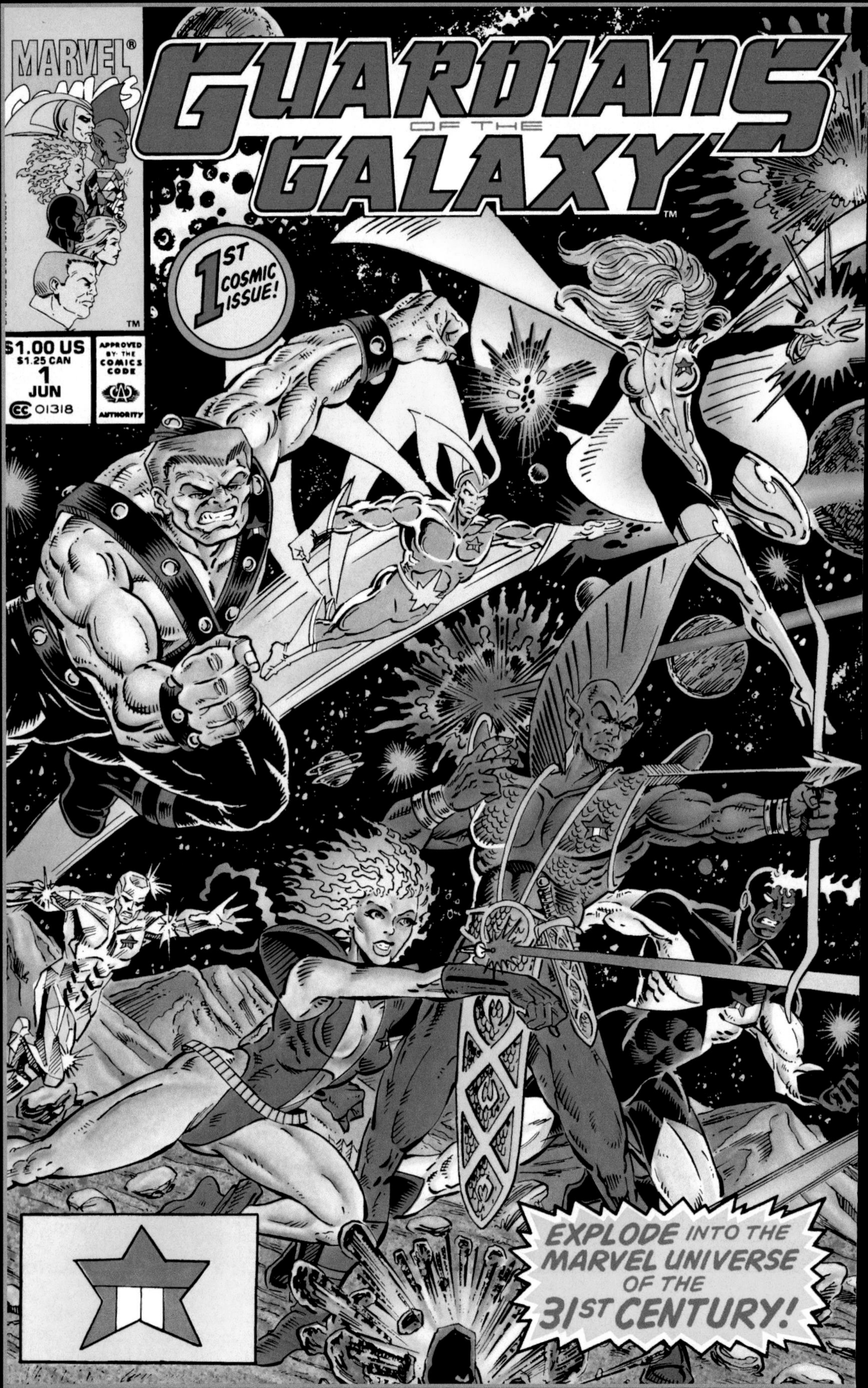
MARVEL® COMICS
GUARDIANS OF THE GALAXY™
1ST COSMIC ISSUE!
$1.00 US $1.25 CAN
1
JUN
01318
APPROVED BY THE COMICS CODE AUTHORITY
EXPLODE INTO THE MARVEL UNIVERSE OF THE 31ST CENTURY!

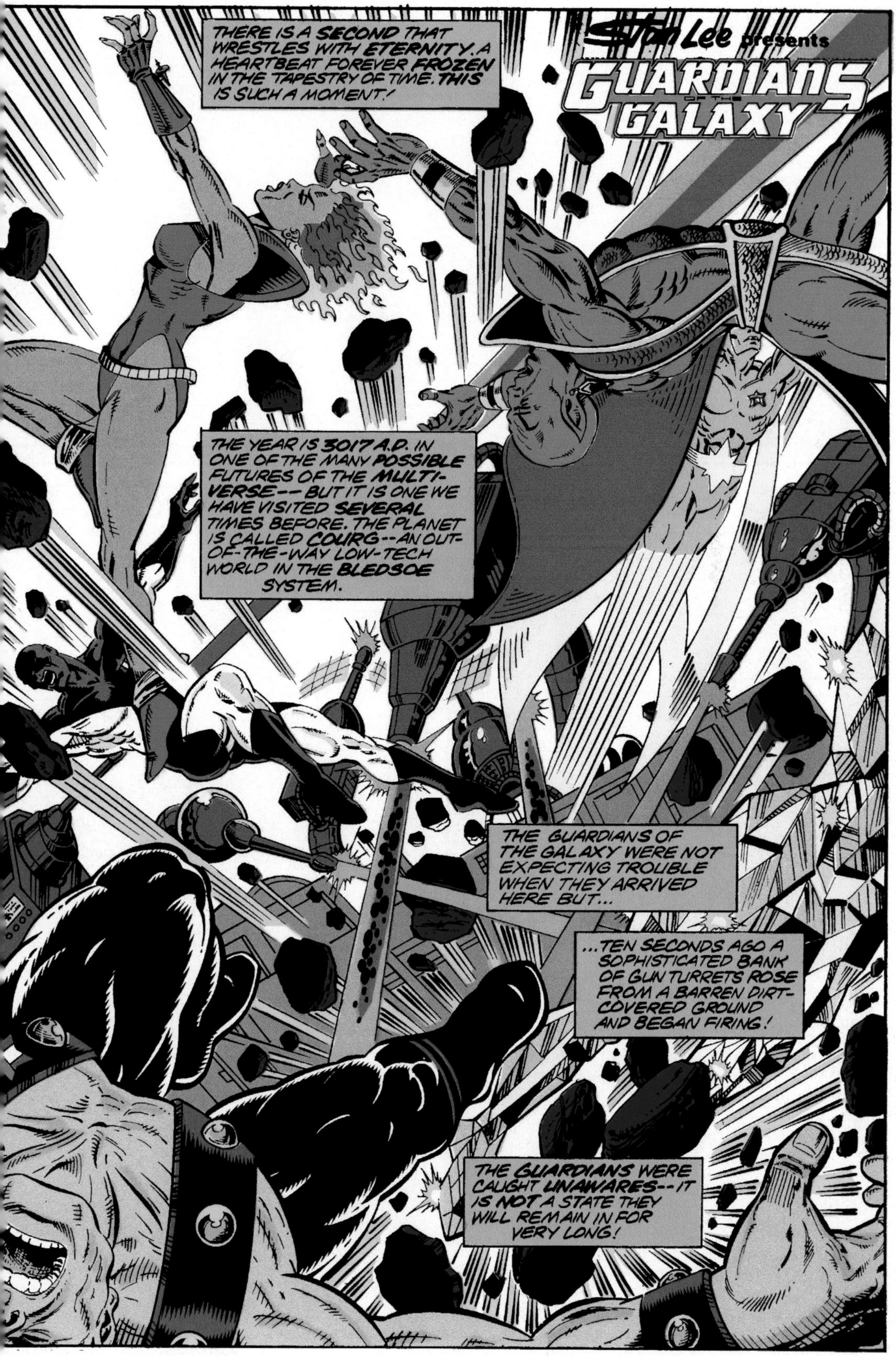
THERE IS A SECOND THAT WRESTLES WITH ETERNITY. A HEARTBEAT FOREVER FROZEN IN THE TAPESTRY OF TIME. THIS IS SUCH A MOMENT!
Stan Lee presents
GUARDIANS OF THE GALAXY
THE YEAR IS 3017 A.D. IN ONE OF THE MANY POSSIBLE FUTURES OF THE MULTI-VERSE-- BUT IT IS ONE WE HAVE VISITED SEVERAL TIMES BEFORE. THE PLANET IS CALLED COURG--AN OUT-OF-THE-WAY LOW-TECH WORLD IN THE BLEDSOE SYSTEM.
THE GUARDIANS OF THE GALAXY WERE NOT EXPECTING TROUBLE WHEN THEY ARRIVED HERE BUT...
...TEN SECONDS AGO A SOPHISTICATED BANK OF GUN TURRETS ROSE FROM A BARREN DIRT-COVERED GROUND AND BEGAN FIRING!
THE GUARDIANS WERE CAUGHT UNAWARES-- IT IS NOT A STATE THEY WILL REMAIN IN FOR VERY LONG!

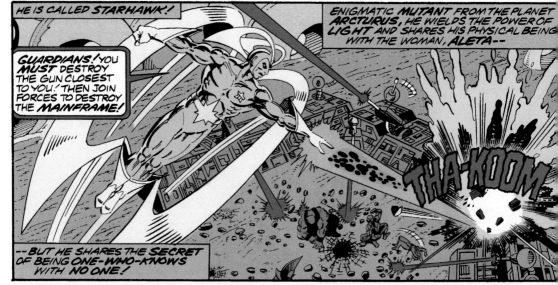

HE IS CALLED *STARHAWK!*

ENIGMATIC MUTANT FROM THE PLANET ARCTURUS, HE WIELDS THE POWER OF *LIGHT* AND SHARES HIS PHYSICAL BEING WITH THE WOMAN, *ALETA*--

GUARDIANS! YOU **MUST** DESTROY THE GUN **CLOSEST** TO YOU! THEN JOIN FORCES TO DESTROY THE **MAINFRAME!**

THA-KOOM

--BUT HE SHARES THE *SECRET* OF BEING ONE-WHO-KNOWS WITH *NO ONE!*

CHARLIE-27. FIFTH GENERATION MILITIA-MAN AND LAST SURVIVOR OF EARTH'S *JUPITER* COLONY...

...GENETICALLY ENGINEERED TO WITHSTAND *ELEVEN TIMES* THE GRAVITY OF EARTH...

GIVE HIM A BREAK, *NIK.* STARHAWK *MAY BE A JERK*, BUT HE'S *RIGHT!*

WHAT DO *YOU* THINK, MARTY?

RRENNO

...WITH THE *STRENGTH AND MASS* THAT GOES WITH IT. HE IS THE GUARDIANS' *PILOT* AND *MILITARY STRATEGIST.*

MARTINEX, SILICON-CELLED MASTER OF *THERMAL ENERGY.* SOLE SURVIVOR OF EARTH'S COLONY ON *PLUTO*...

YOU'RE THE MILITARY MAN, CHARLIE.

IF IT SOUNDS GOOD TO *YOU*, IT'S OKAY BY *ME*, YONDU?

I AM CLEARING A PATH FOR *VANCE* NOW.

BUT ARE THEY READY FOR... **TASERFACE!**

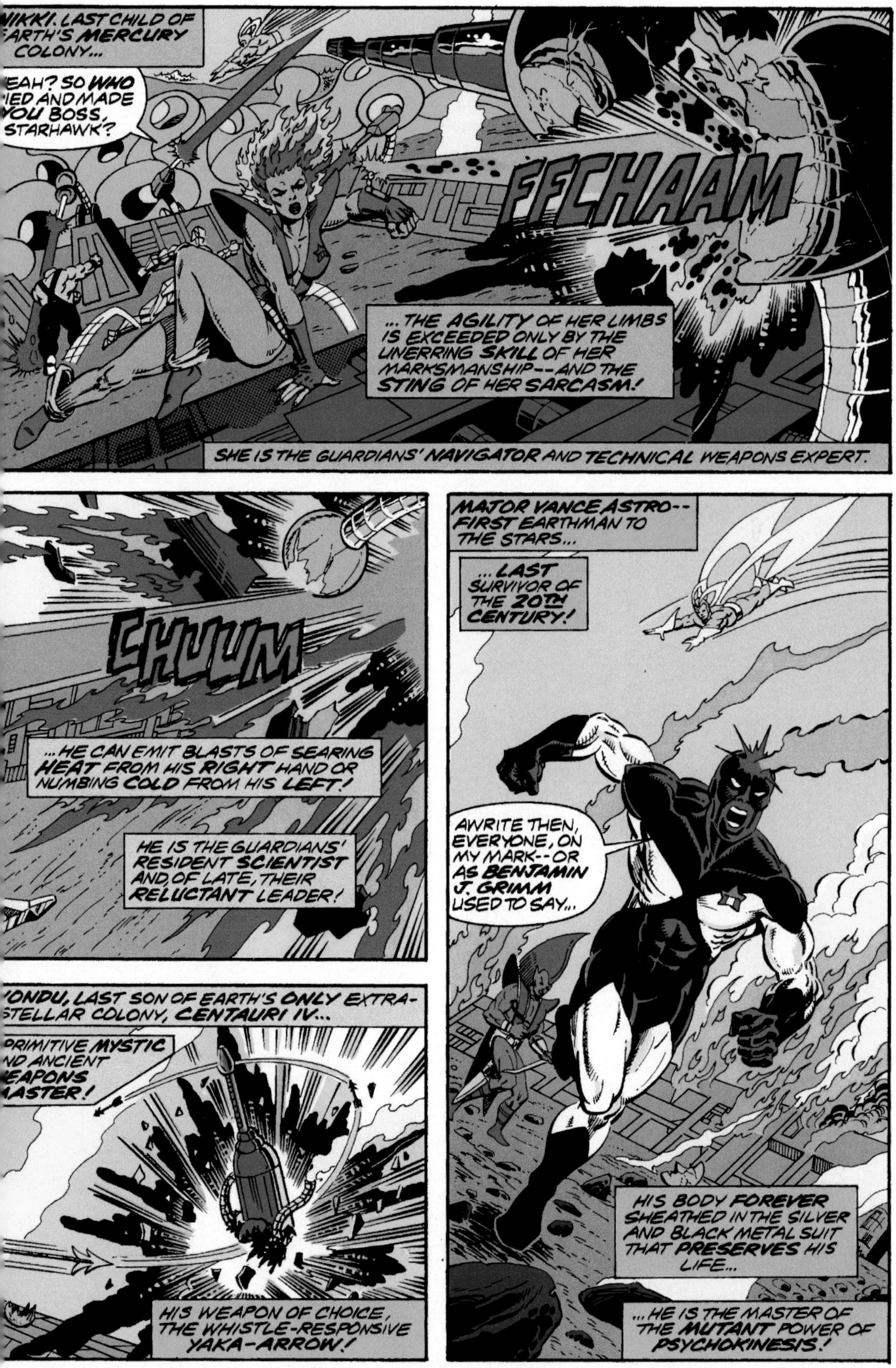
IKKI. LAST CHILD OF
ARTH'S MERCURY COLONY...
EAH? SO WHO IED AND MADE YOU BOSS, STARHAWK?
...THE AGILITY OF HER LIMBS IS EXCEEDED ONLY BY THE UNERRING SKILL OF HER MARKSMANSHIP-- AND THE STING OF HER SARCASM!
FFCHAAM
SHE IS THE GUARDIANS' NAVIGATOR AND TECHNICAL WEAPONS EXPERT.
CHUUM
...HE CAN EMIT BLASTS OF SEARING HEAT FROM HIS RIGHT HAND OR NUMBING COLD FROM HIS LEFT!
HE IS THE GUARDIANS' RESIDENT SCIENTIST AND, OF LATE, THEIR RELUCTANT LEADER!
ONDU, LAST SON OF EARTH'S ONLY EXTRA-STELLAR COLONY, CENTAURI IV...
RIMITIVE MYSTIC
ND ANCIENT
EAPONS
ASTER!
HIS WEAPON OF CHOICE, THE WHISTLE-RESPONSIVE YAKA-ARROW!
MAJOR VANCE ASTRO-- FIRST EARTHMAN TO THE STARS...
...LAST SURVIVOR OF THE 20TH CENTURY!
AWRITE THEN, EVERYONE, ON MY MARK--OR AS BENJAMIN J. GRIMM USED TO SAY...
HIS BODY FOREVER SHEATHED IN THE SILVER AND BLACK METAL SUIT THAT PRESERVES HIS LIFE...
...HE IS THE MASTER OF THE MUTANT POWER OF PSYCHOKINESIS!

JIM VALENTINO WRITER/ARTIST | STEVE MONTANO INKER | KEN LOPEZ LETTERER | EVELYN STEIN COLORIST | CRAIG ANDERSON EDITOR | TOM DeFALCO EDITOR-IN-CHIEF | TASERFACE CREATED BY AARON VALENTINO

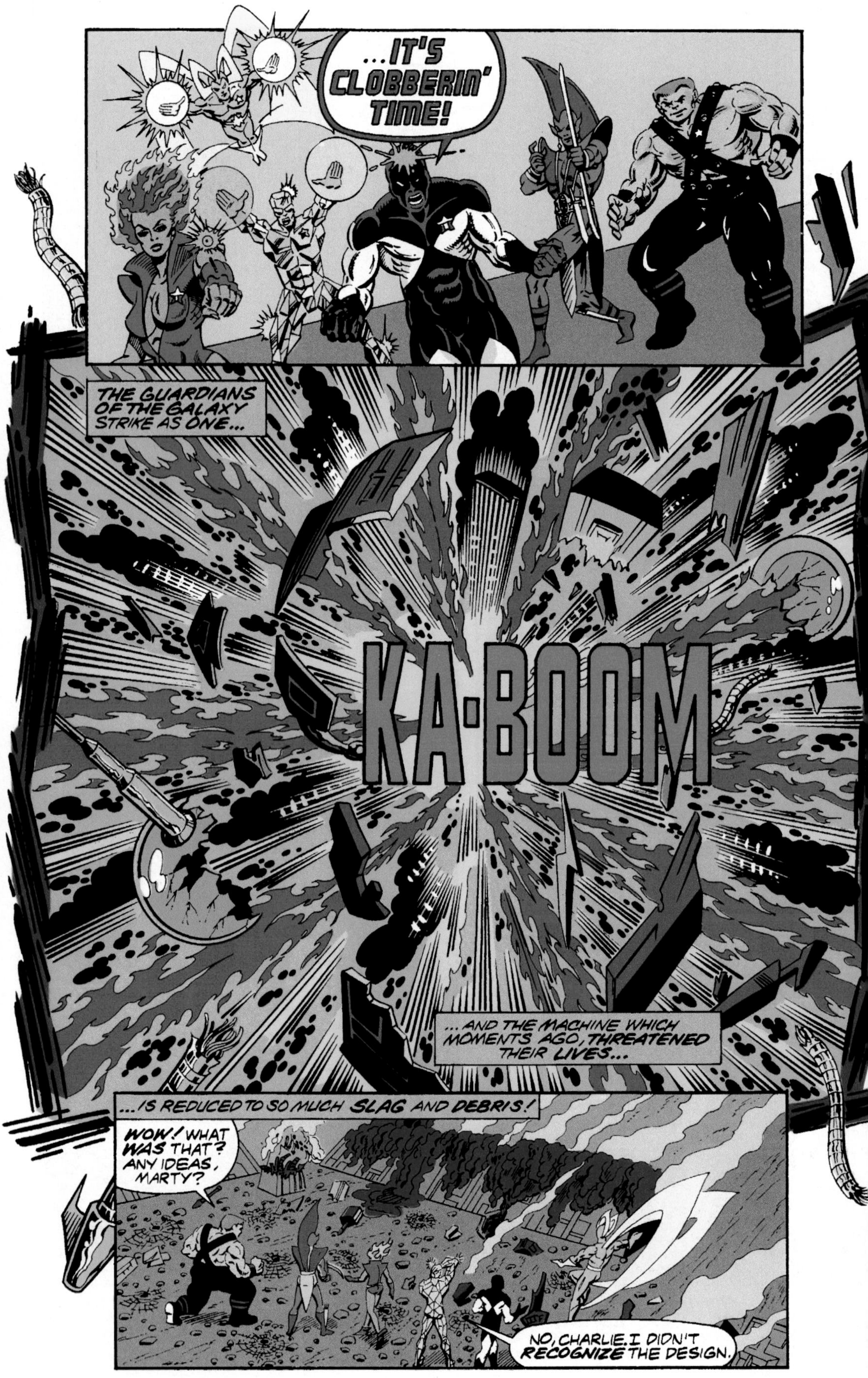
...IT'S CLOBBERIN' TIME!
THE GUARDIANS OF THE GALAXY STRIKE AS ONE...
KA-BOOM
...AND THE MACHINE WHICH MOMENTS AGO, THREATENED THEIR LIVES...
...IS REDUCED TO SO MUCH SLAG AND DEBRIS!
WOW! WHAT WAS THAT? ANY IDEAS, MARTY?
NO, CHARLIE. I DIDN'T RECOGNIZE THE DESIGN.

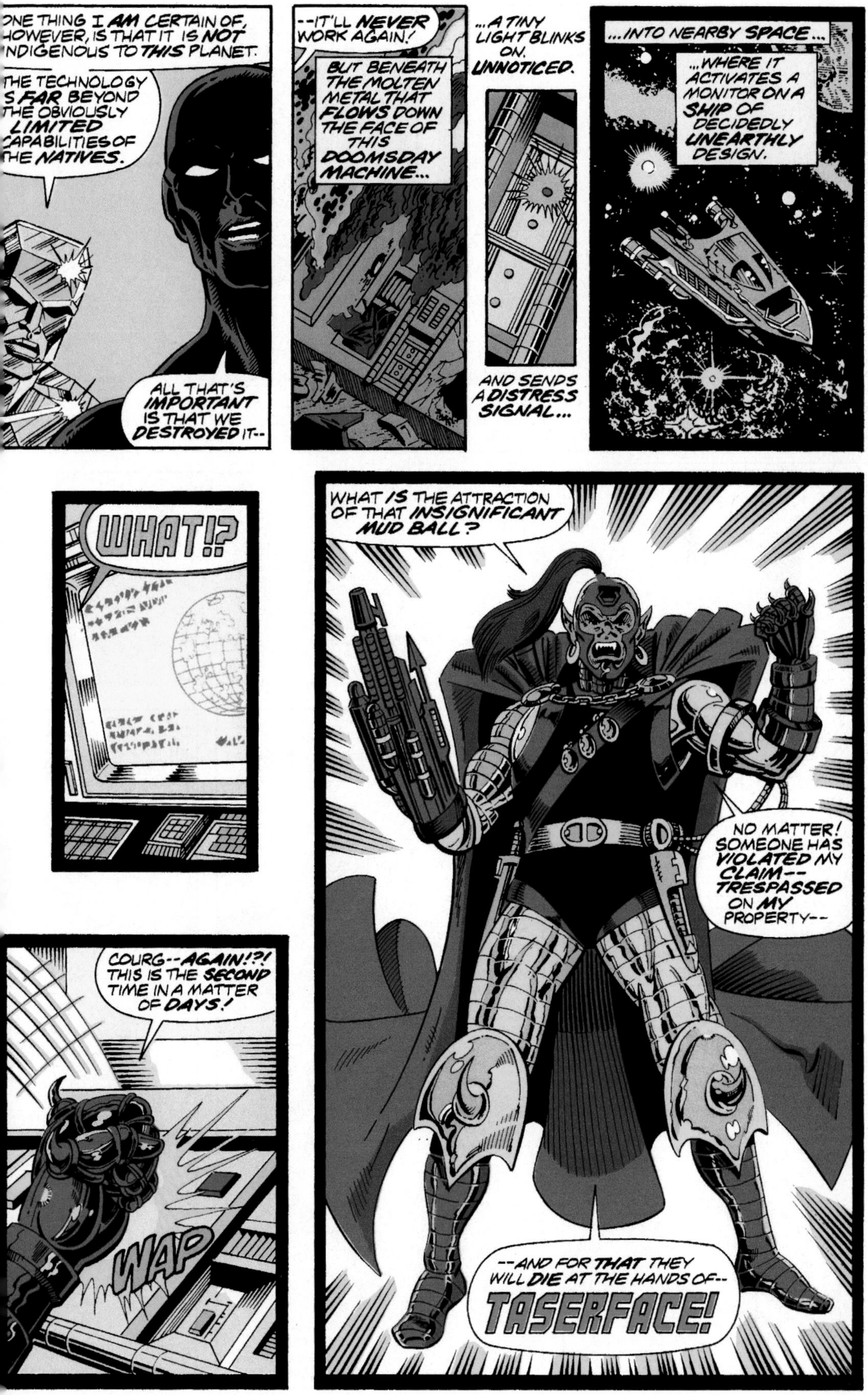
ONE THING I AM CERTAIN OF, HOWEVER, IS THAT IT IS NOT INDIGENOUS TO THIS PLANET.
THE TECHNOLOGY IS FAR BEYOND THE OBVIOUSLY LIMITED CAPABILITIES OF THE NATIVES.
ALL THAT'S IMPORTANT IS THAT WE DESTROYED IT--
--IT'LL NEVER WORK AGAIN!
BUT BENEATH THE MOLTEN METAL THAT FLOWS DOWN THE FACE OF THIS DOOMSDAY MACHINE...
...A TINY LIGHT BLINKS ON, UNNOTICED.
AND SENDS A DISTRESS SIGNAL...
...INTO NEARBY SPACE...
...WHERE IT ACTIVATES A MONITOR ON A SHIP OF DECIDEDLY UNEARTHLY DESIGN.
WHAT!?
WHAT IS THE ATTRACTION OF THAT INSIGNIFICANT MUD BALL?
NO MATTER! SOMEONE HAS VIOLATED MY CLAIM--TRESPASSED ON MY PROPERTY--
--AND FOR THAT THEY WILL DIE AT THE HANDS OF--
TASERFACE!
COURG--AGAIN!?! THIS IS THE SECOND TIME IN A MATTER OF DAYS!
WAP

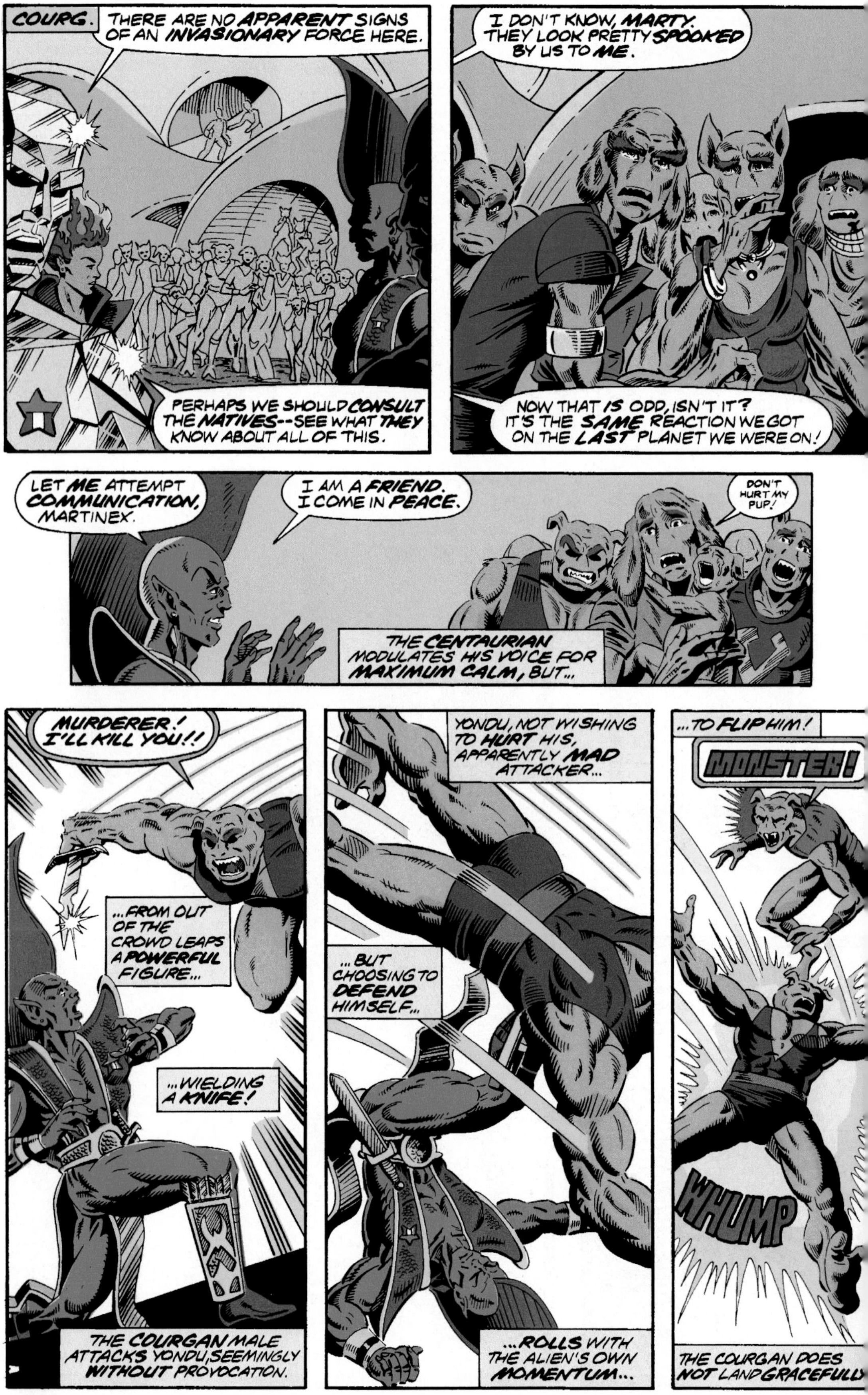
COURG.
THERE ARE NO APPARENT SIGNS OF AN INVASIONARY FORCE HERE.
PERHAPS WE SHOULD CONSULT THE NATIVES--SEE WHAT THEY KNOW ABOUT ALL OF THIS.
I DON'T KNOW, MARTY. THEY LOOK PRETTY SPOOKED BY US TO ME.
NOW THAT IS ODD, ISN'T IT? IT'S THE SAME REACTION WE GOT ON THE LAST PLANET WE WERE ON!
LET ME ATTEMPT COMMUNICATION, MARTINEX.
I AM A FRIEND. I COME IN PEACE.
DON'T HURT MY PUP!
THE CENTAURIAN MODULATES HIS VOICE FOR MAXIMUM CALM, BUT...
MURDERER! I'LL KILL YOU!!
...FROM OUT OF THE CROWD LEAPS A POWERFUL FIGURE...
...WIELDING A KNIFE!
THE COURGAN MALE ATTACKS YONDU, SEEMINGLY WITHOUT PROVOCATION.
YONDU, NOT WISHING TO HURT HIS, APPARENTLY MAD ATTACKER...
...BUT CHOOSING TO DEFEND HIMSELF...
...ROLLS WITH THE ALIEN'S OWN MOMENTUM...
...TO FLIP HIM!
MONSTER!
WHUMP
THE COURGAN DOES NOT LAND GRACEFULLY

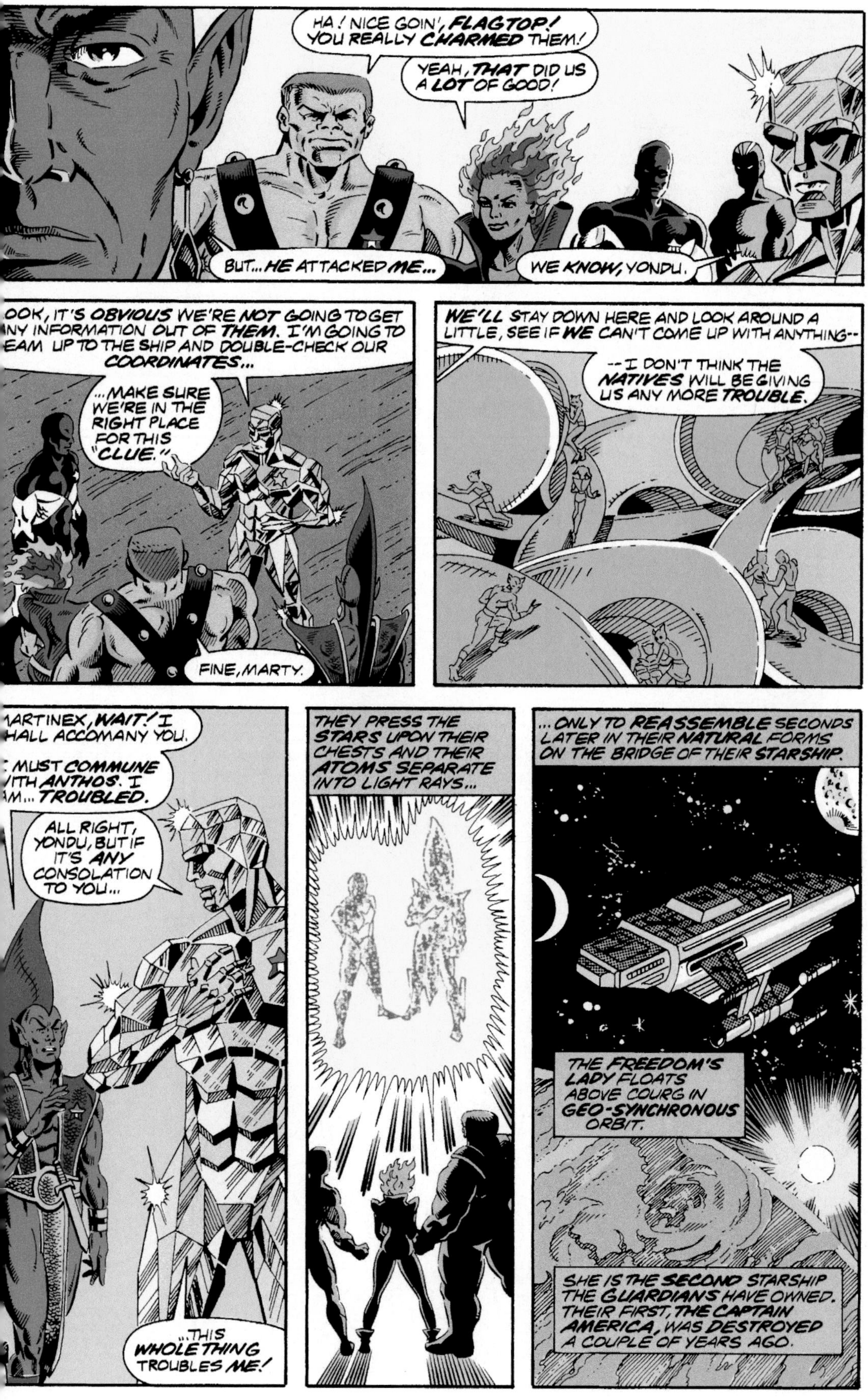

HA! NICE GOIN', FLAGTOP! YOU REALLY CHARMED THEM!
YEAH, THAT DID US A LOT OF GOOD!
BUT... HE ATTACKED ME...
WE KNOW, YONDU.
OOK, IT'S OBVIOUS WE'RE NOT GOING TO GET NY INFORMATION OUT OF THEM. I'M GOING TO EAM UP TO THE SHIP AND DOUBLE-CHECK OUR COORDINATES...
...MAKE SURE WE'RE IN THE RIGHT PLACE FOR THIS "CLUE."
FINE, MARTY.
WE'LL STAY DOWN HERE AND LOOK AROUND A LITTLE, SEE IF WE CAN'T COME UP WITH ANYTHING--
--I DON'T THINK THE NATIVES WILL BE GIVING US ANY MORE TROUBLE.
MARTINEX, WAIT! I HALL ACCOMANY YOU.
MUST COMMUNE WITH ANTHOS. I M... TROUBLED.
ALL RIGHT, YONDU, BUT IF IT'S ANY CONSOLATION TO YOU...
...THIS WHOLE THING TROUBLES ME!
THEY PRESS THE STARS UPON THEIR CHESTS AND THEIR ATOMS SEPARATE INTO LIGHT RAYS...
...ONLY TO REASSEMBLE SECONDS LATER IN THEIR NATURAL FORMS ON THE BRIDGE OF THEIR STARSHIP.
THE FREEDOM'S LADY FLOATS ABOVE COURG IN GEO-SYNCHRONOUS ORBIT.
SHE IS THE SECOND STARSHIP THE GUARDIANS HAVE OWNED. THEIR FIRST, THE CAPTAIN AMERICA, WAS DESTROYED A COUPLE OF YEARS AGO.

PLANETSIDE.

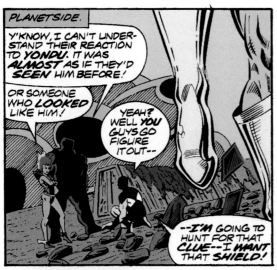

Y'KNOW, I CAN'T UNDER-
STAND THEIR REACTION
TO YONDU. IT WAS
ALMOST AS IF THEY'D
SEEN HIM BEFORE!

OR SOMEONE
WHO LOOKED
LIKE HIM!

YEAH? WELL YOU
GUYS GO FIGURE
IT OUT--

--I'M GOING TO
HUNT FOR THAT
CLUE--I WANT
THAT SHIELD!

SUITS ME, VANCE. I'VE BEEN WAITIN' FOR A
CHANCE TO GET NIK ALONE FOR A WHILE NOW

YOU'RE STILL NOT
OVER THE
BURNS FROM THE
LAST TIME, BIG
BOY!

AM I
COMPLAININ'?

HEY! WHERE DID STARHAWK GO?
I WANT TO ASK HIM SOMETHING.

HE JUST WALKED
AWAY FROM US--AS
USUAL! HE THINKS HE'S
TOO GOOD FOR US,
Y'KNOW.

YEAH, WELL, I
WISH HE'D TURN
INTO ALETA
PERMANENTLY!

...ALETA!

FREE
AGAIN!

"HER I CAN
DEAL WITH!"

YOUR WISH
MAY COME TRUE
SOONER THAN
YOU THINK,
CHARLIE-27.

I FEEL THE
CHANGE UPON
ME. I HAVE
KEPT HER IN
FAR TOO LONG!

HE CLOSES HIS EYES TO
CONCENTRATE...

...AND FEELS THEM
MELT WITHIN THEIR
SOCKETS!

HIS ATOMS
LIQUIFY--
FLOWING
INTO ONE-
ANOTHER...

...AND LIKE A BUTTERFLY
IN ITS CHRYSALIS,
REARRANGE THEIR
CONFIGURATION!

AND
WHERE ONCE
STARHAWK
STOOD, NOW
STANDS...

THE AIR FILLS HER
LUNGS AND SHE
RELISHES ITS
SWEET TASTE.

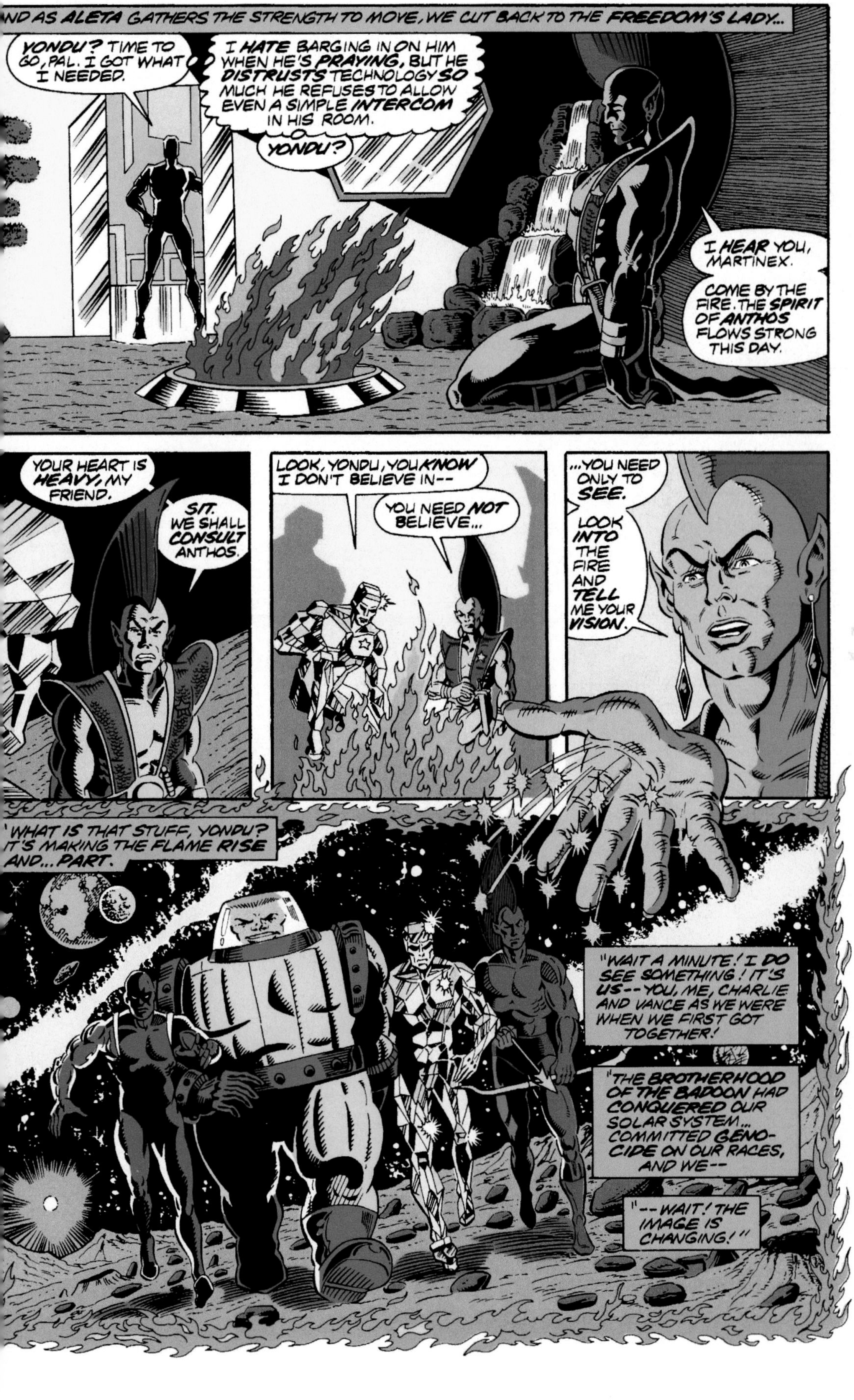

...AND AS ALETA GATHERS THE STRENGTH TO MOVE, WE CUT BACK TO THE FREEDOM'S LADY...
YONDU? TIME TO GO, PAL. I GOT WHAT I NEEDED.
I HATE BARGING IN ON HIM WHEN HE'S PRAYING, BUT HE DISTRUSTS TECHNOLOGY SO MUCH HE REFUSES TO ALLOW EVEN A SIMPLE INTERCOM IN HIS ROOM.
YONDU?
I HEAR YOU, MARTINEX.
COME BY THE FIRE. THE SPIRIT OF ANTHOS FLOWS STRONG THIS DAY.
YOUR HEART IS HEAVY, MY FRIEND.
SIT. WE SHALL CONSULT ANTHOS.
LOOK, YONDU, YOU KNOW I DON'T BELIEVE IN--
YOU NEED NOT BELIEVE...
...YOU NEED ONLY TO SEE.
LOOK INTO THE FIRE AND TELL ME YOUR VISION.
"WHAT IS THAT STUFF, YONDU? IT'S MAKING THE FLAME RISE AND... PART.
"WAIT A MINUTE! I DO SEE SOMETHING! IT'S US--YOU, ME, CHARLIE AND VANCE AS WE WERE WHEN WE FIRST GOT TOGETHER!
"THE BROTHERHOOD OF THE BADOON HAD CONQUERED OUR SOLAR SYSTEM... COMMITTED GENOCIDE ON OUR RACES, AND WE--
"--WAIT! THE IMAGE IS CHANGING!"

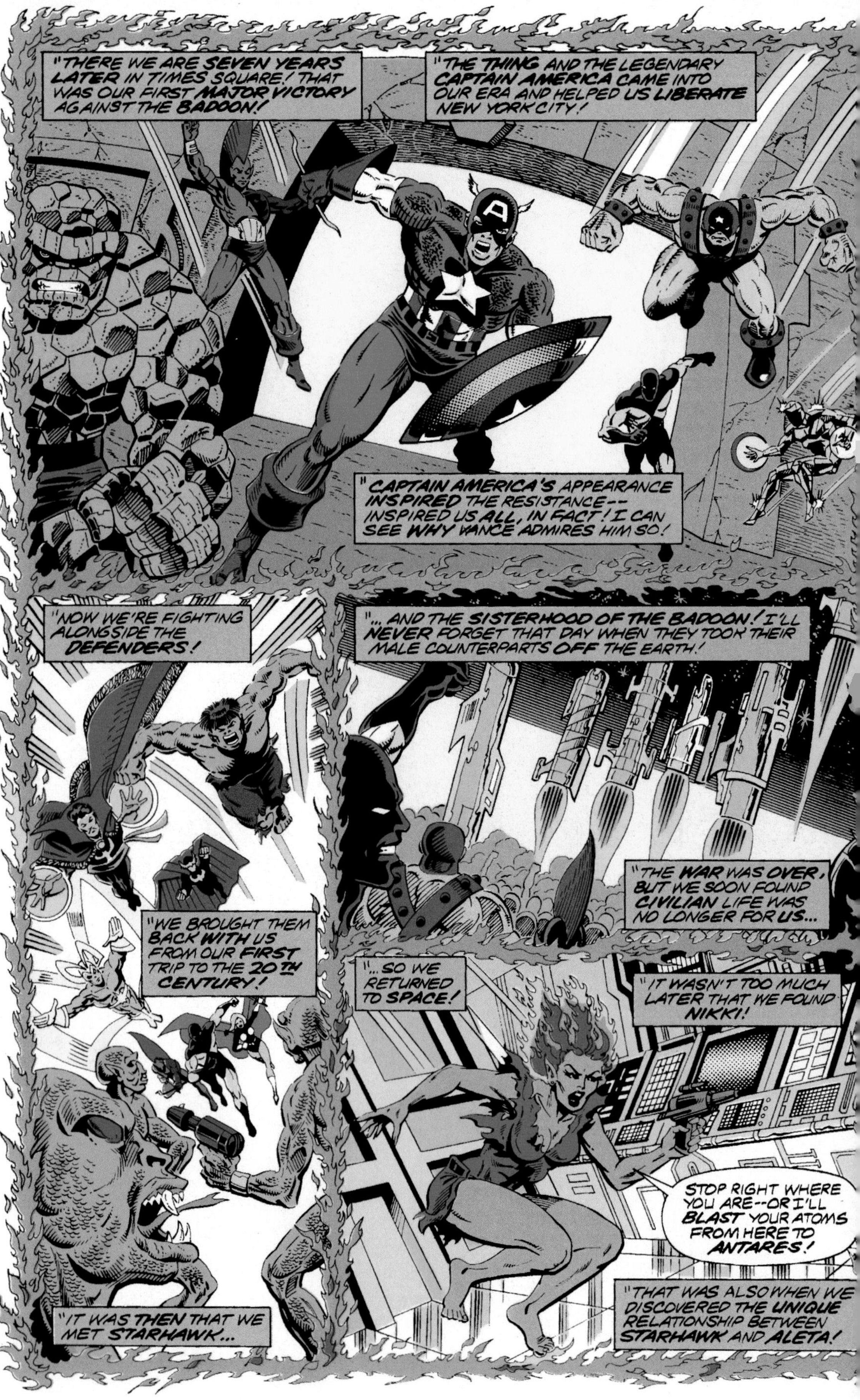
"THERE WE ARE SEVEN YEARS LATER IN TIMES SQUARE! THAT WAS OUR FIRST MAJOR VICTORY AGAINST THE BADOON!
"THE THING AND THE LEGENDARY CAPTAIN AMERICA CAME INTO OUR ERA AND HELPED US LIBERATE NEW YORK CITY!
"CAPTAIN AMERICA'S APPEARANCE INSPIRED THE RESISTANCE-- INSPIRED US ALL, IN FACT! I CAN SEE WHY VANCE ADMIRES HIM SO!
"NOW WE'RE FIGHTING ALONGSIDE THE DEFENDERS!
"WE BROUGHT THEM BACK WITH US FROM OUR FIRST TRIP TO THE 20TH CENTURY!
"IT WAS THEN THAT WE MET STARHAWK...
"... AND THE SISTERHOOD OF THE BADOON! I'LL NEVER FORGET THAT DAY WHEN THEY TOOK THEIR MALE COUNTERPARTS OFF THE EARTH!
"THE WAR WAS OVER, BUT WE SOON FOUND CIVILIAN LIFE WAS NO LONGER FOR US...
"...SO WE RETURNED TO SPACE!
"IT WASN'T TOO MUCH LATER THAT WE FOUND NIKKI!
STOP RIGHT WHERE YOU ARE--OR I'LL BLAST YOUR ATOMS FROM HERE TO ANTARES!
"THAT WAS ALSO WHEN WE DISCOVERED THE UNIQUE RELATIONSHIP BETWEEN STARHAWK AND ALETA!

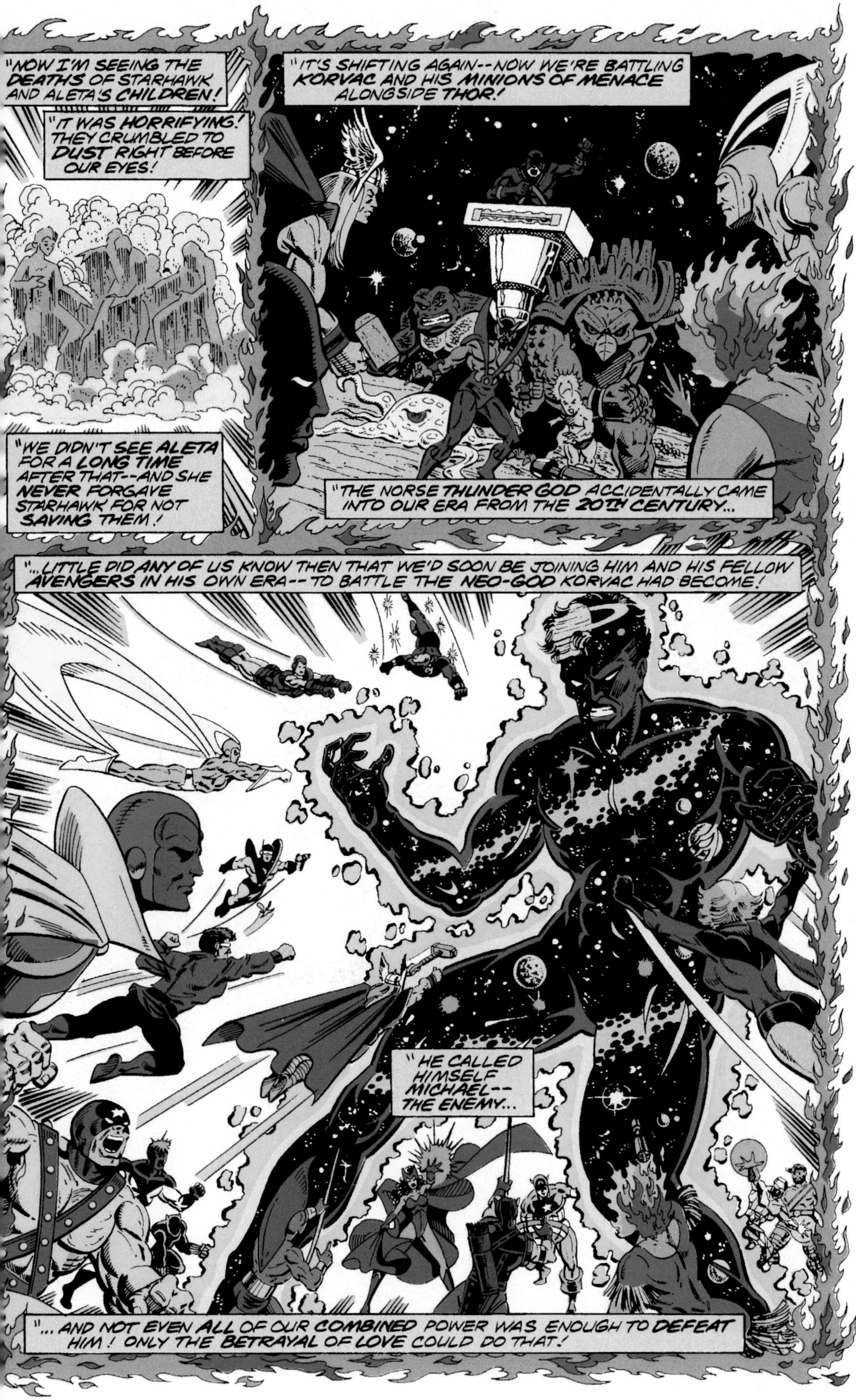
"NOW I'M SEEING THE DEATHS OF STARHAWK AND ALETA'S CHILDREN!
"IT WAS HORRIFYING! THEY CRUMBLED TO DUST RIGHT BEFORE OUR EYES!
"WE DIDN'T SEE ALETA FOR A LONG TIME AFTER THAT--AND SHE NEVER FORGAVE STARHAWK FOR NOT SAVING THEM!
"IT'S SHIFTING AGAIN--NOW WE'RE BATTLING KORVAC AND HIS MINIONS OF MENACE ALONGSIDE THOR!
"THE NORSE THUNDER GOD ACCIDENTALLY CAME INTO OUR ERA FROM THE 20TH CENTURY...
"...LITTLE DID ANY OF US KNOW THEN THAT WE'D SOON BE JOINING HIM AND HIS FELLOW AVENGERS IN HIS OWN ERA--TO BATTLE THE NEO-GOD KORVAC HAD BECOME!
"HE CALLED HIMSELF MICHAEL--THE ENEMY...
"...AND NOT EVEN ALL OF OUR COMBINED POWER WAS ENOUGH TO DEFEAT HIM! ONLY THE BETRAYAL OF LOVE COULD DO THAT!

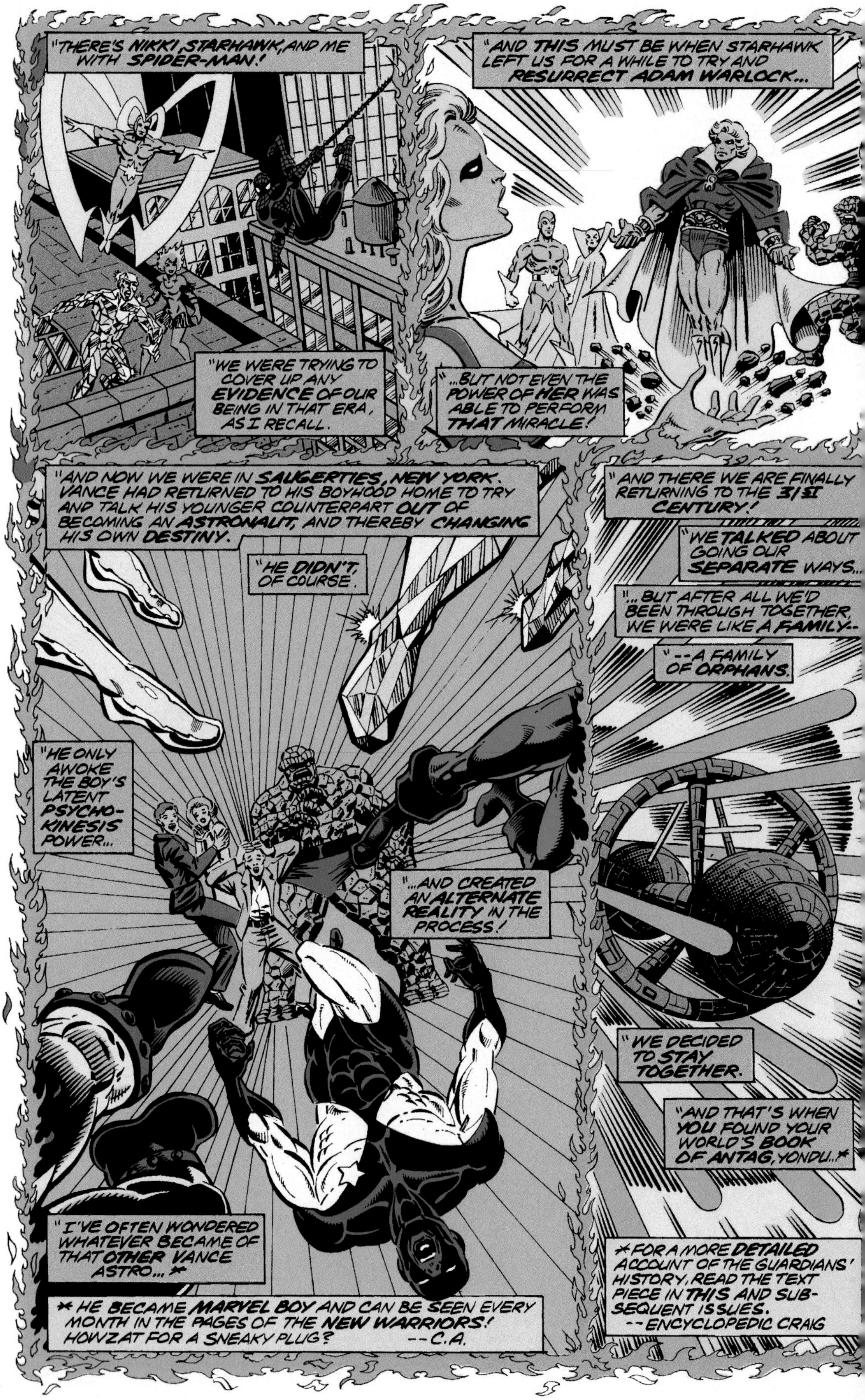
"THERE'S NIKKI, STARHAWK, AND ME WITH SPIDER-MAN!
"WE WERE TRYING TO COVER UP ANY EVIDENCE OF OUR BEING IN THAT ERA, AS I RECALL.
"AND THIS MUST BE WHEN STARHAWK LEFT US FOR A WHILE TO TRY AND RESURRECT ADAM WARLOCK...
"...BUT NOT EVEN THE POWER OF HER WAS ABLE TO PERFORM THAT MIRACLE!
"AND NOW WE WERE IN SAUGERTIES, NEW YORK. VANCE HAD RETURNED TO HIS BOYHOOD HOME TO TRY AND TALK HIS YOUNGER COUNTERPART OUT OF BECOMING AN ASTRONAUT, AND THEREBY CHANGING HIS OWN DESTINY.
"HE DIDN'T, OF COURSE.
"HE ONLY AWOKE THE BOY'S LATENT PSYCHO-KINESIS POWER...
"...AND CREATED AN ALTERNATE REALITY IN THE PROCESS!
"I'VE OFTEN WONDERED WHATEVER BECAME OF THAT OTHER VANCE ASTRO... *
* HE BECAME MARVEL BOY AND CAN BE SEEN EVERY MONTH IN THE PAGES OF THE NEW WARRIORS! HOWZAT FOR A SNEAKY PLUG? --C.A.
"AND THERE WE ARE FINALLY RETURNING TO THE 31ST CENTURY!
"WE TALKED ABOUT GOING OUR SEPARATE WAYS...
"...BUT AFTER ALL WE'D BEEN THROUGH TOGETHER, WE WERE LIKE A FAMILY--
"--A FAMILY OF ORPHANS.
"WE DECIDED TO STAY TOGETHER.
"AND THAT'S WHEN YOU FOUND YOUR WORLD'S BOOK OF ANTAG, YONDU.*
* FOR A MORE DETAILED ACCOUNT OF THE GUARDIANS' HISTORY, READ THE TEXT PIECE IN THIS AND SUB-SEQUENT ISSUES. --ENCYCLOPEDIC CRAIG

"YOU FOUND A CHAPTER IN IT THAT SPOKE OF A BRIGHTLY COLORED DISK THAT WOULD GRANT IT'S POSSESSOR INVINCIBILITY IN BATTLE!"

"WE FIGURED IT WAS JUST ONE OF YOUR PEOPLE'S SUPERSTITIONS..."

"...BUT NOT VANCE! HE KNEW WHAT IT WAS!"

DON'T YOU SEE? IT'S CAPTAIN AMERICA'S SHIELD!!!

"HE WAS CONVINCED HE WAS RIGHT, AND NOTHING OR NO ONE COULD CONVINCE HIM OTHERWISE. WE SOON BEGAN FOLLOWING THE BOOK'S CLUES..."

THAT'S IT! THE VISION IS OVER!

"...WHICH HAVE, SO FAR, BEEN NOTHING BUT DEAD ENDS!"

AND WHAT DID YOU LEARN FROM IT?

MARTINEX, DO YOU NOT SEE THAT OUR FATES ARE INEXORABLY LINKED TO THE 20TH CENTURY?

EVERY ONE OF OUR MAJOR VICTORIES HAS INVOLVED THAT ERA!

LEARN? WHY, NOTHING. I ALREADY KNEW ALL OF THAT! I LIVED IT!

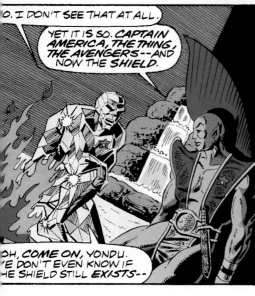

O, I DON'T SEE THAT AT ALL.

YET IT IS SO. CAPTAIN AMERICA, THE THING, THE AVENGERS--AND NOW THE SHIELD.

OH, COME ON, YONDU. 'E DON'T EVEN KNOW IF HE SHIELD STILL EXISTS--

IT DOES. --AND, FRANKLY, ALL THE REST IS JUST CONJECTURE ON YOUR PART.

YOU HAVE A TENDENCY TO READ INTO THINGS, TO SEE...

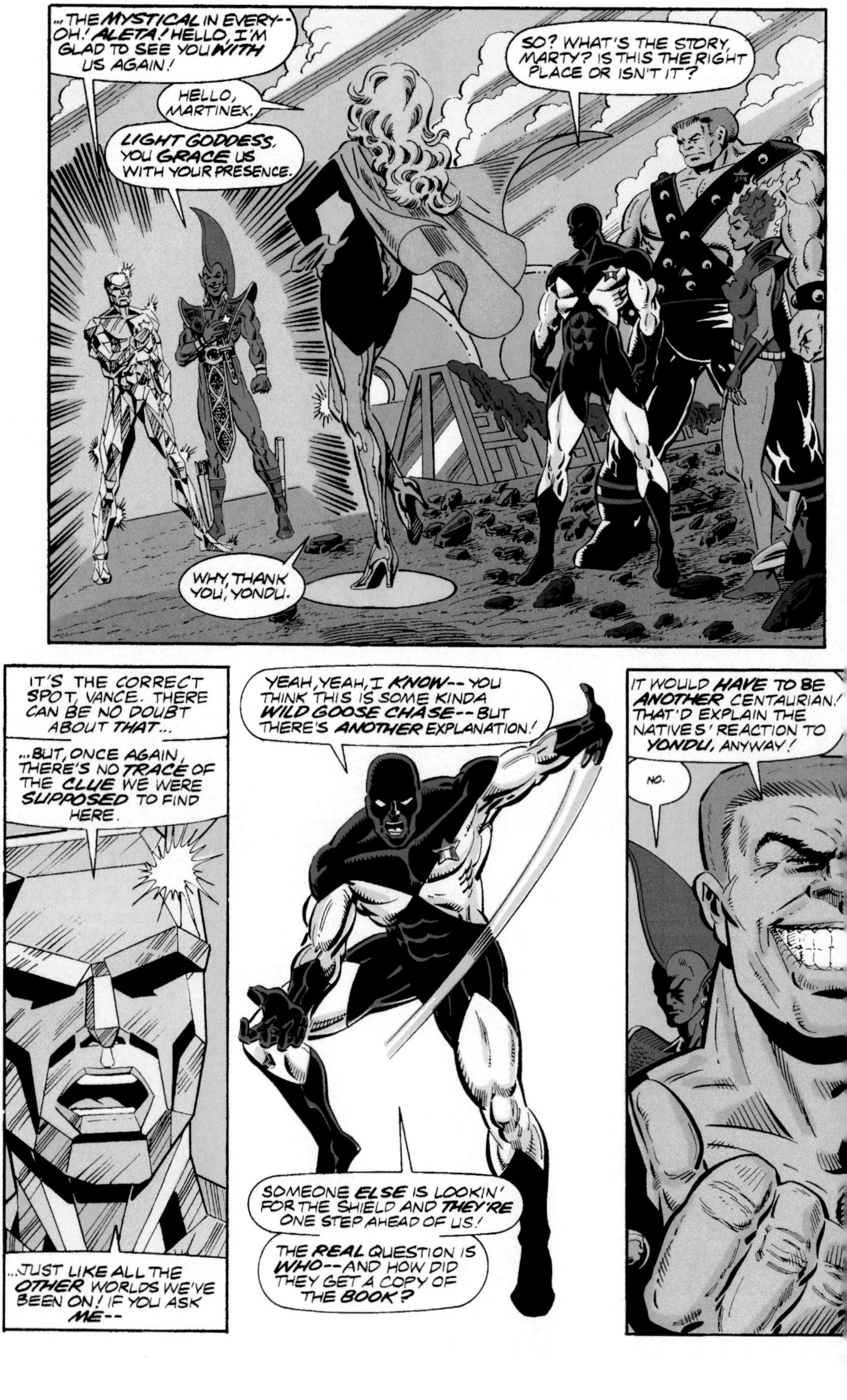
...THE MYSTICAL IN EVERY--OH! ALETA! HELLO, I'M GLAD TO SEE YOU WITH US AGAIN!
HELLO, MARTINEX.
LIGHT GODDESS, YOU GRACE US WITH YOUR PRESENCE.
WHY, THANK YOU, YONDU.
SO? WHAT'S THE STORY, MARTY? IS THIS THE RIGHT PLACE OR ISN'T IT?
IT'S THE CORRECT SPOT, VANCE. THERE CAN BE NO DOUBT ABOUT THAT...
...BUT, ONCE AGAIN, THERE'S NO TRACE OF THE CLUE WE WERE SUPPOSED TO FIND HERE.
...JUST LIKE ALL THE OTHER WORLDS WE'VE BEEN ON! IF YOU ASK ME--
YEAH, YEAH, I KNOW-- YOU THINK THIS IS SOME KINDA WILD GOOSE CHASE--BUT THERE'S ANOTHER EXPLANATION!
SOMEONE ELSE IS LOOKIN' FOR THE SHIELD AND THEY'RE ONE STEP AHEAD OF US!
THE REAL QUESTION IS WHO--AND HOW DID THEY GET A COPY OF THE BOOK?
IT WOULD HAVE TO BE ANOTHER CENTAURIAN! THAT'D EXPLAIN THE NATIVES' REACTION TO YONDU, ANYWAY!
NO.

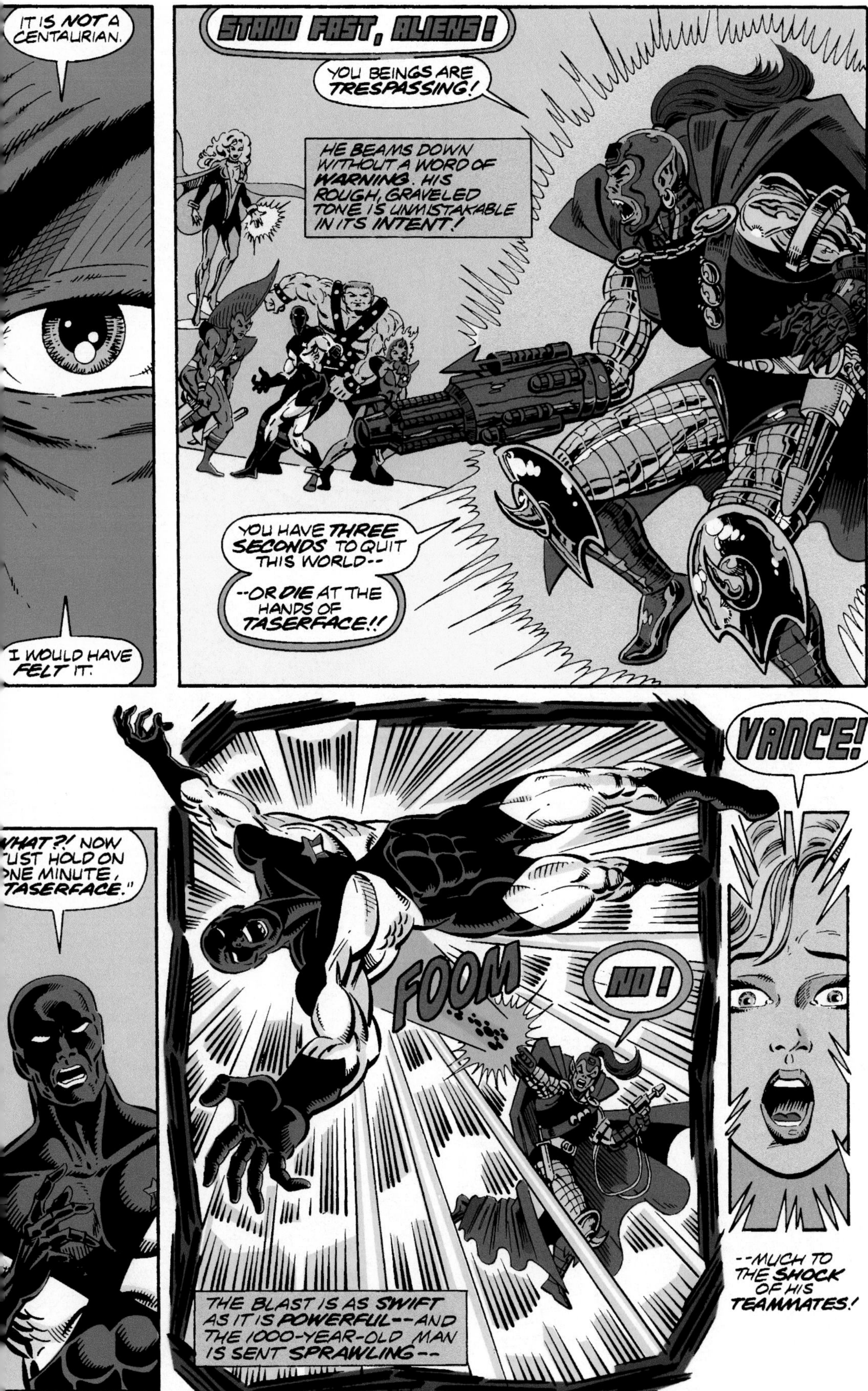
IT IS NOT A CENTAURIAN.
STAND FAST, ALIENS!
YOU BEINGS ARE TRESPASSING!
HE BEAMS DOWN WITHOUT A WORD OF WARNING. HIS ROUGH, GRAVELED TONE IS UNMISTAKABLE IN ITS INTENT!
YOU HAVE THREE SECONDS TO QUIT THIS WORLD--
--OR DIE AT THE HANDS OF TASERFACE!!
I WOULD HAVE FELT IT.
WHAT?! NOW JUST HOLD ON ONE MINUTE, TASERFACE."
FOOM
NO!
VANCE!
THE BLAST IS AS SWIFT AS IT IS POWERFUL--AND THE 1000-YEAR-OLD MAN IS SENT SPRAWLING--
--MUCH TO THE SHOCK OF HIS TEAMMATES!

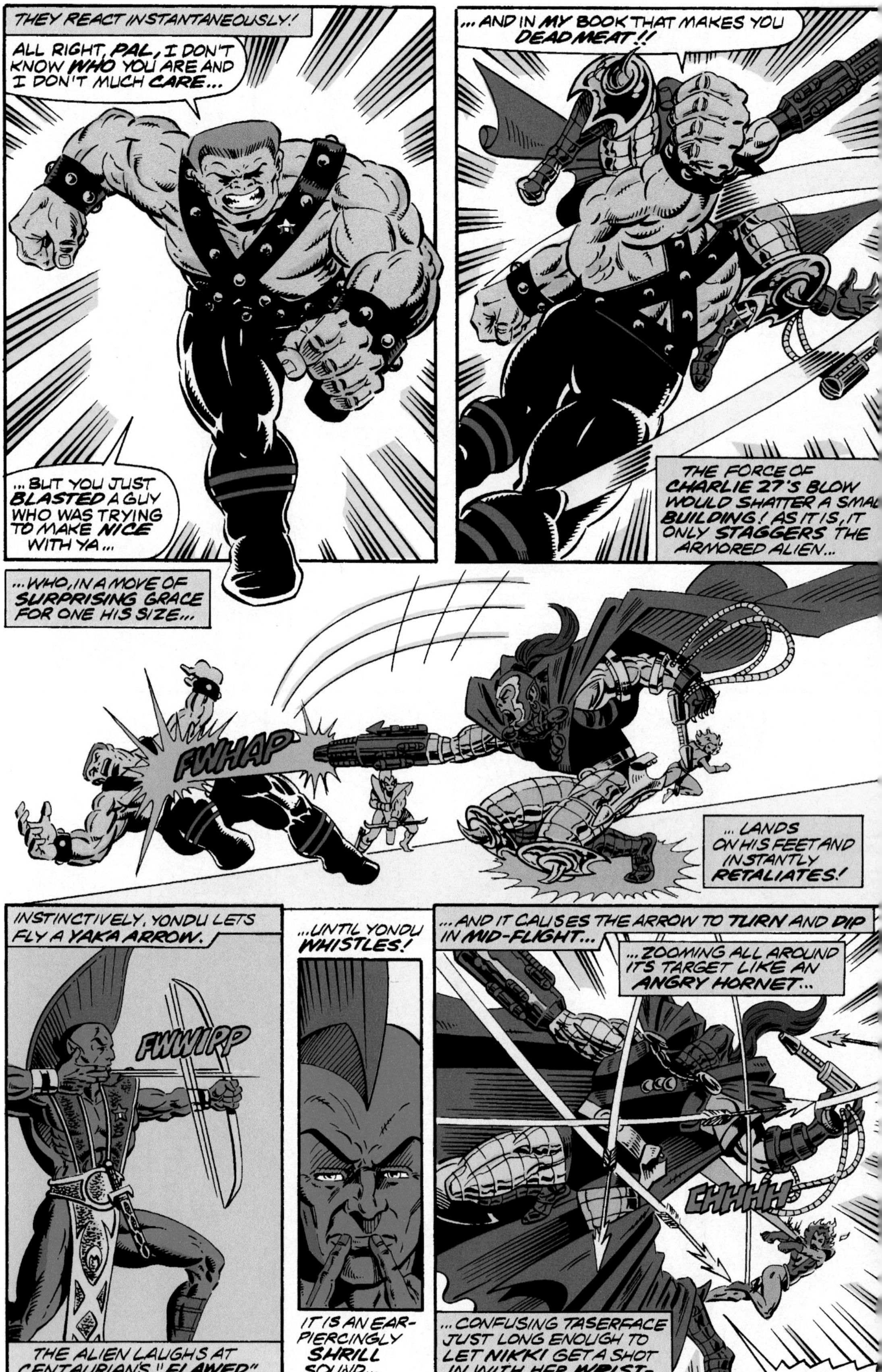
THEY REACT INSTANTANEOUSLY!
ALL RIGHT, PAL, I DON'T KNOW WHO YOU ARE AND I DON'T MUCH CARE...
...BUT YOU JUST BLASTED A GUY WHO WAS TRYING TO MAKE NICE WITH YA...
...AND IN MY BOOK THAT MAKES YOU DEAD MEAT!!
THE FORCE OF CHARLIE 27'S BLOW WOULD SHATTER A SMAL BUILDING! AS IT IS, IT ONLY STAGGERS THE ARMORED ALIEN...
...WHO, IN A MOVE OF SURPRISING GRACE FOR ONE HIS SIZE...
FWHAP
...LANDS ON HIS FEET AND INSTANTLY RETALIATES!
INSTINCTIVELY, YONDU LETS FLY A YAKA ARROW.
FWWIPP
THE ALIEN LAUGHS AT CENTAURIAN'S "FLAWED" MARKSMANSHIP...
...UNTIL YONDU WHISTLES!
IT IS AN EAR-PIERCINGLY SHRILL SOUND...
...AND IT CAUSES THE ARROW TO TURN AND DIP IN MID-FLIGHT...
...ZOOMING ALL AROUND ITS TARGET LIKE AN ANGRY HORNET...
CHHHH
...CONFUSING TASERFACE JUST LONG ENOUGH TO LET NIKKI GET A SHOT IN WITH HER WRIST-BLASTERS!
AARGGHH!

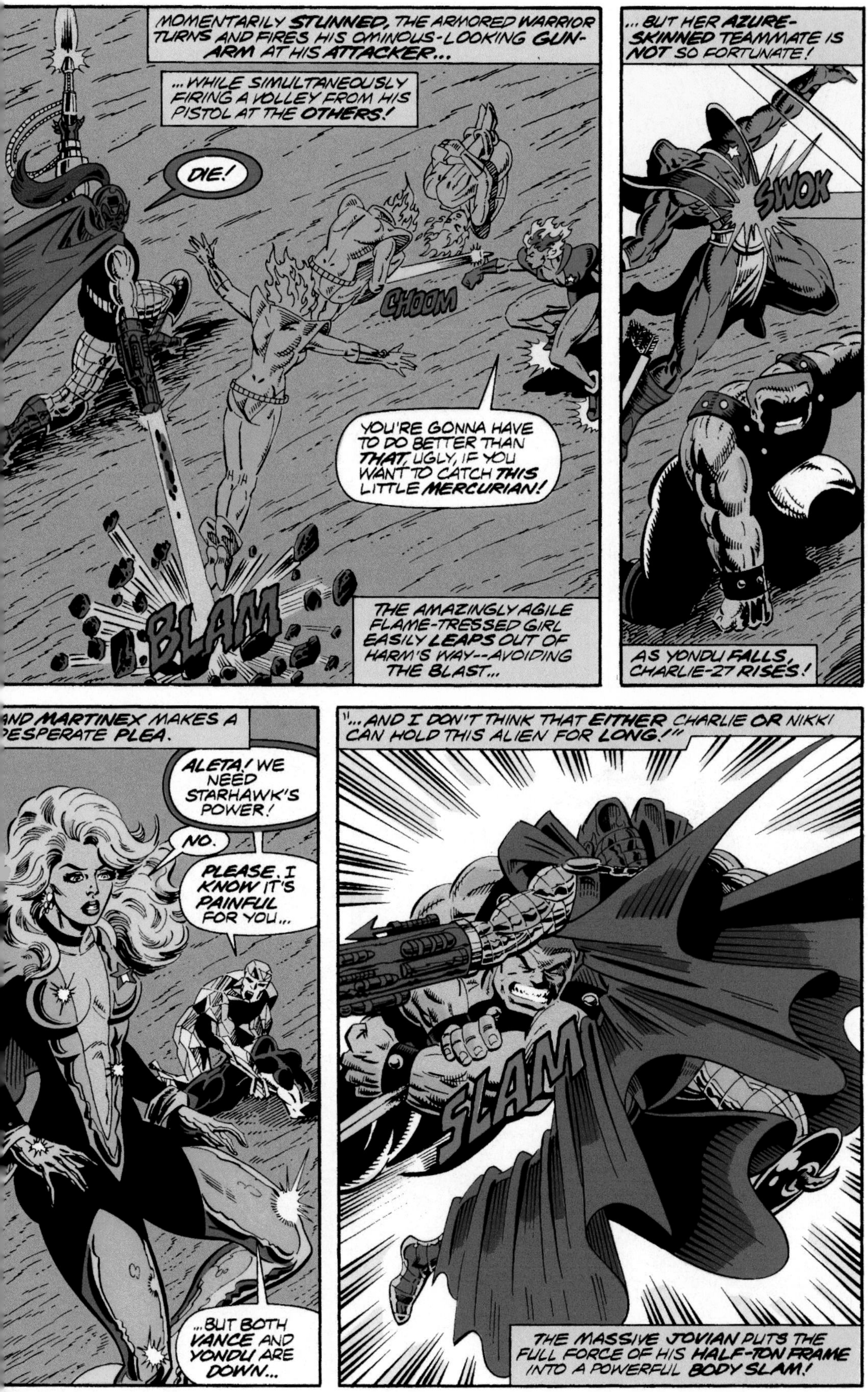

MOMENTARILY STUNNED, THE ARMORED WARRIOR TURNS AND FIRES HIS OMINOUS-LOOKING GUN-ARM AT HIS ATTACKER...
...WHILE SIMULTANEOUSLY FIRING A VOLLEY FROM HIS PISTOL AT THE OTHERS!
DIE!
CHOOM
YOU'RE GONNA HAVE TO DO BETTER THAN THAT, UGLY, IF YOU WANT TO CATCH THIS LITTLE MERCURIAN!
BLAM
THE AMAZINGLY AGILE FLAME-TRESSED GIRL EASILY LEAPS OUT OF HARM'S WAY--AVOIDING THE BLAST...
...BUT HER AZURE-SKINNED TEAMMATE IS NOT SO FORTUNATE!
SWOK
AS YONDU FALLS, CHARLIE-27 RISES!
AND MARTINEX MAKES A DESPERATE PLEA.
ALETA! WE NEED STARHAWK'S POWER!
NO.
PLEASE. I KNOW IT'S PAINFUL FOR YOU...
...BUT BOTH VANCE AND YONDU ARE DOWN...
"...AND I DON'T THINK THAT EITHER CHARLIE OR NIKKI CAN HOLD THIS ALIEN FOR LONG!"
SLAM
THE MASSIVE JOVIAN PUTS THE FULL FORCE OF HIS HALF-TON FRAME INTO A POWERFUL BODY SLAM!

EVEN WHILE *STARHAWK*, RELUCTANTLY RELEASED BY *ALETA*, ENTERS THE FRAY!

THIS HAS GONE ON *LONG* ENOUGH!

CHARLIE, CAN YOU *GRAB* THE CREATURE AND *HOLD* HIM WHILE THE OTHERS PREPARE TO ATTACK *EN MASSE!*

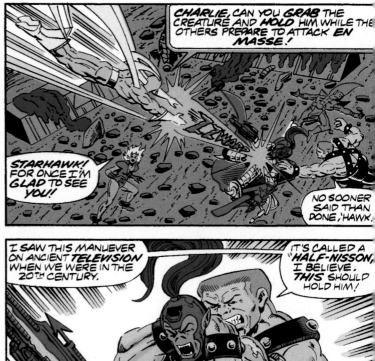

STARHAWK! FOR ONCE I'M *GLAD* TO SEE YOU!

NO SOONER SAID THAN DONE, 'HAWK.

I SAW THIS MANUEVER ON ANCIENT *TELEVISION* WHEN WE WERE IN THE 20TH CENTURY.

IT'S CALLED A "*HALF-NISSON*," I BELIEVE. *THIS* SHOULD HOLD HIM!

FOOL! YOU HOLD *NOTHING!*

THERE IS A REASON *WHY I* AM CALLED *TASERFACE!*

AARRGH!

ZZERRAP

A BEAM OF DEADLY *ELECTROMAGNETIC* ENERGY EMITS FROM THE ALIEN'S *FACE...*

... AND THE *ONE-WHO-KNOWS* IS SENT REELING WITH THE BRUNT OF ITS FORCE!

I AM *TIRED* OF PLAYING GAMES WITH THIS GUY!

YOU WANT TO PLAY ROUGH, "*TASERFACE*, OKAY, LET'S PLAY *REAL* ROUGH!

NOW YOU'RE TALKIN', *MARTY!*

A BURST OF *FREEZ* COLD ISSUES FROM THE *PLUVIAN'S* SILICON APPENDAGE...

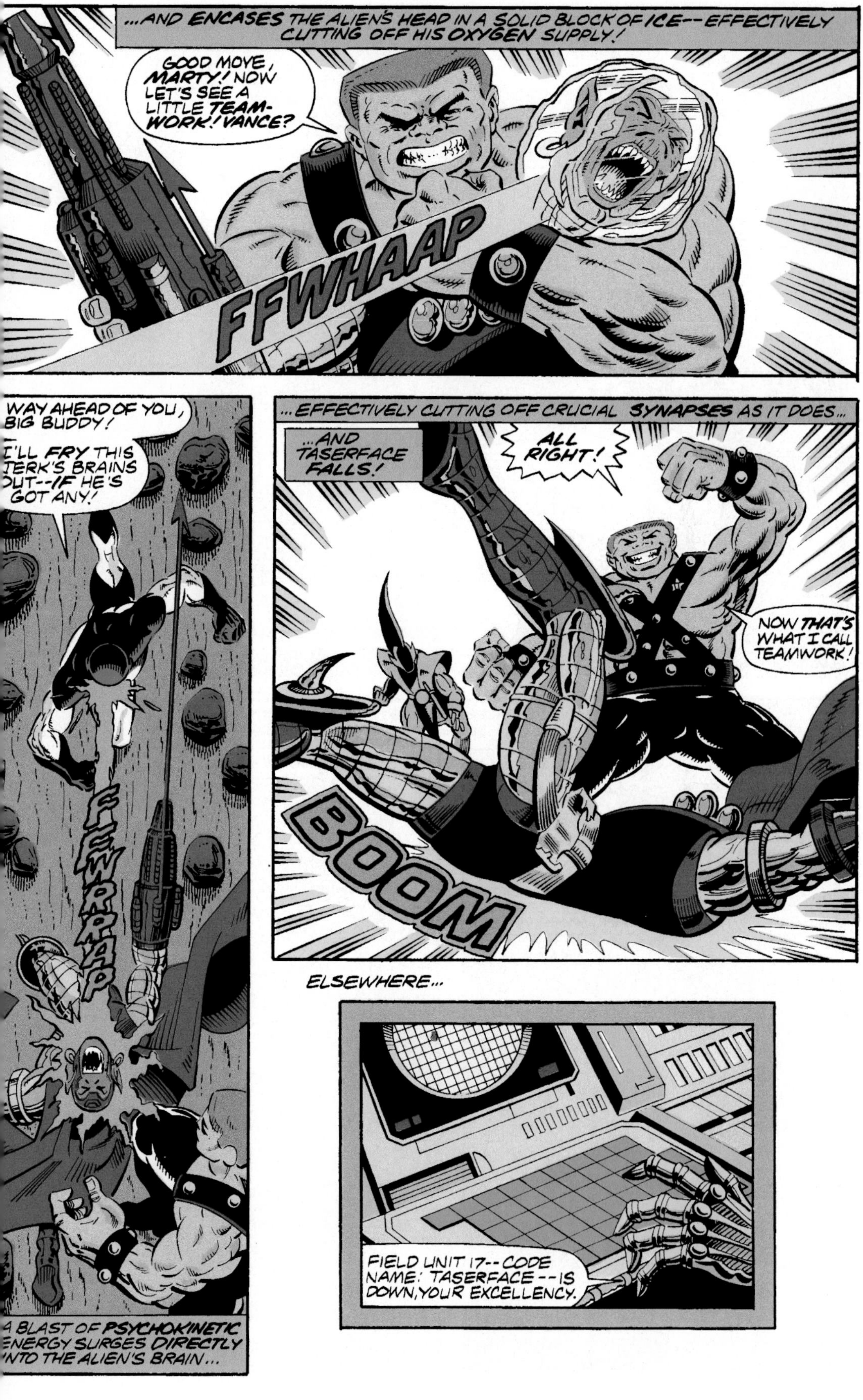
...AND ENCASES THE ALIEN'S HEAD IN A SOLID BLOCK OF ICE--EFFECTIVELY CUTTING OFF HIS OXYGEN SUPPLY!
GOOD MOVE, MARTY! NOW LET'S SEE A LITTLE TEAM-WORK! VANCE?
FFWHAAP
WAY AHEAD OF YOU, BIG BUDDY!
I'LL FRY THIS JERK'S BRAINS OUT--IF HE'S GOT ANY!
FFWRRAAP
A BLAST OF PSYCHOKINETIC ENERGY SURGES DIRECTLY INTO THE ALIEN'S BRAIN...
...EFFECTIVELY CUTTING OFF CRUCIAL SYNAPSES AS IT DOES...
...AND TASERFACE FALLS!
ALL RIGHT!
NOW THAT'S WHAT I CALL TEAMWORK!
BOOM
ELSEWHERE...
FIELD UNIT 17--CODE NAME: TASERFACE--IS DOWN, YOUR EXCELLENCY.

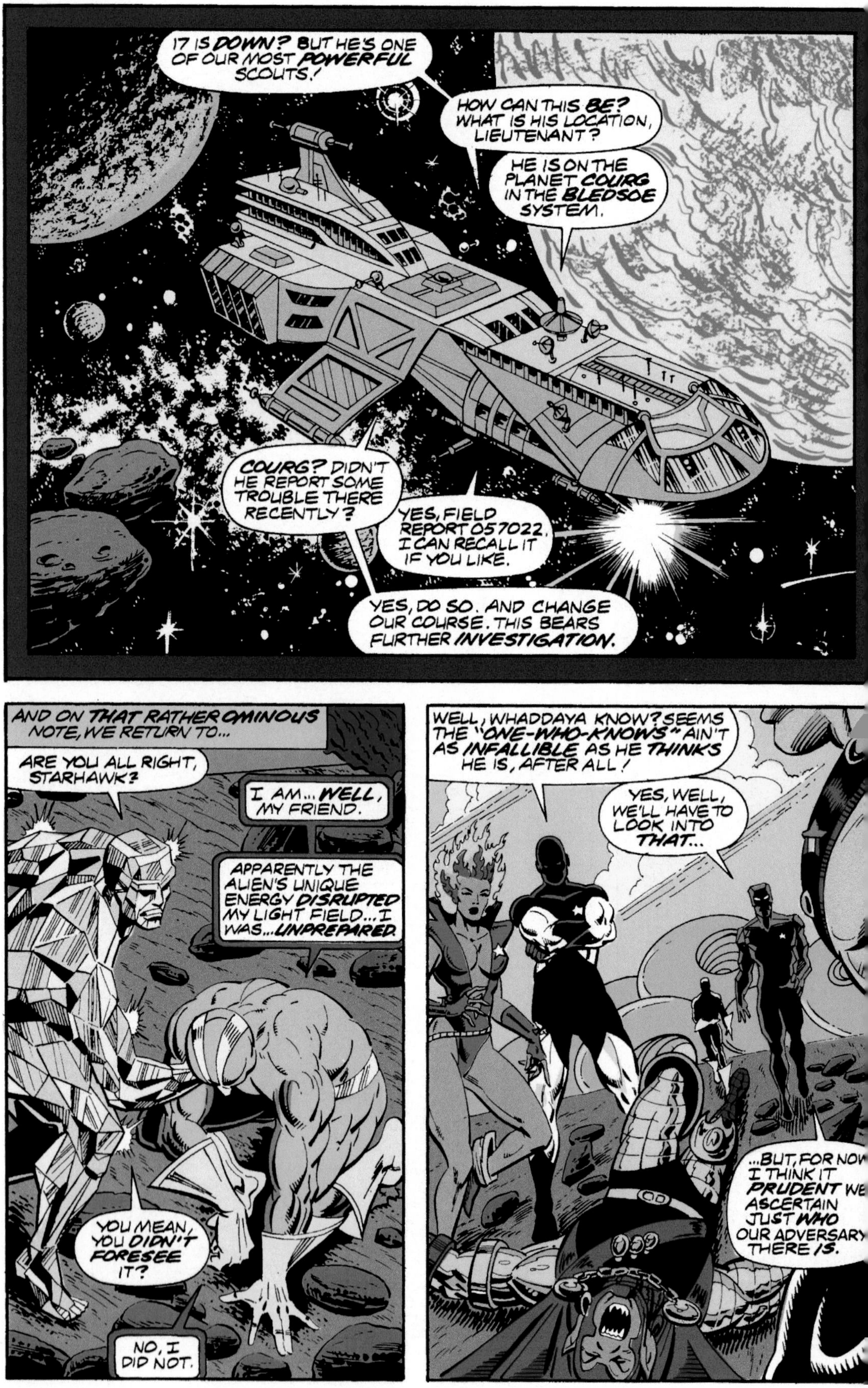
17 IS DOWN? BUT HE'S ONE OF OUR MOST POWERFUL SCOUTS!
HOW CAN THIS BE? WHAT IS HIS LOCATION, LIEUTENANT?
HE IS ON THE PLANET COURG IN THE BLEDSOE SYSTEM.
COURG? DIDN'T HE REPORT SOME TROUBLE THERE RECENTLY?
YES, FIELD REPORT 057022. I CAN RECALL IT IF YOU LIKE.
YES, DO SO. AND CHANGE OUR COURSE. THIS BEARS FURTHER INVESTIGATION.
AND ON THAT RATHER OMINOUS NOTE, WE RETURN TO...
ARE YOU ALL RIGHT, STARHAWK?
I AM... WELL, MY FRIEND.
APPARENTLY THE ALIEN'S UNIQUE ENERGY DISRUPTED MY LIGHT FIELD... I WAS... UNPREPARED.
YOU MEAN, YOU DIDN'T FORESEE IT?
NO, I DID NOT.
WELL, WHADDAYA KNOW? SEEMS THE "ONE-WHO-KNOWS" AIN'T AS INFALLIBLE AS HE THINKS HE IS, AFTER ALL!
YES, WELL, WE'LL HAVE TO LOOK INTO THAT...
...BUT, FOR NOW I THINK IT PRUDENT WE ASCERTAIN JUST WHO OUR ADVERSARY THERE IS.

ANY IDEAS, PEOPLE? VANCE? CHARLIE?

HE'S A TOUGH LITTLE SOD, THAT'S ALL I KNOW!

WELL, THIS IS GONNA SOUND CRAZY, BUT...

...HIS ARMOR, HIS BLASTERS... HE SORT OF REMINDS ME OF... IRON MAN!

THE 20TH CENTURY AVENGER? BUT THAT'S IMPOSSIBLE, ISN'T IT? HOW COULD AN ALIEN THIS FAR FROM EARTH GET IRON MAN'S TECHNOLOGY?

I DUNNO, NIK. I GUESS WE'LL JUST HAVE TO WAKE HIM UP TO FIND OUT WHO HE IS!

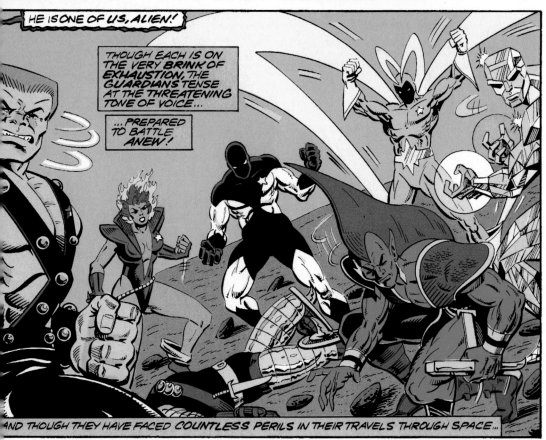

HE IS ONE OF US, ALIEN!

THOUGH EACH IS ON THE VERY BRINK OF EXHAUSTION, THE GUARDIANS TENSE AT THE THREATENING TONE OF VOICE...

...PREPARED TO BATTLE ANEW!

AND THOUGH THEY HAVE FACED COUNTLESS PERILS IN THEIR TRAVELS THROUGH SPACE...

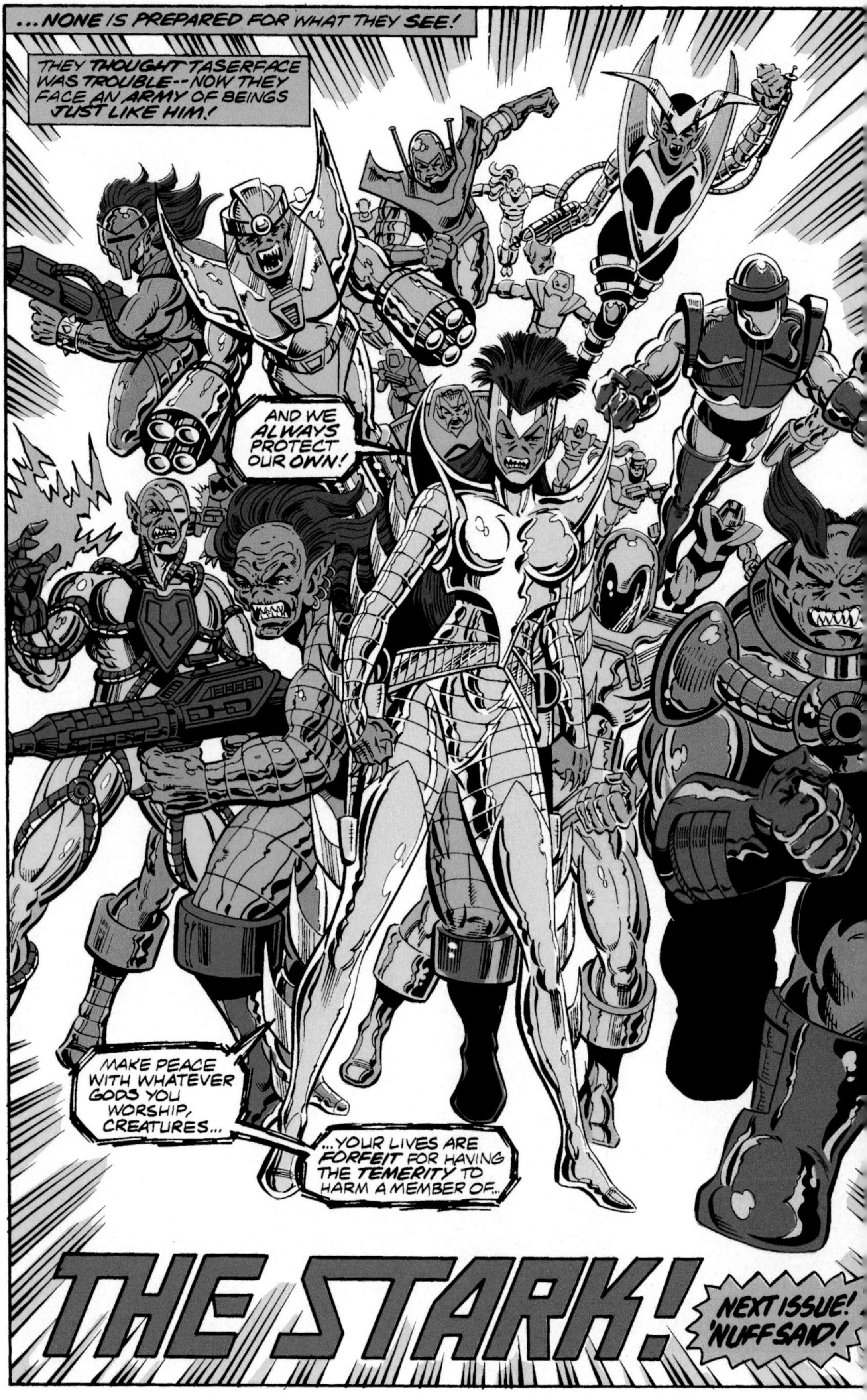
...NONE IS PREPARED FOR WHAT THEY SEE!
THEY THOUGHT TASERFACE WAS TROUBLE--NOW THEY FACE AN ARMY OF BEINGS JUST LIKE HIM!
AND WE ALWAYS PROTECT OUR OWN!
MAKE PEACE WITH WHATEVER GODS YOU WORSHIP, CREATURES...
...YOUR LIVES ARE FORFEIT FOR HAVING THE TEMERITY TO HARM A MEMBER OF...
THE STARK!
NEXT ISSUE! 'NUFF SAID!

Two titanic teams unite like you've never seen before as the Guardians of the Galaxy assemble side-by-side with the mighty Avengers!

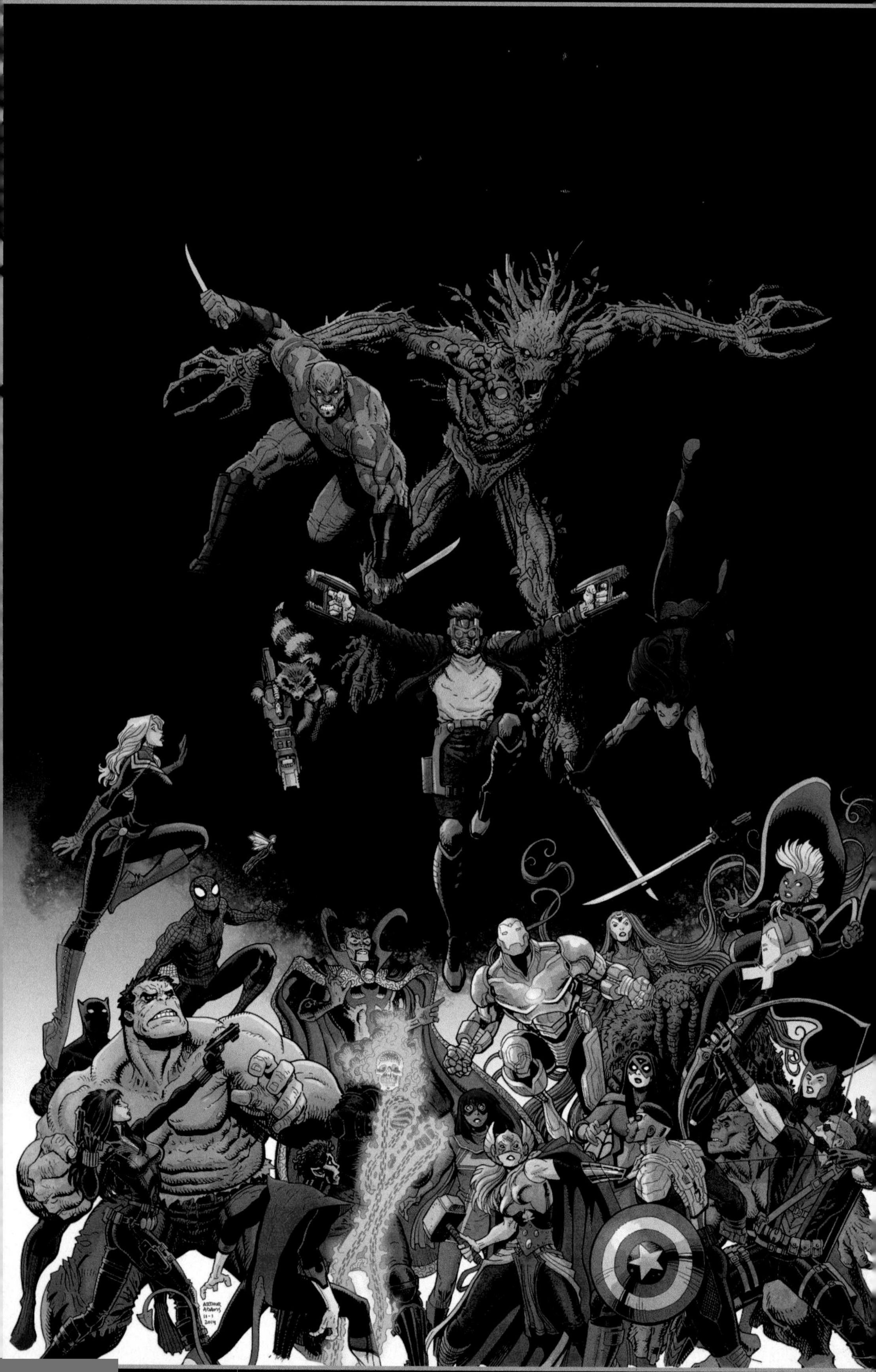

ARTHUR ADAMS 11-1 2014

GU R #1

E ENTIRE GALAXY IS A MESS. WARRING EMPIRES AND COSMIC TERRORISTS PLAGUE ERY CORNER. SOMEONE HAS TO RISE ABOVE IT ALL AND FIGHT FOR THOSE WHO HAVE NO ONE TO FIGHT FOR THEM.

E GUARDIANS OF THE GALAXY ARE PETER QUILL A.K.A. STAR-LORD, GAMORA, THE ST DANGEROUS WOMAN IN THE UNIVERSE, DRAX THE DESTROYER, THE MYSTERIOUS WARRIOR ANGELA, VENOM, CAPTAIN MARVEL, ROCKET RACCOON AND GROOT.

PREVIOUSLY IN...

GUARDIANS OF THE GALAXY

E GUARDIANS THEMSELVES HAVE BEEN STRAINED OVER RECENT CONFESSIONS OF PAST INS. PETER OUSTED HIS CRIMINAL FATHER AS THE PRESIDENT OF THE SPARTAX EMPIRE.

| AR-LORD | GAMORA | DRAX | ANGELA | VENOM | CAPTAIN MARVEL | ROCKET RACOON | GROOT |

RIAN M. BENDIS
WRITER

PAUL MOUNTS
COLORIST

**ART ADAMS &
IAN HERRING**
COVER

KATIE KUBERT
EDITOR

ART ADAMS
PENCILLER

VC'S CORY PETIT
LETTERER

**SKOTTIE YOUNG,
PASQUALE FERRY
& JOSE LADRONN**
VARIANT COVERS

MIKE MARTS
GROUP EDITOR

with SPECIAL THANKS to
JOYCE CHIN

AXEL ALONSO EDITOR IN CHIEF **JOE QUESADA** CHIEF CREATIVE OFFICER
DAN BUCKLEY PUBLISHER **ALAN FINE** EXECUTIVE PRODUCER

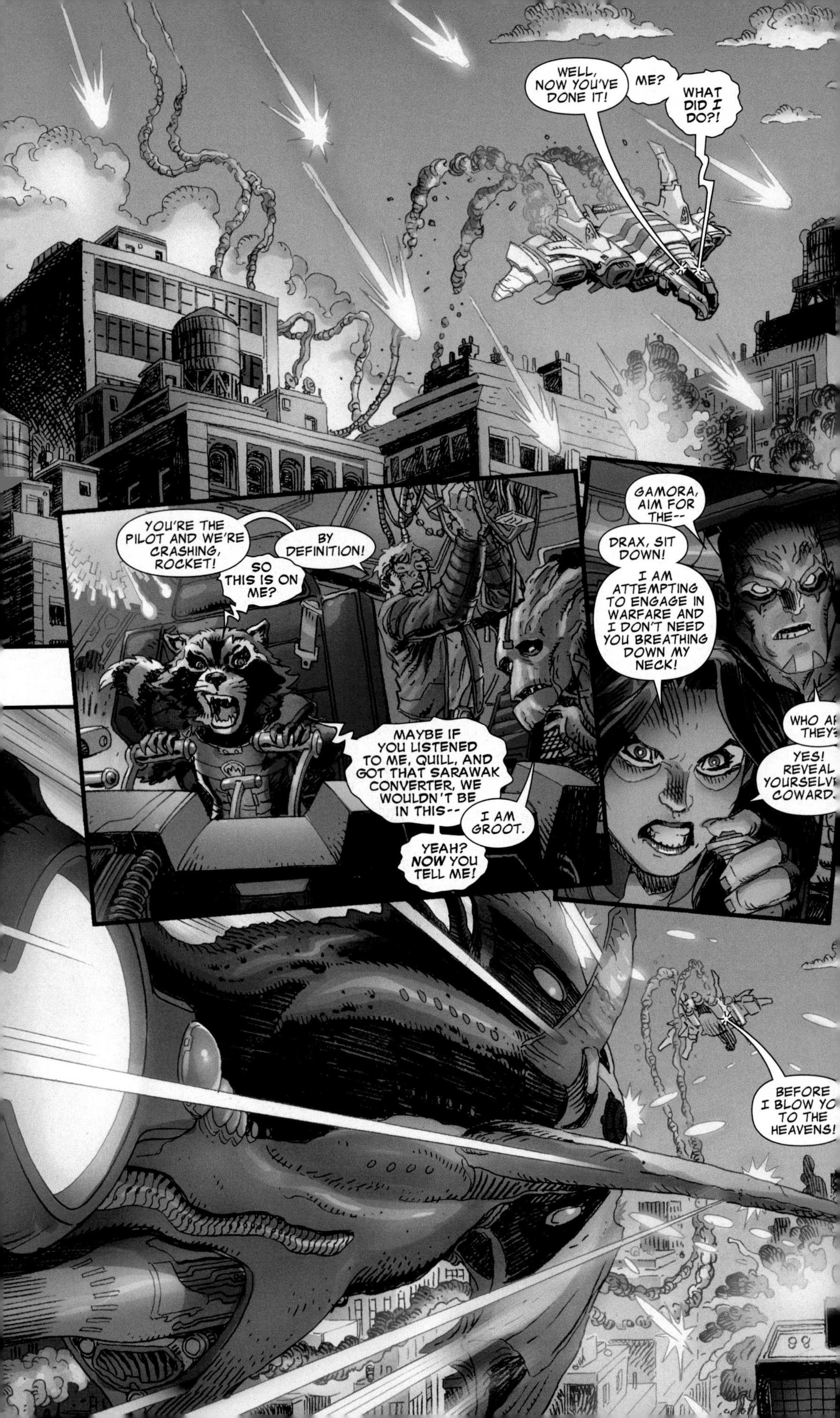
WELL, NOW YOU'VE DONE IT!
ME?
WHAT DID I DO?!
YOU'RE THE PILOT AND WE'RE CRASHING, ROCKET!
BY DEFINITION!
SO THIS IS ON ME?
MAYBE IF YOU LISTENED TO ME, QUILL, AND GOT THAT SARAWAK CONVERTER, WE WOULDN'T BE IN THIS--
I AM GROOT.
YEAH? NOW YOU TELL ME!
GAMORA, AIM FOR THE--
DRAX, SIT DOWN!
I AM ATTEMPTING TO ENGAGE IN WARFARE AND I DON'T NEED YOU BREATHING DOWN MY NECK!
YES! REVEAL
COWARD.
BEFORE
TO THE HEAVENS!

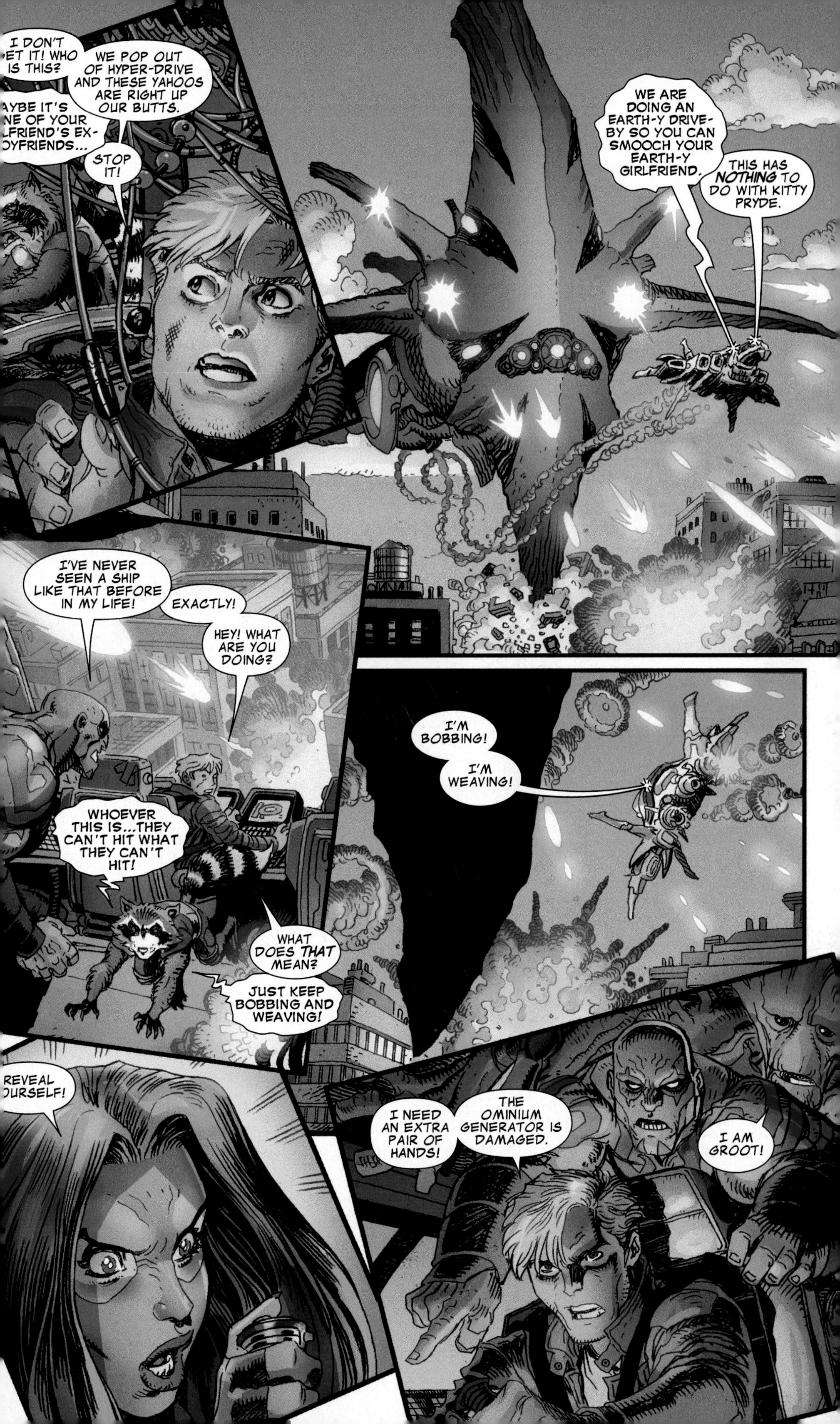

I DON'T ET IT! WHO IS THIS?
WE POP OUT OF HYPER-DRIVE AND THESE YAHOOS ARE RIGHT UP OUR BUTTS.
AYBE IT'S NE OF YOUR LFRIEND'S EX- OYFRIENDS...
STOP IT!
WE ARE DOING AN EARTH-Y DRIVE-BY SO YOU CAN SMOOCH YOUR EARTH-Y GIRLFRIEND.
THIS HAS *NOTHING* TO DO WITH KITTY PRYDE.
I'VE NEVER SEEN A SHIP LIKE THAT BEFORE IN MY LIFE!
EXACTLY!
HEY! WHAT ARE YOU DOING?
WHOEVER THIS IS...THEY CAN'T HIT WHAT THEY CAN'T HIT!
WHAT DOES *THAT* MEAN?
JUST KEEP BOBBING AND WEAVING!
I'M BOBBING!
I'M WEAVING!
REVEAL OURSELF!
I NEED AN EXTRA PAIR OF HANDS!
THE OMINIUM GENERATOR IS DAMAGED.
I AM GROOT!

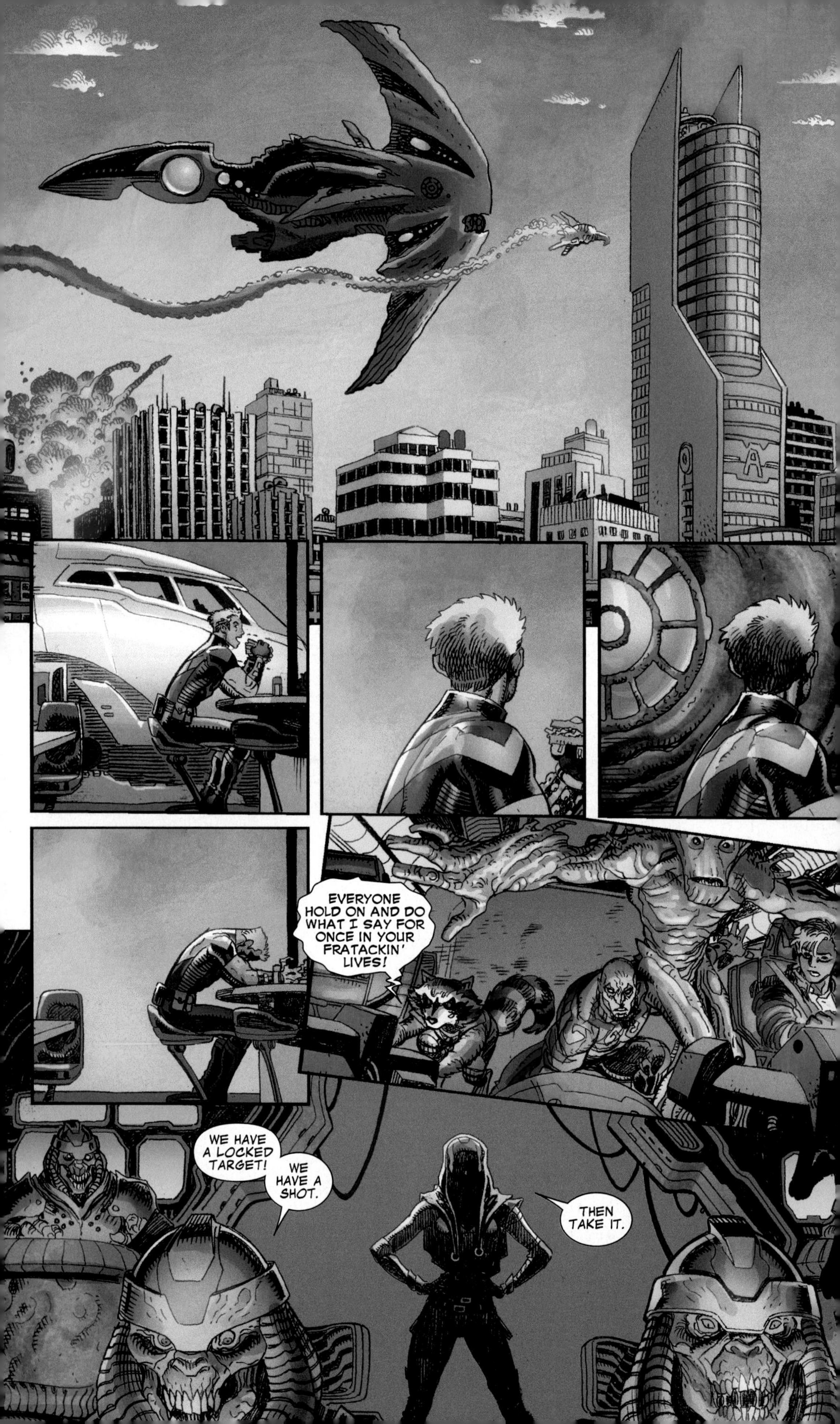
EVERYONE HOLD ON AND DO WHAT I SAY FOR ONCE IN YOUR FRATACKIN' LIVES!
WE HAVE A LOCKED TARGET!
WE HAVE A SHOT.
THEN TAKE IT.

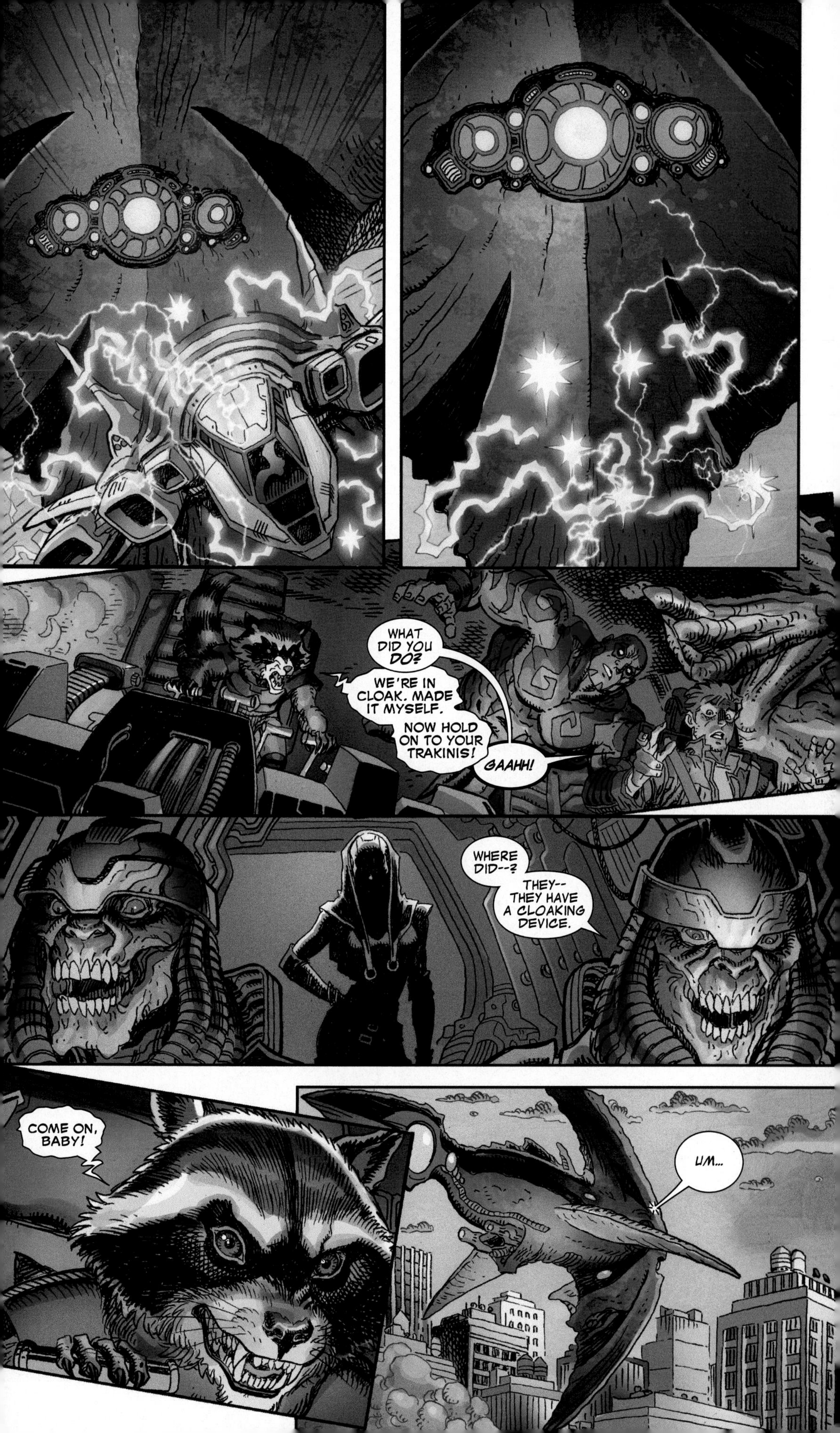

WHAT DID YOU DO?
WE'RE IN CLOAK. MADE IT MYSELF.
NOW HOLD ON TO YOUR TRAKINIS!
GAAHH!
WHERE DID--?
THEY-- THEY HAVE A CLOAKING DEVICE.
COME ON, BABY!
UM...

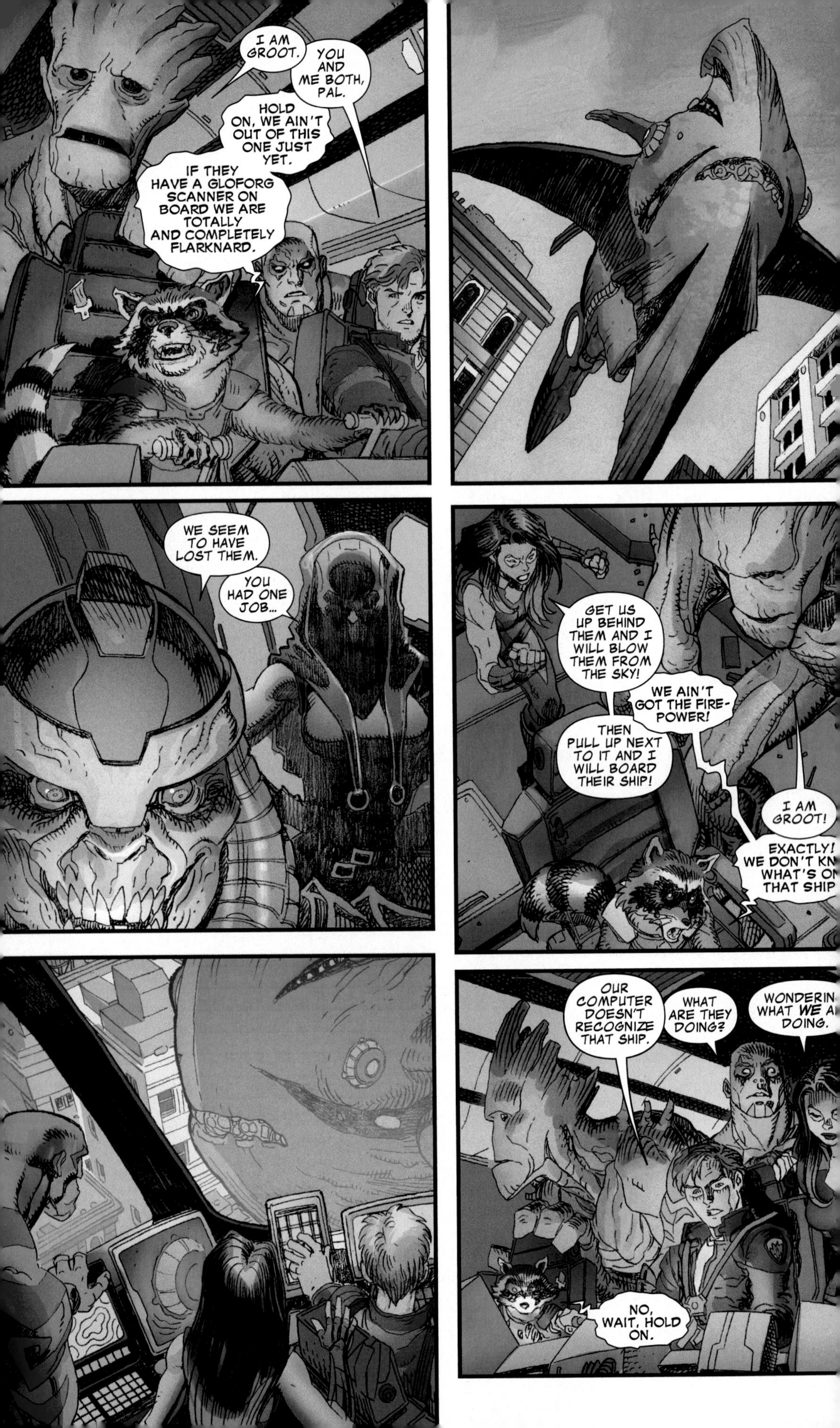
I AM GROOT.
YOU AND ME BOTH, PAL.
HOLD ON, WE AIN'T OUT OF THIS ONE JUST YET.
IF THEY HAVE A GLOFORG SCANNER ON BOARD WE ARE TOTALLY AND COMPLETELY FLARKNARD.
WE SEEM TO HAVE LOST THEM.
YOU HAD ONE JOB...
GET US UP BEHIND THEM AND I WILL BLOW THEM FROM THE SKY!
WE AIN'T GOT THE FIRE-POWER!
THEN PULL UP NEXT TO IT AND I WILL BOARD THEIR SHIP!
I AM GROOT!
EXACTLY! WE DON'T KN WHAT'S O THAT SHIP
OUR COMPUTER DOESN'T RECOGNIZE THAT SHIP.
WHAT ARE THEY DOING?
WONDERIN WHAT WE A DOING.
NO, WAIT, HOLD ON.

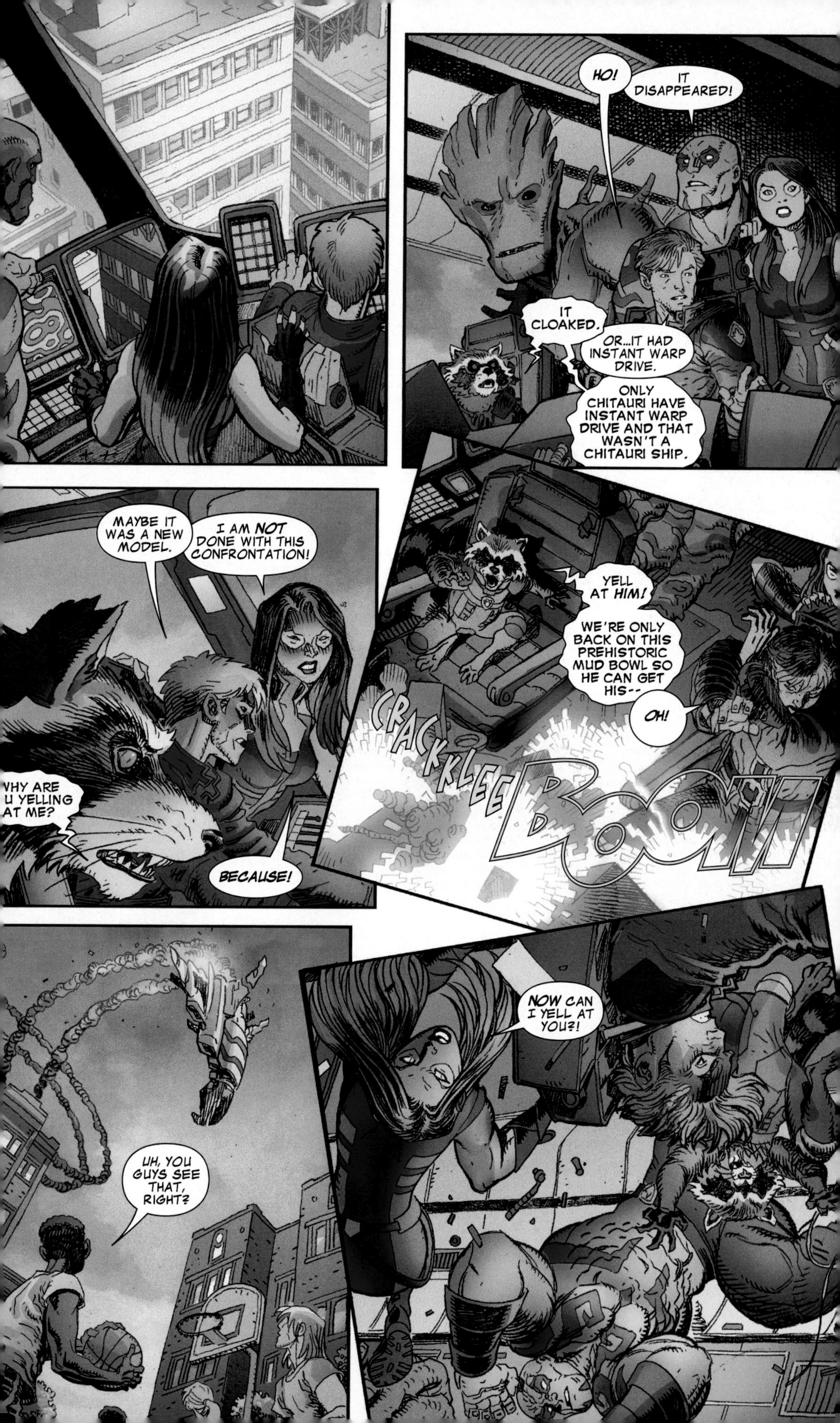
HO!
IT DISAPPEARED!
IT CLOAKED.
OR...IT HAD INSTANT WARP DRIVE.
ONLY CHITAURI HAVE INSTANT WARP DRIVE AND THAT WASN'T A CHITAURI SHIP.
MAYBE IT WAS A NEW MODEL.
I AM NOT DONE WITH THIS CONFRONTATION!
WHY ARE U YELLING AT ME?
BECAUSE!
YELL AT HIM!
WE'RE ONLY BACK ON THIS PREHISTORIC MUD BOWL SO HE CAN GET HIS--
OH!
CRACKLEE
BOOM
UH, YOU GUYS SEE THAT, RIGHT?
NOW CAN I YELL AT YOU?!

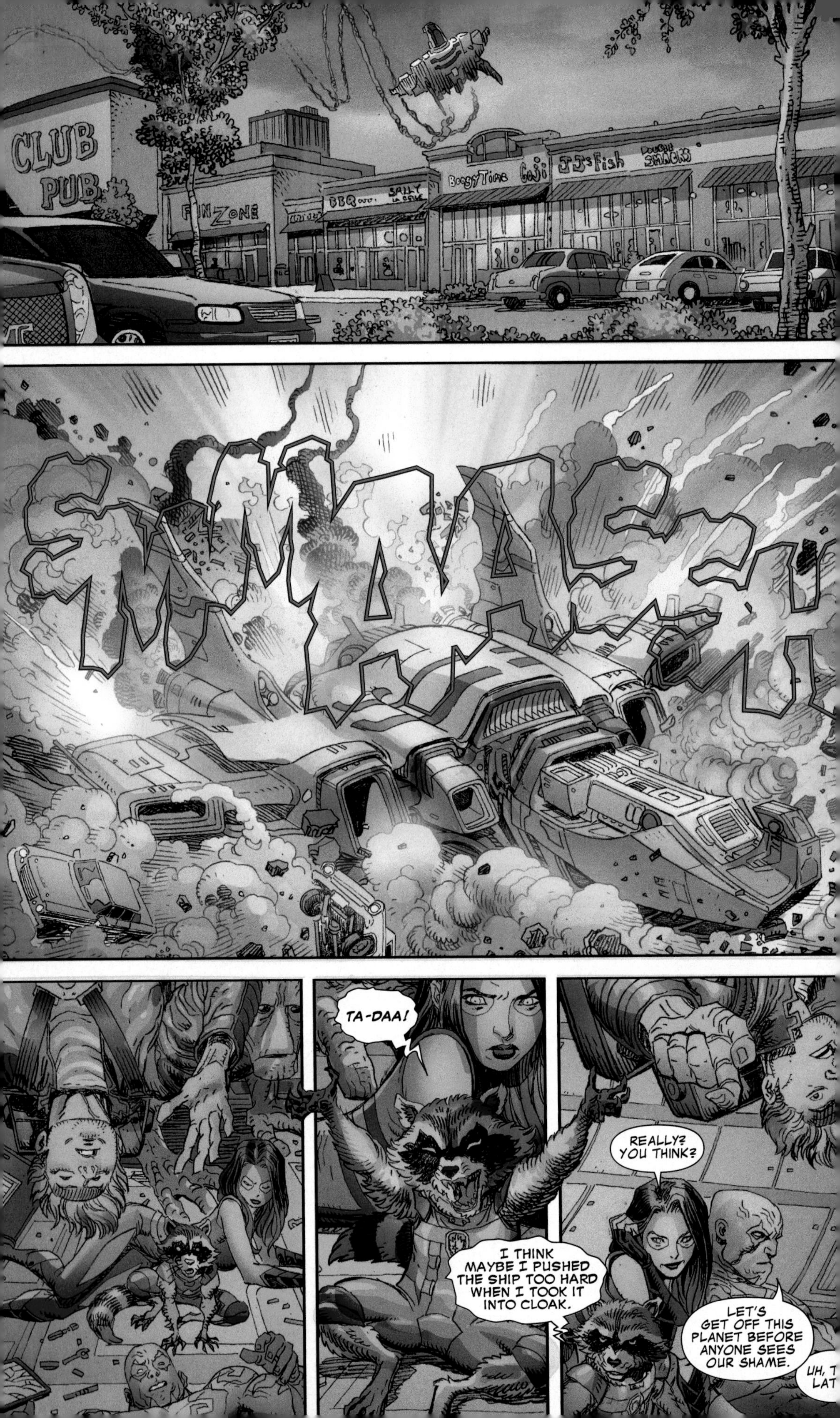
CLUB PUB
FUN ZONE
BBQ
SALLY
Boogy Time
Goji
JJ's Fish
DOUBLE SNACKS
TA-DAA!
I THINK MAYBE I PUSHED THE SHIP TOO HARD WHEN I TOOK IT INTO CLOAK.
REALLY? YOU THINK?
LET'S GET OFF THIS PLANET BEFORE ANYONE SEES OUR SHAME.

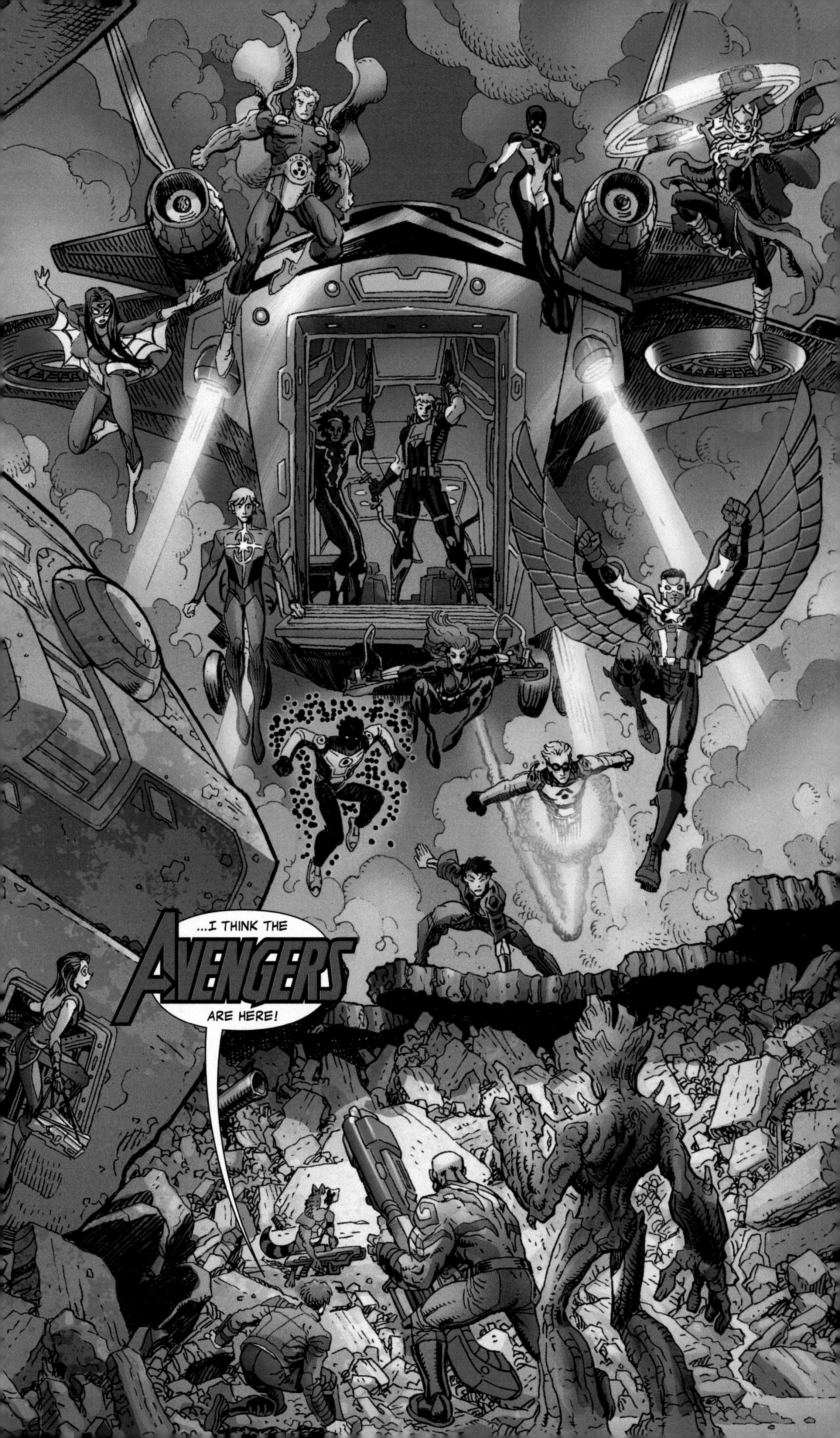

...I THINK THE AVENGERS ARE HERE!

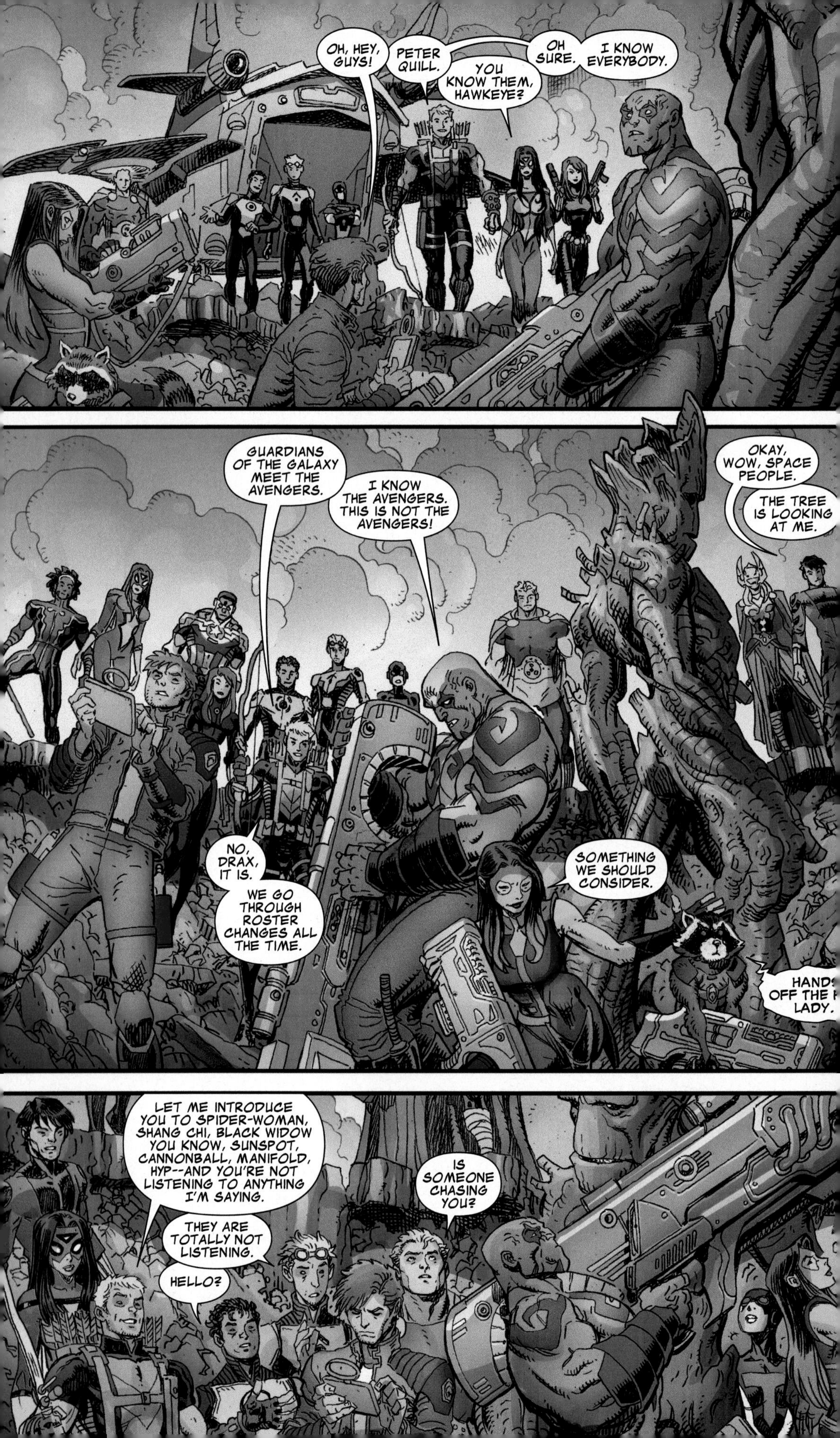
OH, HEY, GUYS!
PETER QUILL.
YOU KNOW THEM, HAWKEYE?
OH SURE.
I KNOW EVERYBODY.
GUARDIANS OF THE GALAXY MEET THE AVENGERS.
I KNOW THE AVENGERS. THIS IS NOT THE AVENGERS!
OKAY, WOW, SPACE PEOPLE.
THE TREE IS LOOKING AT ME.
NO, DRAX, IT IS.
WE GO THROUGH ROSTER CHANGES ALL THE TIME.
SOMETHING WE SHOULD CONSIDER.
LET ME INTRODUCE YOU TO SPIDER-WOMAN, SHANG CHI, BLACK WIDOW YOU KNOW, SUNSPOT, CANNONBALL, MANIFOLD, HYP--AND YOU'RE NOT LISTENING TO ANYTHING I'M SAYING.
IS SOMEONE CHASING YOU?
THEY ARE TOTALLY NOT LISTENING.
HELLO?

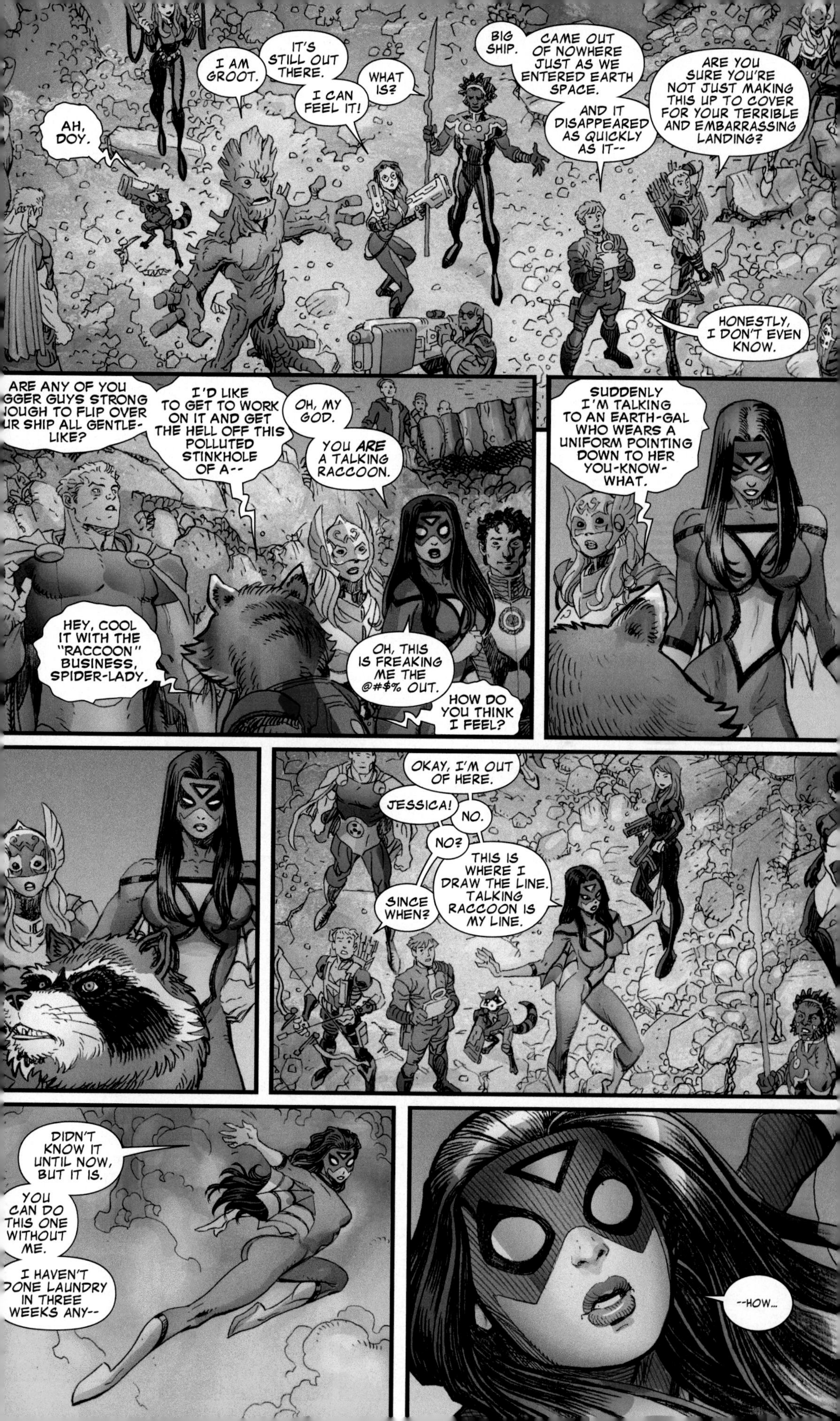
AH, DOY.
I AM GROOT.
IT'S STILL OUT THERE.
I CAN FEEL IT!
WHAT IS?
BIG SHIP.
CAME OUT OF NOWHERE JUST AS WE ENTERED EARTH SPACE.
AND IT DISAPPEARED AS QUICKLY AS IT--
ARE YOU SURE YOU'RE NOT JUST MAKING THIS UP TO COVER FOR YOUR TERRIBLE AND EMBARRASSING LANDING?
HONESTLY, I DON'T EVEN KNOW.
ARE ANY OF YOU GGER GUYS STRONG NOUGH TO FLIP OVER UR SHIP ALL GENTLE-LIKE?
I'D LIKE TO GET TO WORK ON IT AND GET THE HELL OFF THIS POLLUTED STINKHOLE OF A--
OH, MY GOD.
YOU **ARE** A TALKING RACCOON.
HEY, COOL IT WITH THE "RACCOON" BUSINESS, SPIDER-LADY.
OH, THIS IS FREAKING ME THE @#$% OUT.
HOW DO YOU THINK I FEEL?
SUDDENLY I'M TALKING TO AN EARTH-GAL WHO WEARS A UNIFORM POINTING DOWN TO HER YOU-KNOW-WHAT.
OKAY, I'M OUT OF HERE.
JESSICA!
NO.
NO?
THIS IS WHERE I DRAW THE LINE. TALKING RACCOON IS MY LINE.
SINCE WHEN?
DIDN'T KNOW IT UNTIL NOW, BUT IT IS.
YOU CAN DO THIS ONE WITHOUT ME.
I HAVEN'T DONE LAUNDRY IN THREE WEEKS ANY--
--HOW...

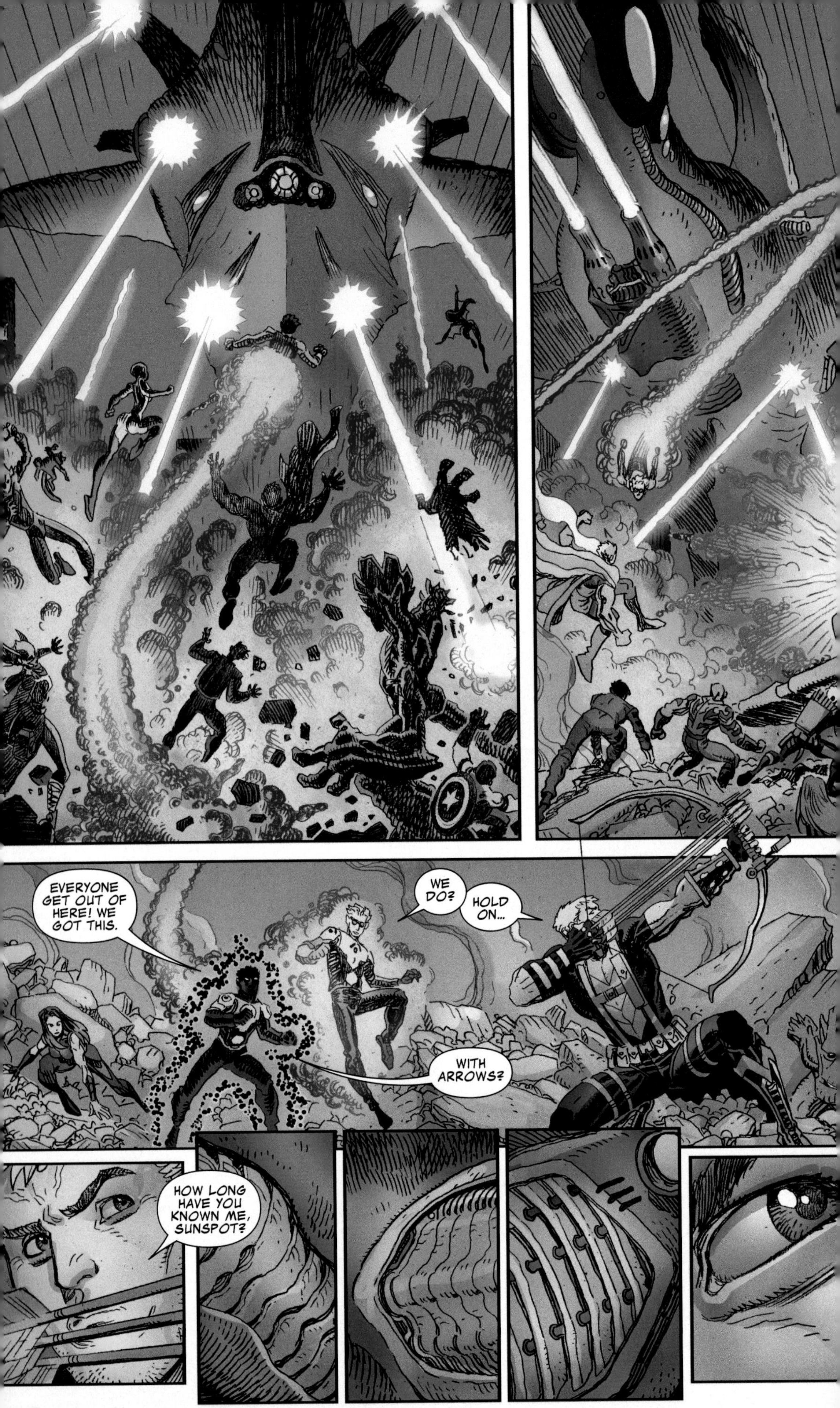
EVERYONE GET OUT OF HERE! WE GOT THIS.
WE DO?
HOLD ON...
WITH ARROWS?
HOW LONG HAVE YOU KNOWN ME, SUNSPOT?

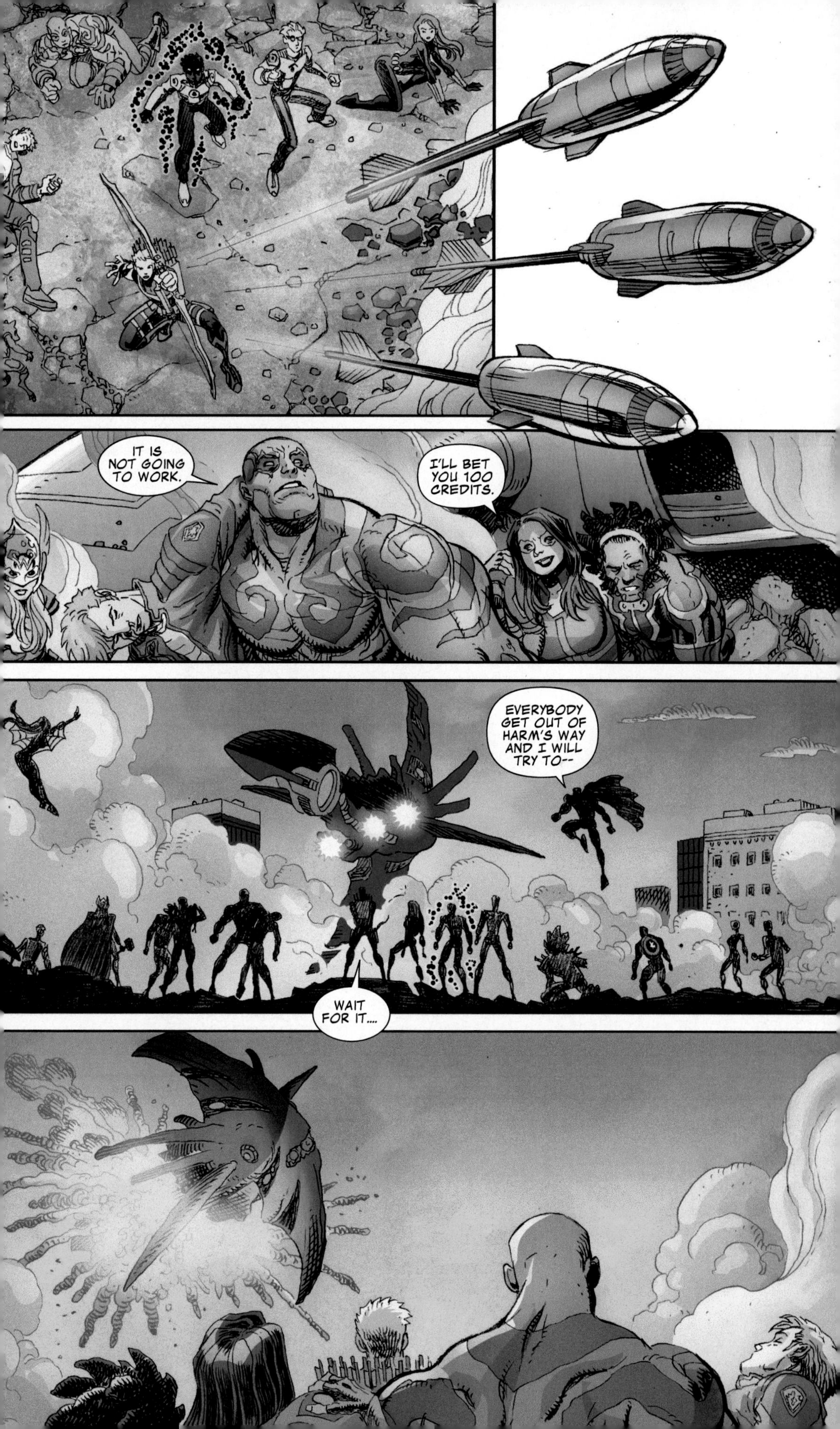
IT IS NOT GOING TO WORK.
I'LL BET YOU 100 CREDITS.
EVERYBODY GET OUT OF HARM'S WAY AND I WILL TRY TO--
WAIT FOR IT....

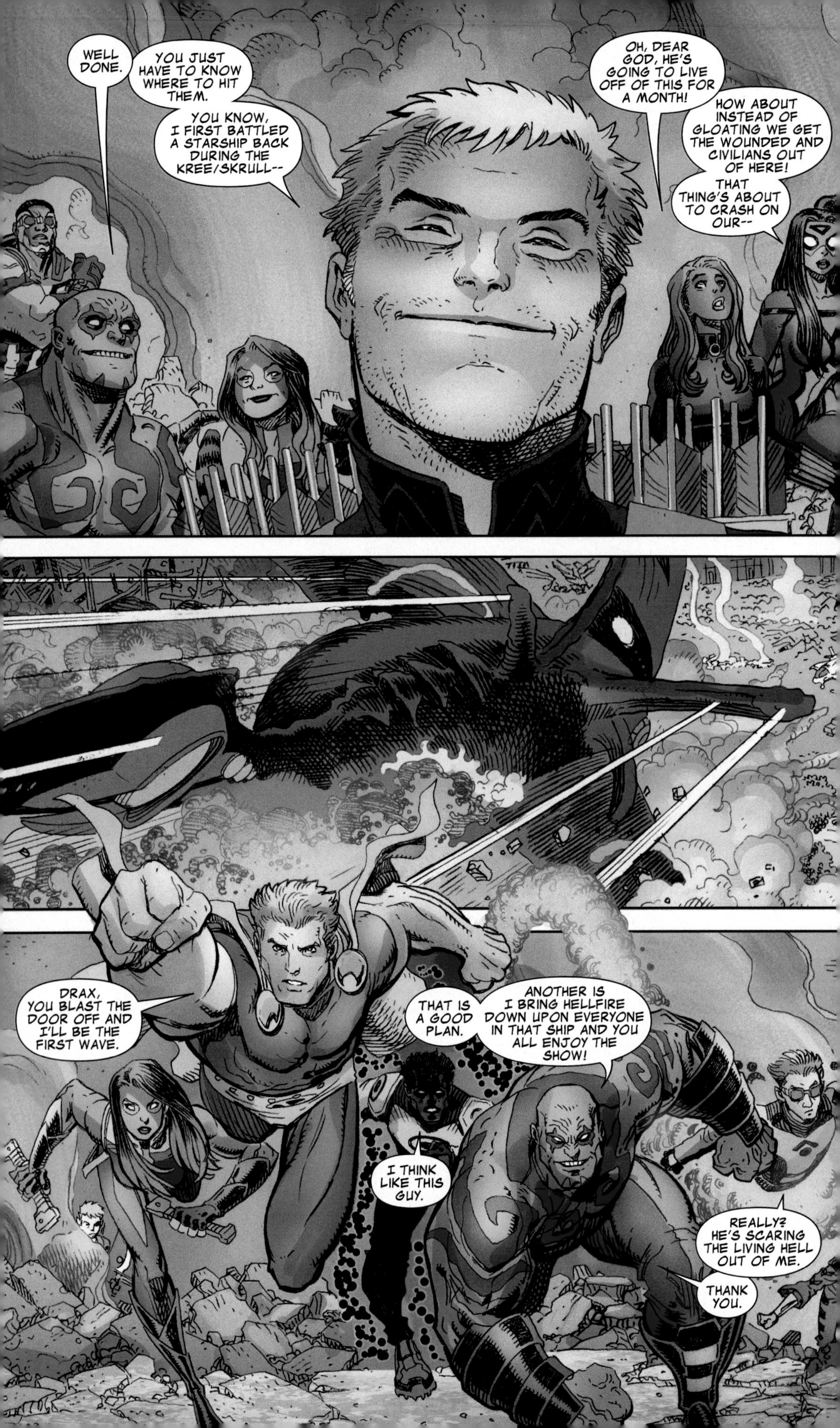
WELL DONE.
YOU JUST HAVE TO KNOW WHERE TO HIT THEM.
YOU KNOW, I FIRST BATTLED A STARSHIP BACK DURING THE KREE/SKRULL--
OH, DEAR GOD, HE'S GOING TO LIVE OFF OF THIS FOR A MONTH!
HOW ABOUT INSTEAD OF GLOATING WE GET THE WOUNDED AND CIVILIANS OUT OF HERE!
THAT THING'S ABOUT TO CRASH ON OUR--
DRAX, YOU BLAST THE DOOR OFF AND I'LL BE THE FIRST WAVE.
THAT IS A GOOD PLAN.
ANOTHER IS I BRING HELLFIRE DOWN UPON EVERYONE IN THAT SHIP AND YOU ALL ENJOY THE SHOW!
I THINK LIKE THIS GUY.
REALLY? HE'S SCARING THE LIVING HELL OUT OF ME.
THANK YOU.

CHITAURI!!

GESUNDHEIT!

ᴴᴼᵞᴱᔕ ᙭ᴹᴬᴸᔕ ᔕᴼᴬ ᴳᴬᴱᴳᴹᔕ ᙭ᴹᴬᴸ

ᴬᴹᴮᴱᴹ ᴵᔕ ᴹᴱᴵᔕᴹ ᙭ᔕ ᴼᴬ ᴹᔕᴵᔕ

H!

WHASGOINON?

ALIEN BATTLE IN A STRIP MALL.

YOU KNOW, SAME OL'.

NO, FOOLISH EARTHER-BABY! CHITAURI!! THAT IS WHO CHALLENGES US.

OKAY, GEEZ, YOU DON'T HAVE TO BE A JERK ABOUT IT.

ᔕᴹᴹ

THIS ESCALATED QUICKLY.

I WAS JUST THINKING THAT.

WHO LEADS YOU DEMONS?

WHO IS YOUR MASTER?!

YOO-HOO!

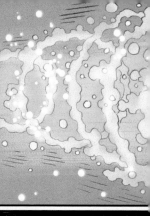

BOOM!

AND *THAT'S* HOW YOU BAKE A-- HEY!

WHAT IS THIS? WHO ARE THESE, UM, PEOPLE?

CHITAURI.

I DON'T KNOW WHAT THAT MEANS.

ALIENS.

I KN... TH...

HAVE AT THEE!

SEE, I COULD NEVER PULL OFF A "HAVE AT THEE."

NOT IN A MILLION YEARS.

WHAT DID YOU DO TO START THIS, STAR-LORD?

I PROMISE YOU, WE DIDN'T DO ANYTHING.

SOMETHING HAPPENED!

THEY JUMPED US. THERE'S NO OTHER WAY TO PUT IT.

I AM...

...GROOT...

TELL ME!

WHY ARE YOU HERE?!

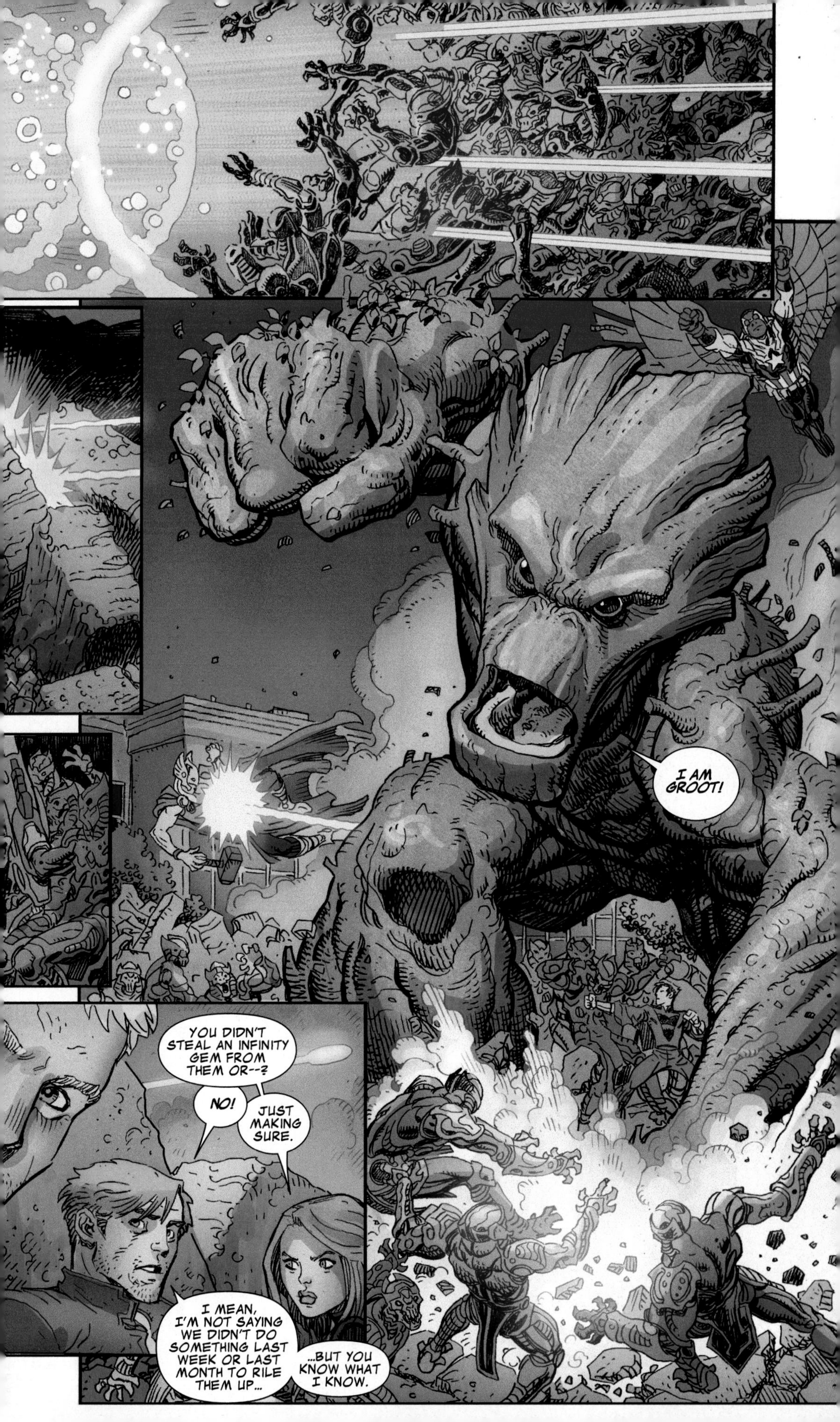
I AM GROOT!
YOU DIDN'T STEAL AN INFINITY GEM FROM THEM OR--?
NO!
JUST MAKING SURE.
I MEAN, I'M NOT SAYING WE DIDN'T DO SOMETHING LAST WEEK OR LAST MONTH TO RILE THEM UP...
...BUT YOU KNOW WHAT I KNOW.

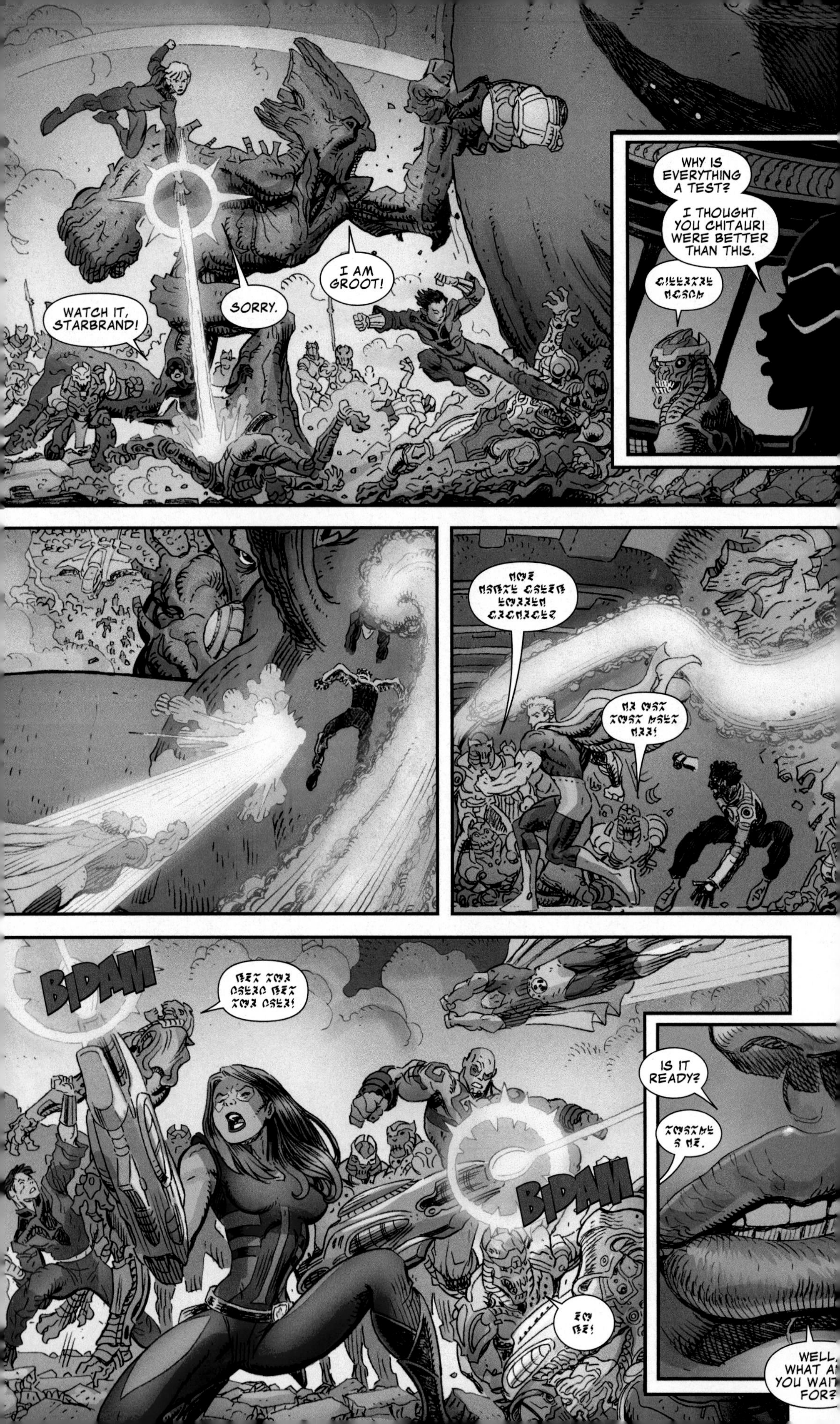
WATCH IT, STARBRAND!
SORRY.
I AM GROOT!
WHY IS EVERYTHING A TEST?
I THOUGHT YOU CHITAURI WERE BETTER THAN THIS.
BIDAM
BIDAM
IS IT READY?
WELL, WHAT A YOU WAIT FOR?

HABEQY IE QAIZM! IYE MEQEYXQ ZOZQMEYX!

BIDAM BIDAM

QIQEX XEKA QIQEX EXQOZX

SXIE! MAME

UM...

ARE THEY RETREATING?

HYPERION! STARBRAND! HELP THEM!

NOW.

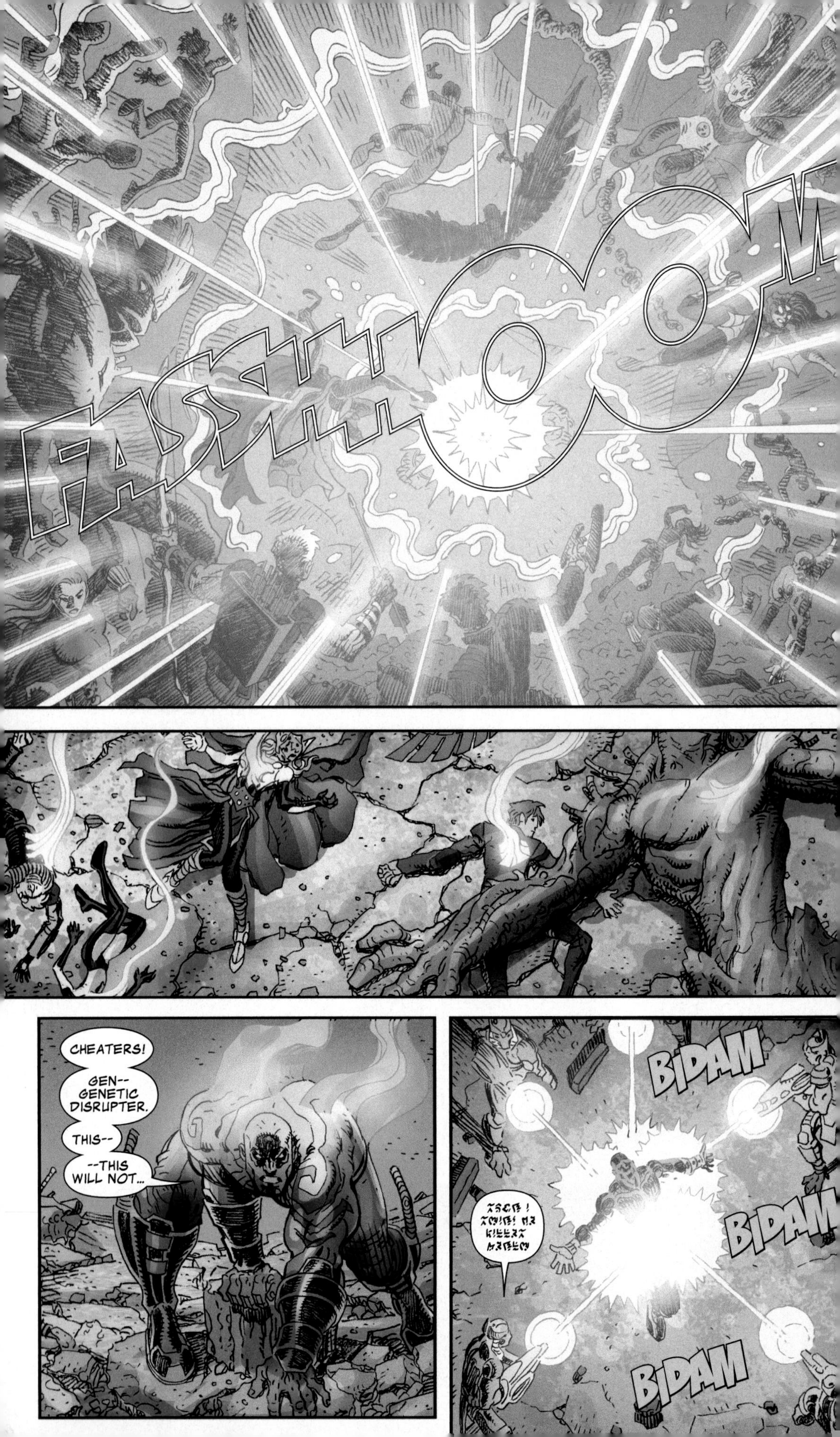
FASSHHOOM
CHEATERS!
GEN-- GENETIC DISRUPTER.
THIS--
--THIS WILL NOT...
BIDAM
BIDAM
BIDAM

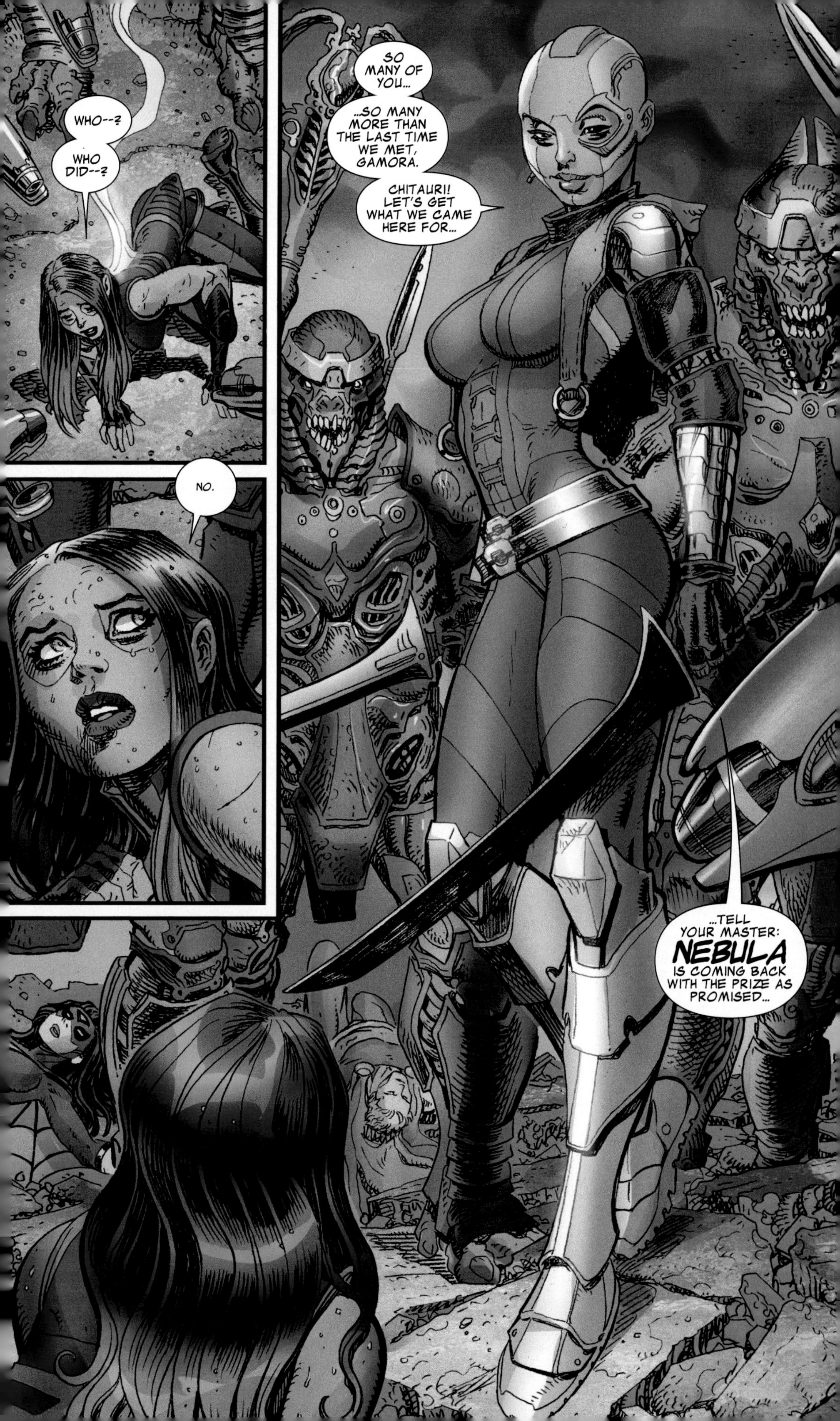
WHO--?
WHO DID--?
SO MANY OF YOU...
...SO MANY MORE THAN THE LAST TIME WE MET, GAMORA.
CHITAURI! LET'S GET WHAT WE CAME HERE FOR...
NO.
...TELL YOUR MASTER: NEBULA IS COMING BACK WITH THE PRIZE AS PROMISED...

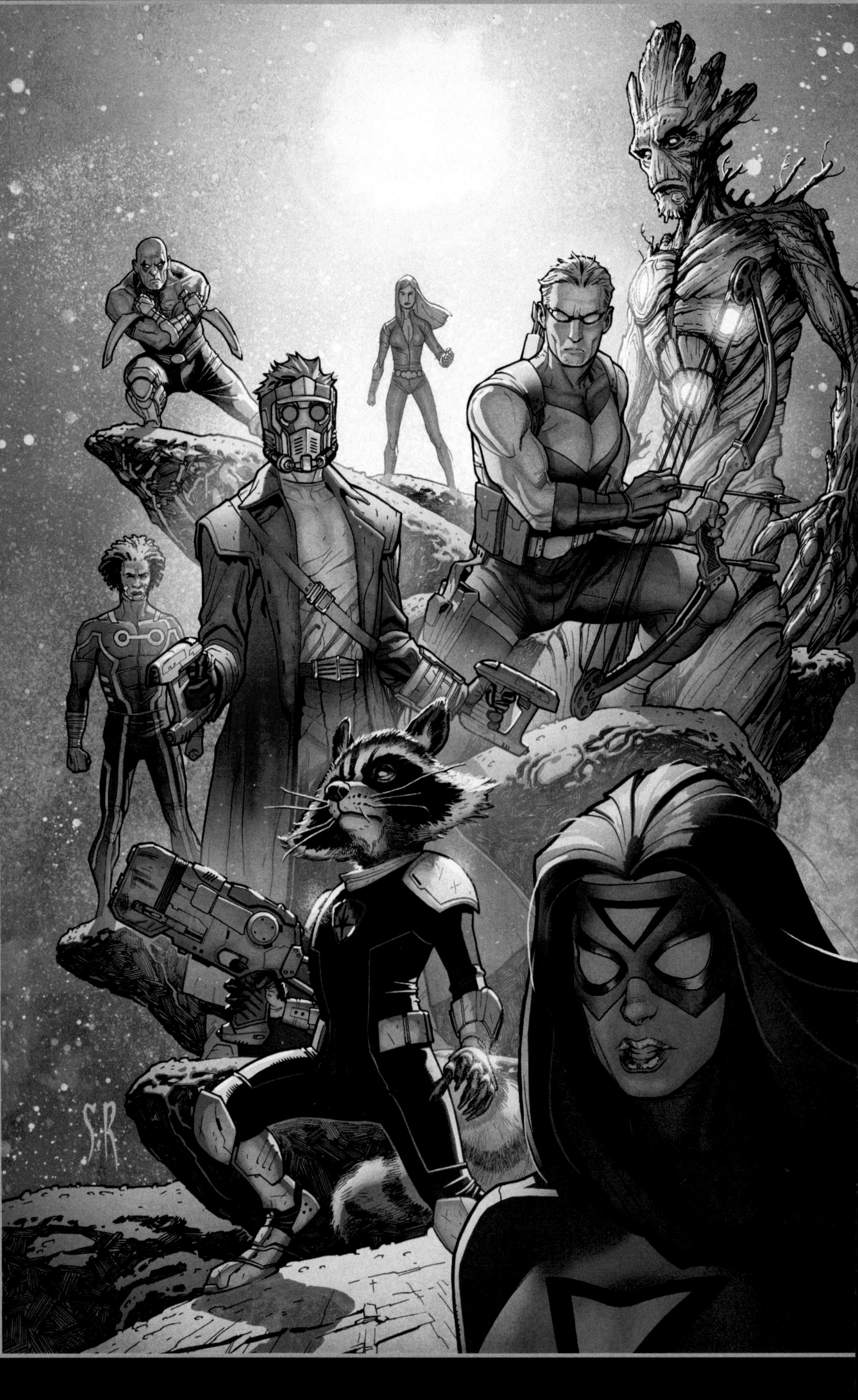

GUARDIANS TEAM-UP #2

THE ENTIRE GALAXY IS A MESS. WARRING EMPIRES AND COSMIC TERRORISTS PLAGUE EVERY CORNER. SOMEONE HAS TO RISE ABOVE IT ALL AND FIGHT FOR THOSE WHO HAVE NO ONE TO FIGHT FOR THEM.

THE GUARDIANS OF THE GALAXY ARE PETER QUILL A.K.A. STAR-LORD, GAMORA, THE MOST DANGEROUS WOMAN IN THE UNIVERSE, DRAX THE DESTROYER, THE MYSTERIOUS WARRIOR ANGELA, VENOM, CAPTAIN MARVEL, ROCKET RACCOON AND GROOT.

PREVIOUSLY IN…

THE AVENGERS AND THE GUARDIANS OF THE GALAXY HAVE A KNOCK-DOWN-DRAG-OUT BATTLE WITH NEBULA AND THE CHITAURI.

       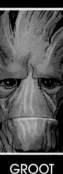

STAR-LORD GAMORA DRAX ANGELA VENOM CAPTAIN MARVEL ROCKET RACCOON GROOT

BRIAN MICHAEL BENDIS
WRITER

STEPHANE ROUX & JAY LEISTEN
ART

BRETT SMITH
COLORIST

VC'S CORY PETIT
LETTERER

STEPHANE ROUX
COVER

PAUL RENAUD
VARIANT COVER

XANDER JAROWEY
ASSISTANT EDITOR

KATIE KUBERT
EDITOR

MIKE MARTS
GROUP EDITOR

AXEL ALONSO EDITOR IN CHIEF **JOE QUESADA** CHIEF CREATIVE OFFICER
DAN BUCKLEY PUBLISHER **ALAN FINE** EXECUTIVE PRODUCER

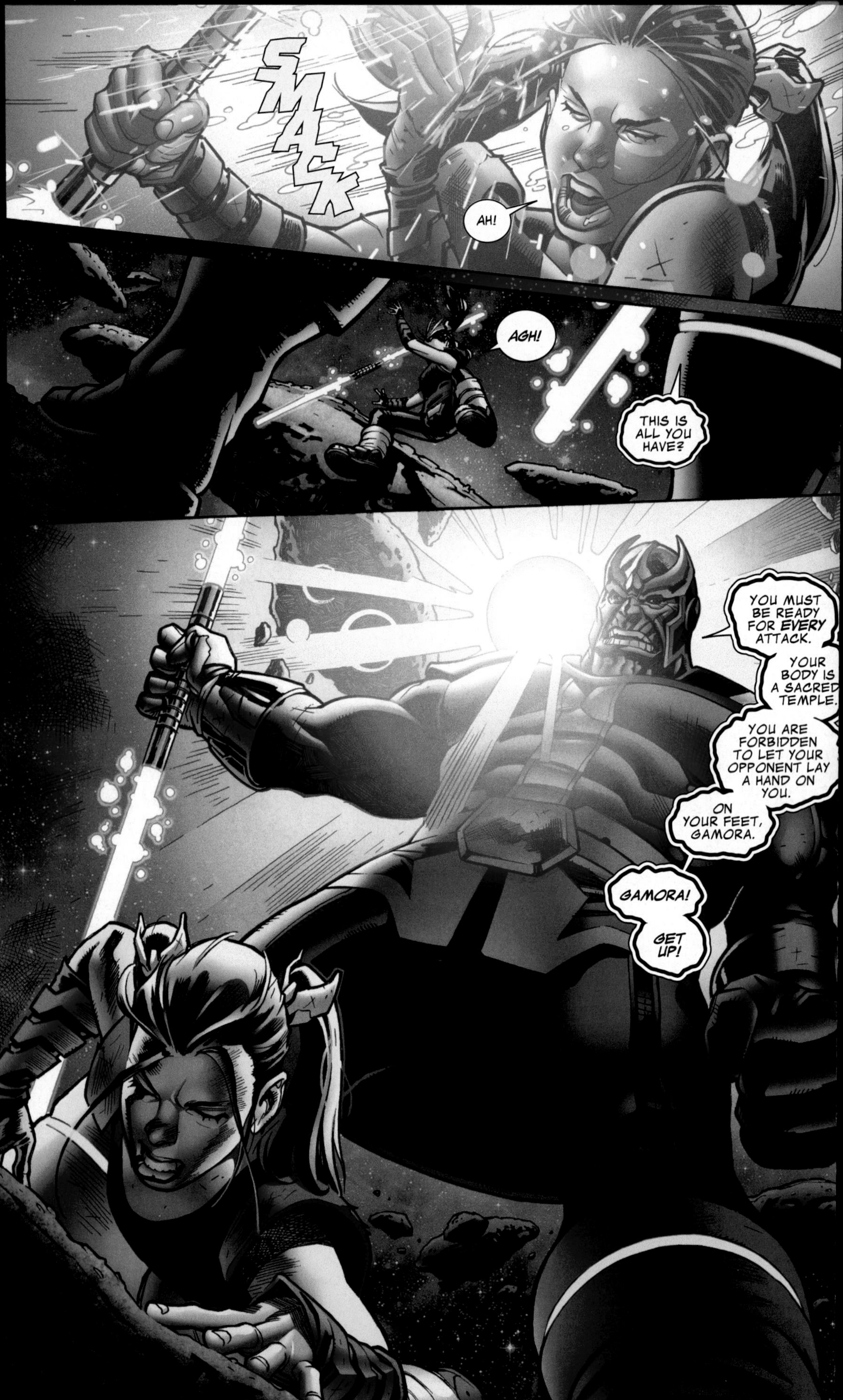
SMACK
AH!
AGH!
THIS IS ALL YOU HAVE?
YOU MUST BE READY FOR EVERY ATTACK.
YOUR BODY IS A SACRED TEMPLE.
YOU ARE FORBIDDEN TO LET YOUR OPPONENT LAY A HAND ON YOU.
ON YOUR FEET, GAMORA.
GAMORA!
GET UP!

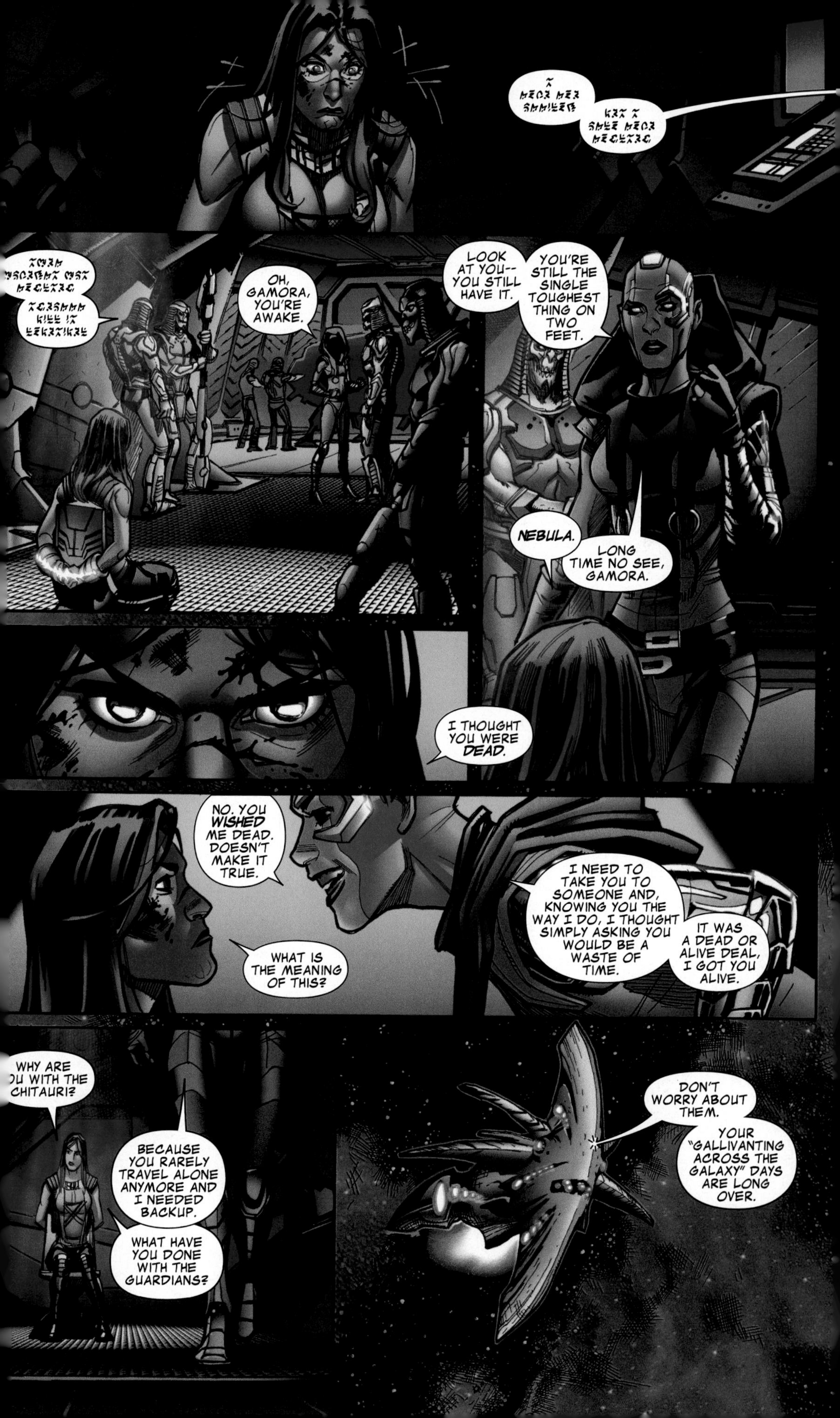
OH, GAMORA, YOU'RE AWAKE.
LOOK AT YOU-- YOU STILL HAVE IT.
YOU'RE STILL THE SINGLE TOUGHEST THING ON TWO FEET.
NEBULA.
LONG TIME NO SEE, GAMORA.
I THOUGHT YOU WERE DEAD.
NO. YOU WISHED ME DEAD. DOESN'T MAKE IT TRUE.
WHAT IS THE MEANING OF THIS?
I NEED TO TAKE YOU TO SOMEONE AND, KNOWING YOU THE WAY I DO, I THOUGHT SIMPLY ASKING YOU WOULD BE A WASTE OF TIME.
IT WAS A DEAD OR ALIVE DEAL, I GOT YOU ALIVE.
WHY ARE OU WITH THE CHITAURI?
BECAUSE YOU RARELY TRAVEL ALONE ANYMORE AND I NEEDED BACKUP.
WHAT HAVE YOU DONE WITH THE GUARDIANS?
DON'T WORRY ABOUT THEM.
YOUR "GALLIVANTING ACROSS THE GALAXY" DAYS ARE LONG OVER.

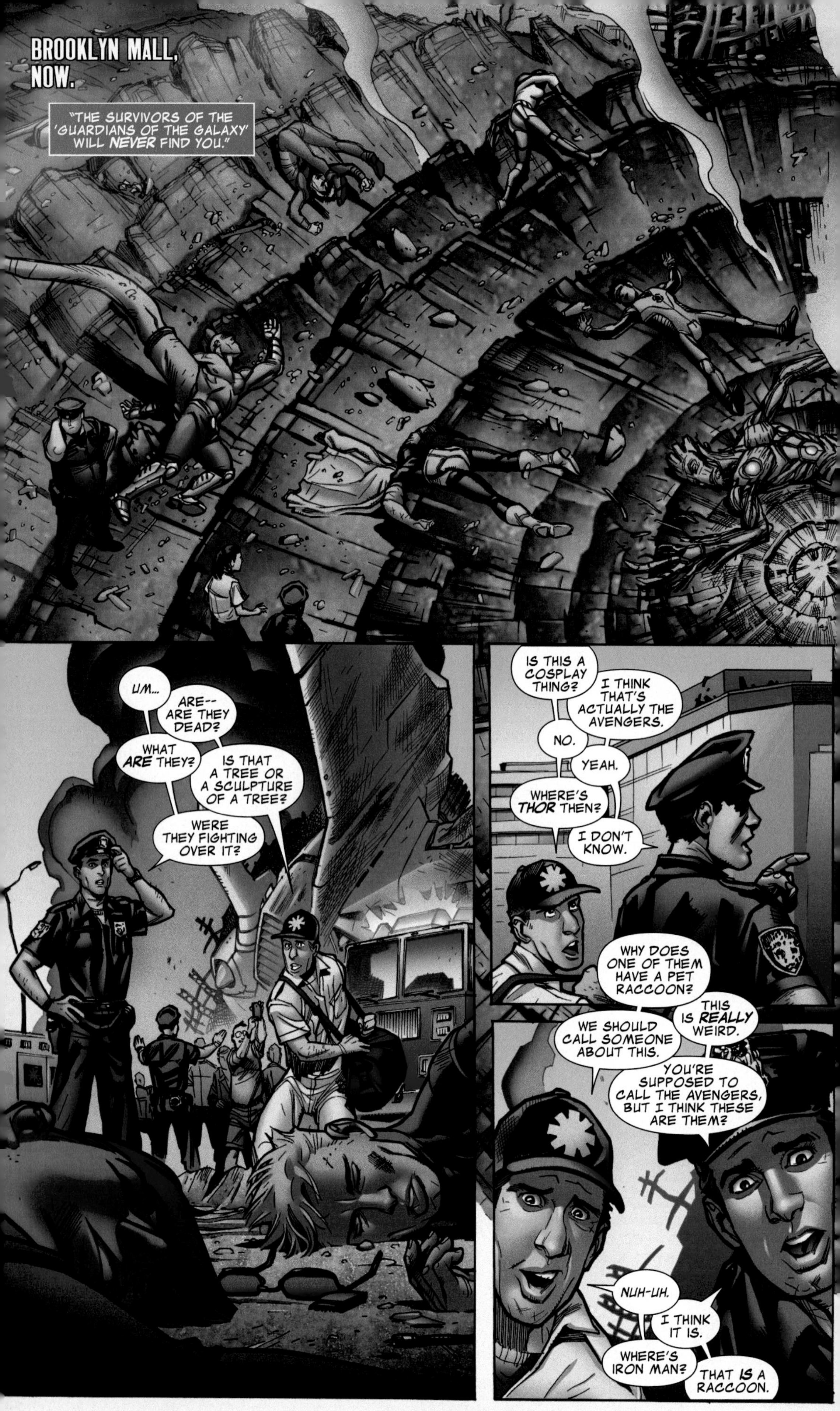
BROOKLYN MALL, NOW.
"THE SURVIVORS OF THE 'GUARDIANS OF THE GALAXY' WILL NEVER FIND YOU."
UM...
ARE-- ARE THEY DEAD?
WHAT ARE THEY?
IS THAT A TREE OR A SCULPTURE OF A TREE?
WERE THEY FIGHTING OVER IT?
IS THIS A COSPLAY THING?
I THINK THAT'S ACTUALLY THE AVENGERS.
NO.
YEAH.
WHERE'S THOR THEN?
I DON'T KNOW.
WHY DOES ONE OF THEM HAVE A PET RACCOON?
THIS IS REALLY WEIRD.
WE SHOULD CALL SOMEONE ABOUT THIS.
YOU'RE SUPPOSED TO CALL THE AVENGERS, BUT I THINK THESE ARE THEM?
NUH-UH.
I THINK IT IS.
WHERE'S IRON MAN?
THAT IS A RACCOON.

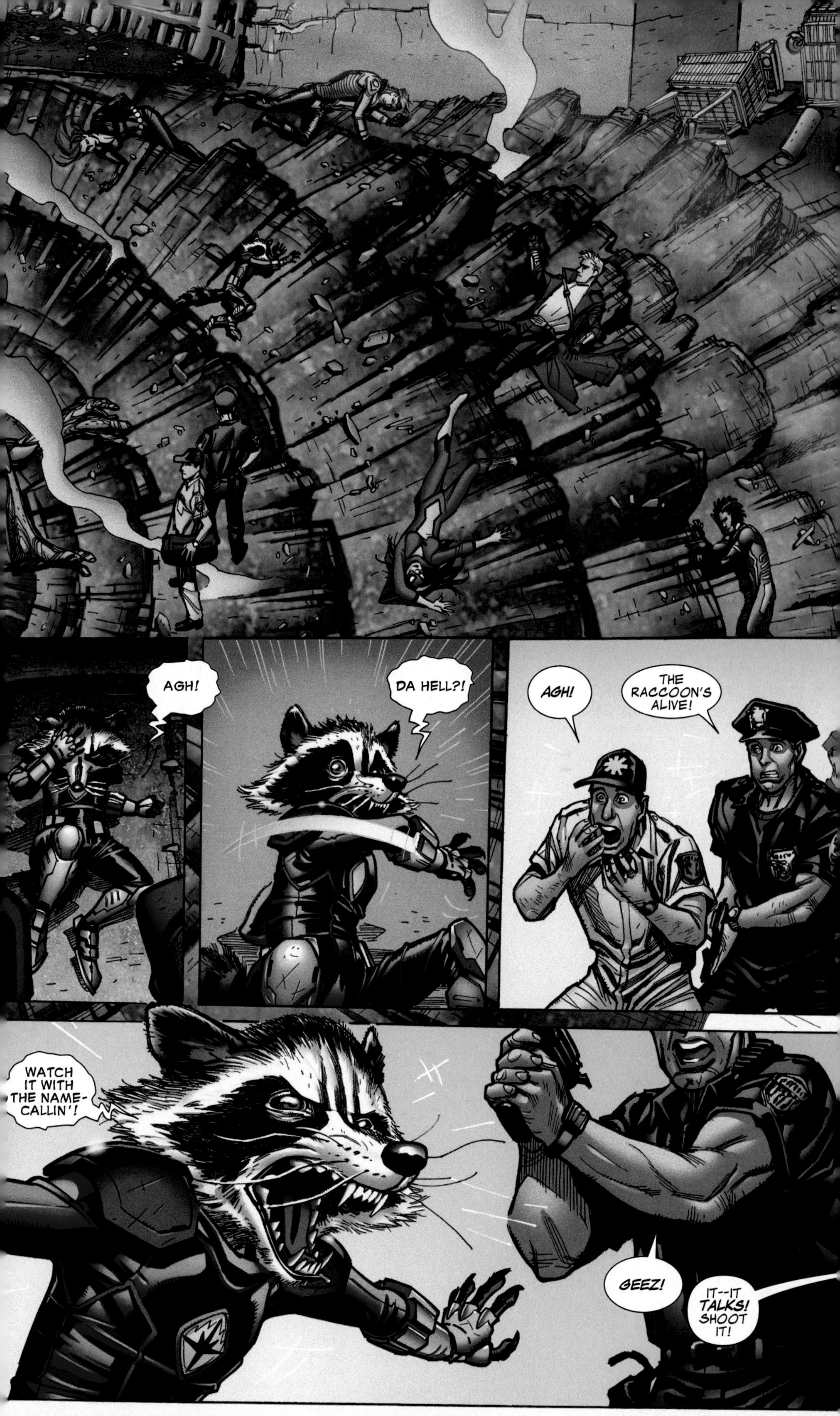
AGH!
DA HELL?!
AGH!
THE RACCOON'S ALIVE!
WATCH IT WITH THE NAME-CALLIN'!
GEEZ!
IT--IT TALKS! SHOOT IT!

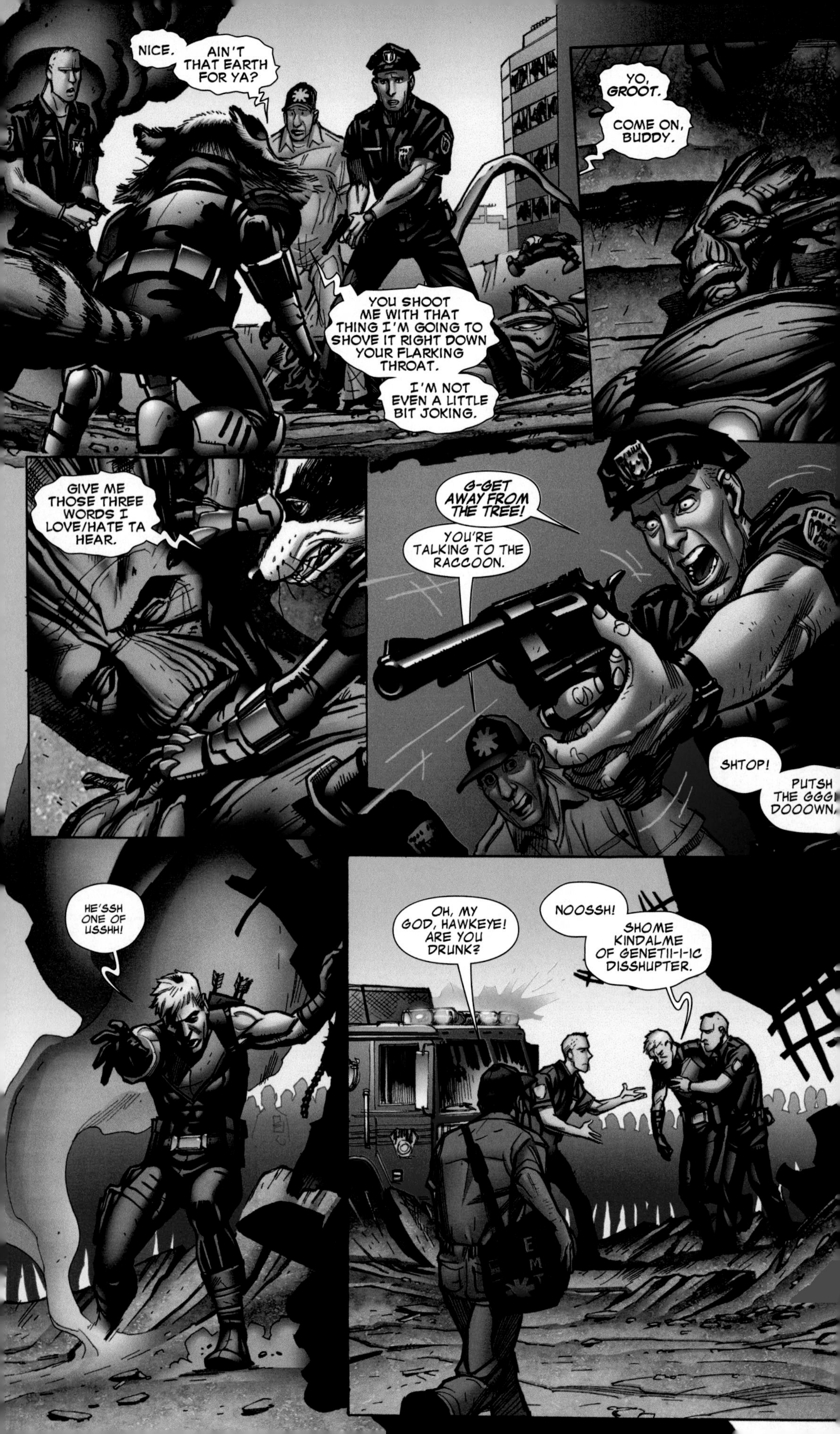
NICE.
AIN'T THAT EARTH FOR YA?
YO, GROOT.
COME ON, BUDDY.
YOU SHOOT ME WITH THAT THING I'M GOING TO SHOVE IT RIGHT DOWN YOUR FLARKING THROAT.
I'M NOT EVEN A LITTLE BIT JOKING.
GIVE ME THOSE THREE WORDS I LOVE/HATE TA HEAR.
G-GET AWAY FROM THE TREE!
YOU'RE TALKING TO THE RACCOON.
SHTOP!
PUTSH THE GGG DOOOWN
HE'SSH ONE OF USSHH!
OH, MY GOD, HAWKEYE! ARE YOU DRUNK?
NOOSSH!
SHOME KINDALME OF GENETII-I-IC DISSHUPTER.

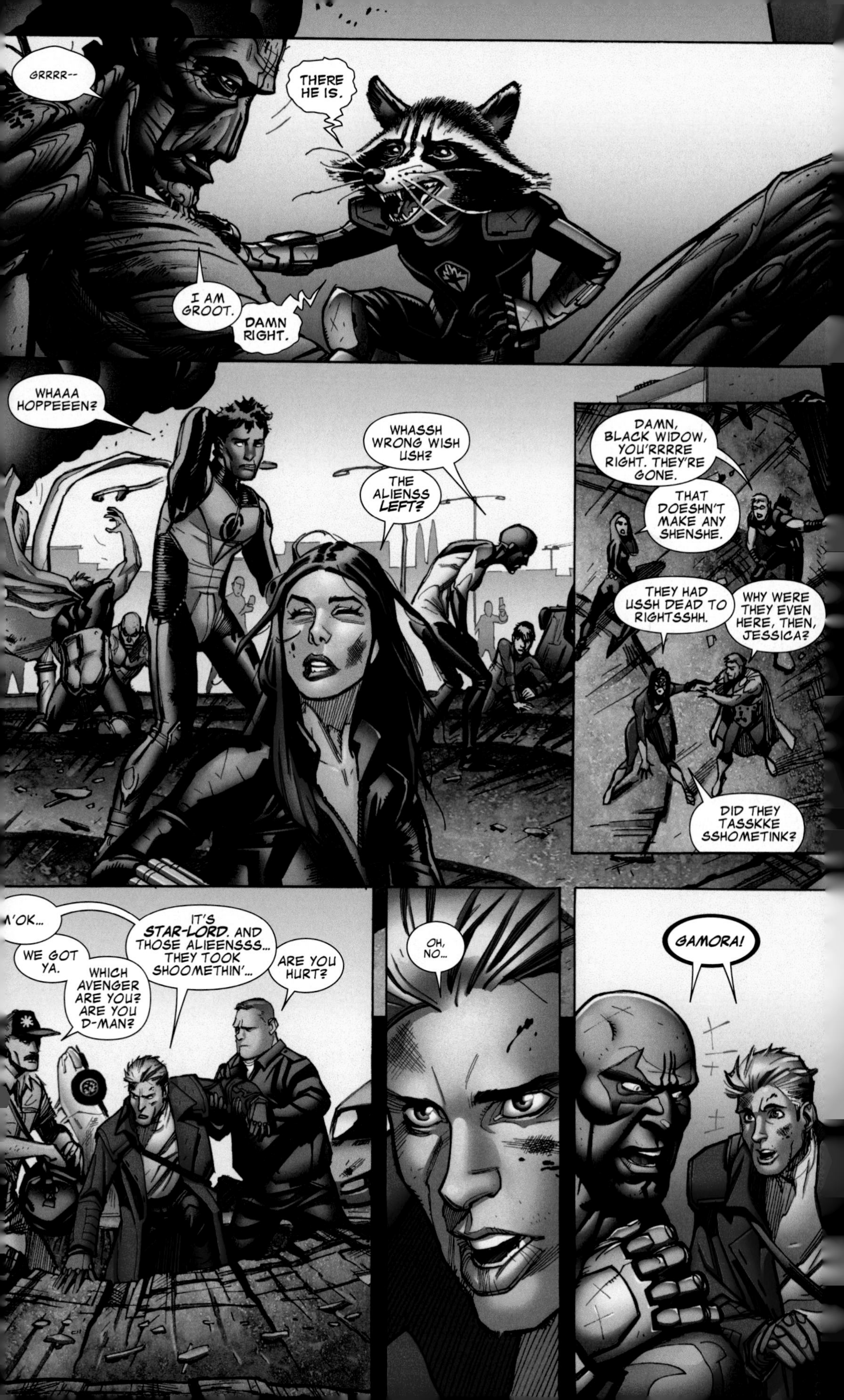
GRRRR--
THERE HE IS.
I AM GROOT.
DAMN RIGHT.
WHAAA HOPPEEEN?
WHASSH WRONG WISH USH?
THE ALIENSS LEFT?
DAMN, BLACK WIDOW, YOU'RRRRE RIGHT. THEY'RE GONE.
THAT DOESHN'T MAKE ANY SHENSHE.
THEY HAD USSH DEAD TO RIGHTSSHH.
WHY WERE THEY EVEN HERE, THEN, JESSICA?
DID THEY TASSKKE SSHOMETINK?
'M'OK...
WE GOT YA.
WHICH AVENGER ARE YOU? ARE YOU D-MAN?
IT'S STAR-LORD. AND THOSE ALIEENSSS... THEY TOOK SHOOMETHIN'...
ARE YOU HURT?
OH, NO...
GAMORA!

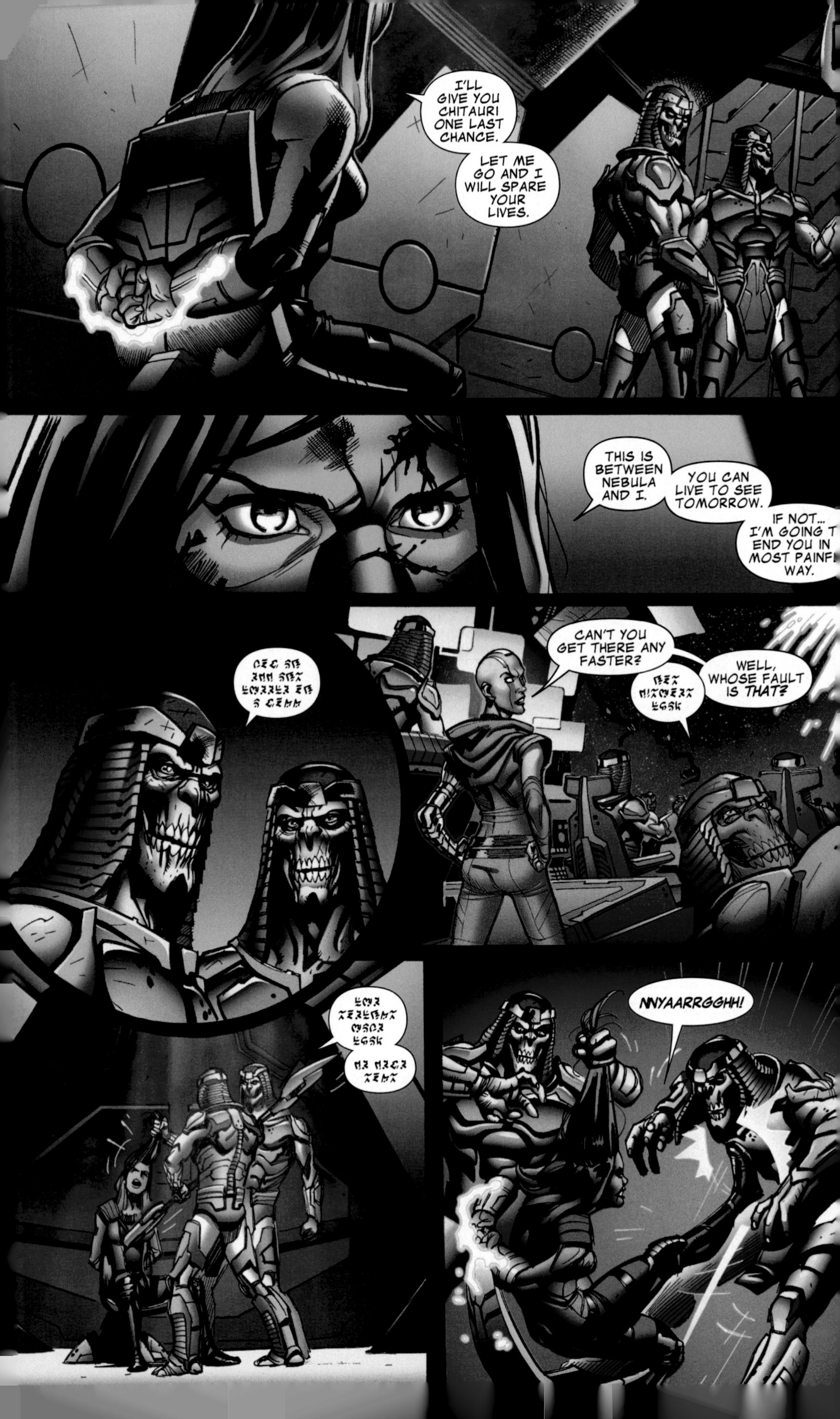
I'LL GIVE YOU CHITAURI ONE LAST CHANCE.
LET ME GO AND I WILL SPARE YOUR LIVES.
THIS IS BETWEEN NEBULA AND I.
YOU CAN LIVE TO SEE TOMORROW.
IF NOT... I'M GOING T END YOU IN MOST PAINF WAY.
CAN'T YOU GET THERE ANY FASTER?
WELL, WHOSE FAULT IS THAT?
NNYAARRGGHH!

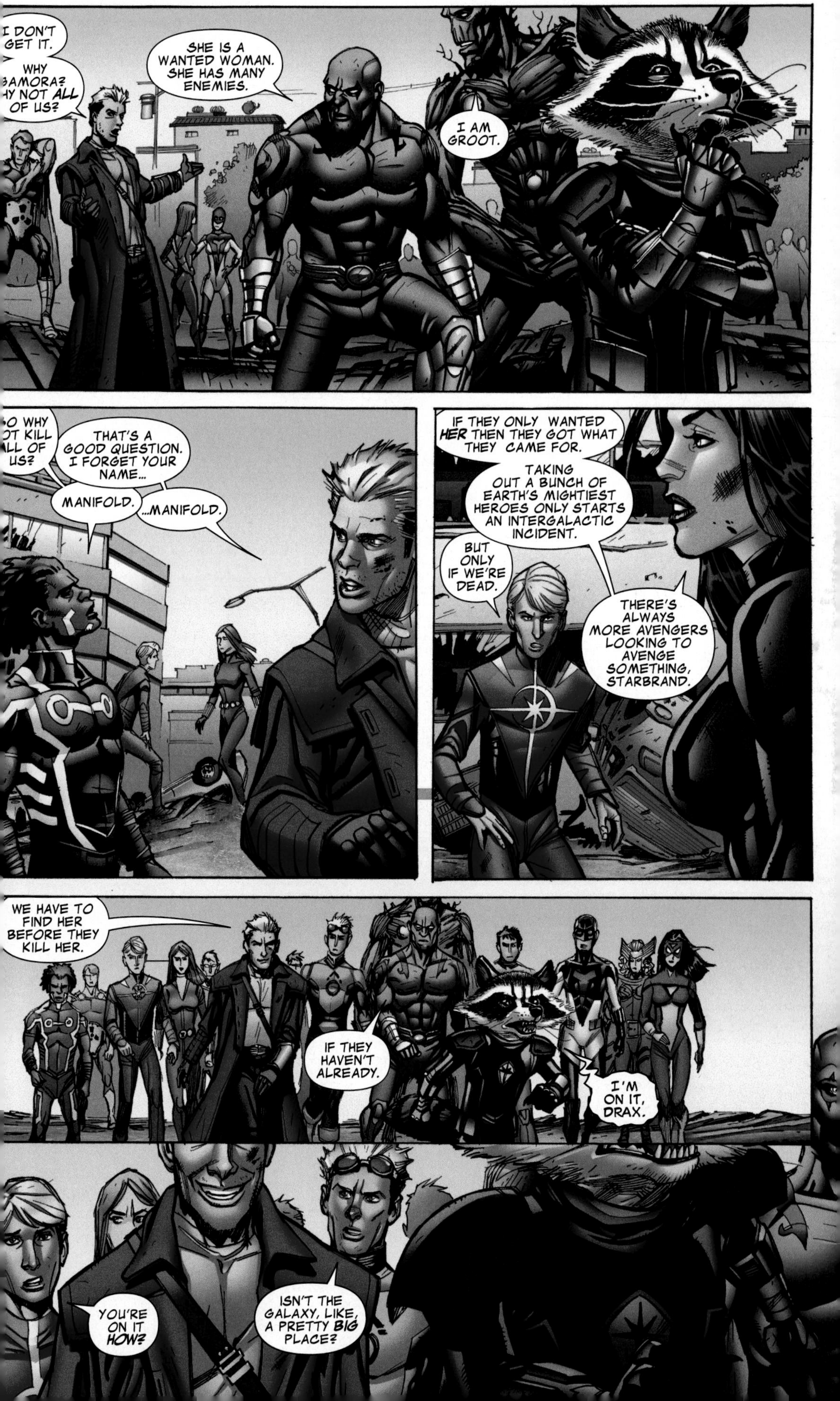

I DON'T GET IT.
WHY GAMORA? WHY NOT ALL OF US?
SHE IS A WANTED WOMAN. SHE HAS MANY ENEMIES.
I AM GROOT.
SO WHY NOT KILL ALL OF US?
THAT'S A GOOD QUESTION. I FORGET YOUR NAME...
MANIFOLD.
...MANIFOLD.
IF THEY ONLY WANTED HER THEN THEY GOT WHAT THEY CAME FOR.
TAKING OUT A BUNCH OF EARTH'S MIGHTIEST HEROES ONLY STARTS AN INTERGALACTIC INCIDENT.
BUT ONLY IF WE'RE DEAD.
THERE'S ALWAYS MORE AVENGERS LOOKING TO AVENGE SOMETHING, STARBRAND.
WE HAVE TO FIND HER BEFORE THEY KILL HER.
IF THEY HAVEN'T ALREADY.
I'M ON IT, DRAX.
YOU'RE ON IT HOW?
ISN'T THE GALAXY, LIKE, A PRETTY BIG PLACE?

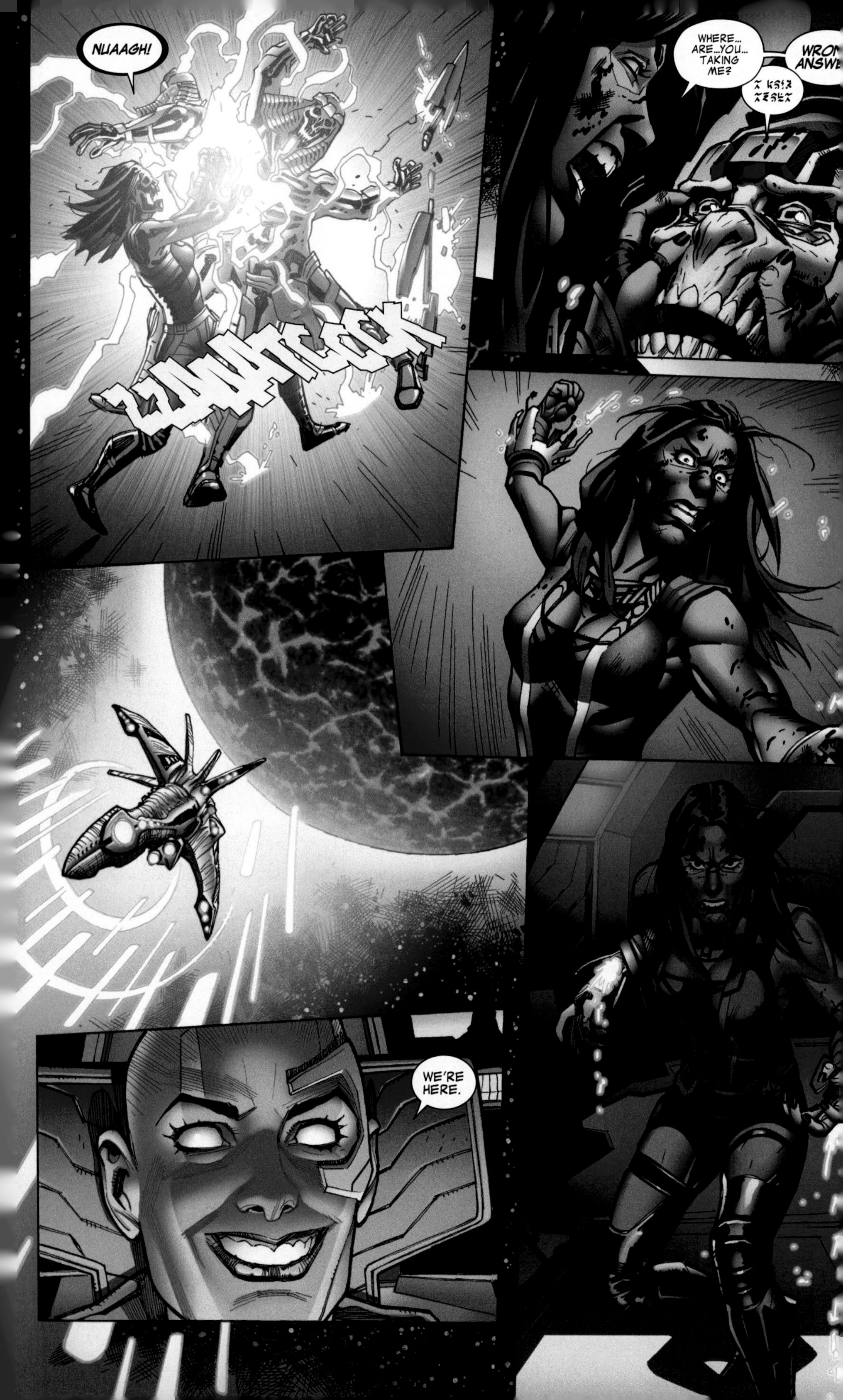
NUAAGH!
WHERE... ARE...YOU... TAKING ME?
WE'RE HERE.

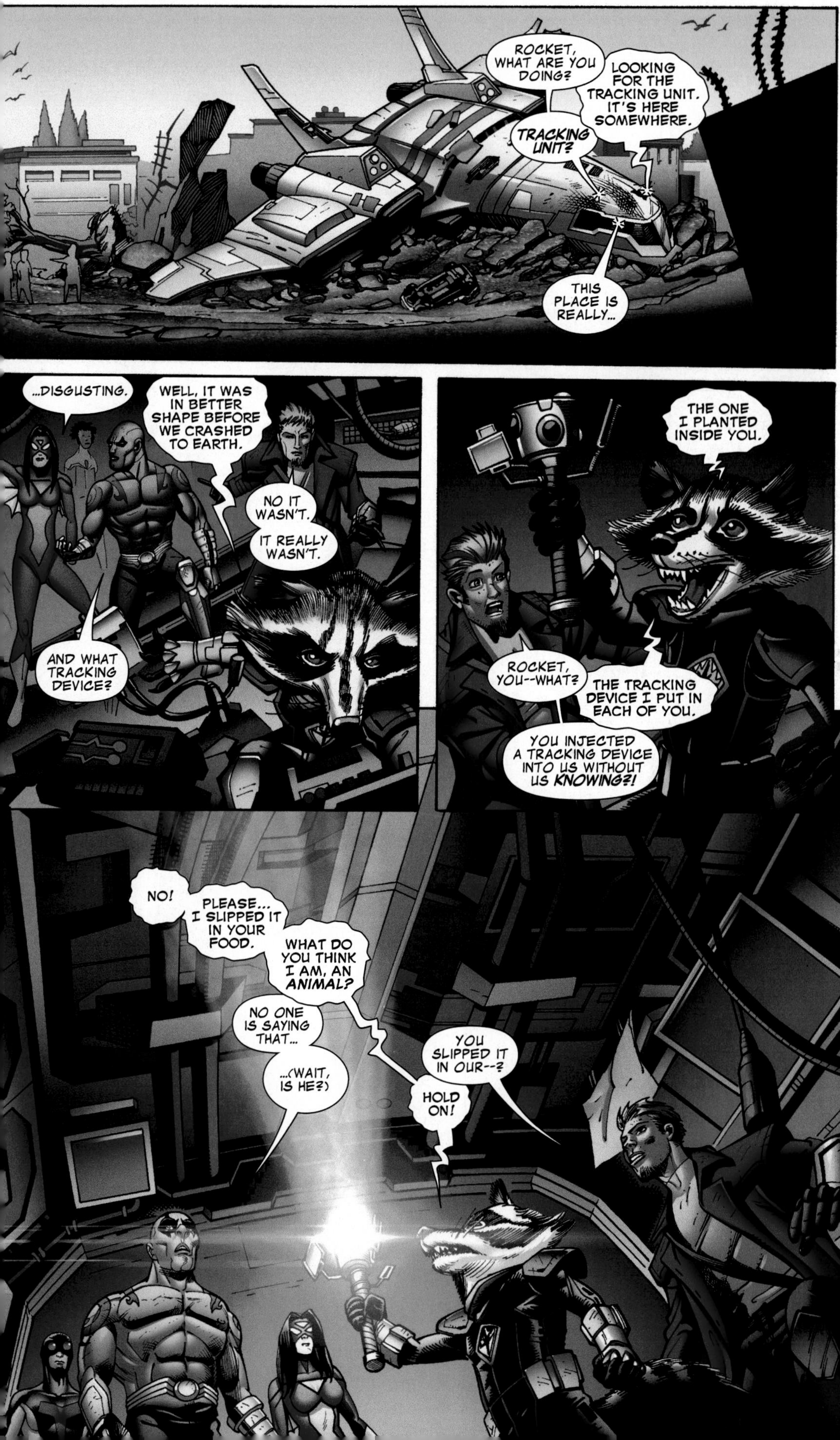
ROCKET, WHAT ARE YOU DOING?
LOOKING FOR THE TRACKING UNIT. IT'S HERE SOMEWHERE.
TRACKING UNIT?
THIS PLACE IS REALLY...
...DISGUSTING.
WELL, IT WAS IN BETTER SHAPE BEFORE WE CRASHED TO EARTH.
NO IT WASN'T.
IT REALLY WASN'T.
AND WHAT TRACKING DEVICE?
THE ONE I PLANTED INSIDE YOU.
ROCKET, YOU--WHAT?
THE TRACKING DEVICE I PUT IN EACH OF YOU.
YOU INJECTED A TRACKING DEVICE INTO US WITHOUT US KNOWING?!
NO!
PLEASE... I SLIPPED IT IN YOUR FOOD.
WHAT DO YOU THINK I AM, AN ANIMAL?
NO ONE IS SAYING THAT...
...(WAIT, IS HE?)
YOU SLIPPED IT IN OUR--?
HOLD ON!

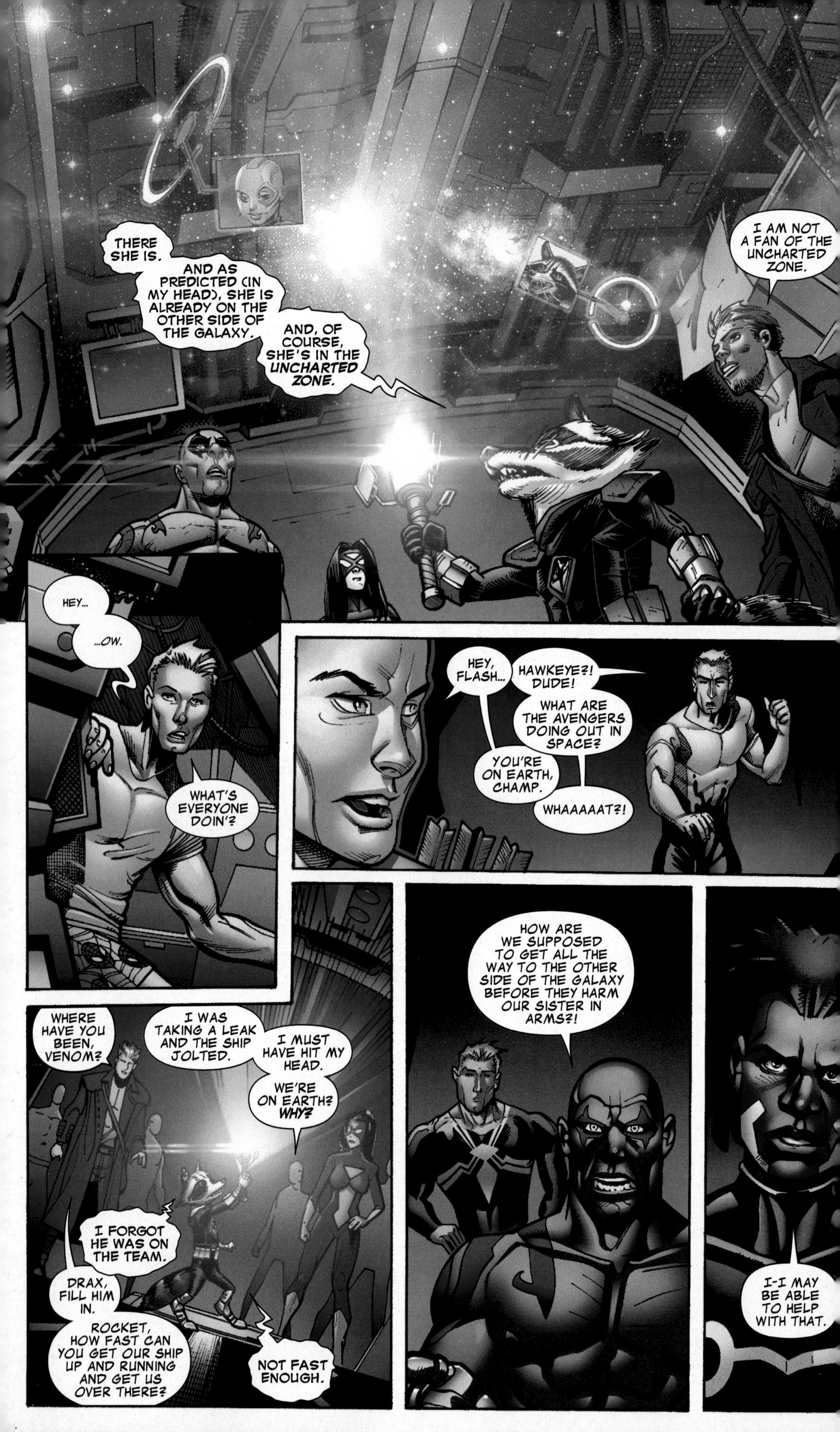
THERE SHE IS.
AND AS PREDICTED (IN MY HEAD), SHE IS ALREADY ON THE OTHER SIDE OF THE GALAXY.
AND, OF COURSE, SHE'S IN THE *UNCHARTED ZONE.*
I AM NOT A FAN OF THE UNCHARTED ZONE.
HEY...
...OW.
WHAT'S EVERYONE DOIN'?
HEY, FLASH...
HAWKEYE?! DUDE!
WHAT ARE THE AVENGERS DOING OUT IN SPACE?
YOU'RE ON EARTH, CHAMP.
WHAAAAAT?!
WHERE HAVE YOU BEEN, VENOM?
I WAS TAKING A LEAK AND THE SHIP JOLTED.
I MUST HAVE HIT MY HEAD.
WE'RE ON EARTH? *WHY?*
I FORGOT HE WAS ON THE TEAM.
DRAX, FILL HIM IN.
ROCKET, HOW FAST CAN YOU GET OUR SHIP UP AND RUNNING AND GET US OVER THERE?
NOT FAST ENOUGH.
HOW ARE WE SUPPOSED TO GET ALL THE WAY TO THE OTHER SIDE OF THE GALAXY BEFORE THEY HARM OUR SISTER IN ARMS?!
I-I MAY BE ABLE TO HELP WITH THAT.

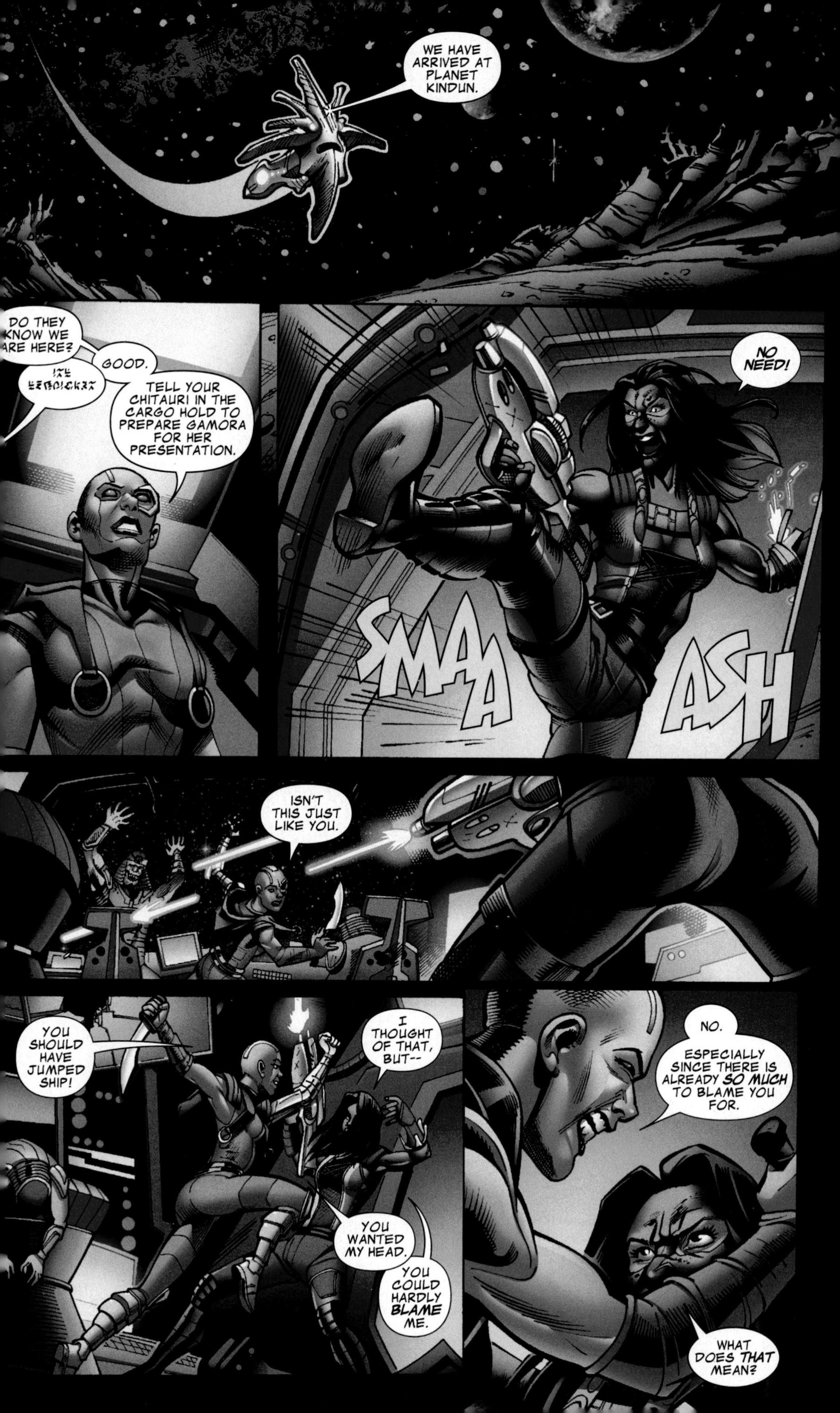
WE HAVE ARRIVED AT PLANET KINDUN.
DO THEY KNOW WE ARE HERE?
GOOD.
TELL YOUR CHITAURI IN THE CARGO HOLD TO PREPARE GAMORA FOR HER PRESENTATION.
NO NEED!
SMAAASH
ISN'T THIS JUST LIKE YOU.
YOU SHOULD HAVE JUMPED SHIP!
I THOUGHT OF THAT, BUT--
YOU WANTED MY HEAD.
YOU COULD HARDLY BLAME ME.
NO.
ESPECIALLY SINCE THERE IS ALREADY SO MUCH TO BLAME YOU FOR.
WHAT DOES THAT MEAN?

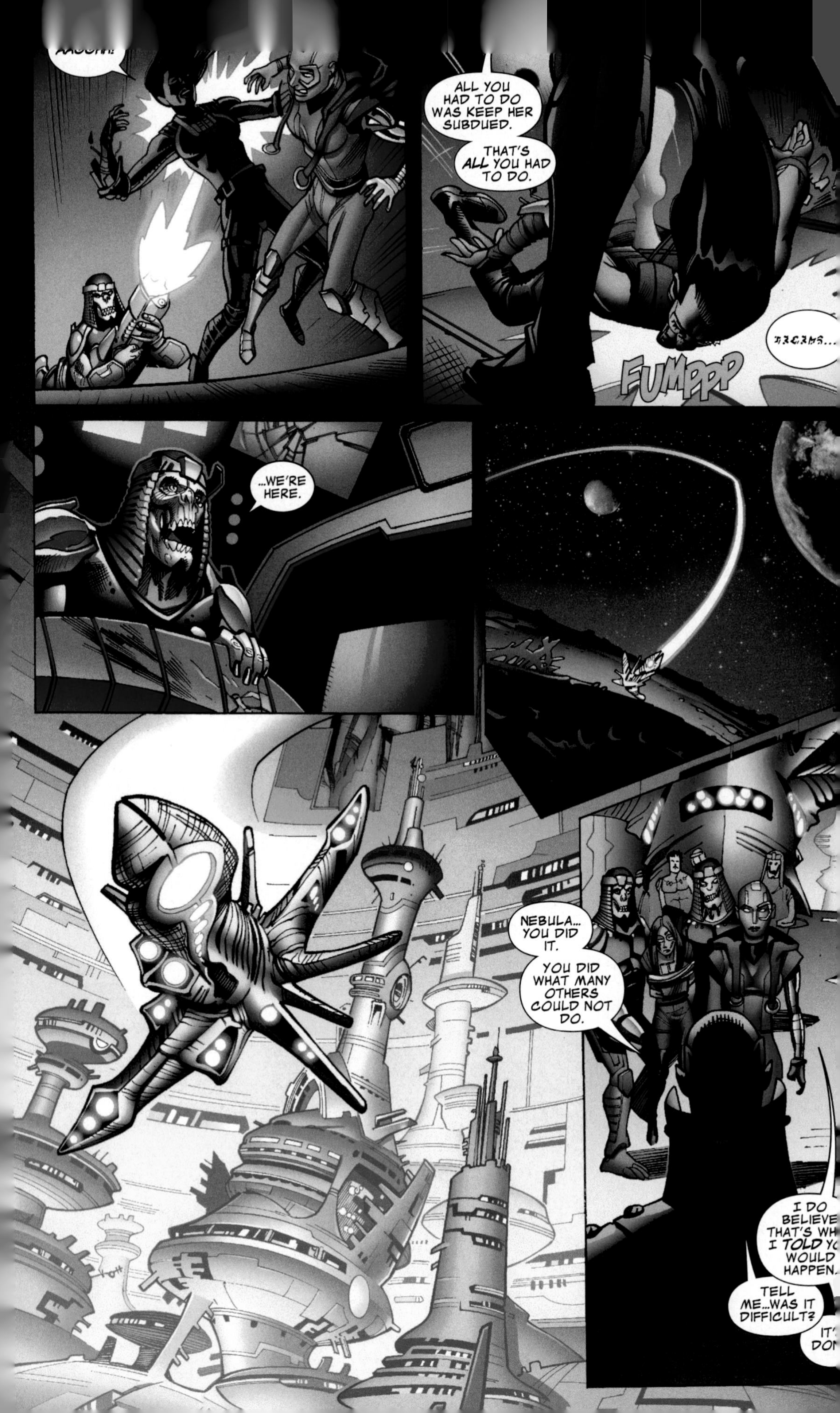
ALL YOU HAD TO DO WAS KEEP HER SUBDUED.
THAT'S ALL YOU HAD TO DO.
FUMPPP
...WE'RE HERE.
NEBULA... YOU DID IT.
YOU DID WHAT MANY OTHERS COULD NOT DO.
I DO BELIEVE THAT'S WH I TOLD Y WOULD HAPPEN.
TELL ME...WAS IT DIFFICULT?

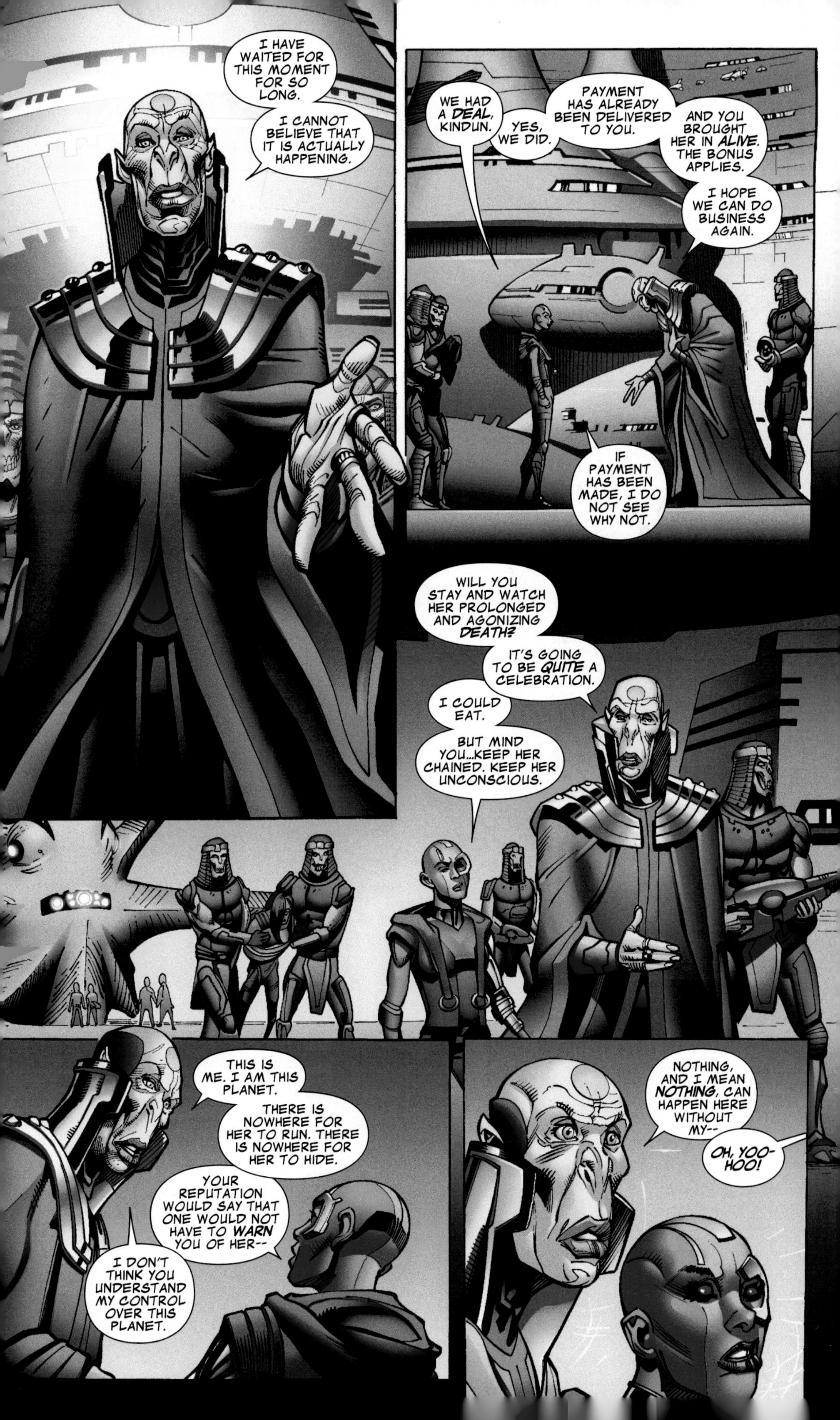
I HAVE WAITED FOR THIS MOMENT FOR SO LONG.
I CANNOT BELIEVE THAT IT IS ACTUALLY HAPPENING.
WE HAD A DEAL, KINDUN.
YES, WE DID.
PAYMENT HAS ALREADY BEEN DELIVERED TO YOU.
AND YOU BROUGHT HER IN ALIVE. THE BONUS APPLIES.
I HOPE WE CAN DO BUSINESS AGAIN.
IF PAYMENT HAS BEEN MADE, I DO NOT SEE WHY NOT.
WILL YOU STAY AND WATCH HER PROLONGED AND AGONIZING DEATH?
IT'S GOING TO BE QUITE A CELEBRATION.
I COULD EAT.
BUT MIND YOU...KEEP HER CHAINED. KEEP HER UNCONSCIOUS.
THIS IS ME. I AM THIS PLANET.
THERE IS NOWHERE FOR HER TO RUN. THERE IS NOWHERE FOR HER TO HIDE.
YOUR REPUTATION WOULD SAY THAT ONE WOULD NOT HAVE TO WARN YOU OF HER--
I DON'T THINK YOU UNDERSTAND MY CONTROL OVER THIS PLANET.
NOTHING, AND I MEAN NOTHING, CAN HAPPEN HERE WITHOUT MY--
OH, YOO-HOO!

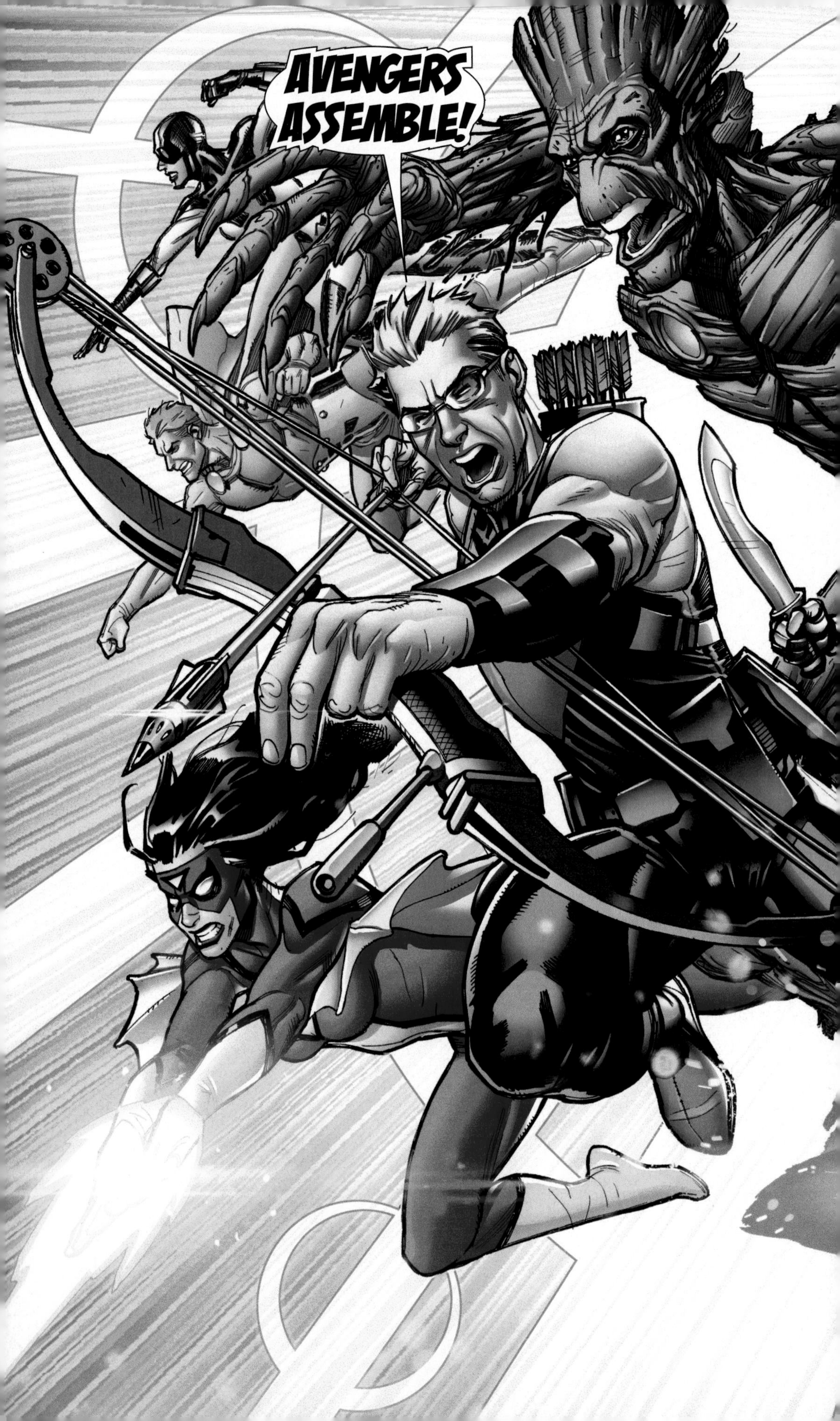
AVENGERS ASSEMBLE!

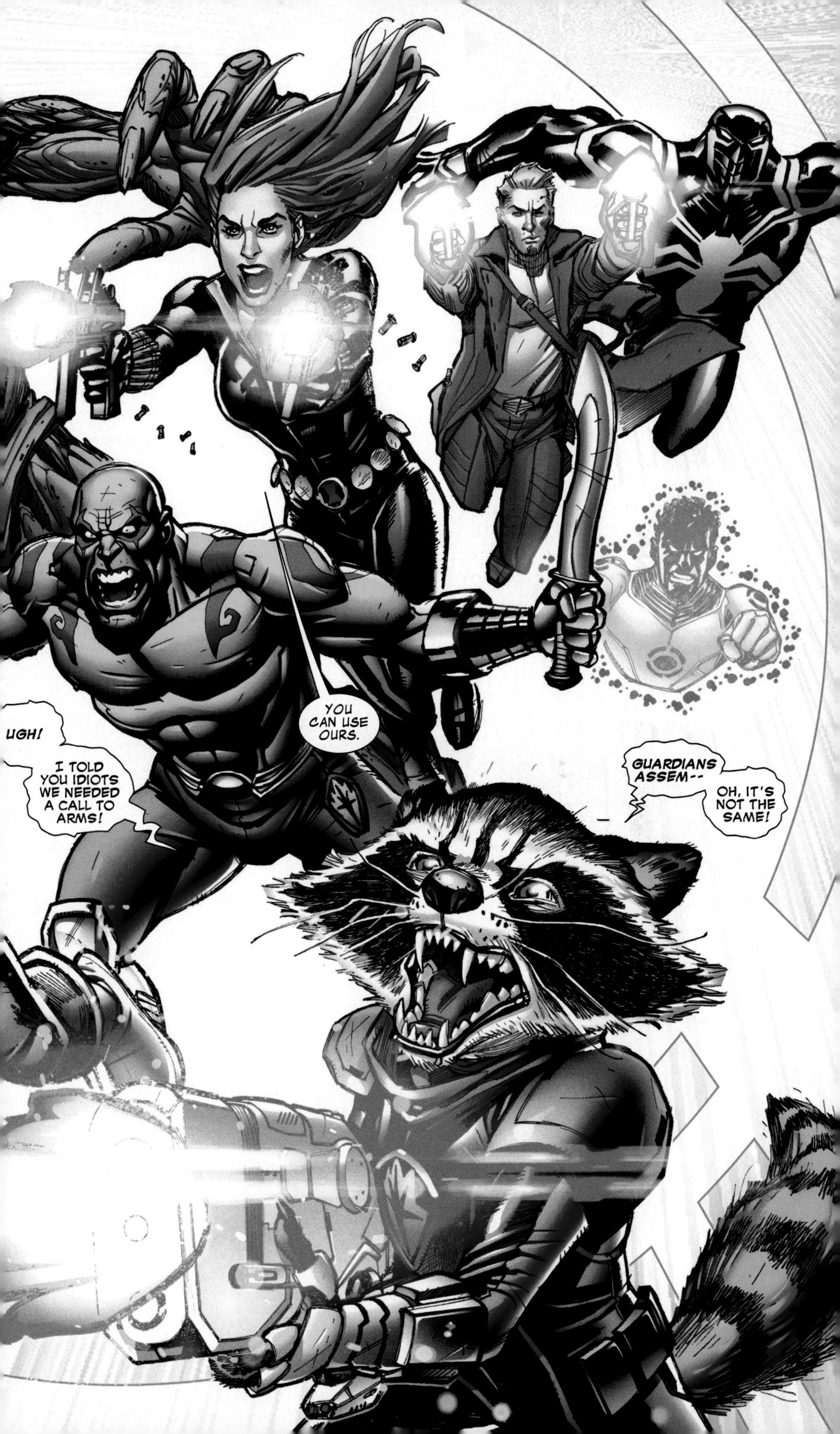
UGH!
I TOLD YOU IDIOTS WE NEEDED A CALL TO ARMS!
YOU CAN USE OURS.
GUARDIANS ASSEM--
OH, IT'S NOT THE SAME!

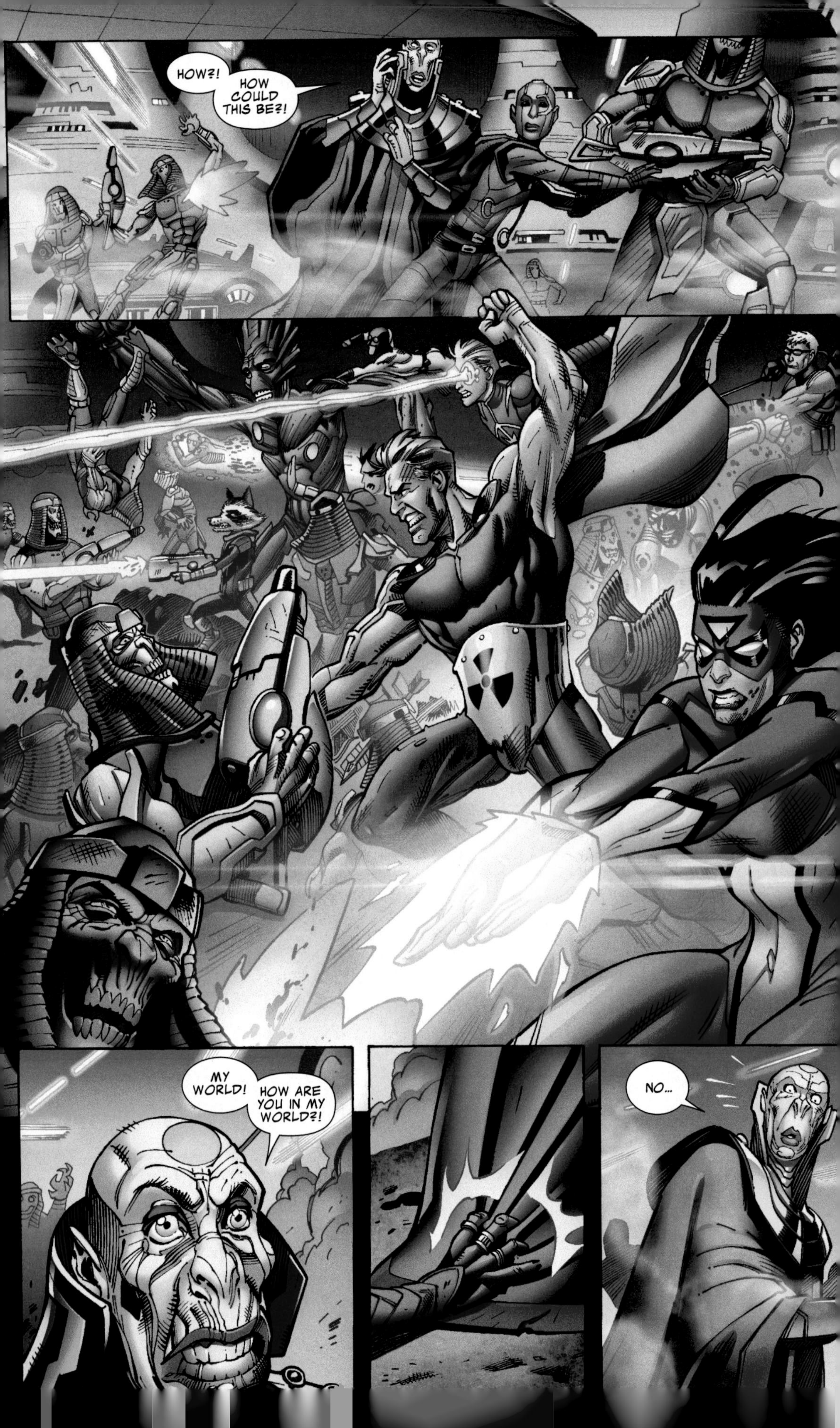
HOW?!
HOW COULD THIS BE?!
MY WORLD!
HOW ARE YOU IN MY WORLD?!
NO...

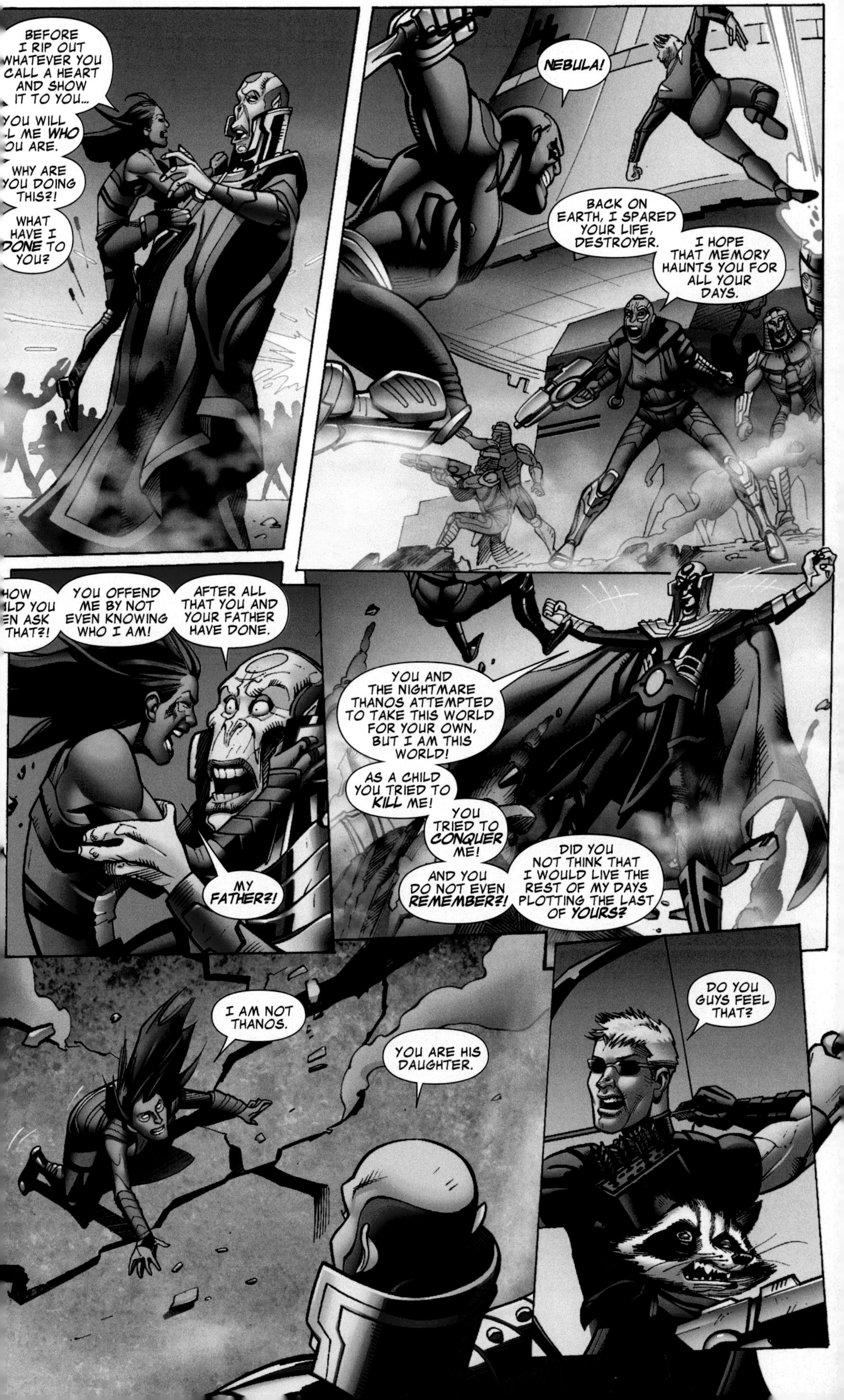
BEFORE I RIP OUT WHATEVER YOU CALL A HEART AND SHOW IT TO YOU...
YOU WILL L ME WHO OU ARE.
WHY ARE YOU DOING THIS?!
WHAT HAVE I DONE TO YOU?
NEBULA!
BACK ON EARTH, I SPARED YOUR LIFE, DESTROYER.
I HOPE THAT MEMORY HAUNTS YOU FOR ALL YOUR DAYS.
HOW LD YOU N ASK THAT?!
YOU OFFEND ME BY NOT EVEN KNOWING WHO I AM!
AFTER ALL THAT YOU AND YOUR FATHER HAVE DONE.
MY FATHER?!
YOU AND THE NIGHTMARE THANOS ATTEMPTED TO TAKE THIS WORLD FOR YOUR OWN, BUT I AM THIS WORLD!
AS A CHILD YOU TRIED TO KILL ME!
YOU TRIED TO CONQUER ME!
AND YOU DO NOT EVEN REMEMBER?!
DID YOU NOT THINK THAT I WOULD LIVE THE REST OF MY DAYS PLOTTING THE LAST OF YOURS?
I AM NOT THANOS.
YOU ARE HIS DAUGHTER.
DO YOU GUYS FEEL THAT?

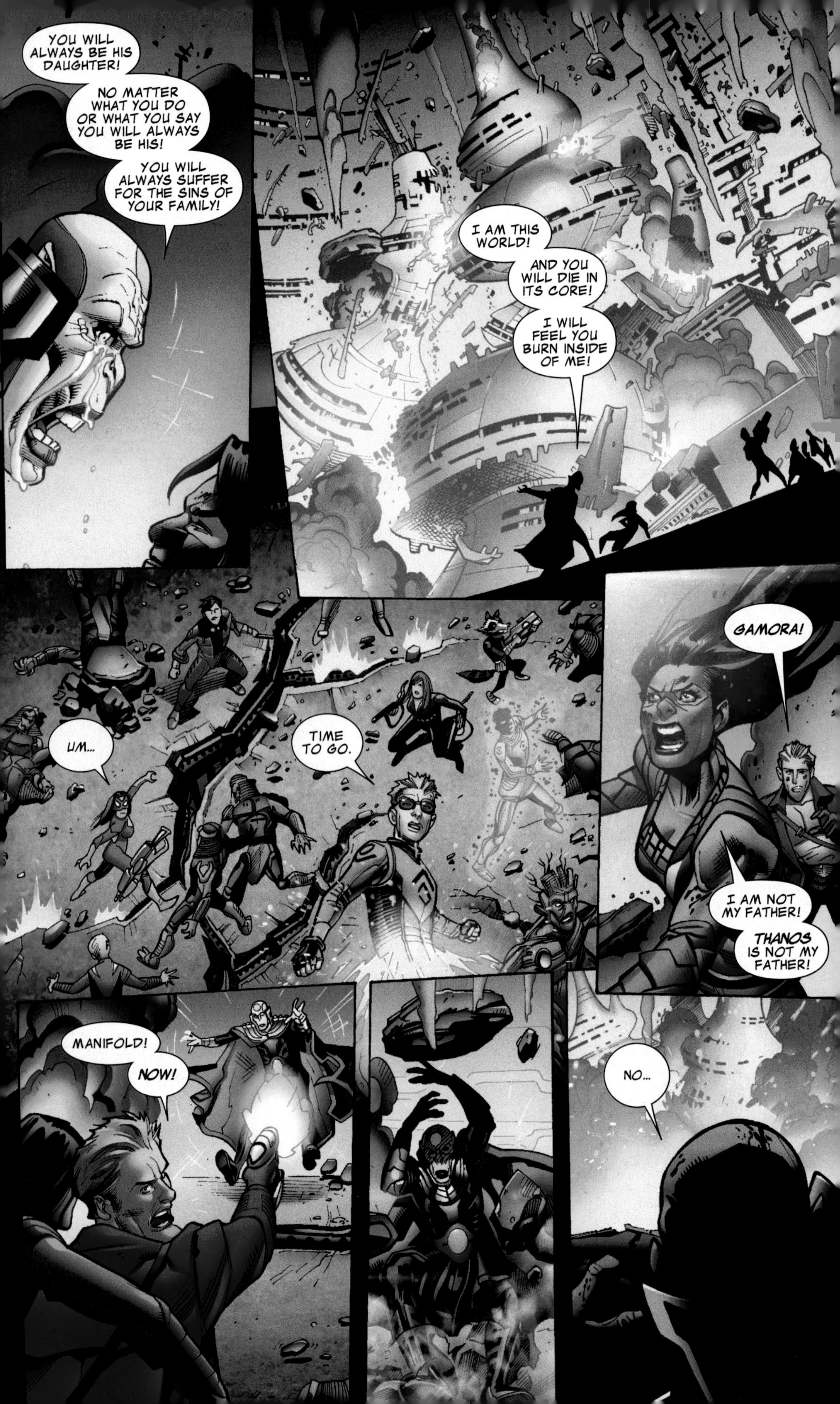
YOU WILL ALWAYS BE HIS DAUGHTER!
NO MATTER WHAT YOU DO OR WHAT YOU SAY YOU WILL ALWAYS BE HIS!
YOU WILL ALWAYS SUFFER FOR THE SINS OF YOUR FAMILY!
I AM THIS WORLD!
AND YOU WILL DIE IN ITS CORE!
I WILL FEEL YOU BURN INSIDE OF ME!
UM...
TIME TO GO.
GAMORA!
I AM NOT MY FATHER!
THANOS IS NOT MY FATHER!
MANIFOLD!
NOW!
NO...

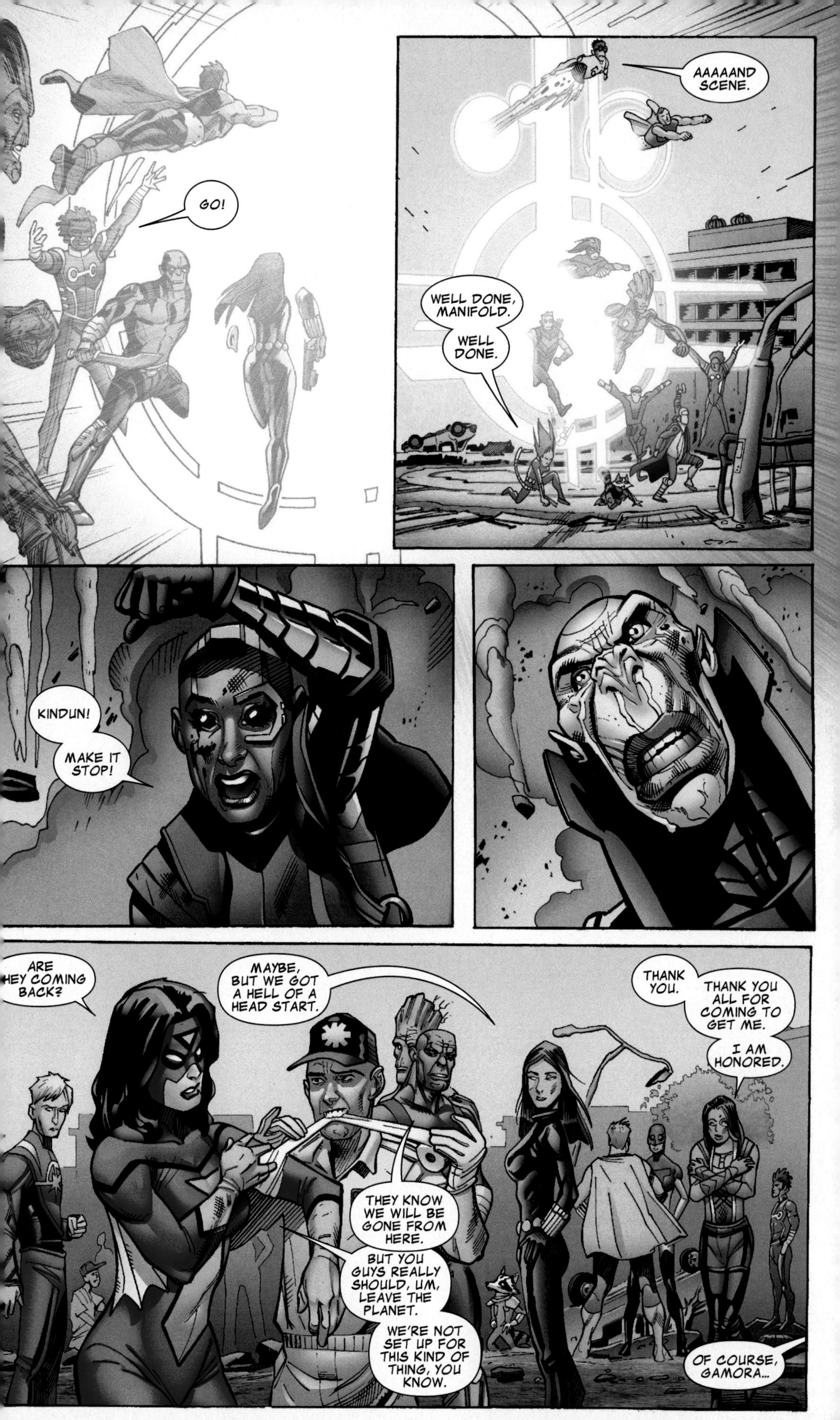
GO!
AAAAAND SCENE.
WELL DONE, MANIFOLD.
WELL DONE.
KINDUN!
MAKE IT STOP!
ARE HEY COMING BACK?
MAYBE, BUT WE GOT A HELL OF A HEAD START.
THANK YOU.
THANK YOU ALL FOR COMING TO GET ME.
I AM HONORED.
THEY KNOW WE WILL BE GONE FROM HERE.
BUT YOU GUYS REALLY SHOULD, UM, LEAVE THE PLANET.
WE'RE NOT SET UP FOR THIS KIND OF THING, YOU KNOW.
OF COURSE, GAMORA...

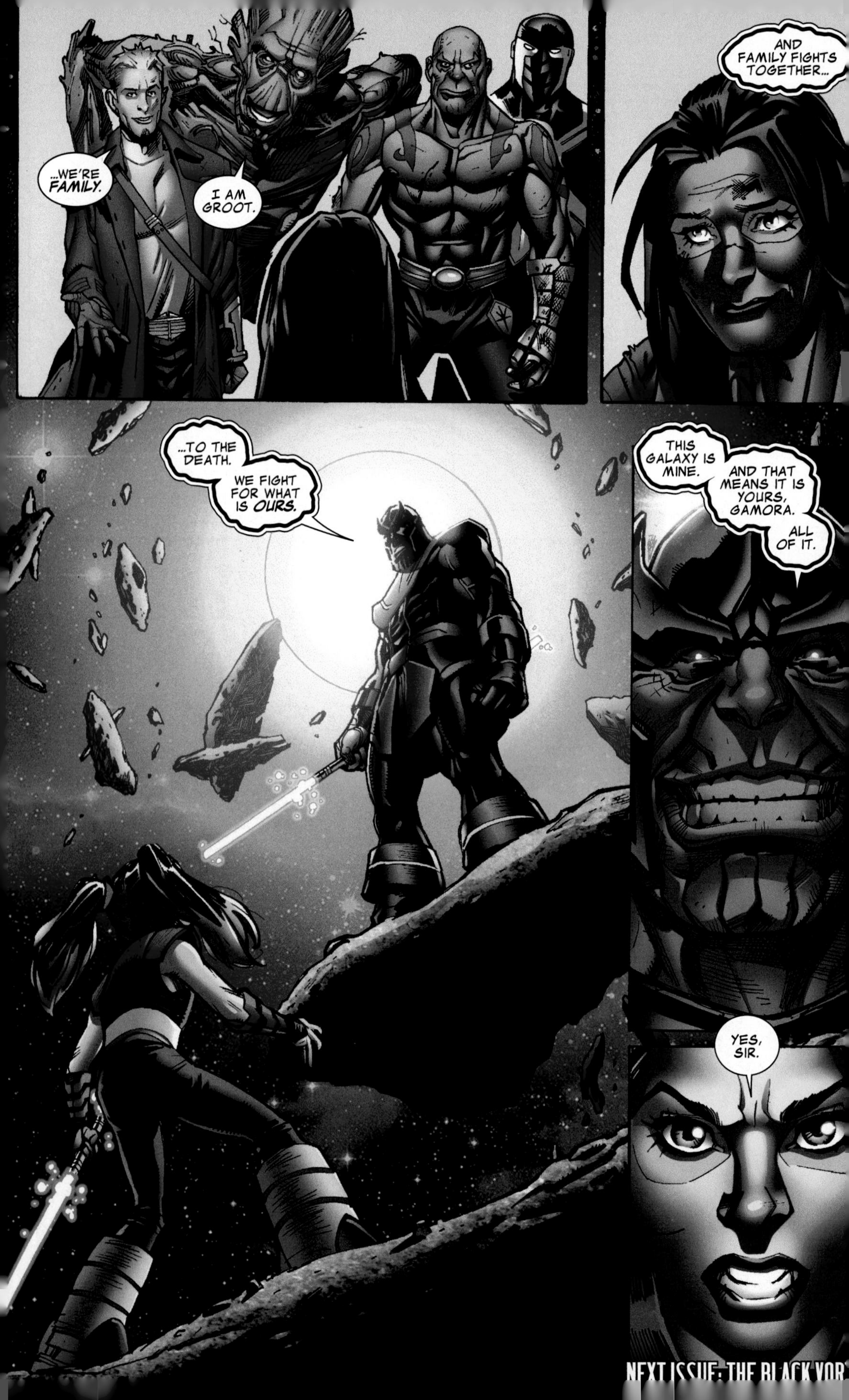
...WE'RE FAMILY.
I AM GROOT.
AND FAMILY FIGHTS TOGETHER...
...TO THE DEATH.
WE FIGHT FOR WHAT IS OURS.
THIS GALAXY IS MINE.
AND THAT MEANS IT IS YOURS, GAMORA.
ALL OF IT.
YES, SIR.

NEXT ISSUE: THE BLACK VOR

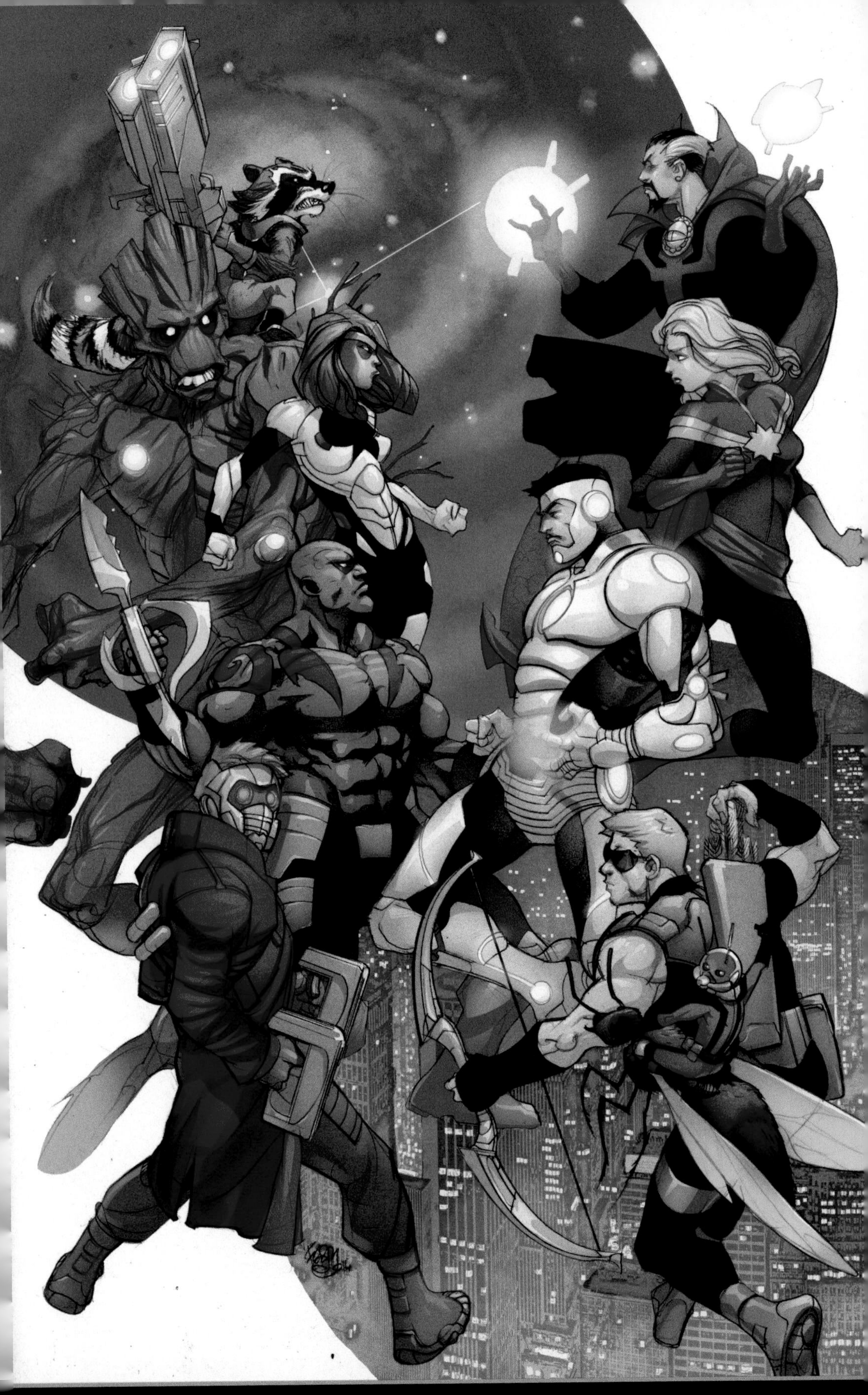

GUARDIANS TEAM-UP #1 VARIANT BY PASQUAL FERRY & JEAN-FRANCOIS BEAULIEU

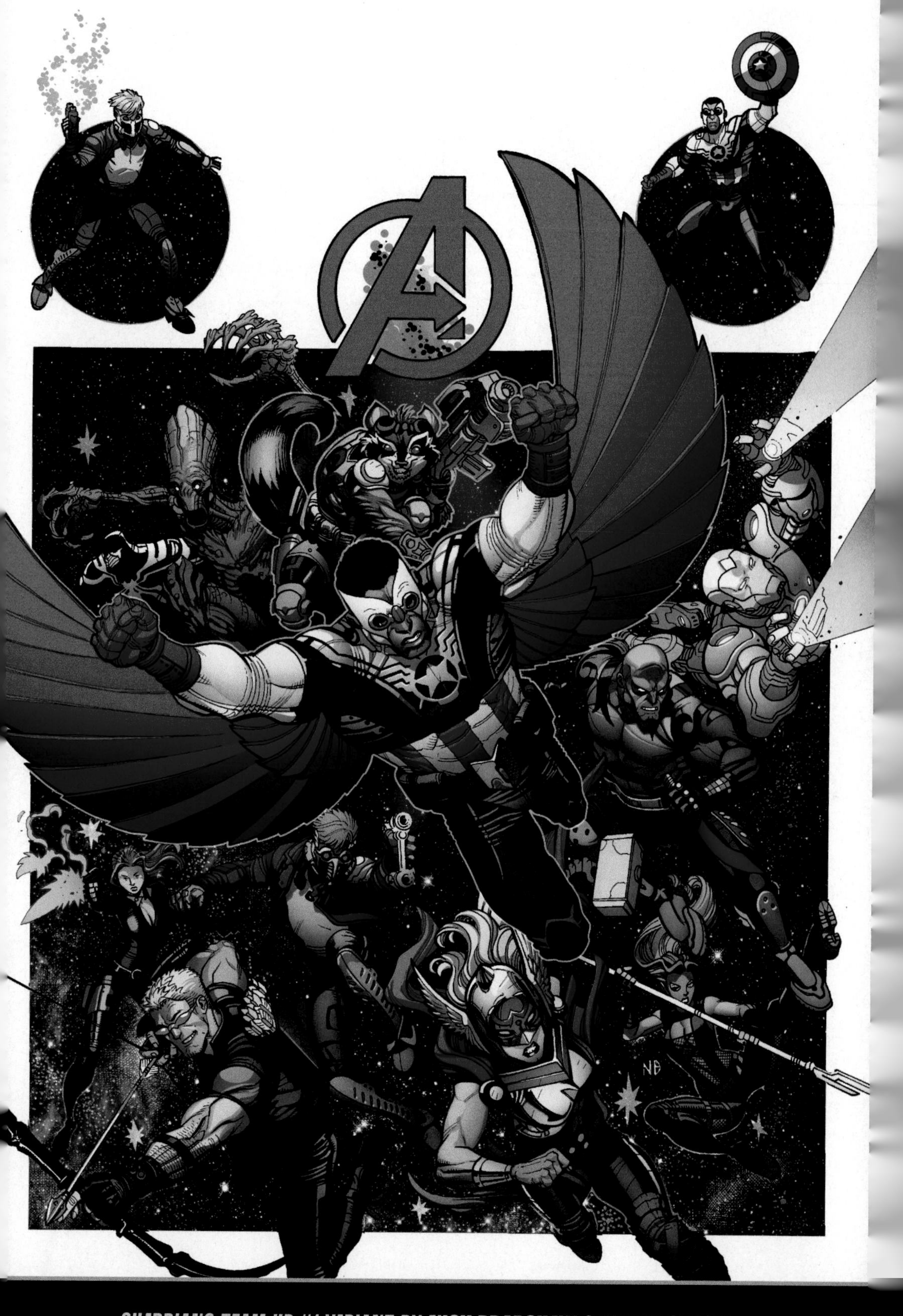

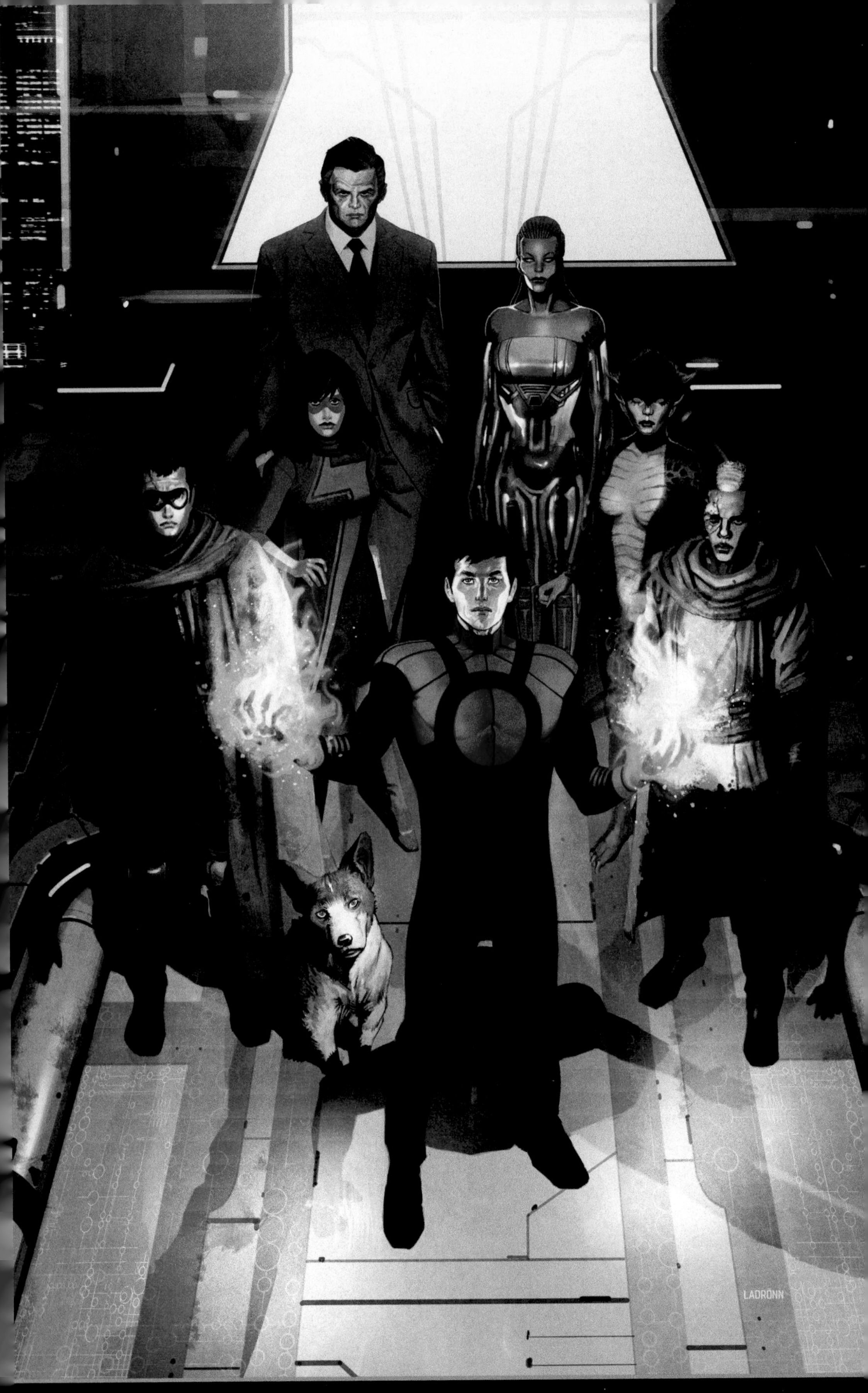
LADRONN

GUARDIANS TEAM-UP #1 50 YEARS OF INHUMANS VARIANT BY JOSE LADRONN

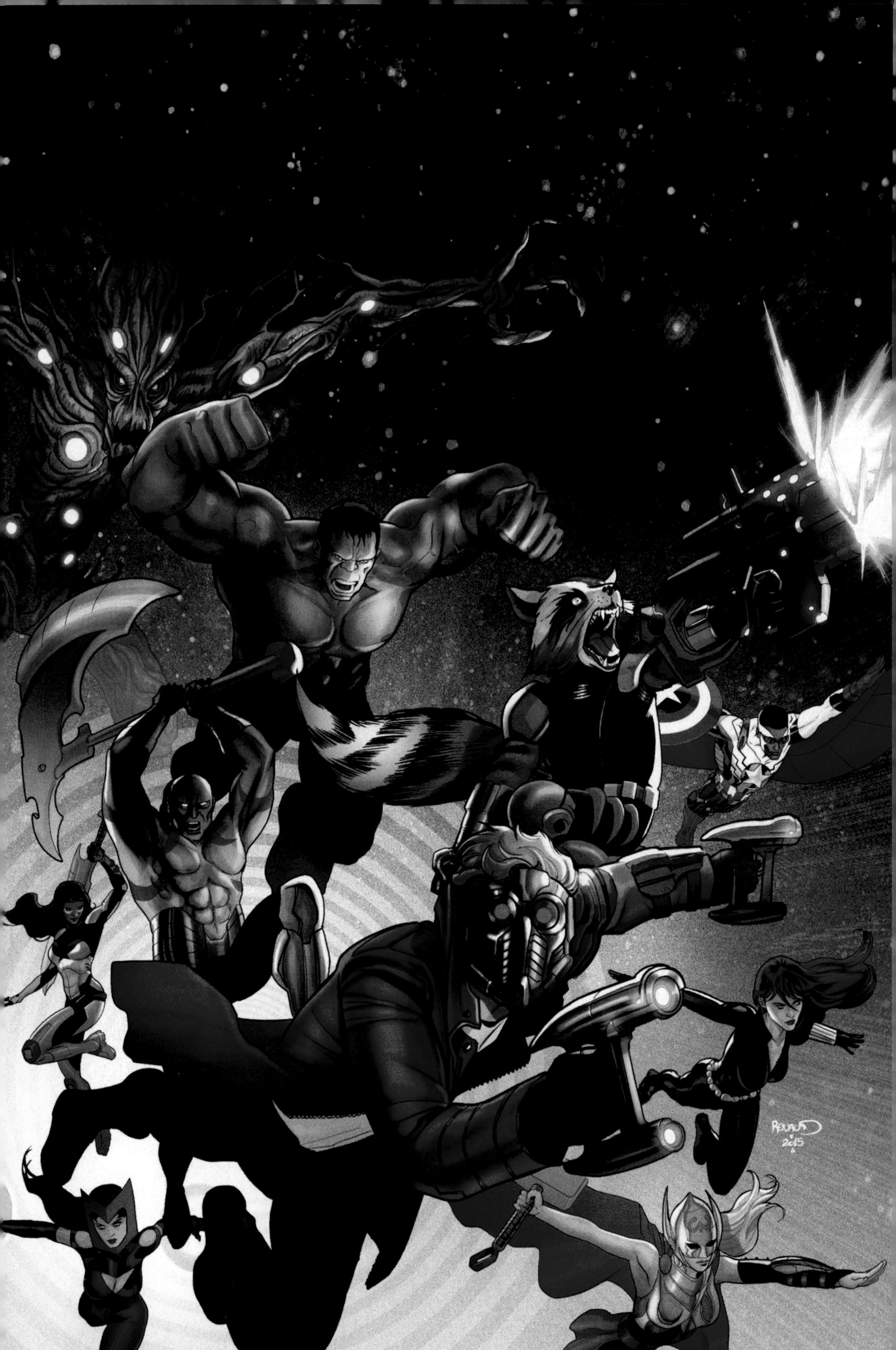